PART TWO   COMMON WRITING PROBLEMS   191

PART THREE   THE BASICS FROM A TO Z   313

Part 3 is an alphabetically organized dictionary of grammatical rules for writers. It also contains cross references to topics covered more fully in Parts 1 and 2.

MLK: To all my family

KHA: For Cole Adams

Easy Access

The Reference Handbook for Writers

SECOND EDITION

Michael L. Keene
The University of Tennessee, Knoxville

Katherine H. Adams
Loyola University New Orleans

Mayfield Publishing Company
Mountain View, California
London • Toronto

Library of Congress Cataloging-in-Publication Data

Keene, Michael L.
      Easy access : the reference handbook for writers / Michael L.
Keene, Katherine H. Adams.
          p.   cm.
      Rev. ed. of: The easy access handbook, c1996.
      Includes index.
      ISBN 0-7674-0656-7
        1. English language—Rhetoric—Handbooks, manuals, etc.
      2. English language—Grammar—Handbooks, manuals, etc.   3. Report
      writing—Handbooks, manuals, etc.   I. Adams, Katherine H.
      II. Keene, Michael L. Easy access handbook.   III. Title.
      PE1408.K425   1998
      808′.042—dc21   98-7816
                                                                            CIP

Manufactured in the United States of America

10   9   8   7   6   5   4   3   2   1

Mayfield Publishing Company
1280 Villa Street
Mountain View, California 94041

Sponsoring editor, Renée Deljon; developmental editor, Barbara J. Armentrout; production editor, April Wells-Hayes; manuscript editor, Carole Crouse; art director, Jeanne M. Schreiber; text designer, Linda M. Robertson; cover designer, Laurie Anderson; illustrator, Robin Mouat; manufacturing manager, Randy Hurst. The text was set in 9.5/12 Stone Serif by Thompson Type and printed on 45# Highland Plus in black and PMS 2727 by R. R. Donnelley & Sons.

Text and illustration credits continue at the back of the book on page 448, which constitutes an extension of the copyright page.

HOW TO USE THIS HANDBOOK

Use the three-part structure and the tabbed dividers.

- Refer to **Part One, Processes and Products** (dark blue tabs), for step-by-step help with writing essays, research papers (including MLA and APA documentation styles), argumentative papers, essay exams, oral presentations, and various kinds of professional communication.

- Turn to **Part Two, Common Writing Problems** (medium blue tabs), to find Quick View Guides and helpful mini-chapters on the most common grammatical errors and problems, including those for ESL writers.

- Flip to **Part Three, The Basics from A to Z** (light blue tabs), for concise coverage of the various aspects of grammar, mechanics, and punctuation, including definitions of important terms—all presented in alphabetical order.

Refer to the Contents Overview (inside front cover).

This at-a-glance outline presents a "snapshot" of the book's contents.

Use the Quick Views to review common writing problems.

Each section in Part Two begins with a Quick View (blue pages) that briefly defines and shows how to fix a common error or grammatical problem.

Look up grammar, punctuation, and mechanics terms in The Basics from A to Z (Part Three).

Like a dictionary, Part Three is alphabetically organized to give you easy access to explanations of the rules, conventions, and exceptions you might have questions about while writing. Many entries in Part Three also contain cross-references to fuller coverage in Parts One and Two.

Check the index (pages 449–476).

The index tells you where to find the most complete discussion of every topic covered in *Easy Access.*

(continued)

v

HOW TO USE THIS HANDBOOK (continued)

Use the reference resources on the back cover, inside back cover, and back cover flap.

Here you'll find Quick View, Box, and Figure Locators (inside back cover); Revision and Correction Symbols (inside back cover flap); A Checklist for Finishing Your Paper (back cover flap); and Frequently Asked Questions (FAQs) (back cover).

Use the Easy Access Features.

1. **Tabbed dividers** mark key sections in Part One (dark blue), Part Two (medium blue), and Part Three (light blue).

2. **Margin tabs** (along pages' outer edges) in Part Two identify each common writing problem.

3. **Part contents pages** provide an overview of the contents of just that part.

4. **Running heads** at the top of each page identify the section or chapter.

5. **Explanations and examples with handwritten corrections** make writing and grammar concepts clear.

6. **Quick Views** in Part Two provide concise reviews of the most common writing problems.

130–132

ESL icons with cross-references highlight points of special concern to ESL writers.

www.

Internet icons signal information about on-line writing and research.

VERB ERRORS

QUICK VIEW

294-304

This Quick View shows the most common problems with verbs: subject-verb agreement, form, tense, and mood errors. The pages that follow explain these problems in more detail. (For a complete discussion of verbs, see *Verbs*, pages 416–27.)

Subject-Verb Agreement Errors

Subjects and verbs must agree in *number*—both singular or both plural. The subject always determines whether the verb should be singular or plural.

The design of the new cars help their gas mileage. *helps*

[A prepositional phrase (*of the new cars*) separating the subject (*design*) from the verb (*help*) has fooled the writer into making the verb agree with the plural object of the prepositional phrase (*cars*) instead of the singular subject (*design*).]

At the front of the procession was the president of the college and the dean of students. *were*

[The inverted sentence order, in which the verb preced[es] [the sub]ject, has fooled the writer into using a singular verb, w[hen the] plural (compound) subject, the *president* of the college ar[e...] of students.]

Form Errors

Verbs change form to indicate time (tense) and conve[y...] other information. *Regular verbs* change only their end[ing...] talked), whereas *irregular verbs* change internally (*sing, s[...]* go, went, gone*). Most verb form errors involve the wron[g...] irregular verbs (especially *lie* and *lay* and *sit* and *set*) o[r...] endings (*s, es, d, ed*). The most common irregular verbs [...] under *Verbs*, pages 418–21. Beyond that, a dictionary i[...] guide to verb forms.

Irina had never swam that fast before. *swum*

THE WRITING PROCESS

THE WRITING PROCESS

---

268 PROBLEMS WITH MODIFIERS

With ice one-inch thick on its wings, an accident was inevitable. *the plane was bound to have*

To take the tournament championship, corners had to be cut when it came to schoolwork. *the students on the team had to cut corners*

Being a high school senior, my parents didn't want to move until the school year ended. *Because I was*

Exception: One construction looks like a dangling modifier, but it is in fact acceptable. An *absolute modifier* is a word or a phrase that modifies a whole sentence:

Jack being an honest person, there was nothing else for him to say.

[The opening phrase places a condition on the rest of the sentence; it follows an earlier discussion of his honesty.]

The judge having considered the circumstances, she ruled that the forensic pathologist's testimony should be allowed.

[An earlier discussion describes the circumstances; the opening phrase modifies the whole sentence.]

That being said, the trial moved on.

[Presumably, the words that were said are cited in the preceding sentence.]

(For more on absolute phrases, see *Phrases*, page 377.)

SQUINTING MODIFIERS

Problems with Modifiers

A *squinting modifier* is unclear because it could modify more than one thing in the sentence—usually the word or phrase before it as well as the word or phrase after it:

Tom told the bank with great difficulty he could get the money.

[Was it hard for Tom to tell them, or hard to get the money?]

or

Tom told the bank with great difficulty he could get the money.

If you find you have written a sentence with a squinting modifier in it, rewrite the sentence to make clear exactly what the modifier refers to.

---

vii

CONTENTS

PREFACE AND ACKNOWLEDGMENTS

When we wrote the first edition of *Easy Access*, we asked ourselves how we could make a reference handbook that would be as easy as possible to use. Such a book's contents, we realized, should be divided so that students could decide which *general* part of the book (more general than chapters or sections) to access. We wanted to create a handbook structure that helped students quickly grasp the book's internal logic and—most importantly—decide which general part of the book to go to for the *kind* of information (not the specific *topic*) they needed.

It was then that we conceived of *Easy Access*, which has a unique three-part structure. Students who have used the first edition of *Easy Access* resoundingly agree that its structure automatically narrows their search to just a part of the book. Now, in the second edition, *Easy Access'* three-part structure is even more apparent because the tabs are color coded. Students can always know at a glance which of the book's three parts they're in.

Part One: Processes and Products (five dark blue tabs) contains all writing process instruction, including guides to specific types of writing—research papers, arguments, essay exams, professional documents and oral presentations.

Part Two: Common Writing Problems (two medium blue tabs) first covers the top ten most common writing problems for all students and then the most persistent writing problems for ESL students. Our colleagues and our students tell us that, because of its concentration on common problems and its inclusion of "Quick View" guides (carefully focused two-page tutorials), Part Two is the section of the book to which students most often return.

Part Three: The Basics From A to Z (one light blue tab) is an alphabetically organized quick-reference section that provides concise coverage of grammar, mechanics, usage, and punctuation. Instead of confusing or overwhelming students, our tabs and the three-part structure of *Easy Access* encourage students to find the information they need and want.

CHANGES TO THE BOOK'S CONTENTS

Extensive coverage of Internet research. This new material covers the use of search engines; the crucial task of evaluating Internet sources; and current methods of documenting these sources, in both MLA and APA styles. A sample student paper that uses both online (including an image from a Web site) and print sources serves as a reliable model. A World Wide Web glossary follows the Glossary of Usage at the end of Part Three.

A new chapter on argumentation. Offering a solid introduction to the principles and elements of argument, the chapter covers argumentative theses and assertions, types of appeals and support, refutation, logical fallacies, and the Toulmin method. We also provide a sample student paper in this section.

A new chapter on professional communication. With guidelines and models for writing e-mail, faxes, memos, direct-request letters, persuasive letters, job-application letters, and résumés, this chapter will prepare students to write outside of school. Use of the Internet to search for scholarships, internships, and jobs is also covered.

A new chapter on oral presentations. This chapter shows students how to adapt their writing for oral presentations. As preparation for either participating in class discussion or delivering a speech, this section will help students confidently make the transition from written to oral communication.

Expanded coverage of run-on sentences and comma splices. Because these common writing problems arise for different reasons, we cover them separately in Part Two.

More help for ESL writers. In response to teachers' suggestions, this section of Part Two now contains additional topics: direct and indirect quotations and questions, participles used as adjectives, and the use of *no* and *not*. We also revised the Quick View for clarity and increased the number of exercises.

Improved cross-referencing. Cross-references now describe the nature of the additional information located elsewhere in the book. We've also added icons to indicate cross-referenced ESL and Internet material.

Various smaller improvements. Reviewers helpfully directed our attention to the need for more information on the rhetorical situation, paragraph development, critical reading, and nonstandard forms of English.

CHANGES TO THE BOOK'S DESIGN

Tabbed section dividers. We have retained the plastic comb binding from the first edition (so that the book lies flat and stays open) and added tabbed section dividers (which indicate the section's contents) so that students can get to the information they're seeking even more easily.

Examples with handwritten corrections and improvements. This new example format allows students to see at a glance what's been changed in the sentence without having to compare different versions. The new format also reinforces the importance of editing and proofreading.

More "quick reference" guides at the back of the book. These guides now appear after the index, on the back cover, and on the back cover's inside and flap: Quick View, Box, and Figure Locators; Revision Symbols; A Checklist for Finishing Your Paper; and Frequently Asked Questions (FAQs).

EASY ACCESS HIGHLIGHTS

- Color-coded, tabbed section dividers that reflect the book's three-part structure *and* direct students to the chapters and subsections they are likely to need most often
- Quick View chapter openers in Part Two
- Comb binding that lets the book lie flat for easy reference
- Contents Overview on inside front cover and first page, as well as full contents on pages ix–xxv
- Contents repeated within the book by part, chapter, and tabbed section

- "How to Use this Book" guide on pages v–vii
- Icons indicating coverage that pertains to ESL writers and to the Internet

ANCILLARY MATERIALS AND RESOURCES FOR STUDENTS

- An electronic hypertext version (Windows and Macintosh formats) is available on CD-ROM (fully networkable)
- *Mayfield's Quick View Guide to the Internet for Students of English* (by Jennifer Campbell and Michael Keene, both of the University of Tennessee at Knoxville) goes into more detail about many of the Internet topics introduced in *Easy Access* and presents more advanced topics, such as the Internet's history, design, and function; listservs; and FTP. This valuable resource is free when shrink-wrapped with *Easy Access*.
- *Additional Exercises to Accompany Easy Access, Second Edition* (by Timothy Miank of Lansing Community College), is available in a print workbook, on disk, and via the World Wide Web.
- *Developmental Exercises to Accompany Easy Access, Second Edition* (by Mary Alice Hardy of Southwestern Michigan College), is available in a print workbook, on disk, and via the World Wide Web.
- *Research Across the Disciplines* (by Kristin R. Woolever and Tiane K. Donahue, of Northeastern University) discusses in detail the role of research across the curriculum, lists the major journals in various disciplines, explains the documentation formats used by different disciplines, suggests research topics, and provides annotated research papers.
- The *Easy Access* Web Site (for students) provides a "Using the Web" tutorial and numerous links to relevant WWW sites.

ANCILLARY MATERIALS AND RESOURCES FOR INSTRUCTORS

- The Instructor's Comprehensive *Easy Access* CD-ROM conveniently provides, in electronic format, transparency masters, PowerPoint files, diagnostic tests, quizzes, the additional exercises, developmental exercises, and the book's instructor's manual, which includes answers to the exercises in Part Two as well as the answers to the additional and developmental exercises.

- The *Easy Access* Web Site (for instructors) provides the same content as the instructor's CD-ROM, as well as the "Using the Web" tutorial for students, student links, and numerous professional links.

- An Instructor's Manual provides assignments for Part One, answers to the exercises in Part Two of the text and in the supplementary workbooks, additional exercises with answers, advice on teaching grammar and writing, and bibliographies on teaching writing.

- Transparency masters

- PowerPoint masters

- Diagnostic tests

- Quizzes

ACKNOWLEDGMENTS

We thank the following individuals, whose incisive comments helped inform the first and second editions of *Easy Access*. For the second edition: Deborah Bradford, University of Massachusetts–Dartmouth; Bennie J. Brown, Kilgore College; Marguerite Helmers, University of Wisconsin–Oshkosh; Mary Frances Hodges, University of Arkansas; Dan Holt, Lansing Community College; David Kann, California State Polytechnic University; Judith Kirkpatrick, Kapiolani Community College; Steven D. Krause, Southern Oregon University; Karen Laing, North Shore Community College; Anthony Petruzzi, University of Nebraska at Kearney; Susan A. Schiller, Central Michigan University; and Julie Segedy, Chabot College. For the first edition: Janice M. Albert, Las Positas College; Cathryn Amdahl, Harrisburg Area Community College; Valerie M. Balester, Texas A&M University; Richard Bullock, Wright State University; Elizabeth H. Curtin, Salisbury State University; Kathy Evertz, University of Wyoming; Judith E. Funston, State University of New York at Potsdam; Gail Garloch, Oklahoma City University; Tharon W. Howard, Clemson University; Fred O. Kemp, Texas Tech University; Emory Maiden, Appalachian State University; James C. McDonald, University of Southwestern Louisiana; Ronald D. Morrison, Morehead State University; Patricia Y. Murray, California State University, Northridge; Virginia J. Nelson, Johnson County Community College; Linda R. Peckham, Lansing Community College; Susan A. Schiller, Central Michigan

University; Paul H. Schmidt, Georgia State University; Judith A. Stanford, Rivier College; Joyce Stauffer, Indiana University–Purdue University at Fort Wayne; Sally Terrell, University of Hartford; Susan Tchudi, University of Nevada, Reno; Kristen R. Woolever, Northeastern University; Nancy Yee, Fitchburg State College; and Holly Zaitchik, Boston University.

Several very talented editors have made invaluable contributions to this book. Editor Renée Deljon helped us to decide on the additions to this edition and envisioned new elements to improve its usability. As she does with every book, developmental editor Barbara Armentrout reviewed every word carefully, always with attention to students' needs. Production editor April Wells-Hayes saw the project through to completion; art director Jeannie Schreiber and designers Linda Robertson and Laurie Anderson created the fine new cover, icons, and tabs. We thank them and their colleagues at Mayfield for their enthusiasm for this project and their unceasing concern for quality.

We also thank our colleagues for their help and support. At the University of Tennessee, Jennifer Campbell's contribution has been major, especially on Internet issues; undergraduate English majors who work as coaches in English 462 have provided valuable feedback on many of the second edition's teaching elements; and the Department of English has generously provided release time from teaching for completion of the new edition. At Loyola University, Paulette Manley proved an incisive critic of the book's layout and its ESL section. Conversations with John Biguenet, Dick Johnson, Mary McCay, Peggy McCormack, John Mosier, Thorny Penfield, Mary Waguespack, and other teachers helped us see how students were reacting to specific sections. Michele Mechta handled the endless mailing involved with two authors and a publisher, each in a different city. We also thank our families: handbook writing requires their endless patience.

Michael L. Keene
University of Tennessee, Knoxville

Katherine H. Adams
Loyola University New Orleans

PART ONE

PROCESSES AND PRODUCTS

THE WRITING PROCESS

THE WRITING PROCESS

Some people seem to find writing easy. The poet Samuel Taylor Coleridge even claimed that verse came to him in his sleep. But most people find writing difficult. Choosing a topic, gathering information, organizing ideas, and correcting grammar errors require real effort for most of us.

You can become more confident about writing by carefully considering the processes that other writers employ. Experienced writers—lawyers, doctors, teachers, journalists, novelists—have individual habits. Some write in the middle of the night, and others choose the early morning or afternoon hours; some read each word to a spouse or friend, and others deal only with editors; some swear by a computer, and others work on legal pads; some compose and revise in their heads, and others put every word down on paper.

Even though their habits vary, experienced writers rely on five steps in writing. These steps are "recursive," meaning that you can move through any of them more than once if you need more information, a better organization, or a more developed draft.

Working in these flexible and repeatable stages can make writing more manageable—and thus more successful. For your assignments, try out the suggestions on the writing process given here in part 1. You will be building valuable writing habits for college and your career.

Steps of the Writing Process

prewriting	deciding on the subject, considering the needs of the reader, gathering information
planning	choosing a preliminary thesis and organization
drafting	writing a first draft to develop the main ideas and discover new ones
revising	making changes in the thesis, structure, content, paragraphing, and sentences
finishing	proofreading for grammar, mechanics, and spelling errors and preparing the final copy

PREWRITING

Before starting a paper, you need to choose or narrow a topic or subject and select the information you want to present. This first stage of the writing process, called prewriting, involves answering six questions and using one or more invention techniques to generate ideas.

QUESTIONS FOR GETTING STARTED

Start your work by considering the following six questions; jot down your answers even if they seem incomplete at this point.

Question One: What Is the Assignment?

Begin by carefully reviewing the writing task. What do you need to know about the assignment? Suppose you were asked to write a paper about some aspect of organized sports at your school. You might choose to write about the women's basketball team, about the importance of sports teams in building school spirit, or about a decision to cut funding for team sports. To narrow the topic and do this assignment well, you need answers to the following questions:

- Who is the **audience** for the paper? Is it students, parents, alumni, teachers, or some other group? What background and characteristics does that group have?
- What types of **research materials** should you use? You could interview current and former team members, coaches, and students; you could do library or Internet research on sports programs at other schools.
- What type of **thesis** should the piece have? Should you argue for or against a certain program or recount the history of one of the teams?
- What **organizational structure** would be appropriate? You could describe a particular game of the women's basketball team and then explain the team's history; you could compare the volleyball team and the football team; or you could argue for increased funding for team sports.
- What is the assigned **length?** When is the paper **due?**

If you're not sure about the answers, ask your teacher or discuss the paper with classmates and writing center tutors.

Question Two: What Should I Write About?

As a first step in choosing a topic if one has not been assigned, consider your interests:

- What subjects do you know well?
- What subjects would you like to know more about?
- What interests you about situations and ideas you have encountered in your classes? at your job? through your hobbies? through your friends and family? in books and magazines? in movies and television shows?
- What are your favorite places?
- What are your best and worst memories?
- What lively debates have you participated in recently?
- What are your career goals?

If you use your interests as a guide to choosing a topic, you are more likely to enjoy working on your assignment, and the paper will reflect your strengths. You might write a paper comparing two bosses you've worked for, several television shows you've seen, or three methods of disciplining children that you have observed at local schools. Your paper on a campus problem might argue against plans to pave over a grassy area or a decision to bar a controversial speaker from participating in a student forum.

Question Three: How Can I Limit My Topic?

Once you have chosen a general topic, you need to narrow it sufficiently so that you can present enough facts and examples to support your main points. If you decide to write about tuition, summer jobs, or television news, for example, try to limit that general topic by listing possible subtopics:

Broad Topics	Subtopics
tuition	increases in tuition
	student loans and grants
	part-time jobs
	scholarships

summer jobs	types of jobs
	job availability
	personal experiences
television news	coverage of political campaigns
	sensationalized stories on violent crime
	the competition caused by CNN
	the styles of different commentators at local stations

After you have made such a list, choose the subtopic

- that best suits the assignment,
- that you already know something about, or
- that you would like to learn more about.

When you have limited your topic once, you may need to limit it further. How all the television news shows cover an election, for example, is probably still too large a topic for a short paper. You might write instead about one network, one political convention, or one news anchor.

Question Four: What Is My Purpose in Writing about This Topic?

As you are deciding on a specific topic, consider your purpose in writing about it. People write for many different purposes, but when we write for others, there are three general aims:

- to **entertain** readers
- to **inform** readers
- to **persuade** readers to accept a particular viewpoint and change their actions

You can begin to formulate your purpose by asking yourself, "What exactly am I trying to accomplish in this piece of writing?" If your paper compares two bosses, you can entertain readers with stories about unorthodox training methods, or you can inform them of the problems caused by disrespect for employees. A paper about school sports teams might inform other students about the women's basketball team or persuade the trustees to increase funding for the soccer team. By considering your purpose before you start writing, you will have a clearer sense of what to include and how to state your points.

Writing for a General Audience or for the Teacher as Audience

In college you will sometimes be writing for a general audience and sometimes for the teacher as audience. In either case, you should consider the reader's needs and interests carefully. The following points should help you to address the reader.

- Both a general audience and a teacher as audience have a basic knowledge of politics, history, entertainment, and other fields, but you should not expect them to be experts on your subject. Thus for both audiences you will need to define specialized terminology, explain the historical background of a problem, or summarize the plot of a story.

- Neither audience may already be interested in your subject—assume that you'll need to create an interest.

- These readers should be able to perceive a clear purpose in your writing. Try to envision a specific goal—to entertain, inform, or persuade.

- They will consider your points carefully and critically.

- They appreciate clear writing and a tone that is neither extremely formal nor extremely informal.

Question Five: Who Are the Readers of My Paper?

Writing involves not only your topic and purpose but also your readers' needs. If you're going to instruct them about how to do something, whether it be sewing, skiing, or job hunting, you must consider their skills and preferences. If you want to persuade them to agree with you on a controversial topic like school discipline, drug testing, or gun control, you should analyze their values and knowledge of the subject.

As part of your prewriting, then, consider the following list of questions about your readers. The answers should help you to more effectively entertain them, inform them of new ideas, or persuade them to accept your judgments.

- What age are my readers?
- How much education do they have?
- What do they value most?

- What do they fear?
- Will they be seeking my information, or will I have to convince them of its importance?
- How do they feel about my topic? How does it affect them?
- How much do they know about it?
- What vocabulary concerning my subject will they already know? Will their definitions agree with mine?
- What examples will they find most disturbing or inspiring?

Question Six: What Is My Role as Writer?

After you analyze your readers, think about how you will appear to them. Writers play many roles—among them, the entertaining storyteller, stern boss, helpful teacher, conscientious reporter, or committed advocate. If you are writing for a general audience or for your teacher, you will take on the role of an informed researcher who presents information clearly and concisely.

Your role helps you to determine what to say and how to say it. Informal language and flippancy don't belong on a job application, for example. If you're applying for a job, present yourself as a respectful and professional candidate:

Too Informal	More Appropriate
I'd like to get that clerking job you put in the paper.	I would like to apply for the clerk's position that you advertised in the *Times Picayune*.

If you're writing an article for the campus paper, you want to seem informed, helpful, and not too formal:

Too Formal	More Appropriate
When the education year commences this September, registration will transpire at the portals of the student center.	When the fall term begins in September, students will register at the student center.

Once you have answered all six of these questions, you will have defined your rhetorical situation—you will know whom you are addressing for what reason. As you move from high school to college, from one college class to another, and from college into professional life, you will write in a number of different rhetorical situations, each one shaping the writing you produce. Answering these six questions before you begin to write will help you to succeed in each situation that you encounter.

INVENTION TECHNIQUES FOR DEVELOPING YOUR IDEAS

After considering the six questions, you will be ready to decide on the specific facts and examples that will entertain, inform, or persuade your readers. To develop your ideas thoroughly, try out the invention techniques preferred by professional writers. As you experiment with the following techniques, *write as much as you can*. You can then choose the best ideas for your paper. If you plan to write on a word processor, begin using it now. Later, you may be able to paste some of your invention notes into a rough draft without recopying them.

Listing

Do you make reminder lists of assignments, errands, or friends' birthdays? Lists can also help you develop your ideas. If you are writing about your father, list thirty of his habits. If you are arguing against capital punishment, write down all the reasons you oppose it. Lists can be made quickly; they allow you to consider all kinds of facts and possibilities.

Freewriting

Put your general topic at the top of a sheet of paper, and then freewrite about the topic for at least five minutes. Don't begin a rough draft; just write down in any order—in sentences or in phrases—all the ideas that come to mind. You can decide later where they will go and how to connect them.

To begin work on a paper about starting first grade, for example, you might record everything that you remember, in any order:

> O.K., the subject is my first day at school. I remember entering the yard to see all these other first graders that I knew from kindergarten, but we were up here with the bigger kids, through a new gate where

we would line up for a flag ceremony by class. My mother held my hand tightly because she was much more nervous than I was, I think. I was back toward the building with my friends (and my mother) when I heard a cry, "Where's Cole?" It was my friend, Micah, from day care who was new at my school. . . .

Using these remembered details in your final draft will help you create a clear impression for your readers.

Looping

Looping is a form of freewriting that may lead to more reflection about your topic. Freewrite for a set amount of time, perhaps five minutes, and then read what you have written. Next, decide on the best point or information in that piece and write about it for another five minutes. If you "loop" three or four times, you will be investigating new ideas and focusing your writing on the best of them.

Reporters' Questions

Write down your topic, and then ask yourself the six questions reporters rely on in their investigations:

- *What* was it?
- *Who* was involved in it?
- *When* did it happen?
- *Where* did it happen?
- *How* did it happen?
- *Why* did it happen?

If you're writing about the soccer team at your school, for example, you might consider who plays on it, why soccer is or is not popular there, and how it is played. These questions will help you find out what you know—and what you need to research further.

Paragraph Development Questions

Once you have a general topic, you may find it helpful to consider the traditional methods of presenting information, such as narration and comparison, to develop new perspectives on your topic:

- **Description:** How would you describe it? What are its traits? physical characteristics? How does it taste, smell, look, feel, sound?
- **Narration:** How did it come about? What history does it have?
- **Examples:** What examples illustrate your topic?
- **Cause and effect:** What caused it? What effects has it created?
- **Comparison:** What is it similar to or different from? Can it be compared to some more familiar item? How is it like or unlike that familiar item?
- **Process:** How does it occur? What processes does it involve? How is it used?

For a paper on summer jobs, for example, these questions might lead you to describe types of jobs, to tell a story about your experience, to cite examples of available jobs, to discuss the causes of a current job shortage, to compare different opportunities, and to review the application process. Your answers might also indicate a format for a paragraph or even for a complete essay. (For examples of these six developmental patterns, see pages 31–36.)

Observation

You may think you understand a place or a situation well, but you can extend your knowledge by observation. If you decide to write about your campus, sit in the library, halls, or campus center and take notes about what you see. What are the age range and the ethnic makeup of the students? Do they spend time socializing or do they only come and go to classes? (For advice on observation, see page 55–56.)

Interviews

Just as you are asking questions of yourself, you should also seek information from others. For a paper on law school admission policies, you could talk to college seniors, law students, and the head of admissions. An interview can consist of one question or many; it can occur on the phone or in person. You can also ask questions of a larger group by creating a survey or questionnaire. (For advice on interviews and surveys, see pages 56–59.)

Reading

You should also investigate your topic by reading about it in books, journals, newspapers, and pamphlets, and perhaps on the Internet. Even if the teacher did not ask you to write a research paper, relevant statistics or quotations may strengthen your arguments. (For suggestions about library, or secondary, research, see pages 59–73.)

Brainstorming and Peer Review

As you investigate your subject, you might talk through your developing ideas with your classmates. Talking about your paper will help you to focus on the best and worst parts and will enable other students to offer suggestions—as your first readers.

PLANNING

After you have gathered information, you will be ready to plan your paper, the second stage of the writing process. This section focuses on choosing a preliminary main idea and creating a visual plan or outline.

CHOOSING A MAIN IDEA OR THESIS

A **thesis** is a sentence that presents the main idea of the paper, an idea that every fact and detail should support. Although you may alter it after you write a first draft, formulating a thesis now will help you to organize your ideas.

A good thesis has two qualities:

- It states the paper's **topic.**
- It states a specific **opinion** or **attitude** concerning that topic.

The thesis will also help you to establish your purpose. In the following examples, the first thesis might introduce a paper intended to *entertain;* the second, a paper intended to *inform;* and the third, a paper intended to *persuade:*

Topic	Thesis Statement (*Topic + Opinion or Attitude*)
1. Two bosses	The two shop managers I worked for last summer had bizarre methods of training workers.
2. The law school admissions process	To complete the law school admissions process successfully, students need to give adequate time to choosing schools, preparing for the LSAT exam, and completing the applications.
3. Residence hall visitation policies	The new visitation policies are causing students to leave the residence halls.

Once you have formulated a specific thesis statement, review your prewriting and choose the best facts and examples to support the thesis. As you write your rough draft, you will be able to create a unified whole by keeping this thesis in mind.

CHOOSING AN ORGANIZATIONAL PATTERN

After you have collected your information and written a preliminary thesis statement, you should begin organizing your ideas, a
process that will continue as you write a first draft. Your subject
matter, purpose, audience, and role will help you to determine
which organizational structure will be best for your paper.

- **Chronological:** You may decide to present events or details in
  a time sequence, from first to last or from past to present. This
  structure might be appropriate for telling a story about a difficult
  boss or for explaining the law school's admission process.

- **Spatial:** A spatial order helps create an exact picture and thus
  enables readers to envision a scene: from left to right, top to bottom, or inside to outside. This choice might be best for explaining the appearance of a residence hall room or of an employee
  training facility.

- **Emphasis or order of importance:** You may want to order
  your details or examples from least important to most important
  so that your readers encounter your strongest points or recommendations—about facts to consider when choosing a residence
  hall, for example—right before the conclusion.

- **General to specific:** You may choose to begin a paper with
  your general judgment—perhaps of current residence hall policies—and then move through the specific cases or points of evidence that support your judgment. This choice provides readers
  with a clear presentation: an overview of a situation and the thesis concerning it, the details that develop the thesis, and a concluding statement that restates key points and further analyzes
  the subject's meaning or impact.

- **Specific to general:** You may decide to discuss several decisions
  made by your boss and then move to your general opinion of
  him or her; instead of encountering the thesis first, readers will
  be actively reviewing the data and coming to the same conclusion that you state.

(The strategies for paragraph development discussed on pages 31–36
can also provide organizational structures for complete essays.)

CREATING A PLAN FOR THE PAPER

After deciding on a preliminary thesis and considering possible
methods of organization, you can begin to structure your paper.

Your decisions may change as you write, but a preliminary plan will help direct your work. After you have finished drafting, you may decide to make a second plan or outline—to evaluate your product and determine the necessary revisions. (For more on outlining, see pages 16–17 and 23–24.)

To plan your paper, read over your prewriting materials and your thesis, and then try one of the following planning devices: clusters, topic outlines, and formal outlines.

Clusters

To create a cluster, write the main idea or thesis sentence in the middle of a sheet of paper and draw a circle around it. Then draw lines out from that circle to smaller circles and write in them the major points that will prove or develop that main idea. Repeat this process to list your supporting evidence for these points.

When you finish, you can decide whether you've placed each example or fact under the right topic and whether you have enough detail supporting each major topic. A cluster can also help you decide on the best order for your ideas.

The cluster shown in Figure 1 concerns campus parking. After making this cluster, the writer can see that she needs more specific information about the location of the new parking lots.

Topic Outlines

If you feel fairly sure about the order of your main points, you may prefer simply listing them instead of creating a cluster. A topic outline, which you can create quickly and modify as you write, provides a general plan to follow. The more details you include, the clearer your course will be.

Sample Topic Outline

Thesis: CNN has redefined our expectations of how international crises should be reported.

role of the news anchor
used by CNN primarily to provide transitions between
reporters in the field
less emphasis on analysis
expectation of coverage to be immediate, on the scene
new emphasis on risk taking
new emphasis on moment-to-moment reporting

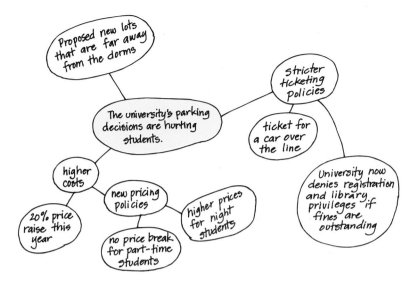

Figure 1. Clustering Diagram for Thesis about Campus Parking

Formal Outlines

For longer and more involved assignments, you might choose a formal outline, which will help you to indicate main ideas and various levels of subordinate ideas and the connections between them. These outlines can consist of phrases or complete sentences.

To create a fuller analysis of CNN, the writer might develop a formal outline, such as the following, before beginning a draft.

Thesis: CNN's reporting of international crises has led to changes in network news.

    I. CNN's reporting style
       A. Reduced importance of the news anchor as reporter
          1. Less news reporting from the newsroom desk
          2. Primary purpose to provide transitions between reports from the field
       B. More immediate, on-the-scene coverage
          1. New emphasis on risk taking
             a. Command stations in dangerous areas
             b. Reporters who travel with army units
             c. Reporters who infiltrate terrorist groups
          2. New emphasis on photography

II. Effect on networks
   A. Changes in the news anchor's job
      1. Relocation of some anchors to on-the-scene reporting
      2. Hiring of news analysts—experts not found on CNN
   B. Changes in network news gathering
      1. Pressure to have expensive crews around the world
      2. Some pooling of resources by networks to compete

III. Conclusion: As CNN continues to improve its worldwide reporting, the networks will have to continue to change, perhaps ultimately going to a news analysis format and contracting for all on-the-scene coverage through CNN or a consortium of stations.

DRAFTING

Once you have considered your subject, audience, thesis, and organization, you will be ready to write a rough draft. In the first draft, your goal should be to develop the main idea of the paper, to put the major points in order—and not much more. Try to write quickly, getting down lots of words and not worrying over each paragraph and sentence. You want to produce not a finished product but a draft (from an Anglo-Saxon word meaning "to draw or sketch"), a preliminary version that will be enlarged upon through revision.

"How can I know what I think until I see what I write?" asked novelist E. M. Forster. By taking chances with this first draft and letting the writing flow, you can find out what you think and how best to say it.

FINDING THE BEST TIME AND PLACE

Before you begin your draft, think about what will help you complete it in one sitting. Does some background noise—perhaps a radio playing in your room—help you concentrate? Or do you like the quiet of a library carrel or a secluded area of the park? Do you need an early-morning burst of energy or late-night solitude? Think back to where and when you wrote a successful paper: early morning in your room, late afternoon in the back booth at McDonald's, or late night at the computer lab. If possible, return there to draft your next paper.

Whatever your favorite writing spot and time, give yourself enough uninterrupted time—at least an hour—to complete the draft. If you have to stop without finishing, you may forget some of what you planned to say.

CHOOSING THE BEST TOOLS

Drafting is easier and more productive if you use the right tools. Some writers prefer fine-point pens; others use felt-tips, ballpoints, or pencil. Experiment to see what you're comfortable with.

Paper is another consideration. You may prefer legal-size pages, which let you put more words on a page, or a spiral notebook, where you can locate everything easily. You may double-space and write on one side of the page; then you can make changes easily as you revise.

You may find that you write more fluently with a word processor than with pen and paper. If your prewriting notes are on disk, you can move some of them into your first draft. Then, as you revise, you will be able to make changes—adding, deleting, and moving text—without starting over.

STARTING YOUR FIRST DRAFT

When you are ready to write, begin the drafting process by reviewing the results of your research and planning. (See pages 14–17.) You might put your thesis, audience analysis, and outline on one sheet of paper. You can then group your notes so that they reflect your intended order.

Although you are trying to produce a complete draft, you don't have to begin at the beginning and write to the end. If you are most confident about some of your supporting data, you can skip the introduction and plunge in at the second or third paragraph. If you have a strong message for the reader, you can begin with the conclusion.

WRITING QUICKLY

As you proceed, keep your thesis and the readers' interests in mind, and follow your outline. If new ideas occur to you but don't seem to fit, write them down anyway to ensure that you don't forget them. In fact, you should try to get down every point that supports your thesis and fulfills your purpose of entertaining, informing, or persuading.

As you work, try to enjoy the writing. This time is for you to explore creative options; nothing you write can be wrong. Ignore the voice inside that says "This is too short," "This sentence sounds stupid," or "This part isn't clear"; revising and proofreading will come later. Your product may be—even should be—uneven and imperfect.

GETTING UNSTUCK AND RESTARTED

You may be able to keep writing smoothly, without any breaks, moving through the outline point by point to your conclusion. Or you may get stuck and feel unable to go on. To get unstuck, return to your prewriting and outline notes or reread what you have written so far—to jar your memory or reveal a new angle.

If you realize you don't have enough information about a particular point, leave a dash—or write down the question that you will need to answer—and keep going. But if this missing fact or opinion could change the entire paper, write down the rest of your ideas quickly and then return to the prewriting stage to continue investigating your topic.

BEFORE LEAVING THE DESK

If you are writing paragraphs out of order, try to get back to all the points in your outline before you stop. Your draft should be nearly complete, even though it may have some blank spots and certainly many rough spots.

Before you leave your first draft, you might make some notes to guide your revisions. Jot down the points that need more research, possible changes in organization, or another good idea that has just come to you.

Then, rejoice. You have created a complete draft of the paper. You are not still pondering the second sentence of the introduction or avoiding your assignment by sharpening pencils or doing your laundry. You will make changes—there is more work to be done—but you should feel a real sense of accomplishment.

REVISING

When your first draft is complete, you will be ready to begin revising, the fourth step of the writing process. *Revising* means "re-seeing" your work in many ways, from the largest elements (its structure, the arguments you make, the examples you use, etc.) to the smallest details. You must be willing to let your own best judgment and instincts suggest how the scope of your revising needs to be defined. Revising may mean starting over from scratch, or it may mean just changing a word here or there and checking for grammatical errors. We present here a very systematic and orderly revising process, starting with the thesis and the overall structure and then moving to each paragraph and each sentence, working through your draft from the largest elements to the smallest. Following this kind of orderly process for revising is important; you shouldn't proofread for grammar and spelling errors until you have settled the larger issues of meaning and structure. (See pages 45–48 for more on when and how to proofread.) But as your own experience has probably already told you, the reality of revising can be both broader in scope and less orderly in sequence than any textbook or handbook could ever faithfully portray.

REVISING: THESIS AND STRUCTURE

The first step in revision is to reread the whole, without stopping to make corrections. If a peer review is not possible, try to read as though you were your intended readers, imitating their knowledge and interest level.

As you read, *make an outline*, not of what you intended, but of what is really there, the major point of each paragraph. Then, with the new outline before you, consider these four thesis and structure questions and jot down your answers:

1. What is my thesis? Did I state it effectively? Should I rewrite it to reflect the information the paper now presents?
2. Will I need more information to support my revised thesis?
3. Have I chosen the most effective method of organization?
4. Do I have a clear outline to follow?

The following sections will help you evaluate and revise your draft.

Evaluating Your Thesis and the Supporting Information

Let's suppose that your rough draft has a general thesis, chosen for the purpose of informing other students in your area about how to plan a beach vacation:

> **Original Thesis:** You need to plan your summer trip to the beach.

After reviewing your paragraphs along with your answers to the six questions on pages 4–9, you can choose a stronger, more focused thesis, consisting of a specific topic and a clear opinion or attitude concerning it. (See pages 13 and 29–30.)

> **Revised Thesis:** Getting a good summer beach rental requires four steps that you should complete during March and April.
>
> or
>
> A fun week at the North Carolina coast can cost as little as $400 if you plan carefully for entertainment, food, and lodging.
>
> or
>
> Because of recent environmental problems, you should avoid the North Carolina beaches in late August.

The next step is to decide whether you have all the information needed to support this revised thesis. If more details seem necessary, return to the prewriting questions and invention techniques discussed on pages 4–12.

Evaluating the Organizational Structure

When you have the information needed to support your thesis, you will be ready to review the outline of your first draft and choose the most effective order for your ideas. Your thesis should help determine the organization of the new draft. The revised thesis sentences about the beach, for example, might lead to three of the structures discussed on page 14:

- With the thesis "Getting a good summer beach rental requires four steps that you should complete during March and April," the writer promises a chronological structure, which requires discussing the steps in order, with a paragraph or more given to each one.
- After reading the thesis "A fun week at the North Carolina coast can cost as little as $400 if you plan carefully for entertainment, food, and lodging," an audience would naturally expect a general-

to-specific structure, with the general assertion stated in the introduction and with separate paragraphs providing the specifics on the three items.

- For an essay with the thesis "Because of recent environmental problems, you should avoid the North Carolina beaches in late August," the writer might choose a specific-to-general structure, in which the problems would first be enumerated and then the recommendation would appear in the conclusion.

Once you decide on the appropriate organizational changes, you will be ready to create a new outline and begin work on a second draft.

Evaluating Your Outline

The next step, then, is to reorganize your information, deciding on the best order for your main ideas. (See pages 15–17 for more information on outlines.)

In the following example, each paragraph would emphasize fun and cost, as does the thesis:

Thesis: A fun week at the North Carolina coast can cost as little as $400 if you plan carefully for entertainment, food, and lodging.

Paragraph 1

By using the special deals advertised in beach newspapers, you can enjoy the best entertainment at reasonable prices.

Paragraph 2

Local fish and vegetable stores as well as the specials offered at non-tourist restaurants provide delicious, economical dining.

Paragraph 3

By investigating "return condos" and other unadvertised real estate options, you can get an excellent house or condominium at a very low rate.

In this next example, the paragraphs would clearly relate to the thesis and to each other:

Thesis: Getting a good summer beach rental requires four steps that you should complete during March and April.

Paragraph 1

Your first step will be to get a list of the reputable real estate offices in the area and work through the "hype" in their catalogues.

Paragraph 2

After you have completed the preliminary analysis, you should talk to the most reputable offices about their rental options.

Paragraph 3

When you have reviewed the catalogues and special options, you should be ready to narrow your choices and make the final decision.

Paragraph 4

Although you are almost finished now, you should carefully review the contract and policies before you rent a house or condominium.

For the third paper, you might begin with a general statement of topic, describe the growing environmental problems, and conclude with the thesis.

Initial Statement of Topic:

Given recent developments on the North Carolina coast, planning a beach vacation requires some knowledge of environmental conditions.

Paragraph 1

The beginning of the hurricane season has in recent years brought huge clumps of seaweed to the shore in late August.

Paragraph 2

Mosquitoes, spawned in standing water at coastal construction sites, also come out en masse at that time.

Paragraph 3

Stinging jellyfish, called sea nettles, come into shallow waters in late August to feed on plankton, a food source that has been greatly increased by recent beach dredging.

Thesis: Because of these recent environmental problems, you should avoid the North Carolina beaches in late August.

REVISING PARAGRAPHS

Along with the thesis and the overall structure, you will want to consider each paragraph of your paper as you revise. In the first draft, some paragraphs may consist of one undeveloped idea or several ideas placed together without a clear connection. The following sections will help you expand and unify these introductory, body, and concluding paragraphs.

Introductions

In the first draft, a couple of sentences may have sufficed as an introduction. As you revise, concentrate on bringing readers into your text, sparking their interest and acquainting them with your topic.

- Many introductory paragraphs open with the essay's **general topic,** explain or limit the topic further in one or more sentences, and then state the thesis of the essay:

  The North Carolina coast is saturated with expensive condominiums and beach houses. Many of the new restaurants and clubs also seem to cater to a wealthy beach clientele. But don't despair. A fun week at the North Carolina coast can cost as little as $400 if you plan carefully for entertainment, food, and lodging.

- Another common opener is **historical background information** that acquaints the readers with the subject and prepares them for the thesis:

  In the last ten years, the United States has become absolutely awash in illegal drugs. Tougher laws, greater efforts at interdiction, and stronger rhetoric at all levels of government and from both political parties have not and will not be able to stop the flow. That is why we must begin to consider what heretofore has been beyond the realm of consideration: decriminalization.

  —Kurt Schmoke, "A War for the Surgeon General, Not the Attorney General"

- You might also state the **sides of the debate** before moving to your viewpoint or thesis:

  The world, as always, is debating the issues of war and peace. Conservatives believe safety lies in more arms and increased firepower. Liberals place their trust in disarmament and a nuclear freeze. I suggest we will be saved by neither fire nor ice, that the solutions being offered by the political right and left miss the mark. Our problem lies not in our technology, but in our minds, in our ancient tendency to create our enemies in our own imagination.

  —Sam Keen and Ann Page, *The Faces of the Enemy*

- You might prefer to engage your readers' interest through an **individual case or anecdote,** which sets the stage for the thesis:

  Historically, my lifetime is important because I was part of the last generation born into a world of total legal separation in the Southern United States. When the Supreme Court outlawed segregation in the public schools in 1954, I was twenty-one. When Congress passed the Civil Rights Act of 1964, permitting blacks free access to public places, I was thirty-one. The world I was born into had been segregated for a long time—so long, in fact, that I never met anyone who had lived during the time when restrictive laws were not in existence, although some people spoke of parents and others who had lived during the "free" time. As far as anyone knew, the laws as they then existed would stand forever. They were meant to—and did— create a world that fixed black people at the bottom of society in all aspects of human life. It was a world without options.

  —Mary E. Mebane, *Mary*

- You can also **address your readers directly:**

  There is no right or wrong way to visit a museum. The most important rule you should keep in mind as you go through the front door is to follow your own instincts. Be prepared to find what excites you, to enjoy what delights your heart and mind, perhaps to have esthetic experiences you will never forget. You have a feast in store for you and you should make the most of it. Stay as long or as short a time as you will, but do your best at all times to let the work of art speak directly to you with a minimum of interference or distraction.

  —David Finn, *How to Visit a Museum*

- Many writers introduce the thesis through a **relevant quotation or paraphrase:**

  "Competition by its very nature is always unhealthy. Rivalry of any kind is both psychologically disastrous and philosophically unjustifiable." These claims made by Alfie Kohn in "Why Competition?" are too strong to be defensible. Although competition has certain negative features, there are positive aspects which should be noted. Competition is neither an unqualified evil, as Kohn would claim, nor an unqualified good, as a Vince Lombardi would have it. But it is on balance more likely to be a good than an evil.

  —Richard W. Eggerman, "Competition as a Mixed Good"

Introductions to Avoid

1. Avoid the flat announcement that "The purpose of this essay is . . ." or "This paper will be about . . ." Stating the obvious will not engage your reader.
2. Don't start with "According to Webster . . ." or another form of dictionary definition. This type of lead-in has been overused, and it rarely adds much to the essay.
3. Don't apologize for your opinions or level of knowledge with a phrase like "I'm not sure, but I think . . ." State your ideas with confidence.

Conclusions

Like introductions, conclusions in first drafts are often left undeveloped, as just a short summary of the main idea. As you revise, shape the conclusion to ensure that your readers understand your main points and the significance of your arguments. The following types of conclusions can make this final section effective and vivid:

- In a conclusion, you can discuss the **results or future impact of your subject,** as in Joyce Maynard's essay concerning the first generation to grow up with television:

  Anguished, frustrated and enraged by a decade of war in Vietnam as we saw it on the news, we became part of the news ourselves—with peace marches, rallies in the streets. But only briefly; we were easily discouraged, quick to abandon hope for change and to lose interest. That, also, comes from a television-watching childhood, I think: a short attention span, and a limpness, an inertia, acquired from too many hours spent in the easy chair, never getting up except to change the channels.

  —Joyce Maynard, "I Remember"

- You may want to provide **a call for action or an attitude change,** as in this conclusion to an essay by a woman whose husband had been killed by a drunk driver:

  I still feel victimized by a system that seems to give more rights to offenders than to victims. I feel unsafe sharing the roads with drivers awaiting court dates while they continue breaking the law. I lack confidence that public safety is upheld when drivers can ignore court sentences without automatic penalty. I also understand that change comes gradually. But the first step is public awareness through education and new legislation. Only then can we hope to change a culture that allows drunk drivers to keep on killing.

—Judith M. Mardorf, "When a Drunk Driver Kills"

- You may choose to state your final judgment, or plea for action, through **a quotation from an authority,** as in this selection calling for greater public attention to the effects of insecticides:

It is the public that is being asked to assume the risks that the insect controllers calculate. The public must decide whether it wishes to continue on the present road, and it can only do so when in full possession of the facts. In the words of Jean Rostand, "The obligation to endure gives us the right to know."

—Rachel Carson, *Silent Spring*

- If you have been using an example or a case study throughout the paper, you might state your final judgment by again alluding to **a particular instance,** as in Michele L. Norris's essay concerning children who grow up in crack houses:

Asked if he would sell or use drugs when he grows up, Dooney shook his head violently and wrinkled his nose in disgust. But the expression faded, and Dooney looked at the floor: "I don't want to sell drugs, but I will probably have to."

—Michele L. Norris, "Growing Up in a World of Crack"

Conclusions to Avoid

1. Avoid the flat statement "In conclusion. . . ."
2. Don't simply restate your thesis or introductory paragraph. Your conclusion should refer to material presented in your body paragraphs—and its larger meaning.
3. Don't start off in an entirely new direction: the conclusion should further develop the content of the essay.

Body Paragraphs

When you revise your rough draft, make sure that each body paragraph clearly presents information about one part of your argument. You may need to work on

- choosing a clear topic sentence,
- developing that main idea thoroughly, and
- presenting the supporting information in a unified format.

Choosing and Placing the Topic Sentence

A topic sentence presents the paragraph's main idea and controls the rest of its contents: every sentence in the paragraph should support this main assertion. Your revisions may involve strengthening each topic sentence to ensure that it states one main idea, eliminating details that don't support that idea, and including more details to back up that one assertion per paragraph.

Most frequently, the topic sentence begins the paragraph, giving the reader a clear idea of what will follow, as in this paragraph about settling America. (The topic sentence is italicized for emphasis.) Notice how each sentence focuses on the specific topic, the role of women in the new settlements:

> *Women were an integral part of the permanent settlements in the New World.* When men traveled alone to America, they came as fortune hunters, adventurers looking for a pot of gold; such single men had no compelling reason to establish communities. Women acted as civilizers for men living alone in the wilderness. Where there were women, there were children who had to be taught. There was a future—a reason to establish laws, towns, churches, schools. The organizers of Virginia understood as much when they sought to attract women to their colony so that the men who came "might be faster tied to Virginia." The labor provided by a wife and children also helped transform the forest into farmland. In the early days of the Georgia settlement the proprietors advertised for male recruits with "industrious wives."
>
> —Carol Hymowitz and Michaele Weissman,
> *A History of Women in America*

Sometimes the topic sentence comes last, to sum up the paragraph's contents. The reasoning proceeds from facts or examples to the main idea that they all support, as in this paragraph about Nepal (the topic sentence is italicized for emphasis):

> Nepal's forests have been pushed so far back from rural populations that it takes, on average, 1.4 additional hours each day for women to collect firewood and fodder than it did just a decade ago. The extra hours are taken, in part, from women's work time in agricultural production, reducing total farm labor by as much as 24 percent per household and thus lowering household productivity. By lowering agricultural productivity, this deforestation has reduced food consumption on average more than 100 calories per capita per day. In addition, time for food preparation and child care has also been lost; this loss furthers the decline in nutrition, especially for children. Expanded planting on hillsides shifts cropping patterns away from rice and other high-quality calorie sources, reducing the nutritional content of the families' diets even more. *The combined effect is a downward spiral of incomes and health, as malnourished individuals are less and less able to overcome the problems caused by deforestation.*
>
> —John W. Mellor, "The Intertwining of Environmental Problems and Poverty"

In other paragraphs, the writer implies but does not specifically provide a topic sentence. Here, Naomi Wolf never directly states her strong dislike for the intimidation of women at department store cosmetics counters:

> On either side of her are ranks of angels—seraphim and cherubim—the "perfect" faces of the models on display. Behind them, across a liminal counter, stands the guardian angel. The saleswoman is human, she knows, but "perfected" like the angels around her, from whose ranks the woman sees her own flawed face, reflected back and shut out. Disoriented within the man-made heaven of the store, she can't focus on what makes both the live and pictured angels seem similarly "perfect": that they are both heavily lacquered. The lacquer bears little relation to the outer world, as the out-of-place look of a fashion shoot on a city street makes clear. But the mortal world disintegrates in her memory at the shame of feeling so out of place among the ethereal objects. Put in the wrong, the shopper longs to cross over.
>
> —Naomi Wolf, "Faith Healers and Holy Oil: Inside the Cosmetics Industry"

Developing the Main Idea

As you sharpen your topic sentences and decide where to place them in your paragraphs, you may need to generate more content to support them. Here are six development strategies for expanding your ideas into complete, unified paragraphs.

Description

When the six o'clock news announces a major earthquake, the numbers (fatalities, rating on the Richter scale, total property damage) don't always provide much impact. But when the newscaster describes a group of injured children whose parents cannot be located, the tragedy seems more real. If you want to convince university administrators that the student cafeteria is unsanitary, describe the filthy kitchen and serving areas. Similarly, if you want them to alter registration procedures, write about long waiting lines.

Effective descriptions acquaint the reader with an actual scene and the people involved, with specifics of a situation as well as your attitude concerning it. Notice here how editorialist Horace G. Davis uses each detail to create the dominant impression he intends, to show readers the horror that is capital punishment:

> A figure, and it could be John Spenkelink, is strapped bolt upright in Old Sparky only two, at the most three, feet beyond the glass. The figure is rigid, unable to move a fraction of an inch. A chin guard, maybe a football or medical jaw support, is firmly strapped around chin and mouth and seemingly cruelly fastens the head to the chair-back. Perched on the head is the hood, brass nut protruding from the top, with the black face flap pulled up. The only flesh visible is the lower arms, a portion of the electrode-wrapped right leg, and four inches of face from nose to mid-forehead.
>
> The scene is a tacky copy of Disney World's haunted mansion. For maybe 30 seconds, this trussed and immobile figure stares into the waiting room. The eyes are wide open, they do not blink. They look neither calm nor terrified.
>
> The figure shares the somewhat smaller room with seven men, not all readily visible. One carries a white towel, to clean up any mess? The top of the executioner's head is visible through a slit in an alcove wall. He is never identified and is getting $150 for this job.
>
> —Horace G. Davis, Jr., "Execution Scene Stark; Death Is Undramatic"

Narration

Writers also develop ideas by narrating a sequence of events. A police officer who wants to prove that her job involves too much

paperwork might create a detailed account of one day. To persuade students to prepare for their final exams, you could tell a
story about one student's lack of preparation and poor scores.

William Buckley narrates this scene to explain the American
fear of confrontation, our tendency toward "passive compliance"
that operates even when the temperature climbs over 100 degrees:

> I watched the train conductor appear at the head of the car. "Tick-
> ets, all tickets, please!" In a more virile age, I thought, the passen-
> gers would seize the conductor and strap him down on a seat over
> the radiator to share the fate of his patrons. He shuffled down the
> aisle, picking up tickets, punching commutation cards. No one ad-
> dressed a word to him. He approached my seat, and I drew a breath
> of resolution. "Conductor," I began with a considerable edge to my
> voice. . . . Instantly the doleful eyes of my seatmate turned tiredly
> from his newspaper to fix me with a resentful stare: what question
> could be so important as to justify my sibilant intrusion into his stu-
> por? I was shaken by those eyes. I am incapable of making a discreet
> fuss, so I mumbled a question about what time we were due in Stam-
> ford (I didn't even ask whether it would be before or after dehydra-
> tion could be expected to set in), got my reply, and went back to my
> newspaper and to wiping my brow.
>
> —William Buckley, "Why We Don't Complain"

Examples

Writers often use specific examples to provide support for a general statement. A few representative cases usually eliminate the
need for many paragraphs of general explanation.

In an essay on shopping, Gilbert Highet uses several short examples to reveal the overwhelming presence in antique stores of
kitsch, which he defines as "anything which took a lot of trouble
to make and is quite hideous":

> To walk along a whole street of antique shops—that is an experience
> which shakes the very soul. Here is a window full of bulbous Chi-
> nese deities; here is another littered with Zulu assagais, Indian ca-
> noe paddles, and horse pistols which won't fire; the next shopfront
> is stuffed with gaudy Italian majolica vases, and the next, even
> worse, with Austrian pottery—tiny ladies and gentlemen sitting on
> lace cushions and wearing lace ruffles, with every frill, every wrinkle
> and reticulation translated into porcelain: pink; stiff; but fortunately
> not unbreakable. The nineteenth century produced an appalling

amount of junky art like this; and sometimes I imagine that clandestine underground factories are continuing to pour it out like illicit drugs.

—Gilbert Highet, *The Clerk of Oxenford*

Cause and Effect

Like John W. Mellor in the paragraph on Nepal (page 30), writers frequently develop their ideas by providing answers to these questions: *Why did it happen? What effects will it create?* Why has the school district cut funding for after-school care? What will happen if this program is discontinued? Readers are more likely to accept your recommendations for change if they understand the causes of a problem and its possible consequences.

The following paragraph begins with its topic sentence—that girl babies are viewed as an economic problem in India—and then explores causes of this attitude. The paragraph ends with the recent effects of this prejudice—sex selection and widespread abortion:

In India, being female is an economic handicap. A girl means trouble. She must be married off at great expense (the custom of dowry was outlawed in 1961 but is still prevalent), only to be lost to her family. Anything she earns belongs to her in-laws. Her parents, who may incur a lifetime of debt to pay for her wedding, can expect to see her only once or twice a year and then in strained, formal visits. The more daughters they have, the worse off they become. It's no wonder then that the idea of sex determination, with abortion as an option if the sex turns out to be "wrong," is so popular here that sex-selection clinics have become a big business.

—Jo McGowan, "In India, They Abort Females"

Comparison

You can also develop a paragraph by comparing one event, object, idea, or person with another, as in the following situations:

- When you are writing about a product with which your readers may not be familiar, you can compare it to something they do know: a computer modem, for example, might be compared to a telephone.
- You can explain a new product or program by contrasting it with an older version: you might describe the new sociology curriculum, for example, by highlighting its differences from the

earlier one; you might contrast an author's latest novel with his earlier works.

- If your paragraph attempts to persuade, you might want to call upon the shared values and beliefs of your audience in making your comparison: a city that does not fight against drug addiction among its adolescents, for example, could be compared to spectators who allow a child to drown.

To create an effective comparison, you need to decide on its purpose, on the point you wish to convey: that, like a phone, a computer modem can be mastered easily; that the new curriculum offers more options to students; that city government must take action. Then you can arrange your specifics, which should all support that judgment, in one of two ways: with the block pattern or with the alternating pattern.

In the **block pattern,** you make all your points about the first subject and then turn to the second one. This organization works well to provide a full picture of each alternative. But, without clear points of comparison or contrast, it can degenerate into two unrelated descriptions. Thus, you need to plan the structure of the two units carefully so that you take up the same points about each subject in the same order. If you want to criticize inequities in county recreation funding, for example, you might plan the following contrast between one suburban and one urban playground:

I. Suburban playground
   A. Play equipment
   B. Grounds maintenance
II. Urban playground
   A. Play equipment
   B. Grounds maintenance

In the second block, you can emphasize similarities and differences through comparison and contrast transitions. (See page 38 for a full list of these transitions.)

Unlike the suburban site, the urban playground . . .

In contrast to the suburban playground, this one . . .

Although both sites have similar layouts, the urban one . . .

The second way to organize comparisons is the **alternating pattern.** Using this method, you first consider one point of comparison concerning the two subjects, and then you move to another, and then to another. If the playground contrast included more items, the writer might choose the alternating pattern to emphasize the specific points being compared:

I. Playground equipment
   A. Suburban playground
   B. Urban playground

II. Grounds maintenance
   A. Suburban playground
   B. Urban playground

III. Recreation staffing
   A. Suburban playground
   B. Urban playground

IV. Special programs
   A. Suburban playground
   B. Urban playground

For the alternating pattern, you can use transition words (listed on pages 37–38) within each paragraph to emphasize the comparison or contrast.

Process

Paragraphs often explain how to do something: how to survive the first day of classes, how to decorate a cake, how to get a good job. If you use this method of development, present each step clearly so that the reader can understand the process and succeed at it.

The following paragraph teaches readers how to bodysurf. Like many other process paragraphs, it follows a chronological order and uses the second person, *you*, to address readers directly:

Stand, or tread water, until you see the right wave far out, gathering momentum. Then position yourself—swim farther out or farther in if necessary—so that you are ready to plunge toward shore in the trough created in front of the cresting wave. Once you are in the trough, swim as hard as you can. Ideally, you will be sucked down into the trough. Suddenly the cresting water above you lifts you, holds you, shoots you forward. At this moment, arch, point your body with your arms like tensed wings down at your sides, flat and bulletlike. You become a missile projected by the churning, breaking wave. If it works, if you are *in*, if you *catch* the wave, you become a part of it, the forward part of the cresting wave, like the prow of a boat made somehow of churning foam, and you can ride all the way home to the sand, and come home *into* the sand like a wedge, grinding into the shore like the wave itself.

—Ruth Rudner, *Forgotten Pleasures*

Presenting the Information in a Unified Paragraph

As you revise, you can bring more information into each paragraph through description, narration, examples, causal analysis, comparison, and process. But an effective paragraph does not consist simply of unconnected information about a topic sentence. The paragraph must be organized—unified—to help the reader assimilate your facts and reasoning. Some ways to unify your paragraphs are by reiterating key terms and by using parallel structure and transitions.

Restatement of Key Words

A paragraph's key terms, or synonyms for them, can be repeated throughout the paragraph to link the ideas in each sentence. Pronouns that refer to those key terms, such as *this, that, they,* or *those,* can also help the reader to follow your arguments. (Always use *this* with a noun, however, to avoid pronoun reference problems. See page 41 for examples.)

In this paragraph, for example, Rachel Carson employs several key terms and pronouns (italicized here for emphasis) to keep the focus on various species of migrating fish:

> In the spring the sea is filled with *migrating fishes,* some of *them* bound for the mouths of great rivers, which *they* will ascend to deposit *their spawn. Such* are the *spring-run chinooks* coming in from the deep Pacific feeding grounds to breast the peak at the Hudson and the Connecticut, the *alewives* seeking their way to the Penobscot and the Kennebec. For months or years *these fish* have known only the vast spaces of the ocean. Now the spring sea and the maturing of *their own bodies* lead *them* back to the rivers of *their birth.*
>
> —Rachel Carson, *The Sea Around Us*

Parallel Structure

Sentences that are grammatically similar can also emphasize a clear progression of ideas. You may want to repeat a structure that places a key term in the subject slot, as in this introduction to an essay on the amazing qualities of warts (italics highlight the parallel structures):

> *Warts are* wonderful structures. *They can* appear overnight on any part of the skin, like mushrooms on a damp lawn, full grown and splendid in the complexity of their architecture. Viewed in stained sections under a microscope, *they are* the most specialized of cellular arrangements, constructed as though for a purpose. *They sit* there like turreted mounds of dense, impenetrable horn, impregnable, designed for defense against the world outside.
>
> —Lewis Thomas, *The Medusa and the Snail*

Thomas opens the third sentence with "Viewed in stained sections under a microscope" to add some variety and thus keep the repeated structures from becoming monotonous.

Transitional Words and Phrases

You can also emphasize the connections between ideas and sentences by using appropriate transitional words and phrases. Here are some of the most common transitions, classified by their uses and with possible additions indicated in brackets:

Time

then, next, afterward

previously, before that, earlier

meanwhile, at the same time, at that point

during [that day]

[several weeks] later

while [I was there]

Sequence of Steps or Causes

first, second, third

then, next, after that

finally

Spatial Transitions

adjacent to, next to, nearby

across from, on the opposite side

above, below, under, beyond

to the right, to the left

in the foreground, in the background

Transitions to Additional Information

additionally, also, furthermore, in addition, moreover

Transitions to Examples

for example, for instance, in one case

Comparison and Contrast Transitions

Comparison	Contrast
both	but
just the same	different from
likewise	however
neither one	on the other hand
similar to, similarly	to the contrary

Causal Transitions

as a result, consequently, for that reason, therefore, thus

Caution: Using too many transition phrases creates a heavy-handed style: the transitions stand out instead of the meaning itself. But well-placed transitional phrases alert readers to the logic of a paragraph, as they do in the following selection about an American's un-American clothes (the transitions are italicized here for emphasis):

> *Returning to the bedroom,* the unconscious victim of un-American practices removes his clothes from a chair, invented in the Near East, and proceeds to dress. He *then* puts on close-fitting tailored garments whose form derives from the skin clothing of the ancient nomads of the Asiatic steppes and fastens them with buttons whose prototypes appeared in Europe at the close of the Stone Age. *This costume* is appropriate enough for outdoor exercise in a cold climate, but is quite unsuited to American summers, steam-heated houses, and Pullmans. *Nevertheless,* foreign ideas and habits hold the unfortunate man in thrall even when common sense tells him that the authentically American costume of gee string and moccasins would be far more comfortable. He puts on his feet stiff coverings made from hide prepared by a process invented in ancient Egypt and cut to a pattern which can be traced back to ancient Greece, and makes sure that they are properly polished, also a Greek idea. *Lastly,* he ties about his neck a strip of bright-colored cloth which is a vestigial survival of the shoulder shawls worn by seventeenth-century Croats. He gives himself a final appraisal in the mirror, an old Mediterranean invention, and goes downstairs to breakfast.
>
> —Ralph Linton, "One Hundred Percent American"

REVISING SENTENCES

Your first draft probably contains awkward or wordy sentences that reflect your initial attempt to get ideas on paper. After working with your thesis, organization, and paragraphing, you can focus on sentence structures and word choices that will make your writing more vivid and exact, more effective for the reader. (See pages 394–399 on sentence variety for more help with creating varied sentence structures.)

Prefer Active Voice

When you write a sentence in the **active** voice, the subject does something and the verb tells what the subject did. The action is straightforward through the sentence, from beginning to end:

Subject	to verb	to object
The girl	hit	the ball.
The student	reviewed	her course notes.

The **passive** sentence is the reverse of the active. In the passive sentence, the verb explains something *done to* the subject. The "do-er" may or may not be named in the sentence. The flow of the passive sentence is backward:

Subject	having something done to it (verb)	by agent (sometimes omitted)
The ball	was hit	by the girl.
The course notes	were reviewed	by the student.
The application	was filled out	

298-301

All passives consist of a form of the verb *to be* (am, is, are, was, were, being, been) plus a past participle. (A *past participle* is the form of a verb that can fill the empty slot in this sentence: "I had _____ it.")

A passive verb may be acceptable if the actor or agent is either unimportant or well known:

Bill Clinton *was reelected* president in 1996.

Sidney *was buried* in the family plot next to his wife.

Additionally, you may choose the passive if you want to avoid casting blame:

Three bicycles and a skateboard *were left* in the yard.

Generally, however, you should avoid passive structures because they make writing wordy and confusing. Active voice allows you to make vigorous and direct statements.

Once you recognize a sentence as passive and decide to change it, you can create an active sentence by finding the do-er (or inserting one) and turning the sentence around:

Passive	Active
Houses *were destroyed* by the storm.	The storm destroyed houses.
Your proposal *has been turned down.*	Our committee turned down your proposal.
The cake *was eaten* by me.	I ate the cake.

(For more examples of active versus passive voice, see *Verbs*, pages 424–25.)

Avoid *It . . . That* Sentences

Some sentences wander aimlessly, taking too long to make a point and thus destroying the flow of ideas. These sentences often contain unnecessary *it . . . that* constructions:

T *seems to have*

~~It seems to be the fact that~~ this dog ~~has~~ worms.

T

~~It is true that~~ the dorms are no longer popular with juniors and seniors.

Eliminate Forms of *Be* and Other Weak Verbs

In first drafts, writers often choose constructions containing weak verbs, especially forms of *be* (am, is, are, was, were, been, being). But in a final draft, a succession of sentences with *be* verbs can be vague and monotonous.

You can easily eliminate one use of *be* that wastes words and delays the action: the *there is* structure.

θ

~~There is~~ one camper ~~who~~ hates milk.

A *was*
~~There was a~~ man lurking in the shadows.

You can eliminate other *be* verbs by making more specific choices. If you say that "the man was in the gym," your reader knows very little. Did he hang from the ceiling? slump in a chair? Think of the different impressions you can create with *strolled, ambled,* and *limped along* to describe the man walking in the gym. Many writers pick the most obvious choice in a first draft but decide on more specific verbs as they revise.

Eliminate Nominalizations

To make your sentences more concise, remove nominalizations— nouns created from verbs—because they can lead to wordiness and a plodding tone:

> *discussed*
> The two leaders ~~held a discussion concerning~~ several peace
>
> alternatives.

> *recommended*
> The director ~~made a recommendation~~ that the student assistant be
>
> rehired.

Other common nominalizations include *give encouragement, make a payment, have admiration,* and *make a judgment.*

Use *This* with a Noun

You may want to use the word *this* to refer to ideas that you have mentioned in previous sentences or paragraphs. But *this* should not be used by itself; instead, it should always be followed by a noun so that the reference cannot be misunderstood. When *this* is the first word of a sentence, you may be able to incorporate the entire idea of that sentence into the preceding one (as in the second example):

> That dealership charges high prices for repairs and doesn't stock
>
> *poor service*
> parts for older cars. This has caused many loyal customers to con-
>
> sider a competitor.

> *Chandra's refusal*
> ~~Chandra refuses~~ to bring her boyfriend over for dinner. ~~This~~ has in-
>
> sulted her family.

Eliminate Empty and Wordy Phrases

You can also write more effectively by avoiding long phrases that provide little information. In the list that follows, the single words on the right replace the wordy expressions on the left:

Wordy Phrases	Revised
along the lines of	like
at all times	always
at this point in time	now
because of the fact that	because
by means of	by
due to the fact that	because
for the purpose of	for
for the reason that	because
have the ability to	can
in a great many instances	often
in order to	to
in spite of the fact that	although
in the event that	if
in the field (or area) of	in
in the final analysis	finally
in the neighborhood of	about
in the not too distant future	soon
in this day and age	today
in today's modern world	today
on account of the fact that	because
similar in nature to	like
situated in the vicinity of	near
until such time as	until
was of the opinion that	believed

Also avoid **tautologies**—the use of two or more words that say the same thing. The unnecessary words appear in brackets:

[true] facts	blue [in color]
large [in size]	attractive [in appearance]
[basic] essentials	each [and every] one

several [in number]   weak [in strength]

rewrite [in different words]   refer [back] to

Make sure that, throughout your paper, you choose the best terms to describe your ideas. Sometimes the more exact choice can replace several words:

persons with knowledge in their field = experts

correcting errors in the final draft = proofreading

unwilling to change his mind = obstinate

speaks words unclearly = slurs

writes quickly and messily = scribbles

Eliminate Clichés

Clichés do not create a specific picture for the reader. Most people don't know the derivation or the precise form of these phrases—is it "toe the line" or "tow the line"? Rather than evoking a sharp image, clichés give a vague and general impression, often an overdramatized one, as in "breathed a sigh of relief," "like a bolt from the blue," or "walking on air." To avoid worn-out abstractions in your writing, describe what happens in specific terms. If the lion moves "slowly but surely," what is he really doing? And if the salesclerk is "busy as a bee" or the sunset is "pretty as a picture," what do you actually see?

Here is a list of some of the most common clichés that you should replace with specific descriptions:

agony of suspense	more than meets the eye
all boils down to	nutty as a fruitcake
as luck would have it	playing with fire
beat a hasty retreat	pretty as a picture
beat around the bush	quick as a flash
blind as a bat	sight for sore eyes
crystal clear	take it for granted
dead as a doornail	trials and tribulations
deep, dark secret	white as a sheet
growing by leaps and bounds	work hand in hand
light as a feather	worth its weight in gold

Peer Review

Just as your classmates can help you with the invention process, they can also help you with revision. Ask the students who read your paper in class or lab sessions to respond to the following questions (preferably in writing so that you will be able to consider their comments carefully as you revise). You might use sections A and B after you complete the first draft and then work with section C after further revision.

REVISION CHECKLIST

A. Thesis and Structure

- What is the thesis? Does it clearly state the writer's subject and an attitude or opinion concerning it? Will it be clear and convincing to the reader? (See pages 21–27.)
- Does the body of the essay support this thesis? Does the supporting evidence seem to be in an effective sequence? Should any information be moved, added, or omitted? (See pages 22–24.)
- Would any other organizational structure be a more effective choice? (See pages 30–36.)

B. Paragraphs

- Does the introduction explain the thesis, involve the reader in the subject, and provide necessary background information? (See pages 25–27.)
- Does each body paragraph clearly relate to the thesis? Does each paragraph have a clear topic and topic sentence? (See pages 23–24.)
- Does each body paragraph contain enough details, examples, or reasons to support its topic sentence? (See pages 30–38.)
- Is each paragraph unified? (See pages 29–30.)
- Does the conclusion state a judgment, provide a call to action, or forecast future events? (See pages 27–28.)

C. Sentences

- Has the writer avoided using ineffective passives and *it . . . that* sentences? Should the writer eliminate nominalizations, *is* verbs, and wordy phrases? (See pages 39–41.)
- Are the sentences clear and vivid? (See pages 42–43.)

FINISHING

Once you have completed your revisions, you will be almost ready to turn your work in. At this stage, you're probably tired of everything about your paper and unwilling to do much more work. But don't get impatient, or you may turn in work with good content and organization that receives a low grade because of errors in grammar, spelling, and typing. Finish your work by proofreading carefully and preparing an attractive manuscript.

PROOFREADING

Before you turn in your paper, proofread it carefully to make sure that the text is error-free.

When to Proofread

Begin to proofread when you are finished writing and revising. You may want to take a break first so that you can return to the task as though you were another person, reviewing a piece of writing you had not seen before.

Allot enough time for proofreading, at least half an hour for a short paper. If you wait until five minutes before class to do a quick proofreading, the teacher will probably return the paper to you with at least several errors marked. Instead of rushing, you should take proofreading seriously.

How to Proofread

To proofread successfully, quit thinking about the ideas and focus on the grammatical correctness of each sentence and the spelling of each word. Try the following techniques to turn yourself from writer into proofreader.

Read Out Loud

If you read the paper silently, you will be remembering what you *meant* to say and will imagine you see words on the page that aren't there. Reading the material out loud slowly will help you to focus on what is really there, on each word and each mark of punctuation.

Read Paragraphs Out of Order

Another helpful technique is to read paragraphs out of order: perhaps the third and then the second or the fifth paragraph. This method will force you to look carefully at the actual words and sentences instead of at your ideas.

Use a Ruler or a Pencil as a Marker

Place a ruler or a pencil below a sentence and then look at that one sentence before moving the marker down the page to the next one. This technique will stop you from reading and thinking ahead and thus will help you to concentrate on the actual sentence structures and words.

Use Computerized Spelling Checkers—Cautiously

If you use computerized spelling checkers, you need to recognize their limitations as well as their strengths.

- Many computer software packages have spelling checkers that you can access as you write or after you are finished writing. Use the checker on the entire document as you proofread instead of having it beep or underline the word if you make an error as you write. You don't want anything to interrupt your composing process.

- Instead of noticing all errors, the spelling checker points out words that are not in its dictionary. If the computer tells you that a proper noun is "misspelled," it may be correct but missing from the dictionary. Verify these spellings in another source. If any other word is tagged that you think is correct, look it up in a dictionary.

- Because the spelling checker tells you only whether a word is in its dictionary, it cannot determine whether you have used the wrong word, such as *affect* for *effect* or *there* for *their*. After you use a spelling checker, you should also proofread for this type of error.

(For help with spelling, see *Spelling,* pages 400–14.)

Use Computerized Grammar Checkers—Cautiously

You can check your grammar by using a computerized grammar or style checker. These programs usually isolate spelling errors, grammatical errors, and poor stylistic choices such as passive constructions and overly long sentences. Some also offer explanations of grammar rules.

Like spelling checkers, however, grammar programs have limitations. Even if you agree with the program's analysis of the error, perhaps in subject-verb agreement, you may want to choose another method of correcting it: the checker may suggest changing a subject and verb to the singular, for example, when you meant for them to be plural. You may have purposely chosen to write in passive voice or to express a complex idea in a lengthy sentence and thus may decide to keep some sentences that the program flags as incorrect. You should also realize that these checkers do not locate all errors. You will still need to review your sentences carefully.

Create a Common-Errors List

To improve your proofreading, you might keep a "common-errors" list in your notebook where you can record both the errors you find and those that are noted by a teacher or tutor. You can also go back through papers from earlier courses and add the errors marked there. To create your list, copy down the word or sentence that you wrote and the correct choice.

As you add entries, you will soon be able to see patterns in your mistakes. You may frequently forget to use apostrophes or to put a comma after an introductory dependent clause; you may be confusing *-ance* and *-ence* words or using *its* for *it's*. At the top of the list, keep track of the prevalent error types. Then you can review the rules and check carefully for similar errors as you proofread.

Get Help

You may have noticed that you can more easily locate errors in someone else's paper because you do not know what the writer intended to say—you are reading what is really there. You may, therefore, want to exchange papers with a classmate or see a tutor—after you have checked everything yourself. If you bring your common-errors list to the session, your proofreader can especially attend to those problems.

PREPARING THE FINAL MANUSCRIPT

When the paper is finished, you should present it to the teacher as the polished work that it is. The final paper layout, like the proofreading, should indicate the care you have taken. Teachers don't like to receive papers that are written on spiral pads, in illegible handwriting, or in a very faint computer print; that have no page numbers; or that have writing on the back of the page. They want manuscripts to show that students have taken the assignment seriously.

Meeting the Specified Standards

Before you prepare the final copy, make sure that you understand the manuscript requirements. If your teacher asks you to use a style manual such as the *MLA Handbook for Writers of Research Papers* (MLA) or the *Publication Manual of the American Psychological Association* (APA), this choice will determine not only the type of documentation but also the physical makeup of the page: margins, paragraph indention, spacing of direct quotations, and placement of page numbers and titles. Refer to pages 93–130 if you will be using one of these style manuals. If your teacher does not stipulate a specific format, you can use the instructions given here to create the finished product.

Document Design Basics

Unless you are following APA or some other style guide, you can use the basic format (based on the MLA format) given here for creating each page. A sample page is provided on page 51. (More information on document design for long research reports is given on pp. 131–42.)

Paper and Print Quality

If you are using **word processing** to compose and print your essay, make sure the printer has a good ribbon or cartridge. Choose a letter-quality printer; it does not have to be a laser printer.

If you are permitted to **handwrite,** make sure that your essay will be legible; print if you need to. Use white, ruled, 8½- by 11-inch, loose-leaf notebook paper. Do not use paper torn from a spiral-bound notebook, unlined paper, or paper with very narrow lines. Write on only one side. Ask your teacher if you should write on every other line, double-spacing, as may be required for typed essays. Do not use pencil.

Type Styles and Sizes

You should print the essay in a twelve-point standard font. Do not use fourteen-point to make the essay look longer; do not choose a special font, like a shadowed or cursive script, that may be difficult to read. If you use continuous-feed paper, make sure that you tear the pages apart and remove the perforated side strips with the tractor holes.

Margins and Page Numbering

Use a one-inch margin on the top and bottom and on both sides. Place the page numbers, preceded by your last name, one-half inch from the top and at the right margin.

The First Page

Unless your teacher indicates otherwise, you will not need a separate title page. Instead, on the first page, put your last name and the page number half an inch from the top and even with the right margin; one inch from the top and even with the left margin, put your name, your professor's name, the course number, and the date, double-spacing between each item. Double-space again and type the title of the piece in the center, using a capital letter to begin each important word. Double-space once more and begin the paper itself. This page will be numbered as page 1.

Paragraphs

Begin each new paragraph five spaces (or half an inch) from the left margin. Do not leave an extra double space between paragraphs. Do not start a new paragraph at the bottom of a page if there is room for only one line. Go to the next page to begin the paragraph.

Spacing

Papers for college courses should be double-spaced unless you are specifically asked to do otherwise. Double-space your name and class information, the text, indented direct quotations, and the reference list. Double-spaced type is easier to read, and it gives the teacher room to make comments.

Quotations

If you are quoting a passage containing more than four lines, indent it ten spaces (or one inch) from the left margin. Do not indent any extra spaces from the right margin. The quotation should be double-spaced and have a double space before and after it. Do not use quotation marks with indented quotations.

Headings

If you decide to use headings within the paper, type them in the center of the page, using a capital letter for the first letter of each important word, as you would for a paper title, and lowercase for all other words. If you have subheadings, type them at the left margin. Add an extra space before headings.

Lists

If you include a list in your text, indent it like a direct quotation, with each entry starting on a new line.

Documentation

To document a research paper, you will need to choose a specific format such as MLA or APA: do not try to remember the one you used in high school. When you have chosen a format or your teacher has suggested one, follow its style of documentation exactly. (For a full treatment of MLA and APA styles, see pages 93–130.)

Morgan 1

Tina Morgan

Professor S. Smith

English 111

September 12, 1997

The R.A. Program: Proceed with Caution

The university chooses students to serve as resident assistants (R.A.'s) for

every dorm floor. These student employees are required to attend weekly training

sessions, organize social programs, maintain hall bulletin boards—and be avail-

able five nights a week. As payment for these services, they are offered free room

and board. Although the student handbook maintains that "anyone fortunate

enough to be the committee's choice would profit from and enjoy this experience,"

anyone thinking of becoming an R.A. should carefully consider the following

questions before seeking this position:

    1. How many hours of work each week will the job involve?

    2. How much does the R.A. make by the hour?

    3. What freedoms does the R.A. have to give up?

    4. What relationship does the R.A. have with fellow students?

    5. How valuable will this experience be for career preparation?

The answers will help you determine whether the R.A. program is for you.

Hours per Week

You first need to consider the real time commitment involved in the job.

All R.A.'s must arrive on campus four days before the other students to complete

training sessions and create a work schedule. Once the term begins, they are

required to be in their rooms, available to help residents, for five nights each week

and on every other weekend. Additionally, they must work at the front desk two

nights a month. When they are on duty, either in their rooms or at the desk, they

may find themselves counseling homesick students, solving disputes between

Figure 2. Sample First Page of a Paper

RESEARCH WRITING

RESEARCH WRITING

An Overview of the Research-Writing Process

- Analyze the assignment.
- Choose a research topic or question.
- Find the right—appropriate and reliable—sources.
- Use primary and secondary sources and, if possible, the Internet.
- Take good notes.
- Choose a preliminary thesis and outline.
- Write the first draft.
- Revise systematically.
- Document sources correctly.
- Incorporate the principles of good document design.

To produce a well-written paper, you must conduct some form of research. Careful investigation of your own opinions, the facts about a situation, or the judgments of others will help you prepare to write a research paper or term paper. Writing this kind of paper requires the skills of investigating a subject, reporting and analyzing information, and acknowledging sources as well as using the steps of the writing process described on pages 3–50.

The paper discussed throughout this chapter, on men's studies, can be found on pages 109–16.

ANALYZING THE ASSIGNMENT

When you begin work on a research paper, first consider the following questions about the assignment itself. They will help you to begin focusing on your subject and research.

- **What type of topic** would be appropriate?
- Does the assignment involve **explaining the research or arguing for a specific viewpoint?**
- **What types of sources** should be used? What processes will you use to judge the sources' reliability? (See pages 70–73.)
- **How many sources** are required?
- **What type of documentation** (acknowledgment of sources) will be needed?
- **What is the expected length** of the paper?
- **When is the paper due?** Are there also deadlines for choosing a topic, for turning in note cards, or for completing a rough draft?

CHOOSING A RESEARCH TOPIC OR QUESTION

In some classes, students can choose any topic relevant to the course—any topic in American history or twentieth-century art, for example. In other classes, more restrictions are placed on the subject: students must write about the Louisiana Purchase or Picasso's blue period. In a composition class, you may be asked to explain the current debate over a social issue, such as affirmative action or animal rights, or you may be asked to take a stand on an issue. For any of these assignments, you should choose your topic carefully, using the three criteria that follow:

1. Pick a topic that interests you or a question you would like to answer. This advice may seem obvious, but many students do not consider their own interests when deciding on class projects. You will enjoy the process more and put more work into your paper if you pick a subject or question that appeals to you. If history, sports, or education interests you, then you might consider one of these questions for an assignment in a course on American culture:

Did pressure from journalists cause President McKinley to start the Spanish-American War?

Have universities become the "minor leagues" for professional sports teams?

Should private companies be invited to run public schools?

If you need help in coming up with a topic, ask your teacher for ideas; browse the subject headings in your library's on-line or card catalogue or in periodical indexes; review course readings. Try not to settle for an "oh, this will do" topic.

2. Choose a topic you can research. When you have decided on a general topic, go to the library or check the Internet to see whether you can find enough material on it. If the information has appeared only in journals that your library doesn't own, if the topic is very new, or if everyone else in the class is writing on the same subject, you may not be able to find enough sources. If you need help, consult a librarian.

3. If necessary, narrow the topic so that you can develop it adequately in the amount of time allotted for research and in the specified number of pages. If entire books have been written on your topic, it may be too broad for a short paper. Certainly, you cannot write a history of health-care or welfare policies. You might begin researching a general subject but then restrict it; current plans to reform American health insurance or current services for the homeless are appropriate topics for research papers. A paper on athletics might center on one sport, time period, or university.

FINDING THE RIGHT SOURCES

When you have decided on a general topic, you will be ready to begin conducting primary and secondary research. As you gather information, you will be narrowing your topic, deciding on a thesis, and collecting the data needed to support that thesis.

Primary Research

Many students go immediately to the library without considering the data they can get "in the field" through observation, interviews, surveys, or other forms of primary research or firsthand investigation.

Observation

Learn to evaluate a situation by using what you see. If you are writing about a new men's studies program, go to one of the classes in the program. If your paper concerns horse racing, visit the track as well as the library. Before you set up an observation, decide on the purpose of the visit. Do you want to observe the interaction between men and women in the men's studies class, to critique the teacher's presentation, or to analyze the course materials? Try to decide what you want to know and give yourself adequate time to learn it; perhaps you'll need more than one visit.

When you are at the site and have decided on whom or what you want to watch, record the physical details, actions, and dialogue. You can also keep a list or chart of repeated actions: of men interrupting women or of students relating their own experiences to the course materials in a men's studies class. Wait until you organize a rough draft to decide on the importance of the material; in the observation session, just get everything down.

Interviews

Other people's firsthand accounts of places or experiences relevant to your topic can make your paper stand out from a stack of papers researched entirely in the library. Ask teachers, friends, and librarians for names of people on your campus and in your community who might be helpful to you. You might also conduct e-mail interviews with people who live far away but can provide important firsthand knowledge.

When you have chosen the people you would like to interview, contact them and tell them what your subject is. You might also ask if you can bring a tape recorder to the session. If someone cannot meet with you, perhaps you can ask that person a few questions over the telephone.

Before the session, research your topic and the person you are interviewing. Then you won't waste time asking questions that you could easily find the answers to elsewhere. Next, with the purpose of your interview clearly in mind, prepare a short list of questions or topics. If you were speaking with the founder of the men's studies program at your college or university, for example, you might ask the following questions:

1. When were the courses started? What teachers were involved? Was there much opposition?
2. What is the purpose of the courses?
3. Does this program follow a national model?
4. What have been the program's strengths and weaknesses?
5. How many men and women students are involved? Is there any difference in men's and women's responses to these courses?
6. How have women's studies teachers and students reacted to the men's studies program?

Your list can combine factual questions, like the first one, with open-ended ones, like the fourth one. Try to avoid questions that might seem insulting to the interviewee ("What makes you think these courses might have some value?") or that might elicit only a "yes" or "no" answer. Listen carefully and be open to new topic possibilities—and thus new questions. You should also observe your subject's physical characteristics and surroundings, which may reflect values and interests.

Surveys

To get information from a larger group, such as all the students in five men's studies classes, you might decide to design a short survey. There are several methods for reaching such a group:

- You can mail students a survey form, but first have the teacher ask them if they are willing for their names and campus addresses to be released. On the form, state the reason that you want the information, assure them of anonymity, and include a deadline and your address. Don't be surprised if only a small percentage of the group, perhaps just 10% or 20%, returns the form.

- You can hand out forms where the group meets: go to the men's studies class and distribute them. Get permission from the teacher before you begin.

- Either in person or over the phone, you can ask a few simple questions of a given group and write down responses. You can call class members or speak at a class session, explaining your project and recording their oral responses.

In all these situations, your questions should be clear and direct, chosen to elicit the information you need for your paper. Before you administer the survey to your target group, test it on several friends or classmates to see if their interpretation of each question matches yours.

Your first questions might identify the respondents by their age or job, depending on what information seems most relevant. Subsequent questions, which should not take up more than one page, should be designed so that your respondents don't have to do much writing and so that you can analyze their answers easily: you might use check-off lists, five-point scales, and yes-no questions. At the end of the survey, you can include one or two questions that require a written answer if you want to encourage respondents to express more of their own viewpoints.

If, for example, you want to find out how various types of students evaluate the purpose and worth of their men's studies classes, you might use a survey like the one shown in Figure 3.

Men's Studies Survey

male _____ female _____   major _____

year in school: freshman ___ sophomore ___ junior ___ senior ___

1. What was your main reason for choosing this men's studies class? (Please check one.)

___ reputation of the teacher

___ fulfills a requirement

___ interest in the subject matter

___ other (please state): _____

2. Which would you say is the main purpose of this class? (Please check one.)

___ to study male aggression

___ to examine the history of men

___ to learn about how to counsel men

___ to learn about relationships between men and women

___ to learn about male roles in our society

___ other (please state): _____

3. How would you rate the text materials?
excellent ___   good ___   o.k. ___   bad ___   awful ___

4. Should the course be required for a counseling major?
yes ___   no___

5. What have been the best features of the class? _____

Figure 3. Sample Survey Questionnaire

After collecting the responses to that survey, you could look at many different issues: how all students rate the textbooks, whether counseling students think the course should be required for their major, how men and women perceive the purpose of the course.

When you report the data in your essay, state exactly what you have: "Of the 170 students enrolled in five men's studies classes in the spring of 1998, 150 filled out the survey; of that group of respondents, 140, or 93 percent, reported that . . . ." You can also quote the written responses of individual students—if you clearly state that you are citing one student's opinion.

Secondary Research

As you collect the appropriate types of primary data, you should also turn to printed or Internet materials, called secondary sources. Encyclopedias, handbooks, journals, newspapers, biographies, research studies, and other secondary sources should contain a wealth of information to explain your topic and support your thesis concerning it. The following sections will help you to use the library and the Internet effectively to locate reference works, books, and periodical articles.

Selecting Reference Works

You should first read several overviews of your subject—to learn about its history, major controversies concerning it, and principal figures involved with it. The reference room of your library contains many valuable sources that provide such general information. Locate them by finding your topic in the library catalogue and then looking under the subheading "Dictionaries," by asking a librarian, or by using Robert Balay's *Guide to Reference Books,* a source that lists 10,000 reference books by subject area. For Internet reference sources, see "Using Search Engines on the Internet" on pp. 67–69. The following discussion will acquaint you with some of the most helpful reference tools.

Specialized Encyclopedias and On-line Subject Trees

You can often find helpful information in general encyclopedias such as *World Book* and *The New Encyclopedia Britannica,* which are written for a general audience and cover a wide variety of subjects. But the reference room also contains encyclopedias devoted to one specific field, era, or country. These specialized encyclopedias, including the ones listed here, provide background information, an overview of current debates, and bibliographies:

Encyclopedia of Beaches and Coastal Environments

Encyclopedia of Black America

Encyclopedia of Chemistry

Encyclopedia of Computer Science and Technology

Encyclopedia of Crime and Justice

Encyclopedia of Management

Encyclopedia of World Art

International Encyclopedia of Higher Education

International Encyclopedia of Social Sciences

McGraw-Hill Encyclopedia of Science and Technology

Many encyclopedias of various kinds are also available on the Internet. You can find ones that deal with traditional academic topics, such as religions, computing, or authors' lives, by typing "encyclopedia" into the text box of any on-line search engine, such as Yahoo! or AltaVista. *But before you use material you discover this way, be sure to read carefully the cautions about the reliability of Internet sources* (see pages 70–73).

A special Internet resource that works much like an encyclopedia is a *subject tree,* such as The Virtual Library at <http://vlib. stanford.edu/Overview.html>. Subject trees are hierarchical indexes of topics that allow you to begin with a broad category and follow the subject tree's branches down to a specific file. Subject trees can be good places to start your research because you can get an idea of the different types of information available on your topic. In The Virtual Library, there are at least three ways to search: by using the Subject Index on the main page, by searching the Category Subtree, or by searching the Top Ten Most Popular Fields.

Biographical Dictionaries

These reference works contain brief accounts of well-known figures, listing such information as family history, educational background, major accomplishments, and significant publications. To find information about the people who played significant roles in the events you are studying, you might look them up in biographical reference works such as the following ones (most of which are in multiple volumes with annual updates):

- *Current Biography* covers people of various nationalities and professions, providing a biographical sketch, short bibliography, picture (with some entries), and address.
- *Dictionary of American Biography* contains short biographies of over 15,000 deceased Americans representing many professions.
- *Dictionary of National Biography* contains biographies of deceased notables from Great Britain and its colonies.
- *Who's Who* offers brief biographies of notable living people. The three major volumes are *Who's Who in America*, *Who's Who* (primarily British), and *The International Who's Who*. The first two have companion volumes for the deceased: *Who Was Who in America* and *Who Was Who*. The series also includes specialized versions that focus on people in particular regions of the United States, in various professions (such as American law, finance and industry, science), and in ethnic and religious groups (such as black Americans and American Catholics).

The "who's who" label has also been used on a variety of other biographical and critical sources:

Who's Who in American Art

Who's Who in American Education

Who's Who in Economics

Who's Who in Faulkner

Who's Who in Horror and Fantasy Fiction

Who's Who in Military History

Who's Who in Rock

Who's Who in the Bible

www.

Of course, you can also type the name of the individual you are researching into the text box of an Internet search engine. (For more about search engines, see pages 67–69.) Or you can look in *biography.com*, an on-line biographical encyclopedia at <http://www.biography.com/find/find.html>.

Almanacs

For the facts and statistics necessary to substantiate your claims, almanacs are an invaluable source. Their tables, charts, lists, and thorough indexes give the researcher quick access to all kinds of data. Here are two examples:

- *The World Almanac and Book of Facts* contains such diverse data as annual gasoline usage, college graduation rates, and divorce rates by state. It includes historical as well as current information.

- *Statistical Abstract of the United States,* which is published by the U.S. Bureau of the Census, contains information gathered each year under such categories as energy, education, income and wealth, and parks and recreation. The *Statistical Abstract* and other statistical sources can be found on-line at <http://gort.ucsd.edu/ ek/refshelf/statistics.html>. The U.S. Census Bureau's home page is at <http://www.census.gov>.

Dictionaries

Unabridged dictionaries enable you to check the meaning of key terms. The *Oxford English Dictionary* explains the derivation of words and their meanings in earlier centuries as well as their current meaning. Specialized dictionaries, such as those in the following list, provide full explanations of the specialized terminology of a particular academic discipline or career:

A Dictionary for Accountants

Dictionary for Computer Languages

A Dictionary for Marketing Research

Dictionary of Advertising and Direct Mail Terms

Dictionary of American Art

Dictionary of Battles

Dictionary of Genetics

Dictionary of Mathematics

A Dictionary of Psychology

A Dictionary of Science Terms

A number of dictionaries are available on-line. Several are listed on a page maintained by the Carnegie Mellon University Department of Computer Sciences at <http://www.cs.cmu.edu/ references.html>, or you can simply type "dictionary" into the text box of your favorite Internet search engine. (For more about using dictionaries, see *Dictionary Use,* pages 350–53.)

Searching for Books

After you have looked in various reference works to get an overview of your topic—and perhaps to narrow it somewhat—you will be ready to turn to other types of books and to periodicals for more detailed information. The steps outlined in the following discussion will help you find relevant data from the books in your library.

Find the Subject Heading for Your Topic

You may waste time and miss sources if you head straight to the on-line or card catalogue, trusting in your own label for the topic. You should first consult the *Library of Congress Subject Headings,* found in book form, on microfiche, or on-line by doing a subject search of the Library of Congress catalogue at <http://lcweb.loc. gov/catalog/browse/bks3subj.html>. This guide will tell you the wording that libraries use to name various topics.

If you looked under *movies,* for example, you would find that the term is not in the system: all entries are under *motion pictures.* If you were looking up *horse racing,* you would see that it is indeed a subject heading and that you could also try narrower terms, such as *doping in horse racing, chariot racing, racetracks, women in horse racing,* and *horse racing—betting. Men's studies* (not *studies, men*) would lead you to information on the new college programs concerning men's history and social problems. You could also try the broader *men—study and teaching* and narrower listings, such as *abusive men.* Consult a librarian if you need help finding the right subject headings.

Use the Library Catalogue

After choosing the correct subject terms, you are ready to head to the library catalogue and begin building a list of possible sources, a working bibliography. If your library's on-line system is new, not all the older books may be listed on it. Ask a librarian if you will need to use the card drawers to search for older books.

The catalogue lists books by *author, title,* and *subject heading.* For most searches, you will be relying on the subject heading entries, which begin with Library of Congress subject labels. You can save time—and find the best materials—if you study the entries carefully. Each card or computer entry, like the sample in Figure 4, contains a great deal of information that should help you decide whether to choose a book or not.

Here are some of the questions you should ask about each potential source. You may not be able to answer all of them, but the answers you generate will help you decide whether the book

```
SEARCH TERM(S) :  SUBJECT = MEN'S STUDIES [HEADINGS SELECTED]
REFERENCES FOUND    1
                                                    Page  1  of  2
----------------------------------------------------------------
CALL NO.:        HQ1090  .C467  1987
TITLE:           Changing men : new directions in research on men and masculinity
                 / edited by Michael S. Kimmel.
PUB INFO:        Newbury Park, Calif. : Sage Publications,   c1987.
                 DESCRIPTION:  320 p. ; 23 cm.
SERIES:          Sage focus editions ; v. 88
NOTES:           Includes bibliographies.
SUBJECT:         Men--United States.
SUBJECT 2:       Masculinity  (Psychology)
SUBJECT 3:       Sex role--United States.
SUBJECT 4:       Men's studies--United States.
LCCN:            86-29754

PRESS YOUR CHOICE:
                                FULL RECORD
SEARCH TERM(S) : SUBJECT = MEN'S STUDIES [HEADINGS SELECTED]
REFERENCES FOUND:    1
                                                    Page  2  of  2
----------------------------------------------------------------
ISN:     080392996XX
OCLC NO.: 14904642
```

Figure 4. On-Line Catalogue Entry

will be worth reading. Again, if you want to see the research paper to which these sources contributed, it is on pages 109–116.

- **Author's name:** Do you know who the writer is? Have you read or seen entries for other books by the writer? Is he or she a well-known expert? The author in the sample entry from the on-line catalogue, Michael S. Kimmel, is a professor of sociology at the State University of New York at Stony Brook. He has written several books and articles on men's studies. Thus the collection of essays that he has assembled might be worth looking at: he is an authority in this field, and the other essay contributors should be also.

- **Title:** Does the title seem related to your topic? "New directions in research" indicates that this book will concern recent studies and findings.

- **Publisher and date of publication:** Does this publishing house specialize in serious scholarship, popular how-to books, religious materials? Is it well respected? When was the book published? A book about genetics written in the 1950s, for example, may provide interesting historical data but not the latest findings. The Kimmel book is part of a series from Sage, a firm that publishes social science research. Because the book came out in 1987, it will not contain information about the newest research and programs.

- **Page numbers and inclusions:** How long is the book? Does it contain illustrations, a bibliography, and an index? An index, which the Kimmel book does not have, allows the researcher immediate access to information on a specific topic.

- **Subject headings:** What other subject headings are listed for this book? These headings may lead to additional books on your topic.

If you study catalogue entries carefully, you can write down or print out information on only those sources that could be valuable instead of wasting time looking for books that are really brief pamphlets, that are outdated, or that are hard to use because they don't contain indexes. Many on-line catalogues can also tell you whether a book is already checked out.

Even if you need only three or four sources, record or print the information about every book that seems applicable to your topic. When you reach the shelving area, called the "stacks" in many libraries, some books may be missing, some will not have anything useful, and two or three may contain the same facts. You will save time if you have a long list of choices.

Searching for Periodical and Newspaper Articles

While you are finding relevant books, you should also search for pertinent material from magazines or journals. Magazines include publications such as *Time, The New Yorker,* and other general-reader periodicals that might be sold at a newsstand. Journals—such as the *Journal of Nursing* or *College English*—contain scholarly articles intended for experts. Both types are called periodicals.

You should look for periodical articles because they contain the most recent scholarship and usually focus on very specific subjects. For papers on recent occurrences or debates, almost all your research will come from periodicals. By checking both magazines and journals, you can choose articles aimed at different readers and thus obtain different perspectives on a topic. For a daily news perspective, you might also want to use stories from major newspapers.

Use Periodical Indexes

To find periodical articles on your subject, you need to use an index. You are probably already familiar with *Readers' Guide to Periodical Literature,* which lists primarily magazine articles, using Library of Congress subject headings. To locate more detailed, scholarly articles, use specialized indexes, also found in the library's reference room. Many of them look like *Readers' Guide,* but they contain entries from journals in a specific field. Some specialized indexes also have short summaries, or abstracts. The following list will give you an idea of the range of specialized indexes that are available:

Art Index	*Humanities Index*
Biological Abstracts	*Music Index*
Business Periodicals Index	*Psychological Abstracts*
Education Index	*Social Science Index*

When you use these annual guides, make sure that you pick the appropriate years. You might want to see how people responded to the Watergate scandal when the story broke, when President Nixon resigned, when President Ford pardoned him, or when President Nixon died. Each would require a different year's index.

As with books, you will want to examine periodical entries carefully to decide if the article will be helpful to you, by looking at the author, the title of the article, the title of the periodical, the length of the article, the date, and certainly an abstract if one is available. You should also find out whether your library receives the periodical and what call number it is listed under: most libraries keep an alphabetized list of their holdings near the online catalogue or the indexes.

Use Computerized Periodical Indexes

With printed indexes, you have to look for your topic in each annual volume. But many of these indexes are also available on computer, where you can search at once for articles published over several years and print out the bibliographic information and abstracts for what you find.

Most libraries have periodical databases on CD-ROM (compact disk read-only memory) that are updated regularly. If your library has Wilsondisc, you can search any of the Wilson indexes, such as *Readers' Guide, Humanities Index, Social Sciences Index,* or *Business Periodicals Index.* Your library may also have InfoTrac I or II, which indexes business, technical, legal, and general periodicals as well as the *New York Times.*

A second type of database transmits information over telephone lines, including annotations of articles and sometimes the complete texts themselves, for an additional charge. Dialog Information Retrieval Service, the largest of these, subscribes to more than 300 indexes. Among other popular computer databases are ORBIT, BRS Information Technologies, and Mead Data Central, which offers LEXIS (a legal database) and NEXIS (for news and public affairs). In addition to libraries, many student groups, businesses, and individuals subscribe to these databases to conduct their own research. Ask your librarian to help you with these on-line services and to explain any charges that you may incur in using them. Of course, there are also indexes and databases on the Internet, described below.

Check Newspaper Indexes

Newspapers provide day-to-day accounts of historical events. Their editorial and living sections can also acquaint you with the opinions and habits of earlier eras and different places. Most major newspapers, such as the *New York Times* and the *Washington Post,* have printed and on-line indexes.

Using Search Engines on the Internet

Search engines are large computer programs that allow you to find information through key-word searches. The search engine provides a *text box* into which you type key words associated with the information you seek. Most search engines also offer more complex searches with the aid of AND, OR, NOT, and NEAR. (Some search engines let + stand for AND and – stand for NOT.) Some offer even more advanced searching, such as limiting a search to specific dates or ranking key words in order of appearance within the document. There are hundreds of search engines for the Internet—far too many to discuss here. Two popular and different types of search engines, Yahoo! (a searchable, browsable directory) and AltaVista (a powerful search engine), are briefly described below. For a more extensive list of search engines, see Netscape's list at <http://home.netscape.com/home/internet-search.html>.

 Yahoo! (<http://www.yahoo.com>) is a good place to start when you want to find general discussions of your topic. It is both a search engine and a directory made of subject trees, a hierarchical index system that allows you to begin with a general subject and follow the branches down to a specific document. Yahoo!'s subject trees begin on its main page, which can be found at the

Tips for Internet Searches

Searching by looking for key words associated with your topic may require some imagination. In most cases your search will be either too narrow or too broad. If you are getting too many hits (successful key-word matches) on AltaVista, which searches through every word of a document, try doing the same search on Yahoo!, which searches only topics and titles. Likewise, if you are not getting enough matches on Yahoo!, try AltaVista. The following tips offer additional suggestions. When you do find the information you want, remember to check its credibility. (See "Evaluating Your Sources" on pages 70–73 for how to judge the reliability of the information on the Internet.)

1. Finding phrases. Use double quotation marks to lock groups of words together into phrases. For example, if you want to find documents containing a specific phrase, such as "Green Bay Packers," put the phrase in quotation marks. Otherwise, you will get thousands of pages that have only "green" or "bay" or "packers" in them.

2. Narrowing a search. If you are getting *too many hits*, try narrowing your search by adding more key terms. Sometimes this will help because most search engines display the pages with the most matches first. With most search engines, you can narrow your search and make sure that all the key terms are found in the document by using AND between them.

Quick tip: In the AltaVista Advanced Search, narrow your search by looking for the most current information (or for the dates of highest controversy about the topic).

URL (the Internet address) given at the beginning of this paragraph. To learn more about how to do a search on Yahoo!, click on the Options link located by Yahoo!'s text box.

AltaVista (<http://www.altavista.digital.com>), unlike Yahoo!, does a thorough full-text search of documents for your key terms. It is a good way to look for obscure items or very specific topics, but if your key term is too general, you will most likely receive hundreds or even thousands of links to pages that may mention your topic only in passing. AltaVista offers both a Simple Search and an Advanced Search. To find out more about both types, click the Help link below the text box on the first AltaVista Page (at the URL at the beginning of this paragraph).

Quick tip: Some search engines such as Yahoo! search for document titles only, allowing you to narrow your search results to sources that are primarily about your topic.

3. Broadening a search. If you are *not getting enough hits,* you need to broaden your search by deleting some of the more specific key terms or substituting synonyms for some of the key words you already have listed. For example, for a search about how to make a Web page, you might try several search strings, such as "Web page design," "creating a Web page," or "making a Web page." You might also try a more general category under which your topic falls. For example, if you want information on the Hopi god Kokopeli but you find only one or two hits with that name as the key word, you could try searching for "Hopi religion" or just "Hopi."

Quick tip: The Web is a big place with millions of documents, and the number increases by the hour. No single search engine can cover the whole Web, because the different search engines do not cover exactly the same territory. If your search does not work on the first engine you use, try running it on several different search engines.

Quick tip: Some search engines are designed to find specific topics, such as Law Crawler (<http://www.lawcrawler.com>) or the Amazing Environmental Organization Web Directory (<http://www.webdirectory.com>).

Gathering Your Sources

With a preliminary bibliography compiled, you will be ready to locate your sources. You can check in the lobby or the reference room of the library to see what call numbers are found on what floor. Some newer magazines and newspapers may be in a reading room; some of the older ones may be on microfilm; many are now on the Internet.

Here are a few tips that can save you time:

1. Make sure the source is relevant. You will waste time if you check out four or five books and then wait until you get home to look at them carefully. Instead, do a bit of prereading. First, check the index to make sure that the book contains information on your topic. Then quickly scan the cited pages to see that the information is relevant. You can then take home—or photocopy pages from—only those books that will be helpful. Similarly, you should scan a periodical article or study its abstract and introduction before deciding to copy it or read the entire piece. Also check to see if these sources mention other sources that you might want to locate.

2. Browse the shelves near the books you have come to get. Because books are shelved by subjects, the ones nearby may also be pertinent to your topic.

3. Think about documentation. If you plan to photocopy parts of articles or books, write down the publication information (author, title, date, publisher, volume, and page numbers) on the photocopy itself and staple the pages together. Then you will have this information when you begin compiling a list of sources. For Internet materials, print out at least the first page of any source you hope to use, and make sure the URL is on the page.

Evaluating Your Sources: The Basics of Critical Reading

As you begin reading the books and articles that you gather, carefully evaluate the arguments presented within them. Consider the following questions to become an *active, critical reader:*

- **The author:** What qualifies the author to speak on the subject? Is the author likely to have a particular bias or be neutral?

- **The source:** Is the publication reputable? biased? Is it recent or out of date?

- **The audience:** To whom does the author seem to be writing? How does the author deal with the audience's opinions and level of knowledge?

- **The arguments:** What points is the author trying to make? Are they all clear or are some relatively hidden?

- **The evidence:** What evidence is offered in support of each point? Is the evidence sufficient?

As you seek answers to these questions, you will be doing critical reading of a sort that will stand you in good stead in all your college classes. As you begin to use more Internet sources, however, that practice of critical reading becomes even more important.

Judging the Reliability of Internet Sources

Students who are accustomed to doing research in college libraries face new issues when they start doing research on the Internet. Before a book or a journal appears in a university library, it has usually gone through a number of checks to make sure the information is reliable. For example, if you find a copy of *Moby Dick*

in your college or university library, you can check the copyright page to be sure you are getting a generally accepted version of the real thing. But if you find a copy of *Moby Dick* on the Internet, you need to give some serious thought as to where you found it, whether the person who put that material on the Internet is a reliable authority on the subject (someone who can be trusted not to enter his or her own personal, political, or scholarly biases into the text), and whether your professor will accept your judgment of the reliability of that material.

There is no centralized regulating body that concerns itself with the reliability of what is on the Internet. Although the Internet can seem like a really big library, it is much more like a huge open-air market. At one place within it, there may be rare, valuable, reliable information. But one click away, there are weirdos and eccentrics from whom anything you obtain is, at best, questionable. *The problem is that no labeling separates the truly eccentric from the rest of us:* on the Internet anyone, absolutely anyone, can post Web pages. Someone who wants to turn *Moby Dick* into a glorification of blood sports can post a rewritten version with no indication of its differences from Melville's original; so can someone who wants to turn it into an animal-rights tract told from the whale's point of view. There's a saying in Latin, *caveat emptor,* or "let the buyer beware." When it comes to doing research on the Internet, the saying should be *caveat internauta,* or "let the surfer beware."

- **Is the information on the page *primary* or *secondary*?** That is, is it a report of facts, such as a medical researcher's article counting cases of "mad cow" disease in England in 1997, or is it an Internet newsgroup discussion about "mad cow" disease? The papers and reports you write for your college classes need to be based on reliable information. The further your own sources are from original research studies, the less reliable the information is.

- **Who is the author or the sponsor of the page? Is contact information provided?** If you're researching the author Jane Austen and find a page done by an English professor at the University of Texas in Austin, it's probably reliable. But if the only source identification is something cryptic, such as "Society for Feruginous Retorts," be suspicious of the page's reliability. A page sponsored by a reputable person or organization should also contain additional ways to verify the sponsor's identity, such as an e-mail or postal address at the bottom of the home page. A page put up by a person or an organization that does not want to be identified is probably not a good source to cite.

Sometimes you can figure out who the actual author or sponsor of the page is if it is copyrighted because the copyright holder will be named in the copyright line at the bottom of the page. You may also be able to tell something about the reliability of the page by the kinds of links it has. Are they to reputable sources, or are they to biased or anonymous ones? Note also that a tilde (~) in the page's address usually indicates a personal home page and thus may require you to look further to find out about the author's credentials.

- **How well written is the page?** Does the page read as if it were created by someone who could speak with an authoritative voice on the topic? Look at the page's grammar—are the language and the style geared toward the intended audience? Who is the intended audience?

- **How well organized is the page?** Does the page look as if it were done by a mature, responsible adult? Although the slickest page is not necessarily the most reliable, if the page looks as if it were put up by a twelve-year-old, chances are it was. Is the page easy to navigate? Is the page complete? When was it last updated? Is the information on it current? Are the layout and the design good? How good are the links it provides, and what kinds of sources or links are being used?

- **What is the purpose of the page?** Why is this material being posted—as information, as a public service, as a news source, as a research tool for academics, as a personal ax to grind, or as a way to gain attention?

- **Are there obvious reasons for bias?** If the page is presented by the Society for the Preservation of Contact with Martians, you must be suspicious of its claims for the existence of Martians. Is there any advertising? If the page is sponsored by Acme Track Shoes, you may want to be suspicious of its claims concerning these shoes' performance.

- **Can you verify the information you found** on the Web page some other way? For example, can you check the page's bibliography (if there is one) against your library's holdings or check the information against a source in the library?

- **If you believe that the information lacks credibility, try starting with a source that is recognized as reputable.** For example, if you have to do a project on the latest in cancer research, you can begin your search at major cancer research institutes, such as Mayo Clinic in Rochester, Minnesota, at <http://www.mayo.edu>.

- **Watch out for zombie pages,** or those considered "walking dead" because the person who posted them no longer maintains or updates them. Even though the information is "alive" in that it is still accessible, it is "dead" because it could well be several years old!

- Finally, remember that **even though a page may not meet your standards as a citable source, it may help you generate good ideas** or point to other usable resources. Besure not to stop your search at the first page you find—shop around and do some comparing so that you have points of reference.

The reliability of information on the Web is like the whispering game children play. A group of children sit in a row and someone whispers a message to the first child, who whispers it to the second, and so on. By the time it gets to the last child, the message is hopelessly distorted. Web pages can work the same way when people get their Web page information from other people's Web pages. The first person who posts information may make only a few small errors; the second unintentionally repeats them and may make one or two more; the third makes a few more; and so on. For information seekers, it can be nearly impossible to tell whether the information is coming from the first person in the chain or the last, but that makes a huge difference in the information's reliability. So it never hurts to double-check with a library reference.

For additional material on how to judge the reliability of Web pages, look at "Bibliography on Evaluating Internet Resources," a Web page with links to a number of other pages with checklists and articles; most of them are sponsored by university libraries. The URL is <http://refserver.lib.vt.edu/libinst/critTHINK.HTM>.

TAKING GOOD NOTES

After you have gathered a group of relevant sources and evaluated the quality of their viewpoints and evidence, you are ready to begin taking notes, either on note cards (perhaps the larger 4- by 6-inch size), in a notebook, or on a computer. As you go through this process, work carefully, recording all relevant material and using your time well.

Write Down the Bibliographic Information

You don't want to find that you've taken notes from several sources but now can't tell which note is from which source. Therein lies late-night panic.

Using the Computer for Notetaking

As you conduct your research, you can use the computer instead of note cards or notebook sheets. You can open a separate file for bibliography entries, thus creating a bibliography in almost final form. You can create another file for your notes, separated by numbers or subheadings for different parts of the paper. If you copy a direct quotation into this file, placing quotation marks around it and noting its source, you will not have to recopy it as you draft and revise. Once you have placed your research information on disk in something like your outline order, you may find yourself well on the way to a rough draft.

When you begin using a source, first record all the bibliographic information (author, title, publisher, volume, pages, and so on), following the documentation form you will be using in the final draft. (See pages 93–130 for a full discussion of bibliographic form.) Some people use separate bibliography cards or separate pages in their notebooks for these lists.

When taking notes, clearly tie them to their source. Start each new card or page with the title, the author's name, or both (if you are using two works by the same author) or with a number that refers to an entry in your bibliography: then you will know which source the notes came from. Write down the number of the first page you are using, and record each additional page number so that you will be able to cite the correct page number as well as the correct source.

Use a Variety of Note Types

Depending on how you want to use the information you find in a source, you will probably take notes in one of four ways: as summary, paraphrase, quotation, or personal response.

Summary

One helpful type of note summarizes the major assertions and evidence of an entire article or chapter. You might outline the principal points of the argument especially as they apply to your topic, as in the example in Figure 5 summarizing Harry Brod's "A Case for Men's Studies," an article from the Kimmel book (shown in the on-line catalogue entry in Figure 4, page 64).

Brod

Brod argues that men's studies can help us to understand the role of men in earlier eras—their relationship
with women and their children, their view of their careers,
the pressures they felt, their view of masculinity—as well
as expectations placed on them today. Such study can
help men to abandon the myth of being "real men," very
macho and sure and in charge. By seeing earlier, gentler
images of masculinity, men can reassess their supposed
need for dominance. Courses in this kind of social history
are defined as men's studies.

Brod (cont.)
        Brod cites reasons for the recent introduction of the
courses and the new research on men.

1. Women's studies programs have led to research on
   gender.
2. The women's movement has led to examination of
   male roles.
3. The nature of male work has changed — away from
   the physical.
4. Changes in warfare have made individual male
   heroism less common.

Figure 5. Summary Note

Paraphrase

In addition to summarizing an entire chapter or article, you may
want to record the major ideas from particular paragraphs and
sentences, noting the page numbers where they occur. Paraphrasing requires you to think carefully about what the author has said
and then to recast the content of the author's sentences *in your
own words and sentence structure*. If some of your notes seem close
to a direct quotation, mark them as poor paraphrases that will
need further work. (See Figure 6 for a sample paraphrase note and

Brod

Pages 267-268: In the 1980s, a gender gap, a difference in male and female voting habits, occurred because men became more conservative. Women's more liberal views on military spending and employment did not change. And different views on these two issues caused the difference in voting habits—not issues like child care or abortion that might be considered as women's issues. The explanation comes from comparative study of the habits of women and men—interesting material for a course.

Figure 6. Paraphrase Note

pages 85 and 77–78 for more help with paraphrasing and avoiding plagiarism.)

Quotation

You may decide to quote some memorable phrases or sentences directly. (See pages 81–86 for help with deciding when to use a direct quotation.) Write down every word exactly and mark the quotation with quotation marks so that later you will not mistake it for a paraphrase. You may also want to make copies of the article or book pages so that you can double-check the quotation later. If you decide to leave out part of the quotation, use an ellipsis mark (. . .) to indicate that you have omitted words from the middle of a sentence, or use a period and an ellipsis mark (. . . .) to indicate that you have omitted one or more sentences from the middle of a quoted passage. (See *Ellipsis Marks,* pages 353–54, for help with using the ellipsis mark correctly.)

When you record a quotation, make a note about how you might use it in your paper. (See Figure 7 for an example.)

Personal Response

As you read source materials, you will be changing your thinking, getting new ideas, agreeing, or even getting angry. Record your responses or any new approach to your paper that comes to

Brod

Page 264: A good definition I could use toward the beginning: "the subject matter of men's studies is the study of masculinities and male experiences in their own right as specific and varying social, cultural, and historical formulations."

Figure 7. Quotation Note

Brod
<u>ME</u>: I am getting the sense of this: these new courses help men and women to understand the social aspects of aggression and violence. Many people think the notion of men's studies is foolish since men are studied everywhere and don't need special attention—but they are usually not studied with this psychology/ social history approach. I could start the paper with the immediate negative response to such classes and go from there to explain the real content and value of these programs.

Figure 8. Personal Response Note

you. Use a separate card or sheet and write *ME* on it (see Figure 8) to distinguish your own thinking from quotations and paraphrases. Do not wait until later or the idea may be gone.

Avoid Plagiarism

Careful notetaking will help you to avoid any possibility of plagiarism in your papers. Failing to cite a source, either intentionally or unintentionally, is called plagiarism. It is a form of stealing because it involves pretending that another person's work is your own.

When you work with source materials, whether they come from the library or the Internet, you must provide a note or citation for the following types of borrowings:

- direct quotations
- paraphrases
- the author's opinions and data
- visuals and graphics

Citations for all four should give appropriate credit to the authors and enable your readers to locate the source. Correct documentation also requires that all direct quotations, placed in quotation marks, be the author's exact words and that all paraphrases be completely in your own words and sentence structure.

The only exception to the requirement to cite all source materials occurs when you decide that a certain fact is common knowledge in the field you are researching. Examples include a president's birth date, a shared definition of a scientific process, and the weight of a certain molecule. If you are in doubt about whether to give credit, however, go ahead and cite the source: no teacher will fault you for being overly careful. (See pages 81–86 for more help with quotations and paraphrases.)

CHOOSING A PRELIMINARY THESIS AND OUTLINE

Once you have investigated your topic thoroughly, you are ready to organize your paper.

Deciding on a Thesis

First, read through your notes and separate them by topic or subtopic to see what material you have, which ideas or facts are connected, and which ones seem extraneous. This review will help you decide on the main idea that your paper will develop. Your thesis should meet the following criteria:

1. Your thesis should deal with the major points you discovered about the topic.

2. Your thesis should interest your readers.
3. Your thesis should take a specific stand about the topic, one that your research materials will support.

For a paper on men's studies aimed at a general audience, for example, you might describe this new curricular development, and if you discover competing program models, you might argue for one over another. A paper intended for an audience of college administrators might focus on the negative publicity that such a program might cause or its cost; a paper for faculty might concern the effects of such classes on male and female students; a paper for students might discuss the appropriateness of such a course as a requirement or an option within a specific major. (See pages 21–22 and 31–38 for additional help with deciding on a thesis. See also the sample research paper on pages 109–16.)

Deciding on an Outline

After choosing a thesis statement, reevaluate your materials, gathering all the information that will be pertinent to it. You will then be ready to create a preliminary organization, which may be altered as you compose and revise. One structure frequently used for presenting research data is thesis/support:

Introduction
    Background information
    Thesis statement
Body
    1. First main point (beginning the proof of the thesis)
    2. Second main point (building on the first point and continuing the proof of the thesis)
    3. Third main point (building on the first and second points and continuing the proof of the thesis)
    (Continuing with additional points)
Conclusion
    Restatement of the thesis
    Address to the reader
    Statement of implications or a call to action

The more specifically you plan your paper, by noting your main points and your evidence to support each one, the easier the actual writing will be. As you decide on the main points, you

How to Avoid Ineffective Writing Practices

For your research papers, you should rely on the techniques for writing a first draft presented on pages 18–20. Since these longer papers require a sustained effort, you should try to avoid the kinds of writing behaviors that do not work.

- **Do not try to write a perfect first draft.** Trying to make your first draft perfect puts too much pressure on you; people who do this usually don't finish any kind of draft at all. You will be much better off doing a fast, loose draft and then relying on your revising and editing skills (and the clear vision that comes from looking at it the next day or from getting someone else's reading of it) to make a later draft the perfect one. Beyond that, doing a good job of research writing requires time for your understanding of the topic to grow and deepen after you've already put a draft on paper. Without that more thorough understanding, you cannot prepare a perfect draft no matter how many times you run the spell checker and the grammar checker on your computer.

- **Do not try to draft when you're too tired.** Writing puts a big burden on anyone's mental faculties: you will write better when you are mentally fresh and physically rested. For some of us, this is first thing in the morning; for others, late at night. Try to do your writing at your best time of day, but whenever you do it, make sure your body and brain are in good shape.

can evaluate their validity just as you examined the arguments in your sources. (For a discussion of evaluating argument, see pages 153–54.) In either an introductory or a final paragraph, you may also want to refute a faulty argument that you encountered in your research, especially if some members of your audience have accepted it in the past. (See pages 14–17 for more help with organizing an essay.)

WRITING THE FIRST DRAFT

Before you start work on a first draft, place your research materials in the same order as your outline so that you can find the relevant information easily. But don't write by recopying your notes. Craft your *own* structure and argument and keep the research ma-

- **Do not try to draft when you lack sufficient knowledge** (of the task, the subject, or the audience). If you run out of things to say when you're doing research writing, your first impulse may be to rack your brain to come up with more. You might do better to talk over the assignment with your teacher or go back to the library and look up more information.

- **Do not let nondrafting activities deplete your time and energy.** We all have a best time of day to write, and doing research writing requires a commitment of time as well as energy. So when your best friend calls five minutes into your writing time to invite you out for pizza, you must say no. When it is time to write, you must write.

- **Do not wait too long to start.** You may be able to dash off a marginally acceptable five-paragraph theme the night before the paper is due; some people can. But planning research, doing research, and writing it up present problems on quite a different scale. Your motto for doing good research writing should be something like *do it early and do it often,* however successful you may have been in the past with *do it at the last minute.*

We can't guarantee that if you follow all six of these recommendations, your writing will be wonderful. But it's a safe bet that if you ignore more than one of them, you will be in trouble when it comes to writing about research.

terials on the side, for reference. Try to develop your thesis but not follow it rigidly; new ideas often come through the drafting process. (See pages 9–12 if you need help with techniques for writing a first draft.)

Using Sources Effectively

As you work on a first draft, you need to decide when to quote directly and when to paraphrase your research sources. The key point to quoting is not to overdo it. Inexperienced writers tend to insert too many quotations, using their own sentences just to link these passages. But readers only glance over long quotations, and they won't understand an essay if the major points are made within quotations. With too many quotations, certainly with more than two or three on a page, the writing will be choppy, the argument will be unclear, and your own voice will be buried by the others.

The first question, then, is whether the material should be quoted directly or whether a paraphrase would be more effective. Direct quotations should be used in only three cases:

1. when you want to provide a sample of a writing style or dialect
2. when a point is particularly well stated
3. when the exact phrasing of a policy or a law is important to your argument

In the following paragraph on the continuing struggle for civil rights, for example, the dialect and speaking style make the quotation powerful:

> Someone said recently to an old black lady from Mississippi, whose legs had been badly mangled by local police who arrested her for disturbing the peace, that the Civil Rights Movement was dead, and asked, since it was dead, what she thought about it. The old lady replied, hobbling out of his presence on her cane, that the Civil Rights Movement was like herself, "if it's dead, it shore ain't ready to lay down."
>
> —Alice Walker, *In Search of Our Mothers' Gardens*

The following excerpts from an essay on bear management at Yellowstone Park provide two examples of effective quotations. The first uses a quotation to emphasize a point; the second uses a quotation to explain official policy:

> Shortly after the study team began its real research, disturbing trends began to surface. The life expectancy of bears was dropping, possibly due to poor nutrition as well as human predation. The average life expectancy of bears studied by the Craigheads was more than twenty-five years. But the team was finding no older animals in Yellowstone Park. "Our bears," the report concluded emphatically, "are dying before they reach sixteen and no one knows why."
>
> A bear injury often resulted in a tort claim against the Park. So when a bear hurt someone, the bear was removed, to prevent further liability. The new policy, as described by Starker Leopold and Durward Allen, both of the National Parks System Advisory Board, was to be one that "protects the people from the bears; protects the bears from the people; and protects the National Park Service from tort cases in the event of mishap."
>
> —Alston Chase, "The Last Bears of Yellowstone"

Choose Short Quotations

When you have decided that a quotation will be effective because it meets one of the three criteria, choose as short an excerpt as possible to keep the quoted material from overwhelming your own developing argument.

If you are writing a paper criticizing college testing methods, for example, you might want to quote some of this paragraph written by a college professor who opposes final exams:

> I suspect that most of us have little conviction that six years or six months after the completion of this or that course, its graduates could pass even a vastly simplified examination on its content. What we might call the "retention quotient" is, in most cases, very low indeed. There is much to suggest that because the final examination presents both a frightening hurdle and an obvious terminus, it actually inhibits retention of the course content. Students at least believe so and often speak cynically of final examinations as a kind of intellectual purge by which the mind is evacuated of all the material that has been stored in it during the course.
>
> —Page Smith, *Dissenting Opinions*

Instead of using the entire excerpt, quote only the part that is essential to your argument and then continue with your own writing, as in these examples employing MLA documentation:

> Final exams generally call on students to recall the most basic factual material covered in the course. Perhaps they will make some judgments, but nothing very taxing. One critic has suggested that the traditional exam "actually inhibits retention of the course content" because it focuses on memorizing facts quickly and not on thinking critically (Smith 42).

> Educators have to face the fact that exams do not help students master the material: "what we might call the 'retention quotient' is, in most cases, very low indeed" (Smith 42). The student may not even remember the material several days or weeks later.

(For a full discussion of MLA documentation, see pages 93–116.)

Use of Ellipsis Mark and Brackets with Quotations

By using the ellipsis mark (. . .), you can eliminate part of a quoted passage and thus produce a shorter quotation—but it must not distort the meaning of the original. If some words need to be changed so that the quotation will fit into your sentence structure, or if you need to add information to clarify the meaning, you can make those small changes within brackets.

Consider, for example, the following sentence about the final exam from the Smith essay:

> Its avowed purpose is to make sure that the student has accomplished something measurable in mastering a certain body of material, that he has increased his efficiency or his knowledge. (42)

In your paper, you might present this material by using both an ellipsis mark and brackets:

> Smith argues that many of the grueling rituals of higher education once had noble goals: "[the] avowed purpose [of the final exam] is to make sure that the student . . . has increased his efficiency or his knowledge" (42).

(See *Ellipsis Marks,* pages 353–54, and *Brackets,* pages 328–29, for more information.)

Punctuation with Quotations

As some of the preceding examples show, *quoted phrases or words* can be incorporated within your sentences in quotation marks. No additional punctuation is required.

> Perhaps the final exam has turned into a "kind of intellectual purge" instead of a sound educational experience (Smith 42).

Use a colon to join a *quoted sentence* with a sentence that introduces it:

> Smith calls on fellow educators to reexamine testing practices: "We are bound to ask ourselves, it seems to me, how well the aims of a particular course or of education in general are served by this ordeal" (42).

(See *Quotation Marks,* pages 383–88, for more information.)

Paraphrasing Sources

Because you should choose direct quotations only in the three situations mentioned earlier, you will generally use a paraphrase when you discuss ideas and facts from sources. To summarize or paraphrase, put the author's ideas completely into your own words instead of creating some odd combination of the text's original wording and your own. Such "plagiaphrasing" should be avoided because it is a form of plagiarism. Consider the differences between the adequate and inadequate paraphrases of this direct quotation:

> The new women's social history focuses on the lives led by the majority of women in all strata of society, using material from a wide range of sources, from diaries to demographics. (Brod 266)

Inadequate Paraphrase	**Adequate Paraphrase**
Today's new social history of women focuses on how women lived in all segments of society, using a wide range of research materials (Brod 266).	In women's studies classes, the concern is not with a few famous historical or literary women but with the daily lives of all types of women, something previously given very little attention (Brod 266).

A good method of paraphrasing is to read the source material, put the book or article down, think through the information, and then write your own version of it.

Introducing Quotations and Paraphrases

One method of introducing the quotation or paraphrase is with a **signal phrase,** which explains to the reader the author's authority or intentions and thus makes the excerpt more meaningful. Signal phrases, like those preceding or following the quotations in the following sentences, commonly appear in research papers.

> "It could not have been worse for local businesses," wrote economist Sheila Parker of the L.A. riot.

> Ronald Dore contends that workers are treated well in companies employing Japanese management theories: "To equate hierarchy with domination and exploitation is clearly illegitimate" (112).

> At the conclusion of his editorial, Mayor Beame noted a dramatic increase in local traffic and maintained that a new bridge must be built on Hester Street (6).

> In seeking causes for Republican victories in 1994, the Cryer Report argues that "voters who rejected the Democratic party did not necessarily endorse the Contract with America" (4).

When you want the subject matter to remain central, you can also use the **dropped-in quotation or paraphrase** and give the author's name only in the parenthetical reference.

Young workers "will find the social security system bankrupt when they need it" (Santayana 237).

More than two-thirds of today's college students feel that graduate study will be necessary for a successful career (Cremedas 92).

Verbs to Introduce Quotations and Paraphrases

When using signal phrases to introduce source materials, you might choose a more specific verb than *said* to indicate the author's attitude or approach. The following verbs create different meanings that may suit your purposes more specifically:

For an Objective Observer

describes	observes	points out
explains	notes	sees

For Making Conclusions and Defending an Interpretation

analyzes	concludes	maintains
alleges	contends	predicts
assesses	insists	suggests

For Agreement

agrees	concurs	grants

For Disagreement

condemns	derides	opposes
criticizes	objects	warns

REVISING SYSTEMATICALLY

When your first draft is finished, you will probably have an uneven piece: some parts will seem unrelated to the thesis, some will be unsubstantiated, and some will be out of place. Your next step is to begin revising. (Before proceeding, you may find it helpful to see the sample research paper on pages 109–16.) After a short break, read your paper carefully and consider the following questions, which will help you to make the necessary changes:

1. **Introduction:** Does the beginning involve the reader? Does it provide the necessary background?

2. **Thesis:** What is the thesis of the essay? Does it seem clear? Does the body of the paper prove this assertion?

3. **Structure:** Make an outline of the paper's contents. Does the order of points seem appropriate? Should any point be added, moved, or deleted?

4. **Evidence:** Does the essay contain sufficient supporting detail? of what types? What faulty evidence—such as one of the common fallacies or an invalid appeal to *ethos* or *pathos*—might be removed or restated? (For a full discussion of evidence, see pages 145–52.)

5. **Use of quotation and paraphrase:** Are the direct quotations and paraphrases woven into the paper? Are there any direct quotations that might be removed or shortened? Are any paraphrases really plagiaphrasing? Are all source materials documented? (See the sections on APA and MLA documentation on pages 90–130.)

6. **Conclusion:** Are the implications of the argument made clear? Is there a call to action or further discussion of the argument's importance? (For a full discussion of conclusions, see pages 27–28.)

For more help with revising and proofreading, see *Revising*, pages 21–44, and *Finishing*, pages 45–51.

DOCUMENTING SOURCES CORRECTLY

As you incorporate quoted and paraphrased materials into your paper, make sure you document those borrowings correctly. Generally, any quotation, paraphrase, summary, or artwork must be noted as the work of another person—both to give credit to the original creator and to help your reader find more information. (See pages 77–78 for a full discussion about avoiding plagiarism.)

When and What to Document

Here are four guidelines to help you decide when and what to document:

1. If you use the exact language of your source, you must use quotation marks and cite the source.

2. If you decide on a paraphrase and thus put the information completely into your own words, you don't use quotation marks but you do cite the source.

3. If you use information that is not common knowledge, you must cite the source. If the information would not be familiar to someone who has not researched the subject, it is not common knowledge, and you must cite its source, whether you are quoting or paraphrasing.

4. Cite sources for all kinds of borrowings, not just for words and facts. You need to cite the sources for anything that is not yours, including drawings, photos, artwork, ideas, and music.

Citing Electronic Sources

Today's students are generally familiar with the traditional elements of documenting sources: articles are cited one way, books another way, and so on. With the advent of electronic sources, however, there are a few new considerations. The most important one is the distinction between two types of electronic sources: CD-ROMs and other portable (or unchangeable) sources and on-line (or changeable) sources.

CD-ROMs and Other Unchangeable Electronic Sources

If you go to your university library and look something up on a CD-ROM in the reference room (such as material on InfoTrac or First Search), that material's source is stable (i.e., unchangeable). Anyone could look it up today, next month, or next year and find the same information. The source has a date and place of publication (although here "publication" may mean "production") and a version number, all of which should be shown in your documentation, just as you would show the comparable information for a page in a book or a journal article. In addition, for these kinds of sources you need to give the title of the database (underlined) and identify the medium (such as CD-ROM).

On-Line (or Changeable) Sources

For materials you find on the Internet, you need to include the date you accessed the Web source as well as the date of its publication or last revision and its Uniform Resource Locator (URL). URLs are usually shown in angle brackets (< >). In the early days of the Web, teachers would not let students break a URL across two lines, but today that is usually acceptable so long as the URL is enclosed in angle brackets and the break is after a slash or a dot rather than between letters. Some teachers may also require you to indicate the path you followed to get to that Web page or even to include a hard copy (a printout) of the page itself. If information you find on the Internet is crucial to your work, it is always a good idea to print out a hard copy just in case you need one.

Different Styles for Different Fields

The method for citing sources varies from field to field; different disciplines, even different teachers within the same discipline, have different requirements. In this book we include two commonly used documentation systems: the MLA (Modern Language Association) style for the humanities, explained in the *MLA Handbook for Writers of Research Papers* (4th ed.), and the APA (American Psychological Association) style for the social sciences, explained in the *Publication Manual of the American Psychological Association* (4th ed.). Professors in higher-level classes or classes in other disciplines may expect you to use some other style, such as the Council of Biology Editors (CBE) style used in the life sciences and described in *Scientific Style and Format: The CBE Manual for Authors, Editors, and Publishers* (6th ed.); the *Chicago Manual of Style* (CMS) numbered notes style often used in business, history, and many of the hard sciences; or the Institute of Electrical and Electronic Engineers (IEEE) style (at <http://www.ieee.org>) used in such fields as computer science. Descriptions of many of these documentation styles may be found on the Web simply by typing the name of the style in your favorite search engine's text box. (MLA's own description of MLA style may be found at <http://www.mla.org/main_stl.htm>.)

Quick View: MLA Style

CITATIONS IN THE TEXT (SEE PAGE 94)

For Paraphrases and Short Quotations

Enclose short quotations (under five lines of prose or under four lines of poetry) in double quotation marks in your paragraphs. Separate lines of poetry with slashes (/). Cite the author's last name either in your text or in parentheses with the page number (or line numbers of poetry) after the quotation marks and before the period: (Quarles 19).

For Longer Quotations

Double-space longer quotations (over four lines of prose or over three lines of poetry or verse plays) and block-indent them one inch (or ten spaces if you are using a typewriter) from the left margin, without quotation marks. Each line of poetry should appear on a new line. If the author's name is not given in the text, cite it in parentheses with the page number (or line numbers of poetry) one space after the final punctuation mark.

FOR THE BIBLIOGRAPHY—ENTITLED "WORKS CITED" (SEE PAGE 99)

Book

Holland, Norman. Five Readers Reading. New Haven: Yale UP, 1975.

Essay or Article within a Book

Tamari, Vera. "Palestinian Women's Art in the Occupied Territories." Palestinian Women: Identity and Experience. Ed. Ebba Augustin. London: Zed, 1993. 63-67.

Scholarly Journal Article, Journal Paginated by Year or Volume

Ganster, Daniel C., and John Schaubroeck. "Work Stress and Employee Health." Journal of Management 17 (1991): 235-71.

Scholarly Journal Article, Journal Paginated by Issue

Campoy, Renee. "The Role of Technology in the School Reform Movement." Educational Technology 32.8 (1992): 17-21.

Newspaper Article

"Roman Catholics: Cardinals, Feminists on Collision Course?" Atlanta Constitution 15 June 1994: C1.

[If the author's name is given, the entry begins with it.]

Electronic Sources (See Pages 99, 105–106)

Quick View: APA Style

CITATIONS IN THE TEXT (SEE PAGE 118)

For Paraphrases
Cite the author's last name either in the sentence or with the publication date in parentheses after the first reference to the material. Place a comma between the name and the date: (Carlson, 1995).

For Short Quotations (Less Than 40 Words)
Enclose short quotations in double quotation marks in the text: do not indent them separately. If the author's name is mentioned in the text, place the publication date in parentheses after it. Cite the page number(s), using *p.* or *pp.*, in parentheses immediately after the quotation marks. If the author's name is not mentioned in the text, include it with the date and the page number in the parentheses: (Harrelson, 1994, p. 32).

For Longer Quotations (More Than 40 Words)
Double-space long quotations and block-indent them five spaces from the left margin, without quotation marks. Place the page reference in parentheses after the final period, along with the author's name and the date if they did not appear in the text.

FOR THE BIBLIOGRAPHY—ENTITLED "REFERENCES" (SEE PAGE 121)

Book
> Ryder, R. (1975). Victims of science. London: Davis-Poynter.

Essay or Article within a Book
> Schilb, J. (1991). Cultural studies, postmodernism, and composition. In P. Harkin & J. Schilb (Eds.), Contending with words: Composition and rhetoric in a postmodern age (pp. 173-188). New York: Modern Language Association.

Scholarly Journal Article, Journal Paginated by Year or Volume
> Welsh, D. (1991). The outlook for a democratic South Africa. International Affairs, 67, 739-753.

Scholarly Journal Article, Journal Paginated by Issue
> Wright, J. D. (1990). Poor people, poor health: The health status of the homeless. Journal of Social Issues, 46(4), 49-64.

Newspaper Article
> Celis, W. (1994, May 18). Forty years after Brown, segregation persists. The New York Times, pp. A1, B8.

Electronic Sources (See Pages 127–128)

MLA AND APA

MLA Documentation Style

MLA Documentation Style

The MLA format for referencing source materials was established by the Modern Language Association. It is used by scholars in English, foreign languages, and other fields of the humanities. The complete format can be found in the *MLA Handbook for Writers of Research Papers,* 4th ed. (New York: Modern Language Association, 1995). It is also available on the World Wide Web at <http://www.mla.org/set_stl.htm>.The MLA format once required note numbers and footnotes. Now it requires short notes, or citations, put in parentheses within the text and an accompanying bibliography, called a "Works Cited" list. The following pages will show you how to do the citations and the bibliography and how to type the paper in MLA style.

Citations in the Text

For a Paraphrase or Short Quotation from Prose (Five Lines or Fewer)

Identify paraphrases of any length or short quotations (no more than four typed lines) from prose by citing *the author's last name and the page number,* either in the text of your sentence or in parentheses at the end of the sentence or paragraph drawn from the source. Citations in parentheses are placed inside the period ending the sentence or paragraph.

- **If you mention the author's name in your sentence,** you need to provide only the page numbers—in parentheses at the end of the sentence within the period. For page numbers over 100, use only the last two numbers of the second number when the two are within the same hundred: 97–98, 272–74, 299–301.

> Richard D. Robinson maintains that in Japan almost all executives began at the lowest positions in their companies: there is only one

MBA program because employers do not seek outside applicants for the top jobs (132–33).

Richard D. Robinson maintains that in Japan "the ratio of a top manager's salary to that of an entry-level blue-collar employee is only 5 or 6 to 1" (133).

- **If you do not mention the author's name in your sentence,** put the last name and page numbers in parentheses at the end of the sentence, with no comma between them.

A survey found that 95% of the members of diet support groups are women (Chernin 196–97).

Endless dieting is, for millions of American women, a "cause of unremitting pain and shame" (Chernin 204).

- **If you are discussing an entire work,** you do not have to cite page numbers.

In his novel <u>Bonfire of the Vanities</u>, Tom Wolfe probed the emptiness of the highest levels of New York society.

- **If you are using more than one work by the same author,** include a shortened version of the title in your citation. Place quotation marks around the title of an article, a short story, or a poem; underline the title of a book or a play. If the citation also includes the author's name, follow it with a comma; there should be no comma between the title and the page numbers.

Sensitivity training would improve the interview techniques of today's journalists (Clark, "The Underside" 139–40).

Clark critiques the "journalism of body bags and stretchers, of funerals and sobbing mothers, of missing teen-age girls and bloodstains in car trunks" ("The Underside" 137).

- **If a work has two or three authors,** list them all either in your sentence or in the citation.

According to Weitzman and Rizzo, only 39% of the people in elementary-school textbook illustrations are women or girls (301).

Studies show that textbook illustrations still feature girls and women primarily in household scenes (Weitzman and Rizzo 300).

- **If a work has more than three authors,** use the same form you use in the list of works cited: either give all the last names, or give the first author's last name followed by *et al.* (from the Latin *et alii,* meaning "and the others"; there is no period after *et*).

> Salholz, Morgan, Greene, and Rosenfeld argue that feminists need to make child-care issues part of their agenda (88–89).

> Wordsworth's <u>Prelude</u> contains a "classic description of the intoxicating spirit of the early 1790s" (Abrams et al. 6).

• **If your citations include two authors with the same last name,** include their full names in the text or their first initials along with their last names in parenthetical documentation. If their first initials are the same, give their first names in the parentheses.

> Edward Hall believes the English person's reserve stems from the nursery: since English children usually share a room with their brothers and sisters, they develop an internalized "set of barriers" (177).

> A careful study of child-raising practices in a certain country can help explain adult behavior there (E. Hall 176–78).

• **If a work has no author listed,** cite it by the title (or the first main word or two of a long title). For a journal article or an essay, use the title of the article (or a shortened version)—not the title of the journal or the book—and place these words in quotation marks. If you are citing a book without a named author, use the book title (or a shortened version) and underline it.

> The new art museum addition combines 18,000-pound concrete panels with reinforced steel beams ("Campaign" 14–15). [The complete article title is "Campaign 2000: Creating a Museum for the Future."]

• **When you use a quotation from an indirect source,** put the abbreviation *qtd. in* ("quoted in") in the parenthetical reference before the source. In the list of works cited, include only the work that you consulted (which would be Braudel in the following example).

> According to Restif de La Bretonne, few people in eighteenth-century France took baths "and those who did confined them to once or twice per summer" (qtd. in Braudel 330).

- **If a concept has two or more sources,** separate them with a semicolon in the parenthetical citation.

> Critical opinion of Dorothy Parker is hardly unanimous (Reynolds 317–22; Stoppard and Haynes 98–102; Tompkins 12–36).

For Prose Quotations of More Than Four Lines

The longer prose quotation, more than four lines, is block-indented one inch (or ten spaces if you are using a typewriter) from the left margin, without quotation marks. Indented quotations are generally introduced by a colon. The entire quotation should be double spaced. If you are quoting one paragraph, or part of one, do not indent the first line more than the rest. If you quote more than one paragraph, the beginning of every paragraph should be indented an additional quarter inch (or three typewriter spaces). The parenthetical citation occurs at the end of the quotation outside the final period. As with shorter quotations, the citation should include author and page number unless the author's name is mentioned in your text.

> Through his characterization of the Yahoos, Jonathan Swift criticizes the eating of meat:
>
>> I saw three of those detestable creatures, which I first met after my landing, feeding upon roots, and the flesh of some animals, which I afterwards found to be that of asses and dogs, and now and then a cow dead by accident or disease. They were all tied with strong withes, fastened to a beam; they held their food between the claws of their fore-feet, and tore it with their teeth. (275–76)

For Paraphrases from Poetry and Verse Plays

As with paraphrases from prose, identify paraphrases from poetry and verse plays by citing the author's last name. Instead of a page number, however, include the line number of the poem, either in your sentence or in parentheses at the end of a sentence or paragraph. For verse plays, include the act, scene, and line number. *Hamlet* 1.2.129, for example, refers to act 1, scene 2, line 129 of the play.

In "The Eve of St. Agnes," Keats places humans in the natural world by comparing the bedesman to the owl, the rabbit, and the sheep (2–6).

Ben Jonson's <u>Volpone</u> criticizes capitalism by naming gold as the modern saint and a money vault as the modern church (1.1.3).

For Short Quotations from Poetry and Verse Plays (Three Lines or Fewer)

If the quotation from a poem or a verse play is three lines or less, enclose it in quotation marks and include the lines within your text. If you quote more than one line, separate the lines with a slash (/), putting a space before and after it. Quotations from poetry are referred to by the line number (not by a page number). Quotations from verse plays are referenced by the act, scene, and line number.

Wordsworth frequently states his faith in the power of the natural world: "To me the meanest flower that blows can give / Thoughts that do often lie too deep for tears" ("Ode: Intimations of Immortality" 203–04).

In <u>A Midsummer Night's Dream</u>, Shakespeare characterizes the poet as one who creates meaning from "forms of things unknown" (5.1.15).

For Longer Quotations from Poetry and Verse Plays

Unless they have unusual spacing, verse quotations of more than three lines should be indented one inch (or ten spaces on a typewriter) from the left margin, without quotation marks or slashes. Each line of poetry should appear on a separate line. The entire quotation should be double spaced. These quotations are generally introduced with a colon. Line numbers can be added in parentheses after the final punctuation of the quotation.

In "Inventory," Vick Adams describes the regimentation and constant anxiety of modern life:

> He calculates time and a half
> while eating and watching the news.
> Drinks minus calories per mile
> deposits minus withdrawals--
> computations compounded constantly. (5–9)

For Nonprint or Electronic Sources

Your reader needs enough information to be able to find these sources in the list of works cited. Usually, the author's name or the title (whichever begins the entry in the list of works cited) will be sufficient.

> "Sissyhood Is Powerful" is the title of one review of Kimmel's Manhood in America in a popular electronic journal (Garner). The reviewer says that . . .

List of Works Cited

At the end of the paper, beginning on a new page, list all the sources that you cited—not everything that you read. For this list, entitled "Works Cited," use the formats given here for the various types of sources. The second and subsequent lines of each entry are indented half an inch (or five spaces on a typewriter); the entire reference list is double spaced and alphabetized.

Books
Book by One Author

> Walker, Alice. The Temple of My Familiar. New York: Harcourt, 1989.

Begin the entry with, and alphabetize it by, the author's last name. If there is no author, the entry begins with the book title, which is underlined or italicized.

Provide only the city (and not the state name) for the place of publication unless it is a small city: thus you would use *New York, Detroit,* or *Paris,* but *Lafayette, LA.* If more than one city is listed on the book's title page, use the first one.

Provide a shortened form of the publisher's name. Omit the first name of a publisher (*Holt,* not *Henry Holt*) and *Company, Publisher,* or *Incorporated* at the end. *Macmillan Publishing Company* should be shown as *Macmillan,* and *Oxford University Press* as *Oxford UP* (*UP* stands for *University Press*). End the entry with the year of publication.

Book by Two or Three Authors

> Dreyfus, Hubert L., and Stuart E. Dreyfus. Mind over Machine: The Power of Human Intuition and Expertise in the Era of the Computer. New York: Free, 1986.

Book by More Than Three Authors

> Belenky, Mary Field, et al. <u>Women's Ways of Knowing: The
> Development of Self, Voice, and Mind</u>. New York: Basic, 1986.

Instead of using *et al.,* you may give the full names of all the authors in the order in which they appear on the title page.

Edited Book

> Tompkins, Jane P., ed. <u>Reader-Response Criticism: From For-
> malism to Post-Structuralism</u>. Baltimore: Johns Hopkins
> UP, 1980.

Translated Book

> Barthes, Roland. <u>The Pleasure of the Text</u>. Trans. Richard Miller.
> New York: Hill, 1975.

Two or More Works by the Same Author

> Fitz, Earl. <u>Clarice Lispector</u>. Boston: Hall, 1985.

> ---. "Freedom and Self-Realization: Feminist Characterization in the
> Fiction of Clarice Lispector." <u>Modern Language Studies</u> 10.3
> (1983): 51–56.

For second and subsequent entries by the same person (whether as author or editor), use three hyphens in place of the name. If the person is the editor or translator, rather than the author, of any of these entries, add a comma and *ed.* or *trans.* after the third hyphen. Alphabetize entries for the same person by title.

Edition Other Than the First

> Nims, John Frederick, ed. <u>Western Wind: An Introduction to
> Poetry</u>. 2nd ed. New York: Random, 1983.

> Brittin, Norman A. <u>Edna St. Vincent Millay</u>. Rev. ed. Boston:
> Twayne, 1982.

Rev. ed. stands for *Revised edition.*

Book by a Corporate Author or Group

> Commission on the Humanities. <u>The Humanities in American Life:
> Report of the Commission on the Humanities</u>. Berkeley: U of
> California P, 1980.

Book without an Author or Editor

> The Chicago Manual of Style. 14th ed. Chicago: U of Chicago P,
> 1993.

When alphabetizing an entry beginning with a title, ignore an initial *A, An,* or *The.*

Book in a Series

> Broome, Edwin C. A Historical and Critical Discussion of College
> Admission Requirements. Columbia Univ. Contributions to
> Philosophy, Psychology and Education 11. New York:
> Columbia U, 1903.

The series name and number follow the title of the book.

Multivolume Work
The Entire Set

> Neather, Carl A., and George Francis Richardson. A Course in
> English for Engineers. 2 vols. Boston: Ginn, 1930.

One Volume

> Battle, Kemp P. History of the University of North Carolina. Vol. 2.
> Raleigh, NC: Edwards, 1912.

Republished Book

> Lamming, George. The Pleasures of Exile. 1960. London: Allison,
> 1984.

The first date is the original publication date; the second is the date of the republished book that is being used as a source.

Parts of Books
Selection in an Anthology

> Vance, John A. "Johnson's Historical Reviews." Fresh Reflections
> on Samuel Johnson: Essays in Criticism. Ed. Prem Nath. Troy,
> NY: Whitston, 1987. 63–84.

Place the name of the selection in quotation marks. Place its page numbers at the end of the entry, after a period. Use only the last two digits of the second number when the two page numbers are in the same hundred: 31–89, 212–43, 271–301.

Two or More Selections from an Anthology or a Collection

First, include the anthology itself in your list of works cited:

> Bailey, Dudley, ed. Essays on Rhetoric. New York: Oxford UP, 1965.

Then add alphabetized entries for each of the selections you use from that anthology, cross-referenced to the anthology.

> Plato. "Phaedrus." Bailey 3–54.

> Weaver, Richard M. "Ultimate Terms in Contemporary Rhetoric." Bailey 234–49.

Article in an Encyclopedia or Other Reference Book
Signed Article

> Harmon, William. "T. S. Eliot." The World Book Encyclopedia. 1992 ed.

With familiar reference books, such as encyclopedia sets, full publication information is not required. With less familiar reference books, provide the full publication information.

Unsigned Article

> "The 'Anusim.'" Encyclopedia of Jewish History. Ed. Ilana Shamir and Shlomo Shavit. New York: Facts on File, 1986.

Introduction, Preface, Foreword, or Afterword

> Moxley, Joseph M. Introduction. Creative Writing in America: Theory and Pedagogy. By Moxley. Urbana, IL: NCTE, 1989. v–vii.

> Auchincloss, Louis. Foreword. The Age of Innocence. By Edith Wharton. 1920. New York: Signet-NAL, 1962. 8–24.

In the first example, the author of the introduction is also the author of the book. In the second example, the author of the foreword is not the book's author.

Reports, Documents, and Dissertations
Government Document

> United States. Internal Revenue Service. 1981 Statistics of Income: Corporate Income Tax Returns. Washington: GPO, 1984.

Give the name of the government first (such as United States or New York State), followed by a period, and then the name of the agency. *GPO* stands for *Government Printing Office.*

Pamphlet

> <u>Careers for the Writing Major</u>. New Orleans: Writing Krewe, 1998.

Dissertation

> Valenti, Jeanette Y. "Delmira Augustini: A Reinterpretation of Her Poetry." Diss. Cornell, 1975.

The example shows an unpublished dissertation. A published dissertation is cited like a book: the title is underlined, and the publication data appear at the end of the entry, after the year of the dissertation.

Legal Case

> Loving v. Virginia. 388 US 1. 1967.

Underline, or italicize, the name of the case in the text but not in the list of works cited.

The example here is for a U.S. Supreme Court decision. If your paper cites many kinds of legal documents, consult *A Uniform System of Citation* (Cambridge, MA: Harvard Law Review Assn.) or *The Chicago Manual of Style* (Chicago: U of Chicago P).

Articles in Periodicals
Article in a Scholarly Journal Paginated by Year or Volume

The entire year's issues are paginated as a unit.

> Murphy, Lawrence W. "Professional and Nonprofessional Teaching of Journalism." <u>Journalism Quarterly</u> 9 (1932): 46–59.

Put the title of the article in quotation marks; underline the journal title. After the journal title, provide the volume number and then the year in parentheses. A colon separates the year and the page numbers of the complete article.

Article in a Scholarly Journal Paginated by Issue

Each issue begins with page 1.

> Cole, Richard R. "Much Better Than Yesterday, and Still Brighter Tomorrow." <u>Journalism Educator</u> 40.3 (1985): 4–8.

Place the title of the article in quotation marks; underline the journal title. Follow the volume number with a period, and give the issue number before the year in parentheses. Put the page numbers of the complete article after a colon.

Popular Magazine Article
Weekly Magazine

> Borger, Gloria. "Can Term Limits Do the Job?" <u>U.S. News and World Report</u> 11 Nov. 1991: 34–36.

Show the date in day-month-year order after the magazine title, and abbreviate the name of the month. Place the page numbers of the complete article at the end of the entry after a colon. If the article is on discontinuous pages, put a plus sign after the first page of the article rather than listing all the pages: 25+.

Monthly Magazine

> Richardson, John H. "Mother from Another Planet." <u>Premiere</u> May 1992: 62–70.

Newspaper Article

> "Combat Stress in Women to Be Studied for the First Time." <u>Times-Picayune</u> [New Orleans] 11 Jan. 1993: A7.

If the article is signed, the writer's name should be the first item in the entry. If the city's name is not part of the title of a locally published newspaper, add it in brackets after the title.

Editorial, Review, Published Interview

> "Broad View of Nature's Losses." Editorial. <u>San Francisco Examiner</u> 16 Feb. 1995: A20.

Identify an editorial, an interview, or a review (*Rev.*) after its title or subject.

> Wang, Wayne. Interview. <u>New York Times</u> 10 Oct. 1994, late ed.: C20.

The name of the interviewee is the first element in the citation for an interview. Include the interviewer's name (*Interview with . . .*) only if it is pertinent to your paper.

> Mackey, Mary. "Don't Know Much about History." Rev. of <u>Lies My Teacher Told Me: Everything Your American History Textbook</u>

Got Wrong, by James W. Loewen. San Francisco Sunday
Examiner/Chronicle Book Review 12 Feb. 1995: 3+.

An entry for a review begins with the reviewer's name and includes
the name of the work being reviewed and its author or originator.

 Electronic Sources

The basic principle for citing electronic sources is that the documentation must be sufficient to allow the reader to retrieve the
material; if the database is revisable or temporary, like much that
appears on the Internet, the documentation must show both
when the material was published and when it was accessed. The
documentation guidelines here are from the current *MLA Style
Manual* (2nd ed., 1998) and the MLA Web page <http://www.mla.
org/main_stl.htm> as supplemented by *The Mayfield Handbook of
Technical & Scientific Writing* (1998).

CD-Roms and Other Unchangeable Databases

Morring, Frank, Jr. "Russian Hardware Allows Earlier Space
Station Experiments." Aviation Week and Space Technology
16 May 1994: 57. InfoTrac: General Periodicals Index. CD-
ROM. Information Access. Aug. 1994.

For material that also has a printed version, provide the publication data (author, title, date) that would be provided for a printed
source. In addition, include the title of the database (underlined),
the publication medium, the name of the vendor (if the name is
available), and the publication date of the database.

Oppenheimer & Co. "Recommendation: Merck & Co. Inc.
Company Report." 19 Oct. 1994. InvesText. CD-ROM.
Dec. 1994.

Identify material that has no printed analog with the following
information (unless it is not given): author's name, title of the
material (in quotation marks), and date of the material. Then provide the database information as in the preceding example.

Internet and On-Line Sources

Walker, Janice R. "Columbia Online Style: MLA-Style Citations of
Electronic Sources." Vers. 1.2, Rev. Nov. 1997. 10. Dec. 1997
<http://www.cas.usf.edu/english/walker/mla.html>.

For Internet and other revisable on-line sources, in addition to the information you would provide for a printed source, give the date of publication or the most recent revision, the date of access enclosed in parentheses, and the full URL address enclosed in angle brackets (< >). Some authorities recommend, to avoid misreading, not interrupting the URL by a line break and not following it with a period; others say that it is all right to break a URL after a period or a slash if it is too long to fit on one line.

> Arnzen, Michael A. "Cyber Citations." Internet World 7.1 (1996): 30 pars. 15 Oct. 1997 <http://www.internetworld.com/ 1996/09/cybercitations.html>.

To identify the location of a specific passage in an on-line document, use its paragraph number. In the citation entry, indicate the number of paragraphs in the entire document. Add that information after the colon following the date of publication; use the abbreviation "pars." for "paragraphs." For an example of documentation for a digitized image, see the MLA sample paper, page 109 and page 116.

A document retrieved from a file transfer protocol (FTP) site or a Gopher site is cited in the same way as Web sites, except that the abbreviation *ftp* or the word *gopher* (rather than *http*) precedes the address, which is not enclosed in angle brackets. For sample citations of these and other kinds of Internet documents, see the *MLA Style Manual* (2nd ed.) or Janice Walker's Web page (endorsed by the Alliance for Computers and Writing) cited as the first example in this section.

Other Sources
Personal Communication (Including E-Mail)

> Calabria, Frank. Personal interview. 7 Feb. 1995.

> Takaki, Ronald. Letter to the author. 28 Mar. 1993.

Other types of personal communication, such as e-mail and telephone conversations, can also be cited with this format. For an e-mail citation, include the subject line in quotation marks after the author's name, as if it were the title of an article.

Lecture, Speech, Live Performance

> Kinstoli, Luigi. "Exploration South." Travel South Convention. Birmingham. 22 Oct. 1994.

If there is no title, use a descriptive label, such as *Lecture* or *Keynote speech*, without quotation marks.

> <u>Empyrean Dances</u>. Chor. Edward Stierle. Joffrey Ballet. Opera
> House, San Francisco. 2 July 1992.

The entry needs to include the site and date of the event, as well as any other pertinent information about originators and performers.

Film or Television or Radio Program

> Zemeckis, Robert, dir. <u>Forrest Gump</u>. Perf. Tom Hanks, Sally Fields,
> Robin Wright. Paramount, 1994.

> <u>TV Nation: Year in Review</u>. Dir. Michael Moore. NBC, 28 Dec. 1994.

Pertinent information, such as performers, writers, and names of series episodes, can be included in an entry; underline the name of a series, and put quotation marks around the title of an episode. If the work of a particular person is the reason for the reference, the entry can begin with that person's name.

Recording

> Verdi, Giuseppe. "Triumphal March." <u>Aïda</u>. Perf. National
> Philharmonic Orchestra. Cond. James Levine. RCA Red
> Seal, 1978.

If you are citing an element of a longer work, such as one piece on a CD or in an opera, place its name in quotation marks and underline the name of the longer work.

Work of Art

> da Vinci, Leonardo. <u>The Last Supper</u>. 1495-1498. Santa Maria delle
> Grazie, Milan.

The date of creation of the artwork, between its title and the site or owner, is optional.

> Shen Chou. <u>Landscape in the Manner of Ni Tsan</u>. 1484. Nelson Gallery-
> Atkins Museum, Kansas City, MO. <u>The Arts of China</u>, 3rd ed.
> By Michael Sullivan. Berkeley: U of California P, 1984. 207.

To cite a photograph or slide of a work of art, add the full publication information, including page or slide number, to the artwork information. For an example of a citation for an image scanned from a Web site, see the MLA sample paper, page 109.

Typing or Word Processing Instructions for MLA

(See Daniel Kimball's paper on pages 109–16 as a sample.)

1. Set one-inch margins on the top, bottom, and sides of each page.

2. Number each page, in the upper right corner, one inch from the right and one-half inch from the top. Type your last name before the number. On a word processor, your name and the page number can be placed in the header.

3. You do not need a title page. (If your teacher requires a title page, follow his or her instructions for format or use the model shown on page 109.) On the first page of the paper, type your name, your instructor's name, the course number, and the date on separate lines beginning at the left margin one inch from the top. Double-space between each line. Then double-space again and type the title—centered—without underlining it or placing it in quotation marks. Then double-space again and begin typing the text.

4. Indent the first word of each paragraph half an inch (or five spaces on a typewriter) from the left; indent block quotations one inch (or ten spaces).

5. Double-space the entire text, including indented quotations and the list of works cited.

6. Use a separate page, at the end of the paper, for your references. Center the words *Works Cited* at the top of the page. Type the first line of each entry an inch from the left margin; each subsequent line should be indented half an inch (or five spaces on a typewriter). Double-space within and between all entries.

Sample Research Paper

After finishing a rough draft and revising carefully, Daniel Kimball turned in the following paper, in MLA format, concerning men's studies.

A cover page is not required by MLA, but many teachers prefer one.

Men's Studies:

Coming of Age, But Not Here

Fig. 1. Plate 11, from William Blake, <u>The Book of Urizen</u>. Copy G (London, 1794); rpt. in <u>The Book of Urizen, by William Blake</u>, 1 Nov. 1997 <http://www.mindspring.com/~jntolva/blake/uriz11.jpg>.

Number all graphics and use the abbreviation *Fig.* for "Figure." Use a caption identifying each figure and its source.

Daniel Kimball

Professor Smithson

English 208, State Tech University

12 November 1997

If you do not use a cover page, put your name, course identification, and paper title at the top of the first page. If you do use a cover sheet, you should omit these four lines.

Daniel Kimball

Professor Smithson

English 208, State Tech University

12 November 1997

Men's Studies: Coming of Age, But Not Here

"Questions of constraining roles, of subtle social expectations and tacit fears, of quiet desperation, of blighted relationships and deadly, silent family dramas are there for both men and women" (Connors 143). So says Professor Robert J. Connors of the University of New Hampshire in his explanation of the need for courses in men's studies. He is one of a growing number of college faculty members who have responded to the need for courses that explore a subject that has grown from only forty courses in 1984 to over five hundred in 1997 (Dobbin E1). This year has seen the creation of the first degree program in men's studies, an undergraduate minor at Hobart and William Smith Colleges in Geneva, New York, another indication of the increasing interest in men's studies.

Ten years ago men's studies may have seemed like an odd notion. Critics of education have long contended that all disciplines concentrate their attention on white men. Even today, women students may feel that men's studies is some kind of backlash against women's studies, an attempt to get even somehow. From the point of view of Harry Brod, one of the most published professors in the field, however, men's studies is "an essential complement to women's studies because neither gender ultimately can be studied in isolation. . . . Masculinities and femininities are not isolated 'roles,' but contested relationships" ("Scholarly Studies" B-2).

The short quotation from Brod is documented at the end of the sentence. Because there are two sources by Brod, a short version of the title is included.

Today's men's studies courses are not a continuation of earlier brands of male-oriented history, literature, or philosophy, nor are they a rebuke to women's studies. These courses are instead a valuable extension of the women's studies movement, giving college students the opportunity to study male behaviors and social patterns and to consider possible ways to alter the traditional male social-

Kimball   2

ization toward aggression and violence. Just as women's studies courses enable
female students to freely discuss the social forces and issues that shape their
relationships with men, men's studies classes can allow male (and female) students to break down the "learned male silence," reexamine relationships between men and women, and consider new possibilities for meeting the
challenges of family and career (Brod, "Case" 266).

These classes, which have been instituted during the last fifteen years,
usually appear in departments of history, sociology, psychology, and English.
Michael S. Kimmel, a sociology professor at SUNY Stony Brook, suggests that full
programs should combine various disciplines to probe key questions about men:

> As an interdisciplinary field, men's studies will draw its objects of
> study and its methodologies from social and behavioral sciences as
> well as from the humanities and from the natural and biological
> sciences. As an academic enterprise, it regroups conventionally
> drawn studies within a new framework and suggests new areas
> for research. And as a corollary to women's studies, it supports
> the radical redefinitions of the social construction of gender rela-
> tions that underlie the field demarcated by its "older sister."
> ("Rethinking" 23)

Kimmel himself has written or edited at least six books related to this subject,
and their titles suggest some of its breadth and depth:

- 1987--Changing Men: New Directions in Research on Men and Masculinity
- 1989--Men's Lives
- 1990--Men Confront Pornography
- 1992--Against the Tide: Pro-Feminist Men in the United States, 1776-1990
- 1995--The Politics of Manhood: Profeminist Men Respond to the Mythopoetic
  Men's Movement
- 1996--Manhood in America: A Cultural History

The quotation
is indented
ten spaces
because it
is more than
four lines long.
The citation
appears after
the final
punctuation,
in parentheses.

A "signal phrase" is used to introduce the opinion of an expert, Daniel Gross. His name is not included in the parenthetical documentation because it is mentioned in the text.

Like these books, courses in men's studies do not focus on great figures of history, but instead they concentrate on "the daily lives led by the majority of men" (Brod, "Case" 267). According to one of the first course founders, Daniel Gross, typical courses cover parental relationships, the portrayal of men in literature, the importance of sports in male identity, masculine images in advertising, obsession with achievement and competition, restrictive emotionality, the male life cycle, reactions to feminism, and attitudes on pornography (11-12).

The feminist movement has proven that gender study can result in sweeping social change. Women ages eighteen to thirty are now earning 90% of the median weekly earnings of men in the same group, and men and women with college educations are even closer together. Twenty years ago, women earned only 70% of men's wages. Sociologists now predict that 64% of the new workers entering the job force over the next ten years will be women (Ehrenreich 83). Never before have women had the options that they enjoy now: a full-time career, full-time family, or some combination of career and family (Farrell, "Men As Success Objects" 125). Much of the credit for the education and empowerment of today's women should go to America's universities and their women's studies programs. Female educators have consistently challenged female students to examine the stereotypical gender roles and traditional patriarchal power structures that have oppressed women and limited their opportunities.

These final sentences of the paragraph are not documented because they are the author's opinion.

The same socioeconomic systems that have oppressed women are wreaking havoc on today's males. Statistics that offer a full view of the carnage are alarming. Today, men are committing suicide at four times the rate of women, with male teenagers being five times more likely to take their own lives than are female teenagers. The rate of male alcohol and drug dependency is three times higher than that of females in the group ages eighteen to twenty-nine. More than two-thirds of all alcoholics are men, and 50% more men than women are regular

Kimball   4

users of illegal drugs. Men account for more than 90% of arrests for alcohol and drug abuse violations (Kimbrell 66).

The traditional roles of American males are now viewed as responsible for their deteriorating physical health and declining rates of longevity. Men live, on the average, 7.8 fewer years than women, giving them a life span that is 10% shorter than women's; they suffer inordinately high rates of heart disease, cancer, and stroke, at least partially because of their ambition and drive (Ehrenreich 60-70). Men suffer a 600% higher incidence of work-related accidents per year, including over 2 million disabling injuries and 14,000 deaths (Farrell, Why Men Are 12). Couple these statistics with the soaring rates of male violence, suicides among Vietnam-era veterans, and the numbers of black men in prison, and it appears, as a culture, we are wantonly destroying the lives of our men.

Gender-specific studies have proven positive for women; the time has come to make the effort on behalf of men. For men's studies to have the kind of impact women's studies has had, it must overcome many obstacles. Not the least is the perception on the part of some men that any man who engages in such studies is to be scorned: "Sissyhood Is Powerful" is the title of one review of Kimmel's Manhood in America in a popular electronic journal (Garner). The reviewer says that Kimmel is "the most visible and prolific example of a new breed I'll call SNAAGs--Sensitive New Age Academic Guys. SNAAGs write big, warm, huggy-bear books that cloak themselves in the rigorous, almost ascetic armor of academia." Professor Connors answers such critics:

> It's easy to portray us as self-pitying oppressors, balding wimps, failed hippies, whining jerks. But think back to the early days of the women's movement and to the completely unsympathetic presenta-tions the media gave it. In the 1960s, feminists were often presented as crazy or evil--bra-burners, Warhol-shooters, ugly girls with grudges, man-haters. There are powerful vested interests threatened by the

Statistics are provided through dropped-in paraphrases that are documented within parentheses.

The Internet source is cited by the author's last name here because that is how the reader can find it in the list of works cited.

Kimball   5

men's movement, and they are the same interests that the feminist

movement threatens. Next time you see someone sneering at the

silliness of the men's movement, ask yourself, cui bono? Who gains

from this representation? (148)

Another site of resistance against men's studies has been established

power structures on some campuses, perhaps where some women may feel

threatened by this new area. As George Mair, professor of criminal justice at

Liverpool's John Moores University, asks, "How many women would want to join

with men in helping to refashion them? Women would certainly be suspicious"

(qtd. in Walker 16). Our own campus library does not subscribe to the leading

journal, the Journal of Men's Studies. We take over twenty journals with

"women's" or "feminist" in the title, but the only two serials with "men's" in

the title (excepting the ones with "men's and women's") are Men's and Boys'

Shirts and Men's Soccer Rules. Yet the Journal of Men's Studies has been pub-

lished four times a year since 1992 and has a circulation of over 500; its sponsor-

ing organization, the American Men's Studies Association, is preparing for its

sixth annual conference in March 1998.

While State Tech has no men's studies offerings, other schools move ahead.

At Colleco State College, as a sample school, the one class in 1985 has developed

into seven offerings today. The courses' founder, Harmon Simmons, says that one

of these classes will be required for a degree in counseling next year. Of the 170

students enrolled in seven men's studies classes in the spring of 1998, 150 filled

out a survey on their course's goals and effectiveness. Of that group of respon-

dents, 140, or 93%, reported that their class's purpose was to help them to under-

stand male roles in our society, and 137 rated the class materials as excellent.

Of course, no university program can immediately alter the kinds of alarm-

ing statistics that characterize men's lives in our society today, but classes in

men's studies are a beginning. Given that there are over five hundred courses

The
interviewee's
name leads to
the reference
to the interview
in the Works
Cited list.

No citation
is provided
here because
the author
conducted
this research.

and now a degree program in men's studies being offered at some schools, is it not time for the curriculum here at State Tech to include at least one such course? Our programs in history, sociology, psychology, English, and counseling would be greatly enriched by men's studies offerings such as those now available at Colleco State. Along with women's studies, in which we offer seven courses and an interdisciplinary minor, men's studies classes will help us to understand and modify behaviors that have traditionally been left unexamined. As Michael Kimmel says, the goal would be "to deconstruct masculinity as a singular, monolithic category . . . and to reconstruct masculinities as a set of possible gender identities, each different, and all equal" (Kimmel, "Invisible Masculinity" 35). The fruits of this effort would be a greater liberation for both men and women and perhaps an alteration to our society's obsession with success and with violence.

Kimball   7

Works Cited

Blake, William. Plate 11. The Book of Urizen, Copy G. 1794. The Book of
    Urizen, by William Blake. 1 Nov. 1997 <http:www.mindspring.com/
    ~jntolva/blake/uriz11.jpg>.

Brod, Harry. "A Case for Men's Studies." Kimmel, Changing Men 263-77.

---. "Scholarly Studies of Men: The New Field Is an Essential Complement to
    Women's Studies." The Chronicle of Higher Education 36, 21 Mar. 1990: B2-3.

Connors, Robert J. "Teaching and Learning as a Man." College English 58.2
    (1996): 137-57.

Dobbin, Ben. "Male Studies--Not Just a Guy Thing." Los Angeles Times, 20 July
    1997: E1, E4.

Ehrenreich, Barbara. The Hearts of Men. Garden City, NY: Anchor, 1983.

Farrell, Warren. Why Men Are the Way They Are. New York: Berkley, 1986.

---. "Men as Success Objects." Family Therapy Networker 4 (1988): 81-84.

Garner, Dwight. "Sissyhood Is Powerful: Man's Journey from Iron John to Ironing
    Johns." Salon Magazine 7, 10 Feb. 1996. 18 Oct. 1997 <http://www.
    salonmagazine.com/07/reviews/manhood.html>.

Gross, Daniel. "The Gender Rap." The New Republic 16 Apr. 1990: 11-14.

Kimbrell, Andrew. "A Time for Men to Pull Together." Utne Reader May-June
    1991: 66-74.

Kimmel, Michael S., ed. Changing Men: New Directions in Research on Men and
    Masculinity. Newbury Park, CA: Sage, 1987.

---. "Invisible Masculinity." Society 30 (Sept./Oct. 1993): 28-35.

---. "Rethinking 'Masculinity': New Directions in Research." Kimmel, Changing
    Men 9-24.

Simmons, Harmon. Personal interview. 10 Nov. 1997.

Walker, David. "In the Shadow of Big Sister." The Times Higher Education Supple-
    ment 1242, 23 Aug. 1996: 16.

This entry identifies the Web page that is the source of the cover-page art.

APA Documentation Style

APA Documentation Style

The APA format for referencing source materials was established by the American Psychological Association. It is used by psychologists, sociologists, and other social scientists. The complete format can be found in the *Publication Manual of the American Psychological Association,* 4th ed. (Washington, DC: APA, 1994). The APA format requires short notes, or citations, put in parentheses within the text instead of footnotes or endnotes. The following section will show you how to create these citations, prepare a bibliography page, entitled "References," and type your paper in APA format.

Citations in the Text

For a Paraphrase

In this system, identify source materials that you are paraphrasing by citing *the author's last name and the publication date,* either in your sentence or in parentheses. You do not have to cite page numbers for paraphrases. Citations in parentheses should appear immediately after you mention the source or information.

• **If you mention the author's name and the publication date in your sentence,** you will not need any additional citation.

> In a 1983 study, Deborah Mayo began questioning the scientific validity of experiments involving laboratory animals.

• **If you mention the author's last name in your sentence,** place the date of publication in parentheses right after the name.

> Mayo (1983) questioned the scientific validity of experiments involving laboratory animals.

• **If you do not mention the author's name or the publication date in your sentence,** put both in parentheses, with a comma between them.

> An early study (Mayo, 1983) questioned the scientific validity of experiments involving laboratory animals.

• **If you use two works by an author in the same year,** cite them within the parentheses with the date and then *a* or *b*. (Also put the *a* or *b* by the date in your bibliography entries.)

> Franklin and Hayes (1992a)

- **If you cite two authors with the same last name,** use their first and middle initials within the parentheses.

> (D. G. Mayo, 1983)

- **If a work has two authors,** combine the names with *and* in your sentence. Use an ampersand (&) instead of *and* in a parenthetical citation.

> Franklin and Hayes (1992) criticized animal testing practices in the cosmetic industry.
>
> One recent study (Franklin & Hayes, 1992) criticized the cosmetic industry for its inaccurate and inhumane testing procedures.

- **If a work has more than two authors,** cite all of them, if there are not more than five, the first time, either in your sentence or in the parenthetical citation. In subsequent references in either location, include only the last name of the first author followed by *et al.* (Latin meaning "and the others"; there is no period after *et*). If a work has six or more authors, use *et al.* after the first author's last name in all references in the text.

First Reference

> Heinrich, Smith, and Blaine (1992) concluded that driver-education programs are woefully ineffective.

Subsequent Reference

> The ineffectiveness of current driver-education programs concerns insurance companies (Heinrich et al., 1992).

- **If a work has no author,** cite it by the first two or three words of the title, starting with the first important word. For a journal article or an essay, use a shortened version of its title—not the title of the journal or the book—and place these two or three words in quotation marks. If you are citing a book, supply a shortened version of its title, underlined.

> To secure good research assistantships, graduate students should learn everything they can about the university's privately funded

grant projects ("Getting the First," 1991). [The complete title of the article is "Getting the First Job: Try for a Research Assistantship."]

In <u>Jobs for Biologists</u> (1990), students can find tips on landing a job at a zoo or museum. [The complete title is <u>Jobs for Biologists in a Changing World.</u>]

• **If you use a quotation from an indirect source,** precede the source information in the parenthetical citation with the words *as cited in.* In the reference list, include an entry only for the secondary source.

• **If you cite two or more works by the same author in one parenthetical citation,** give the author's name, followed by the years in chronological order, separated by commas.

(Stiles, 1991, 1994)

• **If you cite two or more works by different authors in one parenthetical citation,** give the works in alphabetical order and separate them with semicolons.

Several researchers have confirmed Erikson's theory of an adolescent identity crisis (Bryson, 1963; Drummond, 1970; Oliphant, 1968).

• **If you cite a personal communication,** such as a letter, an e-mail message, or a telephone conversation, you do not need to include a reference list entry because the information is not accessible to your readers. Cite the communication in the text, giving the initials as well as the last name of your source and as exact a date as possible.

According to museum official F. Calabria (personal communication, May 22, 1994), the renovations will be completed by 1998.

For Quotations of Fewer Than Forty Words

These shorter quotations should be incorporated within your paragraphs: they should not be indented separately. To document them, include the author's name and the date of publication as you would for a paraphrase, either within your sentence or in parentheses. You should also cite the page number(s), using the abbreviation *p.* or *pp.,* in parentheses immediately after the quotation. If the citation also includes the name or the date, these items are separated by commas.

Combrinck-Graham (1991) asks the essential question for revamping current counseling techniques: "How can there be family therapy without children?" (pp. 373–374).

When "Brutus is making his rounds" (Rosenkoetter & Bowes, 1991, p. 277), nursing home patients exercise, converse, and relax with a well-trained dog.

For Quotations of More Than Forty Words

The longer quotation, over forty words, is block-indented five spaces from the left margin and typed without quotation marks. The quotation should be double spaced. If you are quoting an entire paragraph, or part of one, do not indent the first line more than the rest. The first line of any subsequent paragraphs within the quotation should be indented an additional five spaces. The page reference (and the author and date, if they are not mentioned in the text) appears in parentheses at the end of the quotation, outside the final period. Long quotations are generally introduced by a colon.

British researchers began experiments concerning a gene that may actually determine maleness:

Tests in mice show that after the gene is switched on, a cascade of genetic events takes place, and the testes begin to form. The testes go on to pump out testosterone, which in humans subsequently provokes the sprouting of beards, the deepening of voices, and the other masculine traits that cause anxiety in adolescent boys. (Kinoshita, 1991, p. 47)

Beard (1969) explains the consequences of the young child's egocentric thinking:

He attributes life and feeling, in the first place, to all objects, though later only to those which move; he believes that natural objects are man-made and that they can be influenced by his wishes or by actions at a distance. (pp. 24-25)

Reference List

At the end of the paper, on a new page, list all the sources that you have cited—not everything that you read. For the entries in this list, entitled "References," use the formats given here for the various types of sources. Double-space both within and between entries, and indent the second and subsequent lines of each entry five spaces. This style of indention is the one *used* in APA journals. However, some instructors may prefer to have the first line indented five to seven spaces and the subsequent lines flush with the left margin; this is the style used for manuscripts *submitted to* APA journals. (APA's explanation for the difference in style between manuscripts submitted for publication and published articles can be found on APA's Web page at <http://www.apa.org/journals/faq.html>.)

Alphabetize the entries by the authors' last names or by the first important word of the title of works that have no author. If two or more works by an author are cited, arrange them chronologically, from the oldest to the most recent. If two or more works by an author were written in the same year, arrange them alphabetically by title and differentiate them by adding a letter after the year (for example, 1989a and 1989b).

Books
Book by One Author

> Markel, M. H. (1992). Technical writing: Situations and strategies (3rd ed.). New York: St. Martin's.

Begin the entry with, and alphabetize it by, the author's last name. Use initials for the author's first and middle names. If there is no author, the entry begins with the book title.

Place the date of publication in parentheses after the author's name.

Capitalize only the first word of the title, proper names, and the first word after a colon. Underline or italicize the title.

Provide only the city (and not the state or country name) for the place of publication unless it is a small city: thus you would use *Chicago, Detroit,* or *Paris,* but *Monterey, CA.* If more than one city is listed on the title page, use the first one.

Provide a shortened form of the publisher's name, omitting the first name of the publisher (*Morrow,* not *William Morrow*) and *Company, Publisher,* or *Incorporated* at the end (but retain essential words, such as *Books* or *Press*). For example, *W. W. Norton & Company* should appear as *Norton; Harcourt Brace, Publishers* should appear as *Harcourt Brace.* Give the full names of associations and university presses.

Book by Two or More Authors

> Decker, D. L., Shichor, D., & O'Brien, R. M. (1982). <u>Urban structure</u>
> <u>and victimization.</u> Lexington, MA: Lexington Books.

Edited Book

> Conoley, J. C. (Ed.). (1981). <u>Consultation in schools: Theory,</u>
> <u>research, procedures.</u> New York: Academic Press.

Translated Book

> Veyne, P. (Ed.). (1987). <u>A history of private life: Vol. 1. From pagan</u>
> <u>Rome to Byzantium</u> (A. Goldhammer, Trans.). Cambridge,
> MA: Harvard University Press. (Original work published 1985)

Edition Other Than the First

> Bennett, L., Jr. (1984). <u>Before the Mayflower: A history of Black</u>
> <u>America</u> (5th ed.). Harmondsworth, England: Penguin Books.

If the book is not the first edition, place the edition number in
parentheses after the title. For a revised edition, use *Rev. ed.*

Book by a Corporate Author or Group

> National Research Council Committee on Diet and Health. (1989).
> <u>Diet and health: Implications for reducing chronic disease</u>
> <u>risk.</u> Washington, DC: National Academy of Sciences.

Book without an Author or Editor

> <u>The control of the campus: A report on the governance of higher</u>
> <u>education.</u> (1982). Lawrenceville, NJ: Princeton University
> Press.

Multivolume Work
The Entire Set

> Neather, C. A., & Richardson, G. F. (1930). <u>A course in English for</u>
> <u>engineers</u> (Vols. 1-2). Boston: Ginn.

One Volume

> Battle, K. P. (1912). <u>History of the University of North Carolina:</u>
> <u>Vol. 2.</u> Raleigh, NC: Edwards and Broughton.

If the volume has its own title, include it after the volume number. If an individual volume has a different editor or author than

the series, give the series editor's name first and then that of the volume editor. Identify the two with the abbreviations *Series Ed.* and *Vol. Ed.* in parentheses after the names.

Republished or Reprinted Book

> García Márquez, G. (1990). <u>The general in his labyrinth.</u>
> (E. Grossman, Trans.). New York: Knopf. (Original work
> published 1989)

Use both years in the parenthetical citation in the text: (García Márquez, 1989/1990).

Parts of Books
Essay or Article in a Book

> Jensen, K. M. (1983). The nurse and the deaf adult. In S. Shanks
> (Ed.), <u>Nursing and the management of adult communication
> disorders</u> (pp. 75-108). San Diego, CA: College-Hill.

The selection title is written without quotation marks and with lowercase letters (except for the first letter of the title, of proper names, and of a subtitle after a colon). The book title is in the same lowercase format but is underlined. Place the page numbers for the complete essay or article in parentheses, preceded by *p.* or *pp.,* after the book title.

Article in an Encyclopedia or Other Reference Book
Signed Article

> Ives, S. (1990). Parts of speech. In <u>Collier's encyclopedia</u> (Vol. 18,
> pp. 487-490). New York: Macmillan.

Unsigned Article

> Gypsies. (1978). In L. Shepard (Ed.), <u>Encyclopedia of occultism
> and parapsychology</u> (Vol. 1, pp. 400-401). Detroit: Gale
> Research.

Reports, Documents, and Dissertations
Government Document, Research Report, Monograph

> U.S. Women's Bureau. (1975). <u>Handbook on women workers.</u>
> Washington, DC: U.S. Government Printing Office.

> Kreshner, L., Addams, B., & Winestein, C. (1995). <u>Use of
> manipulatives in teaching mathematics in grades four</u>

through six (Rep. No. 6). New Orleans: State Mathematics
Service.

A report or document number, if there is one, should appear in
parentheses immediately after the title.

Material from an Information Service

Kurth, R. J., & Stromberg, L. J. (1984). Using word processing in
composition instruction. Paper presented at the meeting of
the American Reading Forum, Sarasota, FL. (ERIC Document
Reproduction Service No. ED 251 850)

Give the document number in parentheses at the end of the entry; do not use a period after the number.

Dissertation

Keck, M. (1986). From movement to politics: The formation of the
Workers' Party in Brazil. Unpublished doctoral dissertation,
Columbia University, New York.

Legal Case

Loving v. Virginia, 388 U.S. 1 (1967).

This is a citation for a decision rendered by the U.S. Supreme
Court in 1967. It was recorded in Volume 388, on page 1, of the
United States Reports, which is abbreviated as *U.S.*

In the text, the names are underlined or italicized: *Loving v.
Virginia* (1967).

If your paper cites many kinds of legal documents, consult
the *Publication Manual of the American Psychological Association,*
4th ed.; *The Chicago Manual of Style,* 14th ed.; or *A Uniform System of Citation.*

Articles in Periodicals
Article in a Scholarly Journal Paginated by Year or Volume
The entire year's issues are paginated as a unit.

Caspary, W. R. (1990). Judgments of value in John Dewey's theory
of ethics. Education Theory, 40, 155-169.

Do not underline the title of the article, and do not capitalize it
(except for the first word, proper names, and the first word after
a colon).

Capitalize and underline the title of the journal.
Underline the volume number. It is followed by a comma
and the complete page numbers of the article.

Article in a Scholarly Journal Paginated by Issue

Each issue begins with page 1.

> Crase, D. (1978). Has physical education achieved a scholarly
> dimension? <u>Journal of Physical Education and Recreation,</u>
> <u>49</u>(8), 21-24.

Underline the volume number. It is followed by the issue number in parentheses, a comma, and the complete page numbers of
the article.

Popular Magazine Article
Weekly Magazine

> Murphy, A. (1991, October 14). Bear on the loose. <u>Sports</u>
> <u>Illustrated, 75,</u> 43-45.

Monthly Magazine

> Owen, D. (1981, March). I spied on the twelfth grade. <u>Esquire, 95,</u>
> 72-78.

In citations for popular magazines, the volume number follows
the magazine title.

Newspaper Article

> Marinucci, C., Winokur, S., & Lewis, G. (1994, December 11). The
> war on youth violence: Ganging up on girls. <u>San Francisco</u>
> <u>Examiner,</u> pp. A-1, A-18.

Give all page numbers, separated by commas, for articles that appear on discontinuous pages. Use *p.* or *pp.* before the page numbers. For an unsigned article, start the entry with the title, and
alphabetize it by the first significant word. In the parenthetical
citation in the text, use a shortened version of the title that starts
with that word; enclose the title in quotation marks, and capitalize the first letter of all important words: ("War on Youth Violence," 1994).

Review of Book, Film, or Video

> Mackey, M. (1995, February 12). Don't know much about history
> [Review of the book <u>Lies my teacher told me: Everything your</u>

American history textbook got wrong]. San Francisco Sunday
Examiner/Chronicle Book Review, pp. 3, 8.

Identify the type of medium (book, film, video, or television program) in brackets.

Electronic Sources

There are two goals for references to electronic sources of information:

- to give the author credit
- to make it possible for the reader to find the material

In general, references to electronic sources use the format for
books and periodicals but also show the electronic medium (such
as on-line serial, database, or CD-ROM) in brackets after the title.
As the publisher's name and location do in a book citation, these
references provide information to enable retrieval of the material.

CD-Roms and Other Unchangeable Databases

Morring, F., Jr. (1994, May 16). Russian hardware allows earlier
station experiments [CD-ROM]. Aviation Week & Space
Technology, 140, 57. Abstract from: InfoTrac General
Periodicals Index-A: Abstract 15482317

In addition to the publication information, give the name of the
source and the retrieval number.

Internet and On-Line Sources

APA citations for electronic sources, like those for print sources,
have five elements: author, date, title, document type, and publication information. For the date that appears in parentheses right
after the author's name, use the date of the page's most recent revision (if available). In square brackets after the title of the page,
identify the type of page (such as on-line serial or on-line database). For the publication information, give the date you visited
the page and the complete URL (the Internet address) enclosed
in angle brackets. (Although the APA does not specify angle
brackets, they are an accepted way to avoid confusion about what
constitutes the URL.) If the URL must be broken between two
lines, break it after a slash or a period. Since the fourth edition of
APA's *Publication Manual* (1995), APA's style for citing Internet
sources has been evolving. For its on-line revision of the form to

use to cite information from the Internet and the World Wide Web, see <http://www.apa.org/journals/webref.html>.

> Central Intelligence Agency. (1997). The World Factbook page on Mexico, Section: People. In 1996 World Factbook [On-line database]. Retrieved October 17, 1997, from the World Wide Web: <http://www.odci.gov/cia/publications/nsolo/factbook/mx-p.htm>.

For large databases (such as the one in the preceding example), you may not find an author's name on each page; in that case, check the database's home page.

> Yoes, C. (1996). The science fiction web project: Adventures in teaching with Storyspace [5 paragraphs]. Computers, Writing, Rhetoric and Literature 2(1) [On-line serial]. Retrieved May 3, 1997, from the World Wide Web: <http://www.en.utexas.edu/~cwrl/v2n1/yoes/yoes.html>.

A similar format can be used for documents retrieved from file transfer protocol (ftp) and Gopher sites. E-mail communications should be cited in the text like personal communications; they do not appear in the reference list.

Other Sources
Paper Presented at a Meeting

> Hendrix, M. (1994, January). Can we get there from here? Paper presented at the annual meeting of the Society for an Architectural Future, Chicago.

Audiovisual Sources
Film, Videotape, Work of Art

> Zemeckis, R. (Director). (1994). Forrest Gump [Film]. Hollywood, CA: Paramount Pictures.

Television Broadcast

> Bikel, O. (Director). (1995, April 4). Divided memories. Frontline. New York: Public Broadcasting Service.

Give the name and, in parentheses, the function of the originator of or primary contributors to the work. Identify the medium in brackets after the title. For works of art and for films and videos with limited distribution, give the location of the work or the address of the distributor in parentheses at the end.

Typing or Word Processing Instructions for APA

(See page 130 for the relevant parts of a sample paper.)

1. Leave uniform margins of at least one inch on the top, bottom, and sides of each page.

2. Number all pages, including the title page, consecutively, with the numbers appearing at least one inch from the right-hand edge of the page in the space between the top edge of the paper and the first line of text. A shortened version of the title should appear five spaces to the left of the page number or a double space above the page number, ending even with the number. On a word processor, use the header to set up the shortened title and page number so that they will print onto each page.

3. The title page, like all other pages, should have the shortened title and page number (which is 1) within the top margin. Immediately below the top margin on the left side, type *Running head* followed by a colon and your shortened title typed in capital letters. Then double-space twice and, with a double space between each line, type the paper's title, your name, and the name of your university in uppercase and lowercase letters centered on the page.

4. If your professor requires an abstract or summary of the paper, provide one on the second page. Below the top margin, type the word Abstract centered on the page. Then double-space and type the abstract itself as a single paragraph that is not indented.

5. On a word processor, do not justify lines; leave the right-hand margin uneven.

6. Double-space the entire text, including indented quotations and the reference list. Indented quotations should be printed five spaces from the left margin.

7. Indent the first line of each paragraph five to seven spaces.

8. End each line of text with a complete word—do not hyphenate to divide words.

9. On the reference page, center the label *References* at the top. Start the first line of each entry at the left margin; each subsequent line should be indented five spaces. Double-space within and between all entries.

Figure 9 shows the APA style for a title page, a first page, subsequent pages, and references.

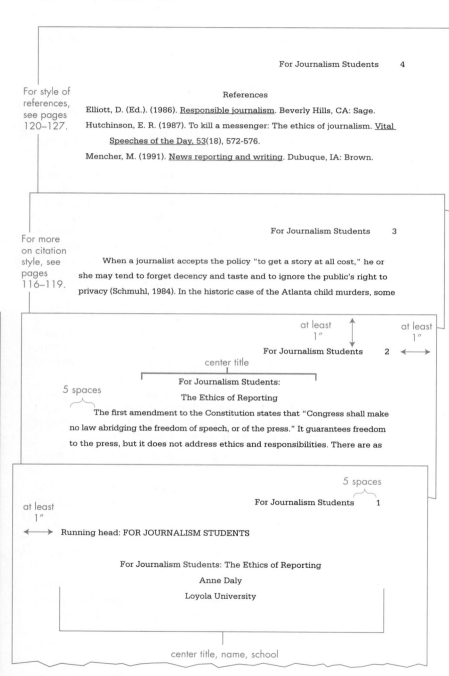

For Journalism Students   4

References

For style of references, see pages 120–127.

Elliott, D. (Ed.). (1986). Responsible journalism. Beverly Hills, CA: Sage.

Hutchinson, E. R. (1987). To kill a messenger: The ethics of journalism. Vital Speeches of the Day, 53(18), 572-576.

Mencher, M. (1991). News reporting and writing. Dubuque, IA: Brown.

For Journalism Students   3

For more on citation style, see pages 116–119.

When a journalist accepts the policy "to get a story at all cost," he or she may tend to forget decency and taste and to ignore the public's right to privacy (Schmuhl, 1984). In the historic case of the Atlanta child murders, some

at least 1"

at least 1"

For Journalism Students   2

center title

For Journalism Students:
The Ethics of Reporting

5 spaces

The first amendment to the Constitution states that "Congress shall make no law abridging the freedom of speech, or of the press." It guarantees freedom to the press, but it does not address ethics and responsibilities. There are as

5 spaces

For Journalism Students   1

at least 1"

Running head: FOR JOURNALISM STUDENTS

For Journalism Students: The Ethics of Reporting

Anne Daly

Loyola University

center title, name, school

Figure 9. Sample APA Layout

DOCUMENT DESIGN AND VISUALS
FOR LONGER RESEARCH PAPERS

The basics of document design for most first-year composition students' papers were covered on pages 50–53. For longer writing projects, such as research papers and reports, teachers and students sometimes agree to do more with document design. Today's sophisticated desktop publishing tools make it easier for students to produce professional-looking reports. Here are three important goals to keep in mind:

- The document should be professional in appearance.
- The document should be consistent in its use of important design elements.
- The document should be easy for readers to use.

Creating a Professional Appearance

Two key factors in giving your report a professional appearance are the binding and the typography. By following the guidelines below, you will ensure that your paper meets the goals of more advanced document design.

Binding

Students often use plastic covers with slide-on plastic binding strips to hold their papers together, but if your document contains more than ten pieces of paper, you may want to consider having your report professionally bound. The easiest way to create a professional binding is to take your manuscript pages to a local copying service and ask for a *plastic comb binding* (like the one this book has). You will need a cover, which the copying service will be happy to sell you. Students often choose a clear plastic cover, which can be followed by their title page or by a color photocopy of an illustration appropriate to the report's subject (with its source duly acknowledged); in the latter case, the title page follows the illustration. The cost of the whole package is usually only a few dollars. You may want to have your report photocopied onto paper that is a little heavier than usual and run "front-and-back," so that what your reader sees is always a two-page spread. That way, if you wish, you can have text on the left-hand pages and the accompanying illustrations (or tables or graphs, or more text) on the right-hand pages.

Typography

Equally crucial is the typography you use. Today's word processors offer a wide range of choices, but for most projects you're better off using *no more than two fonts*—one a font with serifs (the short cross-lines at the ends of the main strokes of the letters), such as Times, for the text, and the other a font without serifs (a *sans-serif font*), such as Arial or Helvetica, for the headings. For academic projects, 12-point type and doublespacing are standard.

Establishing Consistency in Use of Design Elements

You can establish a consistent "look" to your report by treating the design of all its pages similarly. Consistency is especially important when it comes to graphical elements—illustrations, artwork, charts, tables, or diagrams. If you have had your report copied front-and-back, so that your reader always sees two-page spreads, you need to envision each pair of pages as shown in Figure 10: two pages give you four blocks of space with which to work.

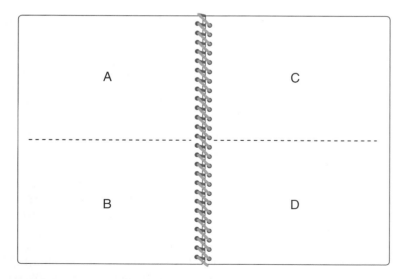

Figure 10. Design of Two-Page Spreads

On one pair of pages you might have text in block A, a sketch in block B, and text in both blocks C and D (with no interruption between blocks). On another pair of pages you might have a graph in block A, text in block B, text in block C, and art in block D. (Note that you wouldn't want text in A and C and art in B and D, or text in B and D and art in A and C—such pages look top- or bottom-heavy.) Of course, on many pages you might want all text, or on some all art. Size each visual appropriately, and make sure the accompanying text is on the page facing the visual. Each visual element also needs a caption—at the minimum, a number and a title (and if necessary an acknowledgment of the visual's source)—and it needs to be surrounded by at least one inch of white space.

Note—Color and White Space: It becomes easier and easier (and cheaper and cheaper) for students to incorporate color into their reports. If you have access to a color printer, you can easily add color to your charts, graphs, and diagrams. The ability to use more than black and white makes line graphs more readable and bar graphs more attractive. And just about any copying service can make a color photocopy for your cover art. Remember, however, that whereas a little color is a wonderful thing for reports, too much can create a visual nightmare. Be conservative in your use of color, especially when it comes to research reports in an academic setting. The opposite is true of white space, however. Newspaper journalists have a saying, "White space doesn't lie." Among other things, that's one way of saying that readers like white space very much. So it's best not to scrimp on white space—the margins, the paragraph indents, the space between lines of text, and especially the white space around visuals (at least one inch all around) are all critical. Be conservative in your use of color, but be liberal in your use of white space. Your readers will appreciate both qualities of your reports.

Types of Visuals

With today's sophisticated computer software, you do not have to be an artist or "good at drawing" to add simple and effective visuals—such as tables, graphs, pie charts, bar graphs, and diagrams—to your reports. Whether you choose to use the kinds of visuals that programs such as Word and WordPerfect offer, to draw your own with a program such as Harvard Graphics, to use clip art from one of the many repositories on the Web, or to use an optical scanner and "pull in" a piece from another source, it has never been this easy to use visuals to greatly increase your writing's effectiveness.

Tables

Tables are especially good at showing the comparisons among specific pieces of information and at showing relationships between categories of information. In fact, the strength of tables lies in their precision and in the ease with which you can create them. Tables come in two varieties, informal and formal. Informal tables (perhaps not more than four or five rows of information in three or four columns) can be placed within the text itself to summarize a small amount of information that would be tedious if it were spelled out in words. Formal tables need to be set off from the text by white space, placed within a box, and appropriately captioned. (For a sample table, see Figure 11). When you put information in a table, there is no need to repeat it all in the text, but just as you might want to highlight the key information in the table, so you might want to repeat that key information in the text.

The weakness of tables is that they tend to become too complex very fast. Be careful not to let your tables get too full of num-

**18- to 24-Year Olds Living at Home, 1960–1990
(Numbers in thousands.)**

	Male		Female	
Year	Total number	Percent	Total number	Percent
1960	6,842	52	7,876	35
1970	10,398	54	11,959	41
1980	14,278	54	14,844	43
1990	12,450	58	12,860	48

Source: U.S. Bureau of the Census, *Current Population Reports*, Series P20-484, "Marital Status and Living Arrangements: March 1994," and earlier reports.

Figure 11. Sample Table

bers; it's always better to use several smaller tables (dividing the information up according to logical categories) than one giant table that no one will want to struggle through.

Line Graphs

Line graphs are very good for showing how one variable relates to another and for showing and comparing trends. Their weaknesses are that they are not by themselves very precise and that they can easily become too complicated. Paying attention to a few simple principles will help you create better, more effective line graphs:

- If you are going to run more than one line, make sure the different lines are easily distinguishable.
- Use only as many grid lines as you need; do not try to make your line graph look like graph paper.
- Label specific points your reader might especially need to refer to.
- Make sure that the vertical axis charts the factor that is changing (the dependent variable) and the horizontal axis charts the factor that is constant (the independent variable). Thus your line graphs will read from left to right and from the bottom to the top.
- Make sure the zero point (where the two axes come together) is in the lower left corner. If the zero point is not shown for some reason, that needs to be explained in the caption ("zero point is not shown because . . .").
- Be careful not to connect data points on the graph with lines if you do not have very good reason to believe that if intermediate data were collected they would bear out the generalization your line suggests.

For a sample line graph, see Figure 12.

Bar Graphs

In bar graphs the lengths of the bars are proportional to the numbers they represent. This visually apparent proportionality makes bar graphs especially good at showing relationships among numbers or sets of numbers, including change over time. (For a sample bar graph, see Figure 13.) As with line graphs, the weakness of bar graphs is that they are not by themselves precise; if you want

18- to 24-Year-Olds Living at Home, 1960-1990

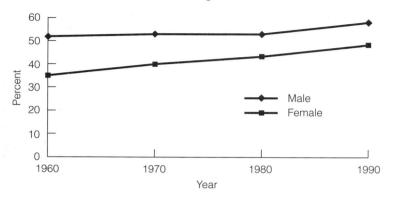

Source: Data from U.S. Bureau of the Census, *Current Population Reports*, Series P20-484, "Marital Status and Living Arrangements: March 1994," and earlier reports.

Figure 12. Sample Line Graph

18- to 24-Year-Olds Living at Home, 1960-1990

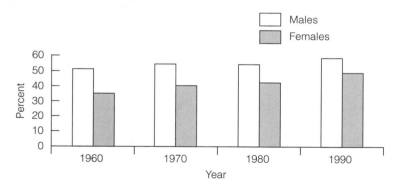

Source: Data from U.S. Bureau of the Census, *Current Population Reports*, Series P20-484, "Marital Status and Living Arrangements: March 1994," and earlier reports.

Figure 13. Sample Bar Graph

readers to learn specific numbers from looking at a bar graph, you usually will need to print the numbers on each bar. When bar graphs are used to represent change over time or distance, they are usually rotated 90 degrees to become horizontal bar graphs. When you are using a bar graph to show changes in quantity over time (that is, the vertical axis charts quantities of something), be sure that scale starts with zero.

Pie Charts

Pie charts are especially good for showing the relative proportions of parts to a whole. The wedges need to be labeled in a legend box or individually. If you label each wedge, keep the labels oriented the same way as the rest of your text (that is, don't try to make the writing angled the same way as each wedge). (For a sample pie chart, see Figure 14.) Pie charts are not a good choice if there are too many wedges (thus making the chart hard to read at a glance) or if the wedges are nearly all the same size (thus

Projection of U.S. Population, by Race and Hispanic Origin: 2050

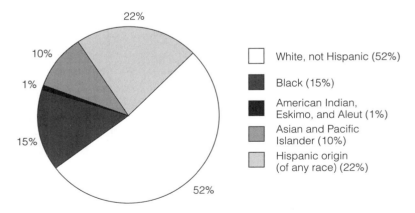

Source: Data from U.S. Bureau of the Census, *Current Population Reports*, Series P25-1104, "Population Projections of the United States, by Age, Sex, Race, and Hispanic Origins: 1993 to 2050."

Figure 14. Sample Pie Chart

making it hard for readers to get any sense of proportionality from the chart).

Diagrams and Drawings

Diagrams and drawings are probably the most common kind of visual in reports. Their strength is that they make it possible for readers to visualize the subject you are writing about. Whether the drawings and diagrams come from clip art, are drawn using a computer program, are drawn by hand, or are traced or photo-copied or scanned from another source, they give writers the op-portunity to control the exact features that are shown or not shown, the size of the image, the kind and amount of detail that is shown, and the orientation (visual point of view) to be used. As with other visuals, the important parts need to be labeled, and sources must be cited (even if the citation is only an "adapted from . . ."). (For a sample diagram, see Figure 15.) The weakness of drawings and diagrams is that they quickly become too com-plex. Make sure you include only the kinds and amount of detail each particular reader needs in each particular setting.

Cranial Features of *Homo Erectus* Compared with Those of Modern *Homo Sapiens*

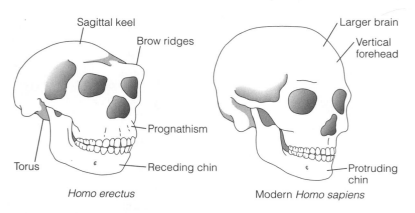

Sagittal keel
Brow ridges
Prognathism
Torus
Receding chin
Homo erectus

Larger brain
Vertical forehead
Protruding chin
Modern *Homo sapiens*

Source: Michael A. Park, *Biological Anthropology* (Mountain View, CA: Mayfield, 1996), 210.

Figure 15. Sample Diagram

Guidelines for Visuals

When you begin using visuals in your reports, check them for the following qualities:
* Are you using the right kind of visual for this situation? Each kind of visual is good for one or two purposes and not good for others. (See the discussion in "Types of Visuals" on the preceding pages.) Make sure you're building on your visual's natural strength, not being hurt by its natural weakness.
* Make sure the text and the visual work well together.

   1. The text does not need to go over everything in the visual, but there will nearly always be one or two key points about the visual that the text needs to stress.

   2. Is each visual also referred to within the text itself? Try to make sure that the visual is placed as soon after the reference in the text as possible. (Collecting all the visuals together at the end of the report is not a good option.)

* Have you adapted the kind of visual and the amount of detail it shows to this setting and this audience? Do not set as your target an appropriate level of complexity; try to achieve an appropriate level of simplicity instead.
* Make sure the visual has good production qualities. Are its lines crisp and clear; is it neatly done; is it easy to read at a glance?
* Is each visual appropriately bordered by white space? For most visuals, that means at least one inch all around. For informal tables and other "spot" visuals, there might be a little less.
* Does each visual have an appropriate caption? Each one needs at the minimum a number and a title; often a short explanation is also good to have.
* Have you cited your sources for each visual? If you downloaded it from the Web, if you scanned it in from somewhere else, if you used clip art, if you photocopied it and pasted it in, if someone else drew it for you—in every case *except* the ones in which you draw the visual yourself or take the photo yourself—you need to cite your sources, even if only with an "adapted from. . . ."

Lists

Although your reader will never explicitly "see" the pattern behind your simple page design, its effect will be one of professionalism and consistency. You can add to that effect by how you treat *lists*. Some will be part of paragraphs (these are called *run-in lists*), and they need no special design treatment. But you may want lists containing important information (such as information your reader may want to refer to later) to show up a little more, and the easiest way to do this is to set off the list typographically, producing a *displayed list* (such as the one that started this section on document design; see page 131). Displayed lists include bulleted, numbered, and alphabetical lists. Use bulleted lists when the ordering of items within the list is not significant, and numbered or alphabetical lists when it is. For maximum design effect, do these lists in a *hanging indent style:* when any item has two or more lines, put the first letter of those lines under the first letter of the first line and not under the bullet or number. (Most current word processing programs offer you this option automatically.) To make your displayed lists stand out even more, you may want to indent them. If you do so, let the indention be bigger than the one you use for paragraphs, perhaps a half inch for paragraph indents and a full inch for displayed lists.

Correct use of all the design elements discussed so far—binding, cover, fonts, graphics, and lists—will go a long way toward making your report easy and even pleasant for readers to use. One final key element is the use of headings and subheadings to indicate the outline of your report. In a twenty-page report it's appropriate to use perhaps three or four levels. Here's an example of how you can make four levels with different sizes and weights of type:

> ### REPORT TITLE
> **Level 1 Heading**
> **Level 2 Heading**
>   *Level 3 heading.*   This lowest level of heading is run into the text paragraph. The other levels of headings are on separate lines.

Use of a simple heading scheme reinforces your readers' sense of the structure of your report, makes it easy for them to find key sections quickly, and provides another way to break up pages that can too often become solid walls of words. Today's word processors let you do much more adventuresome things with typography than the heading examples shown above. However, we recommend that for academic projects you play it safe unless your teacher has clearly invited you to create a nontraditional look.

Coupled with your use of the appropriate style guide (such as APA or MLA), these simple design tips will help you produce attractive reports whose appearance reinforces the good writing inside them. Although no amount of fancy design work can cover up (much less make up for) bad writing, a research report that is both well written and well produced is a worthwhile goal for any writer.

A Note on Page Numbering: One last thing you can do to make your report easy to use is to be sure to number *every* page. Unless you have specific instructions to the contrary, once you place an Arabic number 1 on a page, every page after that should be numbered. Leaving a number off a page or set of pages, for whatever reason, invites problems for your readers.

ARGUMENTATION

ARGUMENTATION

Argumentation is the presentation of verbal (and visual) material intended to change the reader's beliefs. An argumentative piece may result in *a new way of thinking* or *a new type of action*. If you accept an author's arguments about the dangers of drunk driving, for example, you may decide that people should not drink at parties and then drive home—and you may volunteer to serve as a designated driver.

To persuade your readers to accept your beliefs and judgments, you must choose a clear, arguable thesis and assertions that develop it; analyze the readers' needs and assumptions; build your arguments through appeals based on *ethos, pathos,* or *logos;* and create an effective structure for your information. Although there are entire books that discuss the complex subject of written persuasion, the material in the following sections provides an introduction to the topic.

CHOOSING A THESIS AND PLANNING KEY ASSERTIONS

The thesis is the main idea of a paper. In an argument, the thesis states the assertion that you want your readers to accept as a new way of thinking or acting.

An arguable thesis meets these three criteria:

- It concerns a point of view with which another person could reasonably disagree.
- It attempts to change someone's beliefs or actions.
- It provides the answer to a specific question or the solution to a specific problem.

These three points rule out arguments over whether *you* like something ("I love nature"); arguments over simple, established facts ("It is Earth Day"); and vague or general arguments that no one could refute ("The fate of the world's environment is important to everyone").

To argue successfully, the writer should choose a thesis that meets the three criteria and, thus, is "arguable":

As a fall project, the sociology club should install and monitor recycling bins on campus.

Water pollution is responsible for the high rates of breast cancer in our community.

Because of recent increases in food poisoning, the city should force restaurants to stop serving raw shellfish.

While you work on the major assertion or thesis that states what the argument is about, you may also begin planning several minor assertions that will develop it fully. For the preceding thesis about the sociology club, for example, the writer might plan to cover the following points: the benefit to the environment, the learning experience, the financial gain from a regular recycling program, and the opportunity for good public relations on campus.

ANALYZING THE AUDIENCE

In argumentation, achieving the purpose of encouraging a new way of thinking or a new type of action requires a thorough knowledge of your readers. The questions on pages 7–8 can help you evaluate your audience's values. You also need to know their position on your topic: whether they agree or disagree with your thesis, certainly, but also their personal experiences that relate to the subject and the types of arguments they will find convincing.

As part of your audience analysis, you should also examine the assumptions underlying your thesis and your readers' probable response to them. If you argue that learning a sport is good for young children because it teaches discipline, you need to determine whether your readers would agree that children should learn discipline. If you say that the new manager will be unsuccessful because he is authoritarian, you need to know what your readers think about various office management styles. Do they agree that a stern manager creates problems? Instead of simply assuming that readers share your underlying assumptions, you may need to offer proof: that teaching discipline helps children or that a dictatorial boss can harm the work environment.

DEFINING TERMS

As you plan a thesis and consider the assumptions behind it, you need to consider the terms that will require precise definitions. In the following thesis, for example, the term "respect" may not provide a clear concept: "College teachers should treat students with *respect.*" Is the writer discussing classroom behavior, accessibility, or grading? She must make her precise meaning clear. Similarly, if a writer's thesis or arguments concern abstractions, such as *equality, justice,* or *morality,* she should define those terms. Definition also may be needed to explain new ideas or programs that a writer may be arguing for or against. In the sample essay included at the end of this section on argumentation, for example, Suzette Adler makes sure that her readers understand what year-round schools are before she argues against them.

CHOOSING SOURCES OF SUPPORT
(*ETHOS, PATHOS, LOGOS*)

After you have crafted an arguable thesis, you will need to decide on the most appropriate sources of support. You should consider all three types:

- **Ethos:** An appeal to the character of the writer. Readers believe and are moved by a thesis or an assertion because of the qualities of the person who makes it.
- **Pathos:** An appeal to readers' emotions, such as fear, pity, or greed.
- **Logos:** An appeal to reason (an appeal based on well-structured assertions and evidence).

For your argument papers, you will need to know how to use each kind of supporting material.

Ethos: Appeals Based on the Writer's Character

If the university's football coach appears on television selling cars, he is making an argument based on his popularity and coaching ability: he is a winner, and so the car he endorses must be a winner, too. Readers may be attracted to a product or a political viewpoint because they are attracted to the individual, whether the person is an expert in that field or not.

A more firmly grounded ethical appeal is that of a mayor pleading for an end to local rioting: the mayor can speak persuasively about a ravaged neighborhood's need for peace and about the police's commitment to end disturbances. Another ethical appeal is that of an engineer carefully explaining her testing of a solution to a design problem. This detailed accounting should make her appear knowledgeable, thorough, and fair, important attributes for any speaker or writer.

Pathos: Appeals to Emotion

It may never be "logical" in the strictest sense to base an argument on an emotional appeal or to let yourself be persuaded by one, but our strong responses to such appeals are very human. When a muscular dystrophy charity features a beautiful poster child, its ad campaign appeals to our sense of pity. When a politician describes the brutal crimes of one parolee, he is using an appeal to fear to gain support for his new jail tax proposal.

An effective emotional appeal must be geared to the emotional needs and preferences of the audience. If citizens are already afraid of young criminals, they may easily be swayed by pictures of gang members in their neighborhoods. Successful appeals also rely on specific portrayals, of individual children with muscular dystrophy or of individual men loose on our streets.

Logos: Appeals to Logic

Besides deciding on the appropriate uses of *ethos* and *pathos,* you will need to present solid assertions and the evidence to support them. Many arguments are formed by collecting data and drawing a conclusion from them, such as "Because my mother, my friend Murray, and *Consumer Reports* speak well of the Ford Taurus, I think it is the car I should buy." People decide whether to see a movie, buy a certain car or stereo, or choose a particular college by using this *inductive* method, which scientists in laboratories also use. To succeed at creating such arguments, you need to understand the appropriate types of evidence and the best methods of judging their reliability.

Types of Evidence

Writers draw on several types of evidence to support their assertions:

- **Facts and statistics:** Verifiable statements and data
- **Examples:** Specific cases
- **Expert opinions:** The judgments of authorities
- **Analogies:** Comparisons that clarify a new situation

Facts are statements that can be verified by library research or by observation:

> In 1952, scientists Thomas King and Robert Briggs achieved the first animal cloning by making frogs from tadpole cells.

> Rainbows occur when tiny droplets of water in the air separate white light into the spectrum of colors of which light consists.

Facts employing numbers are called **statistics:**

> Women make up 79% of the people over 100 years old.

> The earth travels in its path around the sun at more than 66,000 miles an hour.

When you find facts and statistics in the library or on the Internet, you should document those sources as your teacher requires. (See pages 93–130 for guidelines to MLA and APA styles of documentation.)

Examples are specific instances of a general point, including historical cases. Relevant examples combined with facts and statistics help readers to understand the true import of the data, thus to see a situation clearly. In "No Place Like Work," an essay about the tendency of Americans to work longer hours because their home life is so hectic, author Laura Shapiro begins with this specific example:

> Gwen works in public relations at a large Midwestern corporation. She loves her job, but life can be frantic, beginning with 4-year-old Cassie's sulky protests at being left in day care at 7:30 a.m. At the end of the day, mother and daughter get half an hour of "quality time" before Cassie goes to bed; then Gwen and her husband collapse. Those 10-hour stints at day care worry Gwen, and she wishes that home life weren't so rushed and unsatisfying. She can't afford to quit work, but luckily her company has been named one of the top 10 most family-friendly corporations in the nation by *Working Mother* magazine. Employees can apply for flexible hours, job-sharing and other benefits. So why hasn't she looked into making

any family-friendly changes in her schedule? How come she's allowed her office day, originally eight hours, to creep to nine?

(For another illustration of using examples to develop a main idea, see pages 23–24.)

Expert opinions are statements made by authorities based on their own examination of the facts. You should include their credentials when you quote or paraphrase their work so that readers will understand their qualifications as sources of information about your topic:

> Sociologist Arlie Hochschild claims that since home time is usually scheduled around children's activities and chores, American parents seek relaxation and comradery at the office.
>
> *Nature* editorialized that "cloning humans from adults' tissues is likely to be achievable any time from one to ten years from now."

To choose appropriate authorities to quote or paraphrase, you should consider the values of your readers. Will they be swayed by the opinions and research of scientists, theologians, editorialists, or politicians? Will any particular authority alienate or impress them?

Comparisons or **analogies** can help readers grasp the meaning of a situation or concepts. Like examples, they can increase the impact of other types of evidence by making the abstract or the unknown seem more concrete or by providing a new perspective on a familiar subject.

In an essay entitled "TV Addiction," for example, author Marie Winn claims that addiction to television is similar to addiction to drugs because both cause people to become dependent on a repeated "fix," to withdraw from reality, to become passive, and to lose discrimination powers. Like other good analogies, this one gains readers' attention and encourages them to think in new ways. (For more information on developing comparisons in your papers, see pages 33–35.)

The Reliability of Evidence

As you amass logical support for your arguments, you need to judge whether readers will find it reliable. For logical arguments to be convincing,

Conducting Research for Argument Papers

As you consider the types of facts, statistics, examples, expert opinions, and analogies necessary to defend your thesis, you may decide that you need to conduct some research.

- To find *facts* and *statistics,* you can study reference books such as almanacs, yearbooks, and encyclopedias; journal articles; and on-line sources such as the *Statistical Abstract of the United States* located at the U.S. Census Bureau's home page. You may also decide to conduct your own surveys.

- Relevant *examples* may come from magazine articles, which frequently include specific cases to explain a general trend, or from your own interviews with people who have experience with the subject.

- You can gather *expert opinions* from relevant books and articles, from on-line sources such as the WWW Virtual Library, or from your own interviews.

- *Analogies* may come from sources you read or experts you interview—or from your own imagination.

(For a thorough discussion about conducting research and documenting sources, see pages 54–141.)

- the individual pieces of evidence must be trustworthy;
- the sources must be authoritative;
- there must be enough evidence; and
- the researcher must draw a logical conclusion from the evidence.

In your own decision making, you have probably seen the necessity of all four conditions. If in buying a car, you trust the opinions of friends who have not owned many cars or of the dealer who is selling the car, you may be relying on evidence that is not trustworthy. If you ask two or three people, even ones who are trustworthy and authoritative, you may not be collecting enough evidence. And once you have collected enough evidence, you have to analyze your data carefully. What if your sources give different opinions, just as lab data are likely to be contradictory? How will you decide? You will have to evaluate the different views, make your own tests, and consider compromises. When you are creating arguments, then, you will need to present *trustworthy evidence in sufficient quantities so that your conclusion will seem like the most logical one.*

RECOGNIZING FALLACIES

As you read and plan your essays, you should especially look for faulty and ineffective arguments. The most common weaknesses in argumentative writing are called "common fallacies"; each has its own traditional name: false cause, false analogy, begging the question, either-or, red herring, oversimplification, ad hominem, and hasty generalization.

False Cause

A writer commits the common fallacy of "false cause" by suggesting that *B* was caused by *A* when in fact the two may be totally unconnected or connected only by coincidence in time and convergence in space. For example, did the black cat that crossed a classmate's path cause him to flunk the test? Did your friend's losing her temper at work cause her to also lose her dog on the same day? Most false-cause arguments are like these two, built on coincidences and connections that don't bear close scrutiny.

False Analogy

This fallacy involves treating *A* and *B* as similar in ways that in fact they are not. For example, suppose the school's football team buys the same equipment as the National Football League team that won the Super Bowl last season—does that mean that it will win a national championship? No, the analogy between the two teams is false because this similarity would not necessarily cause a team to win.

Begging the Question

An argument begs the question when it assumes that part of what has to be proved is true. If a student applies only to small schools because she thinks that teachers at large schools do not give students enough attention, she may be committing a fallacy: she should first investigate whether her attitude about teachers is correct. If a politician claims that she could not have given contracts to her friends because she is honest, she may need to prove her record of honesty: she is simply refuting the charge by claiming the opposite. When a store owner claims that she cannot possibly refund a customer's money on a malfunctioning CD player because three months have passed, she needs to prove that her responsibility has ended.

Either-Or

Most issues have more than two solutions. Reducing a complex issue to two simple alternatives creates an either-or fallacy. If a student thinks that he must get into one particular business school next fall or he will not have a successful career, he is probably overlooking other possibilities. A politician's claim that "the U.S. government must raise taxes or cut social services" may ignore other alternatives, such as cuts in defense spending or a reorganization of service agencies.

Red Herring

Drawing its name from a method of throwing a bloodhound off the scent, the red herring fallacy consists of introducing an element into the argument that has nothing to do with the issue at hand. This fallacy occurs, for example, when a lawyer blames the guilty verdict on the "media circus" or when a husband blames his wife's forgetfulness on her being a woman.

Oversimplification

This fallacy consists of oversimplifying the relationship between a cause and an effect. For example, someone being interviewed on a news program might claim that the environment has been ruined by coal-burning power plants. Yes, they do hurt the environment, but ruining it takes a lot more than that. Similarly, a sportscaster might say that the basketball game was lost because the center missed that last shot; but a game involves more than one shot.

Ad Hominem

This fallacy, whose name is Latin for "to the man," is an attack on an opponent's character to arouse the emotions or prejudices of the audience. A candidate for public office might argue that her opponent was seen with Mafia leaders or has fascist relatives. A politician might stereotype supporters of a family-leave bill as "feminist" or "radical" so that others will oppose it without careful study. A person's character or private life may influence his or her actions and beliefs, but unfair stereotyping or labeling diverts attention from the important issues.

Hasty Generalization

Hasty generalization occurs when someone leaps from too little evidence to too big an assertion. If a writer has talked to three disgruntled students, he creates a hasty generalization if he then claims that the student body feels discontented. If four of your neighbors are supporting the same mayoral candidate, you cannot assume this person will win: your neighbors may not be representative of the city's voters.

ANSWERING OPPOSING VIEWS (REFUTATION)

As you craft your arguments, you need to consider whether your analysis of the audience's beliefs and assumptions indicates some point of disagreement that you should address directly in your paper.

In general, consider two means of dealing with the readers' key objections:

1. **Oppose the assertion directly.** You may want to note the point of disagreement and then respectfully explain why the objection isn't valid. If you are arguing in a neighborhood association's newsletter that an empty building should be used as a homeless shelter, you should not ignore the members' fears that crime will increase. Instead, recognize that fear and provide evidence from other neighborhoods to refute their belief.

2. **Concede an assertion's validity through a "yes, but . . ."** **strategy.** In other cases, you may want to note that an objection is factually correct but that factors the audience may not have considered render it unimportant or irrelevant. If you are advocating that high school students participate in an afterschool internship program, you may need to admit that students would have less study time, but you could then note that they would be required to attend study periods during which adult monitors would help them with homework and teach timemanagement skills.

Building Consensus Rather Than Barriers

As you create arguments, you need to consider the values and goals that you share with your readers, not just points of opposition. The more you oppose people head to head, the more resistance you create. Thus you may want to use your evidence to be less adversarial and more conciliatory. For example, if country A analyzes its weak border forces and doubles its weapons budget, neighboring country B may well feel forced to buy more guns and planes. But if A invites B to discuss arms reductions, B may consider disarmament. If you are writing to college officials about residence hall policies, you should recommend a change that they could accept; otherwise, they may not pay attention to your evidence. Opposition leads to opposition; compromise leads to compromise.

USING THE TOULMIN METHOD TO ANALYZE AN ARGUMENT

As you read and write arguments, you might find it helpful to use a method of analysis developed by British philosopher Stephen Toulmin. Toulmin's method focuses on the *structure of argument* and can help you to make sure that each part of an argument (including your own) is related to the whole, ensuring that your paper is developed logically and soundly.

- **Analyze the Thesis:** What general thesis statement, or claim, is the author defending? Is it arguable? Is the thesis qualified with words or phrases such as "on the whole" or "typically"? Careful arguers are wary of making absolute claims. Thus they frequently use qualifying words or phrases to restrict an assertion and improve its defensibility.

- **Analyze the Assertions and the Evidence:** After you look at the thesis, then look at the main assertions, or grounds. Is each one relevant to the thesis? How close is the connection? Then ask, "How do you know that?" What kind of evidence (facts, statistics, examples, citations from authority) is offered as support for each reason? Does any of the evidence seem irrelevant, insufficient, or fallacious?

- **Analyze the Audience's Assumptions:** Assertions and the evidence that supports them have to be accepted by a particular group of readers. What are their interests and beliefs? Will they be convinced? Will they make specific objections that must be refuted? What assumptions, or warrants, underlie the author's assertions? Will the readers accept those assumptions, or will some discussion of them be needed?

- **Summarize Your Analysis:** To help you assess the strengths and weaknesses of your own arguments or those you read, summarize your analysis in a few sentences, noting your judgment of the assertions, evidence, and audience analysis.

STRUCTURING ARGUMENTATIVE PAPERS

Once you have decided on a thesis and the appropriate evidence, you will be ready to structure your paper. Argumentative papers generally follow either a direct or an indirect pattern.

In the **direct pattern,** you assume that your readers are going to present you with no initial resistance, that you are arguing in favor of a point that has not occurred to them or discussing an issue about which they have no strong opinion. In these situations, you should make a clear early statement of your thesis and then present each piece of evidence to support it.

In the **indirect pattern,** you assume that the readers are opposed to your position and have to be led to acknowledge your viewpoint. Thus you might start by introducing the topic generally and save your thesis for the end, stating it after you have presented all of your evidence.

Refutation: With either pattern, you need to anticipate the strongest arguments against you. Before you state your own evidence, you may need to refute those arguments. At the end of your paper, you may also want to offer points of compromise.

(As you consider these options and plan your organization, you might use the outlining techniques discussed on pages 14–16.)

SAMPLE ARGUMENT PAPER

Suzette Adler became interested in year-round schools when her education professor strongly advocated them. She decided to write an argument paper for her composition class against this recent method of transforming education.

Adler   1

Suzette Adler

Professor C. Mayron

English 122

November 13, 1997

The Case Against Year-Round Schools

When year-round education is discussed, many people assume that school
boards are attempting to add more school days, perhaps increasing from 180 days
to the 240 mandated in some German and Japanese schools. While some educators favor such an increase, most of the 1.8 million students in 37 states enrolled
in year-round schools attend for 180 days but do not adhere to the traditional
school calendar. Most of these students participate in year-round learning on a
45-15 or 60-20 track, the first number signifying instruction days, the second
indicating vacation time (Worshop 435-36). The student population splits into a
certain number of calendar tracks—not to be confused with ability tracks—each
with its own separate vacation.

In theory, multi-tracking eases overcrowding without requiring additional
construction costs. Proponents of such plans also claim that eliminating so-called
summer learning loss will enhance students' academic performance. Such arguments may seem appealing in cash-strapped school districts where residents
want to accommodate more students and improve test scores without raising
taxes. In fact, however, multi-track, year-round education creates massive scheduling problems in schools and elsewhere and fails to provide an inexpensive and
more efficient way of educating an expanding population of students.

Alternate vacation times complicate the planning of almost all school activities involving a large group. Some scheduling problems can be avoided with
advance arrangements. For instance, a football coach might require all players to
attend during the same school session. However, if multi-tracking does not in-

---

A *definition* of
"year-round
schools"
acquaints
readers with
the subject.

The author
here mentions
the specific
arguments for
which she will
provide
refutation.

The *thesis*
states the
author's
opinion
and seeks
a change in
the reader's
attitude.

Adler   2

volve relatively equal distribution of students, classes remain crowded. And
conflicts invariably occur: the band director cannot recruit members who want to
rehearse during their vacation, computer class and drama class may not be offered on the same track, or rehearsals for the class play may stall because <u>Our
Town's</u> narrator has gone to Disney World. Policies that weaken and disrupt such
groups often discourage students from developing their interests, learning responsibility, and building their credentials for college.

*Examples
explain the
scheduling
problems.*

Year-round schooling also complicates life beyond campus. Districts often
try such reforms on an experimental basis so that an elementary school may be
multi-tracked while a middle school in the same neighborhood remains on the
traditional school calendar. Consequently, a family with several siblings on different academic calendars may have problems arranging family trips. More important, because of the staggered break times, parents can no longer rely on older
siblings to tend brothers or sisters during the day. Such a change can pose serious economic problems, especially for single parents. Students in year-round
schools also have difficulty scheduling educational summer activities like nature
camp, art camp, or computer camp, and many students on the new academic
calendar lose the learning opportunity a summer job provides. A 60-20 or 45-15
tracking diminishes nearly all job prospects for students because hardly any
employer wants to train a worker who can stay for only two or three weeks before returning to school.

Even with all these problems, some districts might still consider adopting a
plan that makes room for more students without entailing major costs related to
new construction. However, many administrators are dismayed by the expenses
of year-round schooling. Difficult and expensive choices arise when administrators and office staff try to arrange multi-track schedules for teachers and students. Such arrangements may seem simple, but just one example illustrates the

Adler   3

possible problems. Suppose nearly all the gifted students sign up for a nine-week
session of advanced math that begins in late August while only three sign up for
such a class starting in mid September. Should administrators allow the teacher
to teach only three students? No savings would result there. With dozens, or
perhaps hundreds, of situations like this, arranging the multi-track schedule
resembles a pay-as-you-go attempt to navigate through a large maze at night.
Simple maintenance costs also rise. Occupying all classrooms the entire year
means more money for simple upkeep like replacing light bulbs and cleaning
buildings. Air conditioning costs, especially in older, poorly insulated classrooms,
siphon away even more of the alleged savings. Ironically, summer electric bills
soar the most in Sun Belt school districts more inclined to adopt year-round programs to accommodate a large influx of students. After accounting for costs such
as these, even a major proponent like the National Association for Year-Round
Education admits that year-round classes are no more cost efficient than less
disruptive alternatives like modular classrooms unless the school age population
exceeds 16% of a school's capacity (Agron 33). Even schools saving some money
with the modified calendar cannot postpone school construction indefinitely, for,
in high growth areas, the student population will still eventually exceed capacity.

Even without major cost benefits, many would be willing to adjust to the
year-round school's inconveniences if such modifications could significantly improve academic performance. Many groups wanting to abandon the traditional
June-to-August break believe this vacation interrupts the educational continuum.
Teachers must then waste valuable time in September and October reviewing
materials students have forgotten; therefore, students with shorter, more frequent breaks supposedly learn and retain more information. This reasoning fails
to address several basic questions. How much does a student forget in a shorter
break of fifteen or twenty days? Does one long review at the end of traditional

*An analogy
to a maze
makes the
frustrations of
this situation
easier to
grasp.*

*Facts and
statistics
provide further
support.*

Adler   4

summer break total more time than shorter reviews at the end of three or four
vacation periods in the new systems? Also, does the argument against the current academic calendar exaggerate the amount of continuum learning? Subjects
like math do build upon previously learned skills. Yet a year of English literature
does not begin with a month reviewing American authors. A year of chemistry
rarely starts with a refresher course in biology. Research does not strongly support advocates' claims about summer disruption of the learning process. Partly
because researchers have difficulty isolating year-round education from other
variables, comparisons of student test scores often provide conflicting results. In
Year-Round Schools: Do They Make a Difference? (1990), the honorary education
fraternity Phi Delta Kappa examines years of research on the issue and concludes
that year-round schooling has little positive or negative impact on test scores—
hardly a ringing recommendation for adopting such a plan (Williams 243).

> In some emergency situations school districts must choose the least of evils
when trying to educate a rapidly increasing school age population. Shortening the
summer break may indeed be preferable to trying to learn in extremely crowded
classrooms or enduring morning/afternoon type tracking. However, communities
should not endorse year-round schooling as a long-term plan for deferring construction costs and enhancing academic performance. Perhaps if entire states or
regions adopted a new academic calendar, many families, day cares, summer
camps, and other institutions could all adjust together. However, year-round
schooling in just one school district, or even worse in just one school within a
district, almost always creates disruptions and inconveniences more significant
than whatever meager benefits such scheduling might provide.

An expert *opinion authoritatively supports the author's claims.*

Here the author further qualifies her thesis and states her final judgments.

Works Cited

Agron, Joe. "Stretching the School Calendar." American School and University 66

(1993): 30-34.

Williams, Scott. Year-Round Schools: Do They Make a Difference? Bloomington,

IN: Phi Delta Kappa Center for Evaluation, Development, and Research,

1990.

Worshop, Richard L. "Year-Round Schools." The CO Researcher 6 (1996): 435-52.

SPECIAL WRITING SITUATIONS

ESSAY EXAMS

You've probably found that your college teachers use essay exams to assess your performance; these tests are a good way to

- see if you have understood the major concepts of the course,
- find out how well you can interpret and apply that knowledge, and
- test your reading and writing skills.

Doing well on an essay exam requires good studying and test-taking skills. Although an hour may not seem long enough for the full writing process, you will need to prewrite carefully, organize complete answers, make necessary revisions, and proofread. The discussion that follows will acquaint you with the writing steps necessary for succeeding at essay exams.

PREWRITING AND PLANNING

Determine the Format of the Exam

When your teacher announces an exam, first make sure that you understand the exam format. The answers to the following questions will help you prepare for the type of test you will take:

- What materials will be covered on the test? lecture notes? textbook chapters? guest speakers? outside readings?
- What does the teacher view as the most important material? Should you devote more study time to any particular chapters or lecture days?
- How much time will the test take?
- What kinds of questions will it include? short answer? matching? essays? How many essay questions will be included? Will the essays be of different lengths?
- How will the answers be evaluated?

Prepare by Careful Study

Your prewriting continues as you study for the test. Review your lecture notes and the text chapters carefully, underlining or circling important items. Then outline or summarize the material from your notes and the chapters.

You can further prepare by assuming the role of the teacher. What would you ask about on the test? You might create possible questions by using these starters:

Describe . . .

Analyze . . .

Compare . . .

Define . . .

How did the . . .

Why did the . . .

Evaluate . . .

Then you can write out your answers or simply think through the major points and examples you would use in answering. If you think that you will probably have to define the Industrial Revolution, for example, write out that definition. If you think your teacher will want you to evaluate the impact of James Watt's steam engines, examine those effects in advance.

Review the Test and Plan Your Time

On the day of the exam, the need for careful preparation will continue. When you are given the test sheet, first read it over carefully and make sure that you understand what is expected of you. Decide how much time to give to each question by figuring its percentage of the overall grade: if you work for too long on the essay that counts 30% of the grade and thus can't complete the one that counts 70%, you are not using your time efficiently. If you have a question about any part of the test or about these percentages, speak to your teacher before you begin writing.

Analyze the Questions

After looking over the test and determining your time schedule, begin working on the first question. Careful analysis of the specific questions—and question starters—should help you to plan your answers so that you *don't just summarize everything you know but, instead, use your information to answer the question that was asked.*

Describe and Analyze or Evaluate

If an education professor asks you to describe a classroom activity and analyze its educational value in terms of Abraham Maslow's theory of human needs, then the thesis of your essay should mention the main features of the activity and your estimation of how well it accords with Maslow's model.

Your essay should have two parts. First describe the most important features of the activity, and then analyze those features— judging them not by whether you like them but by whether they meet criteria set by the theorist.

Compare

If a history professor asks you to compare the public's responses to the Korean and Vietnam wars, list your specific points of comparison in the thesis. Then choose the block or alternating method of development to explain each one. (For a discussion of comparison, see pages 33–35.)

Define and Explain

If a biology professor asks you to define the role of photosynthesis, start with a clear definition as your thesis. Then describe the process, give examples of it, and explain its importance. (For a discussion of description, see page 31; for a discussion of examples, see pages 32–33.)

How

If an economics professor asks you how the federal deficit was created, answer with a thesis that mentions the key political decisions or market conditions that created the current situation. Then proceed chronologically in your answer, discussing the most important occurrences and explaining their impact on the deficit. (For a discussion of process writing, see pages 35–36.)

Why

If a political science professor asks why the influence of labor unions declined in the 1980s, summarize the *key* reasons in your thesis and then explain each one of them separately in your essay. (For a discussion of cause and effect, see page 33.)

Plan Your Answers

After analyzing the question, you can plan your answer. A quickly made outline of the key ideas will help you to stay on track and respond fully. Your answer might follow the three-part format described in the following sections.

First Short Paragraph

Assume that the reader is generally acquainted with the material: do not begin an essay on General Patton's strategy, for example, by summarizing World War II. Instead, begin your first paragraph with a thesis statement that answers the test question. Here are three examples of thesis statements:

> The Korean War was more popular with the American public than the Vietnam War because the public was more afraid of Communism in the 1950s, the goals of the Korean War seemed clearer and more noble, and the Korean War involved much less time and fewer fatalities.

> The influence of labor unions declined in the 1980s because of plant closings and the relocation of industry into nonunion areas.

> Photosynthesis is a process occurring in green plants that causes all natural food production.

Body

After the introduction, you might develop each major part of your answer in a separate paragraph, with the most important points covered first. Then if you run out of time, you will not have to omit your best material.

Begin each paragraph with a clear topic sentence and then provide supporting evidence—description, narration, examples, causal analysis, comparison, process—to explain the parts of your answer.

If you're writing about photosynthesis, for example, one paragraph might describe the basic process:

> The photosynthesis process involves light entering leaves and being transformed into a sugar. Light from the sun is absorbed into a green pigment in leaves called chlorophyll that is contained in small bodies on the plant surface called chloroplasts. In the chloroplasts, light energy causes water drawn up from the soil through the roots and trunk of the plant to split into molecules of hydrogen and oxygen. The hydrogen combines with carbon dioxide from the air, forming a simple sugar. This sugar combines with nutrients from the soil to make the starch, fats, proteins, and vitamins necessary for plant growth.

Subsequent paragraphs could discuss how photosynthesis creates oxygen and why all plants and animals depend on this process. (See pages 24–38 for a full discussion of paragraphing.)

Conclusion

End with a short conclusion that restates the thesis and notes possible consequences or a plan for future action, as in this conclusion to the essay on photosynthesis:

> Our food and oxygen supply comes from the energy-converting activity of photosynthesis. Since this process is necessary for our survival, we must be concerned about maintaining the forest, farm, prairie, and swamp lands needed for this process to occur.

(For a full discussion of conclusions, see pages 27–28.)

COMPOSING

As you write each part of your answer, follow your outline, paying attention to the clock to keep from spending too much time on any one part.

For the education exam question ("Describe a classroom activity and analyze its educational value in terms of Abraham Maslow's theory of human needs"), student Clara Joyner used her thesis statement—the answer to the question—as her introduction:

> Peer interviews, leading to oral and written profiles of class members, work well to start Mrs. Parmenter's high school journalism course because they follow Abraham Maslow's views on safety and belonging.

After quickly planning her essay, she wrote a paragraph of description, focusing on what the students did in the class activity and why they did it:

> In this class, the first assignment is for students to interview each other. Each student picks a partner and then spends twenty minutes asking the partner about his or her family, reasons for taking journalism, plans for college, ambitions, hobbies, and other classes. Each interviewer is asked to take notes during the session, write a short article for the next class, and then read the essay to the group. Then the classmates can ask questions of both the writer and the student who was interviewed. After completing the assignment, students

should know more about conducting an interview, writing a profile, and speaking before the group; they should also know more about each other.

For the next paragraph, she analyzed the assignment by using ideas from Maslow, a theorist her class had been studying:

This questioning and oral reporting follow Maslow's theories on safety and belonging. For students to learn, Maslow contends, they need to feel safe and valued: the interviewing technique shows that in this class their ideas will be central; the informal, unevaluated oral presentations help students to feel safe about having their voices heard. This exercise also leads students toward the group involvement that Maslow endorses since they work with partners and present positive information about their partners to the group.

Clara ended her essay with a short statement on the value of Maslow for shaping class assignments:

This interviewing assignment was successful because it encouraged students to feel safe and included. Maslow's theories are helpful: our students will achieve more if they feel like valued members of a group of learners.

REVISING AND PROOFREADING

Reserve a few minutes to read over each answer. If you need to scratch something out, do so neatly. If you need to add a word or two, use a caret mark ($_\wedge$) and write the new words above the line. For a longer addition, write "see the insert on the last page" and put an extra sentence or paragraph there.

ORAL PRESENTATIONS

"Most of the speeches top executives give stink." So said *The Wall Street Journal* (August 2, 1993). Study after study reports that people fear standing up and talking in front of other people more than nearly anything else. Yet with planning, just a little careful preparation, and a healthy dose of practice, you can deliver an effective short oral presentation. We're not talking about becoming a $5,000-dollar-per-speech after-dinner speaker, traveling around the country doing 45-minute motivational presentations for corporate America. We're talking about the 5 to 7 minutes you are given at the first staff meeting of your new internship to "tell us a little bit about yourself and your professional interests," or the 7- to 10-minute talk you're expected to give after three months on your first professional job to "report to management what your task group has been up to," or the 5 minutes in first-semester composition to "tell us about your research paper." With the right planning, preparation, and practice, you can do just fine in these short, relatively informal settings.

There are entire courses devoted to the subject of oral presentation; what follows here is best seen as only an introduction to a very complex topic.

PLANNING YOUR PRESENTATION

The first element in planning is to consider the situation itself. Prepare a planning document in which you write out answers to the following questions—the more fully developed your answers are, the better your planning will be:

- What, exactly, have you been asked to do?
- Why are you doing it? (This question has two parts: what is your purpose, and what is the purpose of the people who asked you to make the presentation?)
- Who is your audience?
- What setting are you doing it in?

What have you been asked to do? What subject are you to talk about, on what day, at what time, and at what length? Are you to answer questions afterward? Is this presentation expected to be formal or informal? What other important characteristics of this task can you identify?

Why are you doing it? What is *your* purpose in making this presentation: to make a good grade on a classroom assignment, to favorably impress a prospective employer, to win co-workers' and management's support for your team's project? What is the purpose of the people who asked you to make the presentation? Are they listening to you because they need to know the substantive content of what you are saying, or are they interested mainly in evaluating *you?*

Who is your audience? Are they your peers, people who outrank you, strangers, friends? If you understand that this is not just a presentation on a subject but also something done for a particular group of people, you will do a better job of planning and preparing.

What setting are you doing it in? The physical location of your presentation can have a profound effect on how well or poorly it goes. Are you in a big auditorium or a classroom with a noisy hallway outside? Will you be standing in the middle of a circle of chairs, sitting at a table with others around it, or standing behind a lectern? All these things may affect your presentation greatly.

Note: Students often think that preparing a planning document is simply a meaningless classroom exercise. In fact, however, few professionals go into any kind of speaking situation without first considering their audience, purpose, and site. We urge you to do your planning on paper. To think you can do it "in your head" and get much benefit from it is to fool only yourself. The goal of planning is to prepare you for every aspect of your presentation, both consciously and subconsciously. Its effect will be greatest if you write out your answers.

PREPARING A TEXT FOR PRESENTATION

Two guidelines will help you prepare a text for oral presentation: *reinforce the structure* and *simplify the content.* Whatever structural cueing is done in writing—a title at the top of a page, paragraph indentions, the ordering of paragraphs, any headings or subheadings—are not apparent to an audience in oral presentations. So to the extent that readers would rely on structure to understand your written message, you need to supply that element artificially for listeners to your oral presentations. Similarly, a text prepared for speaking cannot normally make the subtle gradations or go into the amount of detail that a text prepared for silent reading does.

Reinforce the Structure

There are a number of ways to reinforce the structure of an oral presentation. One way is to use *structural visuals*. In a classroom setting, you can come in early and put a short outline on the board. In a boardroom, you can use anything from the simplest flipchart to the most complicated computer-generated overhead projection. Or you can prepare a handout showing your name, the date, the title of your presentation, and the outline. Simply seeing an outline is often enough to allow listeners to follow what you're saying. Another way to reinforce the structure is to create both an *introduction* that clearly forecasts it ("This presentation has three parts: ____, ____, and ____") and a *conclusion* that recapitulates it ("Once we have looked at ____, ____, and ____, we can see that . . .").

Simplify the Content

An informal, five- to seven-minute presentation limits the degree of complexity you can present. Especially if you are working from a paper you have already written, you need to be conscious of simplifying the content. You might take out material you think your audience wouldn't be interested in or that is too complicated to explain in the time allotted—one way or another, you must simplify the content. You can achieve much of this simplification just by making the sentences themselves less complicated, as the box "Sample Text Marked Up for Reading Aloud" shows.

Sample Text Marked Up for Reading Aloud

Ten years ago men's studies ~~may have~~ seemed like an odd ~~notion. Critics of education have~~ *idea.*
~~long contended that all disciplines concentrate their attention on white men.~~ Even today, women students may feel that men's studies is some kind of backlash against women's studies, an attempt to ~~get even~~ somehow. From the point of view of ~~Harry Brod~~, one of the most published professors in the field, however, men's studies and women's studies are actually necessary for each other's existence: "I believe the field is an essential complement to women's studies because neither gender ultimately can be studied in isolation. Gender is, itself, a relational concept. ~~Masculinities and femininities are not isolated 'roles,' but contested relationships~~" (Brod, "Scholarly Studies" B-2).

So far, we have been talking about simplifying the content by eliminating material. You can also simplify the content by adding emphasis through *content visuals*. For example, the quotation at the end of the previous passage is a little too long to be effective in oral presentation. So it could be shortened for reading aloud. Or, as a content visual, the whole thing could be put on an overhead transparency:

> I believe the field is an essential complement to women's studies because neither gender ultimately can be studied in isolation. Gender is, itself, a relational concept: Masculinities and femininities are not isolated "roles," but contested relationships.
>
> Professor Harry Brod

CHOOSING VISUALS TO ACCOMPANY YOUR TALK

Even the most informal oral presentation can be made much more effective through the wise use of visuals, whether they are *structural visuals* (used to reinforce your talk's structure for listeners) or *content visuals* (used to simplify content by adding emphasis). In college classrooms, especially in lower-division courses, those visuals usually take one of four forms:

- material written or drawn on the chalkboard
- poster board visuals
- flipchart visuals
- overhead transparencies

Note: Using more complicated kinds of visuals for an informal and brief classroom talk is generally unwise and inappropriate: unwise because as the complexity of the visual aid increases, the setup and knockdown time increases arithmetically and the likelihood that something will malfunction increases geometrically; inappropriate because something like a two-slide pro-jector presentation with integrated voiceover and music is too much for a simple five-minute talk. It might be great in a corporate boardroom, but it is out of place in a first-year composition classroom.

Each of the media listed above has its own peculiarities and its own strengths and weaknesses, but the general guidelines shown in the next box apply to all of them.

Guidelines for Visuals in Short Presentations

- **Limit yourself to one idea per visual.** You cannot explain all of the Mars Pathfinder mission's "faster, better, and cheaper" philosophy in one visual. You *can* compare Pathfinder's costs with those of earlier missions.

- **Limit the number of words you put on each visual.** You cannot write a three-paragraph narrative history of the Pathfinder mission, put it on a poster board, and expect anyone to read it that way. You *can* do a timeline, listing five or seven or nine key dates in the mission. (That narrative history should be part of your talk, during which you refer to the timeline on the poster board.)

- **Make sure the letters you use can be read from the back of the room.** Titles should be in letters at least an inch high, headings three-quarters of an inch, and text at least a half inch. If you use smaller letters than those, you're just wasting your time.

- **Use color or boldface type to accentuate key points.** A nice touch is to add the highlighting with a color marking pen as you speak. Make sure that it's a pen that works on the kind of visual you're using and that people in the back of the room can see the marks you make.

- **Practice your talk with the visual aids, and if at all possible do so in the room you'll be delivering the talk in.** Of course, practice is important, but practicing "under game conditions" is even more important. Find a time when the room you'll be speaking in is unused, and deliver your presentation there exactly as you intend it to happen before your live audience. And while you're practicing, remember one final point: *Look at your audience, not at your visuals!*

Beyond those general guidelines, here are pointers for using each type of visual:

- **Chalkboards.** The strength of the chalkboard is that it is simple and can be found everywhere. As a nice added touch, colored chalk is very inexpensive and, of course, easy to use. The drawbacks to the chalkboard are that you may have to share space on it with other students and that putting material on it usually takes more time than a short presentation allows. You will have to come to the room early to put your material up, and it will then be there through everyone else's presentations as well. Finally, using the chalkboard during your talk will not strike other students as special; for a student audience, the chalkboard is a routine visual. That doesn't mean you should not use it; it just means that there's no glamour to it.

- **Poster boards.** Students can do wonderful presentations with poster boards. Two or three students can share the cost of a few boards, then take turns using them. The visuals can be drawn or lettered on separate sheets of paper and can be big and in color; you can even generate them on disk and have a campus copying shop such as Kinko's print them on sheets of paper large enough to cover the poster board. Then attach the visuals to the board with rubber cement or some other removable adhesive so it can be reused. Most classrooms have chalktrays in them, which are ideal for displaying poster boards. You do need to get the rigid kind of poster board, not flexible construction paper (which will always fall down). Rigid poster boards cost several dollars each.

- **Flipcharts.** If you have access to a flipchart, you have another powerful tool. As with the chalkboard, you'll usually need to do your writing or drawing on the sheets in advance, but you can make your lettering as big as you want and use as much color as you want. If you're careful, you can tear each sheet off as you use it and tape it up on the wall behind you; at the end of your presentation all the visuals will be displayed simultaneously. In most cases, the flipchart and stand should already be in the room you're talking in; they're too expensive to buy for one talk and too cumbersome to carry around campus all day.

- **Transparencies and slides.** Transparencies give you easy access to crisp images, color, and professional-quality charts, tables, and graphs. (See pages 133–140 for more on these.) With software programs such as PowerPoint, you can also create slides on a computer and show them on an LCD projector connected to it. All the guidelines listed above still apply, though. And when you use transparencies, it is especially important to think about where you are going to stand in relation to the screen and the projector. Standing next to the screen is good, but be careful to place yourself where the projector won't blind you. Standing next to the projector usually won't work because the noise of the projector's fan will probably make you inaudible. With either technology, remember to focus your attention on your listeners. They want to see your visuals, true, but they want and need to see your face too.

PRACTICING YOUR TALK

You may choose to *read* your presentation. For an especially nervous person, that is sometimes the best way to start getting practice. But your goal should be to know the subject well enough that you can, perhaps with the help of prompting from your notes, just talk it instead. You may want to "script" the introduction and the conclusion because they are so important. For the rest, however, you want to have practiced the material enough that you are perfectly comfortable just *talking* from your notes, not *reading* them.

You should plan on taking about two minutes to talk through one double-spaced, twelve-point page. If you take less time, you are going too fast. The best way to rehearse is with a tape recorder. Do exactly what you will do the day your make the presentation.

If at all possible, you should practice once or twice in the place where you will be making the presentation. Use the voice you intend to use, bring the props or visuals you intend to use, and have a tape recorder running. If you can get a classmate or a friend to listen and give you feedback, that's a valuable addition.

Dealing with Stagefright

It is natural to feel some nervous tension before an oral presentation. The question is whether to let that tension slide into fear and unhappiness, as for some people it naturally does, or to turn it by a deliberate act of planning and will into positive energy. If you find yourself becoming negative, do more preparation. If that doesn't work, do more practice. By being overprepared, by having excellent material, by having practiced and practiced, you can turn that negative energy into positive performance. The better prepared you are, the less there is to worry about.

DELIVERING YOUR TALK

When it comes to delivering your talk, there are three p's to re-member: props, pacing, and personality. You may be tempted to use the most complex forms of visual aids, but for an informal presentation, that is nearly always a mistake. You will do much better to rely on things you can put on the board, tape to the wall, or write in advance on a flipchart. It can be especially pow-erful to bring in props—actual objects to build your talk around. An architecture student can bring in a three-dimensional scale model of "the home of the future," or a composition student do-ing a paper on men's studies can bring in a stack of men's studies textbooks or of journals devoted to the subject. These props not only enhance the effect of the presentation but also help to calm you down.

Pacing is crucial. The vast majority of speakers speak too fast—always. Take your time, pause between sentences, stop between paragraphs. If you have timed your practices, you can have con-fidence that what may seem to you like a hundred years between paragraphs is actually only fifteen seconds. People take informa-tion in much more slowly through their ears than through their eyes, and you need to adjust your oral presentations to their pace.

What do people take away from such presentations? Do they remember what you said? Not much. Do they even remember what your topic was? Only sometimes. What people recall is the kind of person you seem to be. If you seem friendly, relaxed, and smile a little bit, people will simply forget problems of content or delivery. If you seem angry, defensive, or just grim, that's what people will think of your presentation too.

ANSWERING QUESTIONS

Most presentations should end with the speaker asking, "Any questions?" Remembering to do that is relatively easy, especially if you write it on your script or note cards. Dealing with ques-tions well, however, is almost a lost art. Here are two important guidelines: (1) listen to the whole question and make sure you understand it before responding, and (2) in your answers don't try to bluff your way through material you don't know or don't understand.

The first of these valuable techniques is so rarely practiced in the kinds of question-and-answer sessions we see on television that we forget its power and rightness. When someone asks you a question after your presentation, lock your mouth shut, look that person right in the eyes, nod when it's appropriate, and don't make a sound until the questioner is completely finished. Then if you are not absolutely sure you understand the question, play it back to the questioner: "Let me see if I understand what you're asking. . . ." This behavior will make it clear that you take the question and the questioner seriously; it will avoid needless misunderstandings; and it will give you extra time to think about your answer.

Not trying to bluff your way through an answer is essential. In an informal presentation, there is nothing wrong with saying, "I don't have that information right now. If you'll give me your phone number (or e-mail address) when this session is over, I'll try to get a good answer for you as soon as I can." Most audiences can tell when a speaker is bluffing, and they resent it. Most questioners appreciate your willingness to be honest and to try to use the knowledge you do have to find an answer for them later on.

PROFESSIONAL COMMUNICATION

Once you begin a career, producing effective written communication will be a daily part of your work. Even while you are in college, you may need to begin writing pieces of professional communication—internship applications, job applications, résumés, faxes to graduate school admissions committees, e-mail to co-workers at your current job or internship. There are entire courses on business and professional writing; the material presented here is only a short introduction to this important topic.

FORM FOR LETTERS, E-MAIL, FAXES, AND MEMOS

You can use the same basic block layout for letters, e-mail, and faxes. Some software programs also provide templates for various kinds of business correspondence.

[Your company]
[Its street address]
[City, state ZIP]

[Date]

[Receiver's title and name]
[Receiver's company]
[Receiver's street address]
[Receiver's city, state ZIP]

[Salutation followed by a colon]

[Body, with each paragraph in a single-spaced block and with a double space after the salutation, between paragraphs, and before the closing. The paragraphs are not indented.]

[Closing followed by a comma]

[Signature]

[Typed signature]

[Supplement line(s) for names of copy recipients and enclosed documents]

- **If you use this form for faxes,** be sure to add a cover sheet that names the person you're sending it to, gives that person's phone number, and gives your phone number in case a re-send is necessary. Remember that even with a cover sheet, nothing in a fax should ever be considered private or confidential.

- **If you use this form for e-mail,** add your e-mail address to the heading. Of course, the message will not include a signature. (Never consider anything you send or receive as e-mail private or confidential.)

- **If you use this form for memos,** you may want to replace the first nine lines (the inside heading, address, and salutation) with the following (many people use a "subject line" in their letters and e-mail, as well):

```
TO: XXXXXXXXXX
FROM: XXXXXX
SUBJECT: XXXXXXXX XXXXX XXXXXX
DATE: XXXXX

[The body of text follows.]
```

THE WRITING PROCESS FOR PROFESSIONAL COMMUNICATION

Even though most letters, memos, e-mail, and faxes are short pieces of writing, they still require careful prewriting and planning, drafting, revising, and correcting. The following steps summarize the writing process as it applies to these forms of professional communication. Obviously, for some short and casual documents it may be too much, and for some very important documents it may be too little.

1. Write down the purpose of the document. What does it need to accomplish? Use the purpose to keep you focused in steps 2–7.

2. Collect the relevant information. You don't want to interrupt your drafting to seek more information, and you certainly don't want to have to try to write around points that should be there.

3. Size up your role and your readers. Who are *you* to the readers of this document: a job applicant? a student requesting information about a graduate program? an employee requesting a raise from a superior? Who is your *audience,* and what is their relationship to you? What will be their likely reaction to this document?

4. From the following sections on pages 178–189, choose the plan you want to use.

5. Quickly compose a first draft.

6. Get someone to read over this draft to make sure that you have accomplished your purpose. Make any necessary changes.

7. Proofread the document, correct any spelling or grammar errors, print the final draft, and send it. Be sure to save a copy!

TYPES OF PROFESSIONAL COMMUNICATION

These documents are generally divided into types based on the writer's purpose and the reader's anticipated reaction. The following sections present patterns for three types of professional transactions as well as suggestions for pursuing jobs, internships, and scholarships on-line.

- **The job- or internship-application letter plus résumé:** Someone has advertised an opening, and you want to be the one to fill it.

- **Direct requests:** You are asking for something.

- **Persuasive documents:** You want to change the reader's beliefs or actions.

Job/Internship-Application Letters and Résumés

A job- or internship-application letter is a specialized form of persuasion: your letter should persuade the employer to consider you for the position. In it, you want to appear serious, well organized, and qualified, to indicate that you want to work at the company and will do the job well. A sample job-application letter is shown in Figure 16.

When you hear about a possible opening, you apply by sending an application letter and your résumé. The letter usually has four paragraphs:

1. Begin your letter by applying for the position and naming your best credential for it.

2. In the second paragraph, give the key details about that best credential. For most college students, that credential is probably education. In this paragraph, you can discuss your major,

1413 State Street
Gainesville, FL 32301
February 15, 1998

J. D. Abercrombie, Senior Biologist
Thompson Biological Systems Research Center
Columbia, FL 32442

Dear Dr. Abercrombie:

I would like to apply for one of the summer-long internships in wildlife biology
that your company has advertised in the biology department at State Tech University. I will be graduating this May with a B.S. in biology and am looking for
worthwhile practical field experience prior to entering graduate school this fall.

As a biology major at State Tech, I took primarily wildlife- and ecosystems-
oriented classes within the wildlife and fisheries science option. I also had a
strong minor in math, 21 hours instead of the usual 15. My long-term career interest is to earn an M.S. in Ecology and to secure employment as a career professional with the U.S. Wildlife and Fisheries Service.

In addition to the usual variety of part-time and summer jobs, my work experience includes a part-time lab assistantship in the raptors unit at State Tech's
Veterinary Teaching Hospital. For the last year, I have been the primary person
in charge of the care and feeding of many injured hawks, eagles, and other raptors brought in by the public for eventual return to the wild or placement in cap-
tive breeding programs.

With my academic and work backgrounds and my career interest in this area, I
can bring a fair amount of knowledge and experience to the position. I am available any time at your convenience for an interview, and I look forward to hearing
from you soon.

Sincerely,

Mary Washington
(555) 555-5555 (after 5 p.m.)
mwashington@sttech.edu

Figure 16. Sample Job-Application Letter
Here is a sample job-application letter from a student applying for a summer internship position in her major field. Notice how her letter clearly applies for the job,
explains her credentials, and suggests the next step—while stressing what she can
contribute to this research center.

coursework, special projects, computer and writing experience, technical training, and awards. Your goal here is to provide enough good information to make your reader pay attention to the additional details and examples on your résumé.

3. In the third paragraph, discuss your second-best credential, probably your work experience. Here you should discuss both volunteer and paid positions, including internships, relating your duties and accomplishments to those of the job that you are seeking. For example, even if you have only cashiered at a fast-food restaurant, you can point out the responsibilities involved, such as helping to train co-workers. If you have not had any paying jobs, you can discuss the duties involved in your club or team memberships. Give the most attention to your more recent experiences, especially those that relate to the job, whether they were paid positions or not.

4. In the fourth paragraph, mention anything additional (such as the résumé) that you are including with the letter and indicate what you think should happen next (how you can be reached and when you will be available for an interview). Close with something simple, such as "I look forward to hearing from you."

Cautions: Throughout the letter, make sure that you are discussing *what you can do* for the employer, not *what the employer can do* for you. Do not write that "this would be a great first job for me" or "I could learn about accounting here." Instead, concentrate on proving that you have the skills to do the job well and that you can make a contribution to the firm. As you state your qualifications, however, do not go too far. You do not want to say that you can solve all the firm's problems or that you have every possible trait of the exceptional worker. You will seem pompous, not qualified.

Résumés

When you send a letter of application, you should include a brief résumé with it. This one- or two-page document should summarize your education and work experience. You can also post your résumé with some of the on-line job-search services described on the following pages. A simple résumé is shown in Figure 17.

To prepare a résumé, you should first write down all your relevant experiences, including your major, coursework, other

MARY WASHINGTON
1413 State Street
Gainesville, FL 32301
(555) 555-5555

Computer Skills
Word, PowerPoint,
Statistical Analysis,
MatLab

EDUCATION
B.S. in Biology, Wildlife and Fisheries Science Option, expected May 10, 1998.
Math Minor. GPA 3.5 (on a 4.0 scale)

Important Coursework
Basic Biology, 9 hours
Chemistry, 9 hours
Botany, 3 hours
Zoology, 6 hours
Wildlife & Fisheries, 6 hours
Biocalculus, 6 hours
Models in Biology, 6 hours
Calculus, 6 hours
Statistics, 3 hours
Technical Writing, 3 hours

EMPLOYMENT
Part-time laboratory assistant, raptors unit, State University Veterinary Teaching Hospital. Fed and cared for 35 birds in various stages of health. Supervised high-school interns. 1997–1998.
Part-time groundskeeper, State University Veterinary Teaching Hospital. Maintained shrubs and other plants. Monitored supplies. Prepared budgets for new planting projects. 1996–1997.
Desk clerk, Somerset Hilton Hotel, Somerset, New Jersey. Helped guests with check-in and check-out. Monitored all cash and charge transactions. Trained new workers. Full time, 1994–1995.

REFERENCES Available on request from State Tech Job Placement Service.

Figure 17. Sample Résumé
Here is an example of one of the many acceptable formats for a one-page résumé. (Some software programs also provide templates for résumés.) Note how Mary used bold print and italics to set off headings and her jobs.

training, jobs, volunteer work, and extracurricular activities. After you have written everything down, you can begin choosing categories for grouping the information. You might pick from the following lists:

Possible Résumé Categories

Education

Relevant Coursework

Work Experience (you might divide it into Professional Work Experience and Other Work Experience)

Skills

Computer (or Technical) Skills

Specialized Training (for additional training courses or workshops)

Hobbies

Extracurricular Activities

Academic Honors

Honors and Awards

Under each category, you should define your experiences clearly. For the most important ones, you can include specific descriptions of your efforts, using verbs such as the following to reflect your active role. These verbs portray you as an active, responsible worker. They will have more impact than "responsible for" or "duties included."

Verbs for Describing Job Duties

achieved	evaluated	presented
administered	gathered	programmed
advised	generated	researched
arranged	guided	reviewed
budgeted	improved	revised
calculated	initiated	scheduled
completed	instituted	selected
computed	instructed	solved
coordinated	introduced	supervised
determined	managed	taught
developed	operated	tested
devised	organized	trained

| directed | planned | updated |
| established | prepared | wrote |

Pursuing Jobs and Internships On-Line

 The Internet offers searchable databases of job and internship postings by employers worldwide. This service is one of the fastest-growing areas of Internet use, and one that is especially important for students. Depending on the kind of job or internship you are looking for, you can search by type of job, by key word, by your skills, or by the city, state, or country where you want to find employment.

Caution: Because this area of the Internet is growing and changing so fast, the names and the URLs (the Internet addresses) of the services given below are only indicative of what is currently available. If you search for one of these services and do not find it, simply type "jobs" or "employment" into the text box of any large search engine, such as Yahoo! or AltaVista, and the most recent sites and their URLs will pop up. *Do not* use the services of any site that requires payment; there are too many good free services available.

Sites to Search for Jobs

With services such as **The Career Search Launch Pad <http://www.anet-dfw.com/~tsull/career/cslp.html>,** you can access several job-search engines. The Web pages available from the Launch Pad are Career Mosaic, NationJob, Net Temps, and Online Career Center. Launch Pad allows you to use the key-word searches for these career-search engines directly from the Launch Pad Web page, or you can link directly to any of them, using the URLs given below.

• **Career Mosaic <http://www.careermosaic.com/>** allows you to search for jobs by any one or any combination of skills description, job title, company name, city, state/province, and country. Career Mosaic will sort job listings by most relevant jobs (best matches) or by most recent jobs. It will also help you to get more information on top companies (by browsing company profiles), alert you to on-line job fairs, and give you access to success stories (letters from people who have used Career Mosaic). The site also includes tips on job hunting and résumé writing, and wage and salary information. Additionally, employers can find you if you post your résumé on ResumeCM.

- **NationJob <http://www.nationjob.com>** allows you to search for jobs by any one or a combination of key word search, field (e.g., general business, engineering), location by U.S. region, education (e.g., high school, bachelor's), job duration (full-time, part-time, temporary, or seasonal) and salary. Personal Job (P.J.) Scout is free and will help you search for a job; it will keep looking for jobs for you and e-mail updates on jobs that fit your qualifications. NationJob will help you get more information on companies (by browsing by field), find specialty job pages (by browsing available jobs by field), and let you read "Thank You PJ!" (success stories using NationJob P.J.).

- **Online Career Center <http://www.occ.com>** allows you to search for jobs by any one or a combination of key words, city, and state. With Online Career Center, you can get more information on member companies (possible employers), companies by category (industry, firms/agencies, contract, franchises), résumé writing, general career advice, corporate college recruiting, and colleges and universities. Job Seeker Agent is free and will search for jobs for you. Each time you log on to your account, the latest jobs fitting your qualifications will be listed. Jobs can find you if you post your résumé to OCC.

- **Net Temps <http://www.net-temps.com>** allows you to search for jobs on the Web by key words and state. Net Temps will help you get more information on employers as well. If you post your résumé to Net Temps (you can post to the whole database or to a particular state), then jobs can also find you.

On-Line Résumés

Many of the job-finding services allow you to post your own résumé in their databanks, which can make it easier for employers who are looking for someone with your unique blend of education and experiences. Usually, for you to post your résumé you will need to have a version written in hypertext markup language (HTML). Most word processing packages now have utilities that will do that for you.

Sites to Search for Internships

A great place to start looking for internships is Yahoo!'s Internships category **<http://search.yahoo.com/bin/search?p=internships>**. Some of the listings are as follows:

- Anchorage Animal Hospital
  http://www.alaska.net/~animhosp
- Campus International
  http://www2.campus-int.de/campus
- Center for Photography at Woodstock
  http://members.aol.com/cpwphoto/index.htm
- Construction Technology for Women
  http://www.contech.wittnn.com
- Environmental Careers Organization
  http://www.eco.org
- Explorations in Travel
  http://sover.net/~explore
- Fund for American Studies
  http://www.dcinternships.com
- Independent Movie Production Jobs & Internships
  http://members.aol.com/crewjobs/index.htm
- Institute for Central American Development Studies
  http://www.icadscr.com
- International Educational Resource Center
  http://www.studyabroadierc.com
- JobSource
  http://www.jobsource.com
- Multicultural Alliance
  http://www.branson.org/mca
- Rising Star Internships
  http://www.rsinternships.com
- Tripod's National Internship Directory
  http://www.tripod.com/work/internships
- Washington Center for Internships and Academic Seminars
  http://www.twc.edu
- WISE—Worldwide Internships & Service Education
  http://www.pitt.edu/~wise
- You and the Smithsonian
  http://www.si.edu/youandsi/start.htm

Sites to Search for Scholarships

To find scholarship opportunities, go to Yahoo!'s scholarship site **<http://search.yahoo.com/search?p=scholarships>**. Some of the listings are as follows:

- ExPAN Scholarship Search
  http://www.collegeboard.org/fundfinder/bin/fundfind01.pl
- Rotary Foundation Ambassadorial Scholarships
  http://www.rotary.org/foundation/educational_programs
- Scholarships & Financial Aid
  http://www.vweb.net/scholarship
- Scholarships for Women and Minorities
  http://members.aol.com/ox13qr/webpages/eyfswm1.html

Direct-Request Letters

A letter of request might ask for information on products or services, a company, or a program. Figure 18 shows a sample direct-request letter. The pattern is a simple one:

1. Present the background of the request, providing as much information as the reader needs to understand why you need help. Begin with your reason for wanting information about, for example, ski equipment or the sociology program. If you supply this background information, the respondent will be better able to meet your needs. If only one sentence of background is required, you might make the second sentence the request itself, without starting a new paragraph.

2. Make the request, in as much detail as the reader needs to be able to fulfill it.

3. Close with any additional details describing steps that will follow the granting of the request. These details could concern the next step in the process.

Persuasive Letters

When you want to use a letter or a memo to change someone's actions, use a persuasive pattern. Figure 19 shows a sample persuasive letter. Because of the difficulty of these types of situations, you will need to plan carefully. First consider these three questions:

102 Cameron Dormitory
Tonapaw College
Lewiston, MO 34226
November 15, 1997

R. J. Watson, Director of Graduate Studies
Graduate Program in Accounting and Business Law
Carlton College
Smithville, AK 43445

Dear Professor Watson:

I will be graduating next May with a B.A. in Accounting from Tonapaw College. I would like to continue my studies by getting an M.A., also in accounting.

Will you please send me the relevant information and application forms for your university's M.A. program in Accounting? I am especially interested in your statistics course requirements, financial aid packages, and internship programs. I would also like to have any information you can send about your former students' job placement.

Once I receive this information, I hope to arrange interviews with the directors of the graduate programs at the schools that look the best suited to me. I look forward to hearing from you soon, and I look forward to the possibility of meeting you in person in the near future.

Sincerely,

Robert Simpson

Figure 18. Sample Direct-Request Letter
Because this type of letter or memo asks for something the reader provides routinely, it does not need to be long or involved. If you feel that persuasion is necessary, you should consider using the persuasive form described on the following pages.

Buddig Dorm, Room 411
Campus
February 7, 1998

Professor Hiram Smith
Box 402
Department of History

Dear Professor Smith:

As you may recall, I was a student in your History 355, Contemporary Issues in Foreign Affairs, course last spring. I remember your interest in the history and politics of the Persian Gulf region, and the comment you made several times during class that it would be nice to have a course just on the history and politics of that region. Because it becomes more apparent every day that the politics of that region will be an important factor in the twenty-first century, I am requesting your approval of a three-hour independent study course next fall, on the topic of the Persian Gulf's history and politics, with particular attention to the circumstances surrounding the 1991 Persian Gulf War.

My own interest in the Persian Gulf was triggered by having spent five months there on active duty with the 577th Combat Engineers. As I came to know the people and the region better, I became more convinced that any understanding of the current political situation there that was not shaped by a thorough knowledge of the region's history was bound to be erroneous.

Completion of this independent study will bring benefits to both of us. I will fulfill another three hours of study toward my B.A. and learn more about a subject that not only interests me greatly but also is important to all of us. For you, directing the independent study will provide an opportunity to test the availability of texts and other appropriate course materials that you could use if you ever do teach this as a regular course.

I will stop by during your office hours next week to discuss this request in more detail. I hope you will agree with me that such a course is well worth doing.

Sincerely,

Rhonda Jane Jones

Figure 19. Sample Persuasive Letter
Here is an example of a persuasive letter. This student had earlier mentioned the possibility of an independent study course to her professor; he had said, "Well, you will have to convince me."

- What is the claim you are trying to make? (For example, that your reader should accept the course substitution you propose in your college curriculum.)

- What is the evidence in support of this claim? (For example, that the proposed substitute course's requirements are more demanding than those of the course the curriculum specifies.)

- What opinions will your readers have about your claims? How resistant will they be? What values or needs can you tap into to convince them? (Perhaps your readers will be more likely to approve the course substitution if you provide syllabi for both of the courses in question.)

To be effective, an argument needs to reach readers' values, attitudes, or beliefs. (The section on argumentation, pages 143–59, develops this idea more fully.) In the case of a student requesting a substitution of one course for another in her college curriculum, arguments that the proposed substitution fits the student's daily schedule better might not be effective. But her arguments might succeed if they are based on the fact that the proposed course is a higher-level course, a more difficult course, or a course that allows the student to significantly enhance her education in some other way.

You might follow this pattern for a persuasive letter or memo:

1. Begin with a reference or an appeal to the shared value, belief, or attitude. Then state your claim, connecting it to that value.

2. In the next paragraphs, state any other evidence in support of your claim.

3. In the final paragraph, more fully explain the benefits that will follow from your reader's adopting this changed belief or course of action.

COMMON WRITING PROBLEMS

PART TWO

Common Writing Problems

SENTENCE FRAGMENTS

QUICK VIEW

This Quick View shows how to identify and correct sentence fragments; the pages that follow explain these steps in more detail. A sentence fragment is a *part* of a sentence that begins with a capital letter and ends with a period, making it look like a complete sentence. But a complete sentence must meet *all three* of these conditions:

- It must contain a *subject.*
- It must contain a *complete verb.*
- It must not begin with a *subordinating word or words.*

To revise a sentence fragment, you can turn it into a complete sentence or make it part of another sentence—often the one just before or after the fragment.

Sentence Fragment

Ranch work was not strange to Audrey. *Being a native Texan.*

[The fragment lacks both a subject and a complete verb.]

Revised

Ranch work was not strange to Audrey. Being a native Texan.

or

Ranch work was not strange to Audrey. Being a native Texan. *made Audrey familiar with ranch work.*

Sentence Fragment

Someone else had already reported the fire. *When I got to a phone.*

[The fragment is a dependent clause beginning with the subordinating word *When.*]

Revised

Someone else had already reported the fire. When I got to a phone.

Testing for Fragments—An Overview

Use the following tests (explained in detail on pages 195–96) to check for sentence fragments in your writing.

1. Make sure the sentence has a subject. If the group of words lacks a subject, it is a fragment. The *subject* of a sentence is a noun (or a noun phrase) that the verb of the sentence makes a statement about or asks something about.

Serena said she was bringing her lunch. ~~Also~~ ^{and} reminded us to

bring ours.

2. Make sure the sentence has a complete verb. A group of words without a verb cannot be a sentence. The verb must also be *complete;* that is, it cannot be the *to + verb* form or the *-ed, -ing,* or *-en* form of the verb by itself.

When the tanker car derailed, it released toxic chlorine gas, requiring

evacuation of residents within a five-mile radius.

3. Make sure the clause is not introduced by a subordinating word. A subordinating word (such as *after, because, that,* or *unless*) usually begins a dependent clause, which cannot stand on its own as a sentence. (See the complete list of subordinating words and phrases on page 000.)

Tomás found his ticket after we had left for the show.

TESTING FOR FRAGMENTS—IN DETAIL

304–05

1. What is the subject? If the sentence lacks a subject, it is a fragment. The subject names the "do-er" of the verb. (The only exception is sentences in the *passive voice*. In this case, the subject receives the verb's action, as in "The book was borrowed by Henry"; here, *book* is the subject, receiving the action of *was borrowed,* and *Henry,* the object of the preposition *by,* is the do-er.)

Jack played all his favorite songs/̲And took requests.

[The fragment "And took requests" lacks a subject.]

The play, ~~was~~ an enormous hit/̲ Was performed on Broadway over 500 times.

or

The play was an enormous hit. Was performed on Broadway over 500 times.

[The fragment "Was performed . . . 500 times" lacks a subject.]

304

Exception: An instruction or a command, in which *you* is the *understood subject,* is not a fragment.

[You] Make a copy of the file.

2. What is the verb? Is it complete? A group of words without a complete verb cannot be a sentence. Testing for a complete verb has two steps:

a. Make sure there is some form of a verb in the sentence.

294–304

b. Make sure the verb form you have found is not a *verbal.* Verbals include infinitives (the *to + verb* form), participles (the *-ed, -ing,* and *-en* forms of verbs used as modifiers), and gerunds (the *-ed, -ing,* and *-en* forms of verbs used as nouns).

Getting greedier all the time/̲Charlie saves more and more of his money.

[*Getting* is a verbal, not a complete verb.]

Chelsea finally made it to the airport/̲Thanks to her neighbor.

["Thanks to her neighbor" does not contain a verb.]

3. Is there an independent clause? Even if both a subject and a complete verb are present, they must be part of an independent clause. (An *independent clause* is a group of words that contains a subject and a complete verb and can stand on its own as a sentence.) Make sure the clause you are testing does not begin with a subordinating word or phrase (*after, because, unless,* and the others listed below). These words introduce *dependent clauses.* If the sentence does begin with a dependent clause, be sure that clause is connected to an independent clause.

304–07

Subordinating Words and Phrases

after	if	that	whereas
although	in order that	though	wherever
as	in order to	unless	which
as if	now that	until	while
as though	once	what	who
because	rather than	whatever	whoever
before	since	when	whom
even if	so that	whenever	whose
even though	than	where	why

(For more on independent and dependent clauses, see *Clauses,* pages 335–37.)

Then came the fall of the Berlin Wall. Which signaled the end of the Cold War.
[*Which* introduces a dependent clause.]

Exception: A few of the subordinating words and phrases listed above—notably *who, what, where, when, why, how,* and *which*—can be used to introduce an independent clause if it is a question (as in "Where will the class meet?").

Then came Professor Longhair. Who put jazz and blues together in a new way.
[*Who,* a subordinating word here, introduces a dependent clause.]

Interrogative Independent Clause
Who put jazz and blues together in a new way?
[*Who* is an interrogative here.]

REVISING FRAGMENTS

You can revise a sentence fragment in many ways. Here are two of the most common:

- Attach the fragment to the sentence right before it or right after it (depending on where it seems to work better).
- Make whatever changes are required within the fragment itself to make it a separate sentence.

These examples illustrate both methods. Notice how the meaning of each sentence in the resulting pairs is slightly different, depending on how the fragment has been revised.

Sentence Fragment

Sarah took out her own hand axe. *Her razor-sharp Estwing.*

["Her razor-sharp Estwing" is a fragment; it lacks a verb.]

Fragment Revised to Combine into One Sentence

Sarah took out her own hand axe, *h*er razor-sharp Estwing.

Fragment Revised to Make Two Sentences

Sarah took out her own hand axe. Her razor-sharp *Estwing was honed*.

Annie Dillard has a magical touch with words *and always gets* their sound just right.

["Gets their sound just right" lacks a subject.]

or

Annie Dillard has a magical touch with words. *She gets* their sound just right.

At times, one method of revision will seem clearly superior to another, either because the resulting construction fits the rest of the paragraph better or because it is stylistically more pleasing. (For additional examples of revision options, see *Sentences*, pages 392–94.)

I will support the law of the land. Being a true American.

or

I will support the law of the land. ~~Being~~ *I am* a true American.

[The fragment is based on a verbal (present participle), *being,* a form of the verb *to be.*]

The Chieftains play traditional Irish music. *w* With great skill.

or

The Chieftains play traditional Irish music. ~~With~~ *They have achieved* great skill.

[The fragment is a prepositional phrase; it lacks both a subject and a verb.]

We enjoyed listening to the Mervins. *a* A classic Seattle bar band.

or

We enjoyed listening to the Mervins. *They are a* A classic Seattle bar band.

When to Use Fragments

Sentence fragments may be used—with care—in a few situations, such as advertising, informal writing, and dialogue.

In Advertising

"Less filling, tastes great!"

For Emphasis

Living in Miami is not so different from living in Maine. Except for the climate.

As an Answer

Would she ever be a writer? Probably not. Would she keep trying? Yes.

In Dialogue

"What are you doing?" Jack asked.
"Nothing."
"When do you expect to start doing something?" he pried.
"Never."
"How do you intend to spend your life, then?" he kept on.
"Loafing at my leisure."

For a Transition

First we won the season opener. And now the second game. We just seem to keep right on winning.

As an Exclamation

With one minute to go in the game and the visiting team driving toward what would be a winning touchdown, the 70,000 home-team fans tried to urge the defensive team on. "Defense! Defense! Defense!"

Caution: If you are tempted to use a fragment, find out how your teacher feels about fragments in writing assignments. Some instructors object to them on principle, but others may allow the occasional fragment used for a particular effect.

PRACTICE

I. Revising Sentence Fragments

Revise each of these fragments two ways: first, to create one sentence; second, to create two sentences. The first fragment is revised for you as an example. (Where necessary, make other minor changes in the sentences as you see fit.) If you feel that one of the two resulting revisions is clearly better (for example, less choppy) than the other, underline the one you prefer.

1. For decades, the assembly line earned Detroit companies billions of dollars. And gave Detroit auto executives huge salaries.

Revised to Combine into One Sentence	Revised to Make Two Sentences
For decades, the assembly line earned Detroit companies billions of dollars and gave auto executives huge salaries.	For decades, the assembly line earned Detroit companies billions of dollars. It also gave auto executives huge salaries.

2. My parents just won a huge prize. Two free weeks in Hawaii!
3. Betty had previously owned the car. That my parents bought for me.
4. I will arrange to take a makeup exam. Being a conscientious student.
5. Bart Simpson took a dare once too often. With disastrous results.

6. The book finally found its audience. People who want to know how to write books.

7. The dream finally took on a life of its own. One that included a cleaner environment for everyone.

8. The challenger dared the incumbent to debate her. In front of a live television audience.

9. I have finally discovered the right house. Which I want to buy.

10. If people want to run their own lives. They need to accept the consequences.

II. Identifying and Revising Sentence Fragments

Rewrite the following short passage to eliminate the fragments.

As a child, I spent one month each summer at a camp in Maine. From the time I was seven until I turned fifteen. Many of my friends remember their camp days with great nostalgia. Recalling the camaraderie of the campfires, the adventures of hiking, canoeing, camping out under the stars, the thrill of a tug on a fishing line or a no-hitter pitched against a rival camp. These are the people who were always eager to attend the camp reunions. Held in dead of winter, usually in the social room of one church or another, and complete with home-baked brownies, slides of activities from the previous summer, and a pep talk from the camp director about what delights lay in store for those of us returning in the summer. When the letter came announcing the date and place for the reunion, calls were made to and received from summer friends little thought of in the intervening months. People whose company I had enjoyed in July, but whom I had rarely thought of since. Caught up in the excitement of another school year and the daily routines of suburban life. Routines that, to be honest, I enjoyed. And even missed during that month away each summer. Somehow, the romance of camp life never took root in my imagination. And while I never said or felt that I did not want to go each summer. Neither did I relish the return as some of my companions did. I always thought of it as "going away." Rather than "going back." A difference of one word reflecting a completely different sense of where I felt my truest and best life was lived.

COMMA SPLICES

■ QUICK VIEW

This Quick View shows how to correct comma splices, an error that occurs when two independent clauses are joined with only a comma. (An *independent clause* contains a subject and a complete verb and can stand on its own as a sentence.) Independent clauses should be connected with a comma plus a *coordinating conjunction* (*and, but, or, nor, for, so,* or *yet*) or a *subordinating word* (such as *although, because,* or *which*), or with a semicolon. The pages that follow this Quick View provide more detail.

A comma splice occurs when two or more independent clauses are connected with only a comma. Sometimes the comma is accompanied by a *conjunctive adverb* (such as *however* or *therefore*) or a transitional word or phrase (such as *in other words*), but the result is still a comma splice.

Comma Splice

He left the house, his wallet was still on the table.

[To connect these two independent clauses correctly, you could use either a comma *plus* a coordinating conjunction or a semicolon.]

Revised

He left the house, *but* his wallet was still on the table.

or

He left the house; his wallet was still on the table.

[A semicolon rather than a comma needs to precede *his wallet.*]

The tax bill was high; however, we found the money somehow.

[A semicolon rather than a comma needs to precede *however.*]

Testing for Comma Splices

1. Check to see if the sentence contains two or more independent clauses. An independent clause contains a subject and a complete verb and can stand on its own as a sentence, such as "The Berlin Wall fell." A dependent clause begins with a subordinating word such as *after, when,* or *if* and can never stand alone as a sentence—for example, "when the Berlin Wall fell."

2. Next, check the way the clauses are joined. There are two acceptable ways to connect independent clauses:

- a comma plus a coordinating conjunction (*and, but, or, nor, for, so,* and *yet*)
- a semicolon (or, in special circumstances, a colon)

Two independent clauses joined any other way make a comma splice.

3. You can also check for comma splices by underlining the clauses. If you are not sure whether what you have underlined is an independent clause, circle its subject and double-underline its verb; then make sure it does not begin with a subordinating word or phrase.

Comma Splice:

A small person still can compete at the very highest levels of soccer,

that person has to be fast and tough.

[The two independent clauses are joined only by a comma.]

(For more on recognizing independent and dependent clauses, see *Clauses,* pages 335–37.)

REVISING COMMA SPLICES

There are four revision techniques for eliminating comma splices:

- Use a period and create two sentences.
- Use a comma and a coordinating conjunction to create a *compound sentence.*
- Use a semicolon (or, in special conditions, a colon) to create a compound sentence.
- Use a subordinating conjunction and a dependent clause to create a *complex sentence.*

Use a Period and Create Two Sentences

One simple way to correct a comma splice is to place a period between the independent clauses, thus making two separate sentences:

Eventually I want to go to graduate school in St. Louis, my goals are

to study journalism and get a job at a small-town paper.

Create a Compound Sentence

You can also correct a comma splice by using a coordinating conjunction (*and, but, or, nor, for, so,* and *yet*) preceded by a comma. Your choice of the right coordinating conjunction can help your readers understand the relationship between the independent clauses more exactly. The result is a compound sentence: a sentence with two or more independent clauses.

At midnight my roommate couldn't find anything to eat in the

room, she went to the convenience store for a dozen doughnuts.

Sherlock Holmes never said "Elementary, my dear Watson" in any

of Arthur Conan Doyle's stories, he did use the word *elementary* to

describe the deductions he made.

One additional way to create a compound sentence is to use a pair of *correlative conjunctions (either . . . or; not only . . . but also)* to create a balance between the two clauses:

> *Either* these negotiations will be successful, *or* fighting may once again break out.

> *Not only* are there many new players on the team this year, *but also* the league has been restructured.

Punctuating Compound Sentences

Use a comma before the conjunction in compound sentences to separate the two independent clauses clearly:

> William Cody's Wild West Shows began in the 1880s, *and* Annie Oakley's mock battles were his biggest draw.

> Jazz originated among black musicians in nineteenth-century New Orleans, *yet* their Dixieland music also gave birth to what we now call rock and roll.

Another Way to Create a Compound Sentence

If the ideas expressed in the two independent clauses are closely related, you may correct the comma splice with a semicolon or with a colon, thus creating a compound sentence.

Use a Semicolon

The semicolon is especially appropriate to connect independent clauses that are closely related and about equal in length. The semicolon can be used on its own or with a conjunctive adverb (listed below). Each conjunctive adverb signals a slightly different relationship between the two clauses.

Conjunctive Adverbs

accordingly	finally	likewise	similarly
also	furthermore	meanwhile	specifically
anyway	hence	moreover	still
besides	however	nevertheless	subsequently
certainly	incidentally	next	then
consequently	indeed	nonetheless	therefore
conversely	instead	otherwise	thus

Note that adding the conjunctive adverb does not change the need for a semicolon to join the independent clauses:

Microwave ovens can interfere with the electronic impulses sent out by pacemakers; *therefore,* stores and restaurants must post warnings wherever these ovens are in use.

When you use a conjunctive adverb after the semicolon, a comma normally follows the adverb, as in the preceding example. Note also that the conjunctive adverb does not always have to follow immediately after the semicolon, as in this revision of the previous example:

Microwave ovens can interfere with the electronic impulses sent out by pacemakers; stores and restaurants, *therefore,* must post warnings wherever these ovens are in use.

Use a Colon

A colon can be used to link independent clauses in one special situation: when the second clause explains or provides an example of the idea stated in the first clause:

Pepper is not very good as a hunting dog: he hates to get dirty.

Being a hospital volunteer has taught me an important lesson: a caring family is as important as medicine itself.

Researchers cannot guarantee that the new drug is safe: not enough tests have been done on it.

Create a Complex Sentence

You can also correct a comma splice by making one of the independent clauses a dependent clause, thus creating a *complex sentence.* To make a clause dependent, add a subordinating word or phrase, such as a subordinating conjunction or a relative pronoun. The subordinating conjunctions and relative pronouns that introduce all dependent clauses can indicate many different relationships among ideas.

Subordinating Words and Phrases

after	as if	before	if
although	as though	even if	in order that
as	because	even though	in order to

now that	that	when	while
once	though	whenever	who
rather than	unless	where	whoever
since	until	whereas	whom
so that	what	wherever	whose
than	whatever	which	why

When
Stephanie walked into the cafeteria, she didn't see anyone she knew.
^

or

although
Stephanie walked into the cafeteria, she didn't see anyone she knew.
^

or

Before
Stephanie walked into the cafeteria, she didn't see anyone she knew.
^

Punctuating Complex Sentences

When the dependent clause begins the sentence, follow it with a comma, as in the first and third sample sentences above. When the dependent clause *follows* the independent clause, as in the second example above, you do not need a comma. (See pages 336–37, 389.)

PRACTICE

I. Creating Compound Sentences

Correct the following comma splices by turning them into compound sentences, adding an appropriate coordinating conjunction (*and, but, or, nor, for, so,* and *yet*) or conjunctive adverb (listed on page 204). The first one has been done for you.

1. The College of Engineering may institute its own yearlong writing course, it may continue to have its students take the writing courses offered by the College of Liberal Arts.

   Revised: The College of Engineering may institute its own yearlong writing course, <u>or</u> it may continue to have its students take the writing courses offered by the College of Liberal Arts.

2. We approached Atlanta about 5:00, we took the I-285 route that bypasses downtown.

Comma
Splices

3. You have never lied to me, I hope you never will.
4. The IQ test should not be used to place children in ability groups, it measures cultural background as well as intelligence.
5. Thompson was not supposed to compete in this event, I brought my camera just in case she did.
6. Students usually like their Spanish classes, they often dislike the audiotape labs.
7. Mary had suffered for years from the pain of rheumatoid arthritis, she retained her optimistic outlook on life.
8. After twenty hours of steady snow and high winds, the highway crews could not clear the roads of the heavy drifts, the turnpike was shut down between Worcester and Albany.
9. We rejected the original plan to drive across the country, we decided to fly to Los Angeles, rent a car, and drive up to Seattle.

II. Creating Complex Sentences

Correct the following comma splices by creating complex sentences. Insert an appropriate subordinating word or phrase (see the list on pages 205–06) and decide whether to place the dependent clause at the beginning or the end of the sentence. You may also need to change or remove a word or two. The first sentence has been done for you.

1. The hills were a uniform light green, they reminded me of where I grew up.

    Revised: <u>Because</u> the hills were a uniform light green, they reminded me of where I grew up.

2. The fire alarm went off, the children all moved quickly out of the building.
3. Sitting on the two chairs were the two leaders, they were tired after talking all night.
4. Molly Ivins has a way with words, Southerners can really appreciate it.
5. A doctor can do wonders for a problem like that, you have to want to be cured first.
6. She likes to dance, she sat down for an hour after the samba.

III. Using Semicolons and Colons

Revise the following comma splices by adding either a semicolon or a colon. The first sentence has been done for you.

1. For kleptomaniacs, stealing is not a matter of personal need or economic necessity, it is a compulsion to take items of no use to them.

   Revised: For kleptomaniacs, stealing is not a matter of personal need or economic necessity: it is a compulsion to take items of no use to them.

2. Flags can represent the goals of a nation, the crossed hammer and sickle of the former Soviet Union were said to symbolize the union of industry and agriculture.

3. High schools in the United States generally want to teach their students about citizenship, today's students really need to learn about community action.

4. Many electronics products decrease in cost after the first model year, personal computers and keyboards now sell for less than half of their introductory prices.

5. Baseball is called America's pastime, most Americans today seem to prefer football or basketball.

6. After rethinking her first impulse and organizing her large collection of tape recordings, Clara decided against buying a CD player, she chose a new tape deck.

IV. Identifying and Revising Comma Splices

Four of the six sentences in the paragraph have comma splice problems. Rewrite the paragraph to eliminate those errors, trying to use all four techniques demonstrated in this chapter.

Komatsu is a company in Japan that builds tractors and other kinds of agricultural equipment. This company has been more successful at innovation than many U.S. firms, it is making Komatsu increasingly successful in the U.S. market. At Komatsu the head of the company establishes each year's goal for innovation, one year it might be to make Komatsu's quality the best in the world. Managers then set specific targets to accomplish that goal, the targets are always based on outperforming specific competitors. Managers don't use general targets like "invent the tractor of the future," instead they set specific goals, one might be to reduce costs 30% below Caterpillar's. Then they start programs to accomplish each goal and institute processes to measure their achievements.

RUN-ON SENTENCES

▦ *QUICK VIEW*

This Quick View shows how to correct run-on sentences (sometimes called fused sentences), an error that occurs when two or more independent clauses have no punctuation separating them. (An *independent clause* has a subject and a complete verb and can stand on its own as a sentence.) Two independent clauses may properly be separated with a period, with a comma plus a coordinating conjunction (*and, but, or, nor, for, so,* or *yet*), or with a semicolon (with or without a conjunctive adverb, such as *however*), or with a colon. Or one clause may be turned into a dependent clause with the addition of a subordinating conjunction or a relative pronoun. The pages that follow this Quick View explain revision of run-on sentences in more detail.

Winter came early this year,~the first snow came before Halloween.

The song was popular~its tune was heard everywhere.

Double-click on *Reload*~the image should come right back.

or

~~Double-~~click on *Reload*~the image should come right back.

Testing for Run-On Sentences

1. Check to see if the sentence contains two or more independent clauses. An independent clause contains a subject and a complete verb and can stand on its own as a sentence, such as "The rain came down in torrents." A dependent clause begins with a subordinating word, such as *after, when,* or *if,* and can never stand alone as a sentence—for example, "After the rain came down in torrents."

2. Next, check the way the clauses are joined. There are two acceptable ways to connect independent clauses:

- with a comma plus a coordinating conjunction (*and, but, or, nor, for, so,* and *yet*)
- with a semicolon (or, in special circumstances, a colon)

209

Two independent clauses joined with only a comma (and no co-ordinating conjunction) are a comma splice (discussed in the previous section); two independent clauses joined without any punctuation or connecting word are a run-on sentence. (For further discussion about recognizing independent and dependent clauses, see *Clauses,* pages 335–37.)

REVISING RUN-ON SENTENCES

There are four revision techniques for eliminating run-on sentences:

- Use a period to create two sentences.
- Use a comma and a coordinating conjunction to create a *compound sentence.*
- Use a semicolon (or, in special circumstances, a colon) to create a compound sentence. A conjunctive adverb (such as *however, nonetheless,* or *therefore*) may be used with the semicolon.
- Use a subordinating conjunction or a relative pronoun to make one of the clauses dependent and thus create a *complex sentence.*

Use a Period to Create Two Sentences

You may choose to correct a run-on sentence by placing a period between the two independent clauses, thus creating two sentences. Use this revision technique when there is not a close relationship between the two ideas.

Jim Thorpe was the best performer in track and field at the 1912

Olympic Games͵*H*he was also a successful college football player.

Use a Comma and a Coordinating Conjunction to Create a Compound Sentence

You can also correct a run-on sentence by inserting a coordinating conjunction (*and, but, or, nor, for, so,* and *yet*) preceded by a comma. The right coordinating conjunction will help your readers better understand the relationship between the clauses of the compound sentence:

Dad hid the presents in the attic͵*for* he didn't want any of us children to find them.

To indicate a balanced relationship between the two clauses, you may also choose to use a pair of *correlative conjunctions (either . . . or; not only . . . but also):*

Not only will the

^The new registration procedures ~~will~~ work better for the registrar's

, *but also*

office the students will be happier ~~too~~.
         ^

Use a Semicolon or a Colon
to Create a Compound Sentence

When the ideas in a compound sentence are closely related, you may join the two independent clauses with a semicolon:

> Three planes were waiting for the same gate^two groups of passengers were going to be unhappy.

To indicate the nature of the relationship between two independent clauses, you can use a conjunctive adverb (see the list on page 204) in addition to the semicolon:

; however,

> The game was already hopelessly lost the band seemed determined
                                         ^
> to keep people cheering.

When the second clause explains or provides an example of the idea stated in the first clause, you may use a colon rather than a semicolon to connect the two clauses:

> Time was always running out on Jim.^today's test was but one more
>
> example.

Use a Subordinating Conjunction or a Relative
Pronoun to Create a Complex Sentence

If you make one of the clauses in a run-on sentence a dependent clause, you have created a *complex sentence.* The subordinating conjunctions and relative pronouns (such as *after, because, if, since, until,* or *which*) create particular relationships between the two clauses (see the complete list of these words on pages 205–06).

Because she

^She was hungry, she got into line right away.
                    ^

, which

Each gene has a particular structure it normally remembers ~~the struc-~~
                                       ^
~~ture~~ every time the gene is duplicated.

PRACTICE

I. Creating Compound Sentences

Correct the following run-on sentences by turning them into compound sentences. The first one has been done for you.

1. Our experimental car approached the wall smoothly the brakes did not activate.

   Revised: Our experimental car approached the wall smoothly, but the brakes did not activate.

2. Women's basketball is taking off on all levels two professional leagues in the U.S. may be one too many.

3. Recently, professional drawing tools have become easier to use new computer programs have simplified the process of creating clear and accurate graphics.

4. Shimano shifters have long dominated the U.S. market today there are several challengers to that dominance.

5. Annie decided not to go to the concert she didn't have enough money for tickets.

6. Company policies can never take the place of good judgment by employees the policies do provide a general place to start.

II. Creating Complex Sentences

Correct the following run-on sentences by creating complex sentences. You may need to change a word or two or to move the dependent clause to a different place in the sentence. The first one has been done for you.

1. Jimmy Carter has been out of the presidency he seems to have become a much more interesting person.

   Revised: Since Jimmy Carter has been out of the presidency, he seems to have become a much more interesting person.

2. The poet William Stafford did not receive the recognition he deserved his politics were out of step with the majority.

3. Few English composers have been famous for writing symphonies that all changed in this century.

4. Television can help you pass the time television can never help you improve it.

5. Ursula LeGuin is a famous author her mother may have led a more creative life.

6. A pine cone was rolled in peanut butter it was then rolled in bird seed.

III. Using Semicolons and Colons

Revise the following run-on sentences using either a semicolon or a colon. The first one has been done for you.

1. For people who are clinically depressed, simply finishing a routine task can be almost impossible doing the dishes or putting away laundry seems like a gargantuan chore.

> **Revised:** For people who are clinically depressed, simply finishing a routine task can be almost impossible: doing the dishes or putting away laundry seems like a gargantuan chore.

2. Four hundred people applied for the twenty jobs many went away disappointed.

3. Esteban was admitted to Cornell Freda was admitted to State Tech.

4. Many people think Key West has become very commercial the urge to turn something unique into profit tends to destroy uniqueness.

5. Salamanders are found in many places the Southern Appalachians may be home to the greatest numbers.

6. Time is a river we swim in it or are drowned by it.

IV. Identifying and Revising Run-On Sentences

Rewrite this paragraph to eliminate the run-on sentences. Try to use a variety of techniques.

The effect of the Internet on college classrooms varies from subject to subject a few elements come up again and again. Research to discover what someone else has said does not have to be done in the library it can be done right in the dorm room. Library hours do not limit student access to many kinds of documents book and movie reviews are just two examples. Along with the vastly improved access students have to documents come some problems an important one is that plagiarism becomes easier. Students who regularly surf the Web can find many term papers that are easily available students need to know that their professors probably spend more time surfing than the students do. Thus we see again the double-edged sword of technology students can easily lay their hands on more information than ever before they can also get in trouble more easily.

VERB ERRORS

■ QUICK VIEW

294–304 This Quick View shows the most common problems with verbs: subject-verb agreement, form, tense, and mood errors. The pages that follow explain these problems in more detail. (For a complete discussion of verbs, see *Verbs,* pages 416–27.)

Subject-Verb Agreement Errors

Subjects and verbs must agree in *number*—both singular or both plural. The subject always determines whether the verb should be singular or plural.

> *helps*
> The design of the new cars ~~help~~ their gas mileage.

> [A prepositional phrase (*of the new cars*) separating the subject (*design*) from the verb (*help*) has fooled the writer into making the verb agree with the plural object of the prepositional phrase (*cars*) instead of the singular subject (*design*).]

> *were*
> At the front of the procession ~~was~~ the president of the college and
>
> the dean of students.

> [The inverted sentence order, in which the verb precedes the subject, has fooled the writer into using a singular verb, *was,* with a plural (compound) subject, the *president* of the college and the *dean* of students.]

Form Errors

Verbs change form to indicate time (tense) and convey certain other information. *Regular verbs* change only their endings (*talk, talked*), whereas *irregular verbs* change internally (*sing, sang, sung; go, went, gone*). Most verb form errors involve the wrong forms of irregular verbs (especially *lie* and *lay* and *sit* and *set*) or dropped endings (*s, es, d, ed*). The most common irregular verbs are listed under *Verbs,* pages 418–21. Beyond that, a dictionary is the best guide to verb forms.

> *swam*
> Irina had never ~~swam~~ that fast before.

He ~~laid~~ *lay* down to rest awhile.

Why don't you ~~set~~ *sit* with her at church?

Some spoken dialects of English regularly drop the final *ed* or *s* from some verbs. Speakers of such dialects and people who grew up reading and writing languages other than English often forget to add those endings when they are writing.

John ~~sing~~ *sings* like a professional.

Inappropriate Shifts in Tense

Tense shifts distort the sequence of actions being described:

> When they received our gift, they ~~had~~ sent a thank-you note
>
> immediately.

In this example, the simple past action of the first verb (*received*) seems to be preceded by the past perfect action of the second verb (*had sent*); that is, they seem to have sent the thank-you note before receiving the gift, a sequence of events contrary to the order in which the events actually happened. The solution to the problem is to put the two verbs in the same tense.

Inappropriate shifts in tense occur not only in single sentences but also in paragraphs and groups of paragraphs. (For a complete discussion of verb tenses, see *Verbs*, pages 421–24.)

Mood Errors

The mood of a verb tells whether the verb expresses

- a fact (*indicative mood*)
- a doubt, a condition wished for, or a condition contrary to fact (*subjunctive mood*)
- a command (*imperative mood*)

The most common mood error is use of the indicative rather than the subjunctive to express doubt or a wish or to describe something that is contrary to fact. (For a complete discussion of mood, see *Verbs*, pages 425–27.)

I wish my refund check ~~was~~ *were* already here.

Inappropriate Shifts in Mood

As with verb tense, make shifts in mood only for good reasons. Especially, be careful not to slip accidentally into the imperative mood, the one used for instructions or commands.

> We should all be grateful for the sacrifices of the people who fought in
>
> *Each of us should take*
> World War II. ~~Take~~ time to remember that freedom comes with a price.

SUBJECT-VERB AGREEMENT ERRORS

Subjects and their verbs always need to agree in *number*—singular or plural. No matter where the subject appears in the sentence, the subject always determines whether the verb will be singular or plural. Errors in subject-verb agreement can occur for several reasons, which are discussed on the following pages.

Subject and Verb Separated by Modifiers

When other words come between the subject and the verb, be careful not to let the number of the verb be determined by the closest noun. The *subject*—which is not necessarily the closest noun to the verb—always controls the number of the verb.

> Of all my compact discs, Nancy Wilson's collection of rainy day
>
> *makes*
> songs ~~make~~ me feel the loneliest.
> [Although *songs* is plural, the subject, *collection,* is singular.]

> The new word processing programs that have every kind of option
>
> *are*
> ~~is~~ the best yet.
> [The subject, *programs,* is plural; the verb should be plural as well.]

> *is*
> Traditional country music played on acoustic instruments ~~are~~ still
>
> popular in many places.

Compound Subjects Joined by the Conjunction *And*

When the parts of a compound subject are joined by *and*, the verb is always plural. It doesn't matter whether the individual parts of that compound subject are singular or plural.

> *Jack and Tom* are going with us.
> *Jack and the other boys* are going with us.
> *Jack and I* are going.
> *Both Jack and I* are going.

Agreement Error Revised

are
My answering machine and my CD player ~~is~~ two electrical appli-
ances I cannot live without.

Exception: Certain pairs of nouns joined by *and* work as a
unit and are treated as if they were one-word, singular subjects:

Research and development is our company's weakness.

Ham and eggs is not the most healthful breakfast.

Compound Subjects Joined by the Conjunctions *Or* or *Nor*

When the elements of a compound subject are joined by *or* or *nor*,
the element closer to the verb determines whether the verb is singular or plural. If the element of the subject closer to the verb is
singular, the verb is singular. If it is plural, the verb is plural.

Either Karen or her daughter is going to pick me up.

Either Karen or her daughters are going to pick me up.

Neither the tires nor the alignment is in good shape.

Neither the alignment nor the tires are in good shape.

Agreement Error Revised

are
Either a school bus or parents' cars ~~is~~ going to be used to take the
students on the field trip.

Subjects That Are Collective Nouns

When the subject is a collective noun (such as *group* or *team*), the
verb may be either singular or plural, depending on the context.
Collective nouns are treated as *singular* when the individuals
within the group are considered as a group, and as *plural* when
the individuals within the group are considered as individuals.

Common Collective Nouns

army	clergy	enemy	jury
audience	committee	family	majority
band	company	flock	number
class	crowd	group	team

Singular Uses of Collective Nouns

Our *band* of happy travelers <u>is</u> leaving now.

The *majority* <u>is</u> always right.

Plural Uses of Collective Nouns

Our *band* of unhappy travelers <u>are</u> going their own ways.

The *majority* <u>are</u> bilingual.

Agreement Errors Revised

The class ~~are~~ *is* going on a field trip to the museum.

The class of 1998 ~~is~~ *are* going their separate ways immediately after

graduation.

Subjects That Are Indefinite Pronouns

When the subject is an indefinite pronoun, the verb may be either singular or plural, depending on the pronoun and its context. Indefinite pronouns are those that do not specify a particular person or thing.

Common Indefinite Pronouns

all	each	much	other
another	either	neither	some
any	everybody	nobody	somebody
anybody	everyone	none	someone
anyone	everything	no one	something
anything	few	nothing	such
both	many	one	

Most indefinite pronouns are singular and take a singular verb:

Nobody <u>is</u> going to the game.

Someone <u>is</u> going to pay for this.

Anyone <u>is</u> better company than Gary.

Such <u>is</u> life.

One <u>is</u> all I want.

Everybody <u>is</u> going.

Some indefinite pronouns (such as *both, few, many, others,* and *several*) are plural and take a plural verb.

Many <u>are</u> volunteering, but *few* <u>are</u> actually showing up.

A few indefinite pronouns (such as *all, some, none, more, most,* and *any*) can be either singular or plural, depending on their context:

Singular Use of Indefinite Pronoun

All of this book <u>is</u> as good as the first chapter.

[*All* can be either singular or plural. Here its number is set by the object of the prepositional phrase that follows it.]

Plural Use of Indefinite Pronoun

All the books <u>were</u> by one author.

Agreement Errors Revised

Some of the Kool-Aid ~~have~~ *has* been spilled.

[Because *Kool-Aid,* the object of the prepositional phrase, is singular, the indefinite pronoun (*Some*) should be treated as singular also.]

Some of the passengers is *are* getting off here.

[Because *passengers,* the object of the prepositional phrase, is plural, the indefinite pronoun (*Some*) should be treated as plural also.]

Subjects That Are Relative Pronouns

When the subject of a dependent clause is a relative pronoun, such as *which, that,* or *who,* the verb should be singular or plural, depending on the number of the pronoun's antecedent.

The presiding officer suddenly had a great <u>idea</u>, *which* <u>was</u> to table the new motion and end the meeting.

[Here *which* refers to *idea*—a singular noun—so *which* is considered singular and is followed by the singular form of the verb, *was.*]

I called up two of my <u>friends</u> *who* <u>seem</u> to understand my problem.

[Because *who* refers to *friends*—a plural noun—*who* is considered to be plural here and is followed by the plural form of the verb, *seem.*]

Verb Errors

FORM ERRORS

Common errors in verb form include errors in irregular verbs and errors in verb endings (*s, es, d, ed*).

Regular versus Irregular Verbs

Most English verbs form their past tense and past participles by adding *ed* or *d*. However, the irregular verbs form their past tense and past participles in irregular ways. The three most common irregular verbs are *be*, *have*, and *do*.

	Present		Past		Past Participle
	Singular	*Plural*	*Singular*	*Plural*	
to be	I am	we are	I was	we were	been
	you are	you are	you were	you were	
	he, she, it is	they are	he, she, it was	they were	
to have	I have	we have	I had	we had	had
	you have	you have	you had	you had	
	he, she, it has	they have	he, she, it had	they had	
to do	I do	we do	I did	we did	done
	you do	you do	you did	you did	
	he, she, it does	they do	he, she, it did	they did	

Other common irregular verbs are *lay, awake, choose, dive, spring,* and *swim*. (For a more extensive list, see *Verbs*, pages 418–21.)

When you use an irregular verb, make sure you're using the correct form:

written
Gerald had ~~wrote~~ a letter to his teacher explaining his absences.

[This verb should be in past perfect tense, formed by *had* plus the past participle, *written*.]

If you are in doubt about the correct form of a verb, you can consult a dictionary. Dictionaries nearly always list all the forms of each verb. For example, the *American Heritage* entry for *write* lists *wrote, written, writing, writes;* those are (in order) the past tense, past participle, present participle, and third-person singular present tense of *write*.

Verb Endings: *s, es, d, ed*

Most regular verbs in English form the third-person singular (*he, she* or *it* does something) by adding either *s* or *es*.

The teacher *requests* your presence in class tomorrow.

Ann *protests* her innocence.

Phish's music *takes* you away.

Susan always *tosses* her coat onto the bed.

Some spoken dialects of English regularly drop the ending *s* or *es* in informal settings.

Spoken Dialect Forms

"The teacher *request* your presence in class tomorrow."

"Ann *protest* her innocence."

"Phish's music *take* you away."

"Susan always *toss* her coat onto the bed."

In standard written English those dropped endings need to be re-stored: *requests, protests, takes,* and *tosses.*

Regular verbs in English form their past tense and past par-ticiples by adding *d* or *ed.* Some spoken dialects do not regularly add these endings.

Spoken Dialect Forms

"She *love* him until he *die.*"

"That book *change* my life."

In standard written English, *d* or *ed* needs to be restored.

Correct Written Forms

She *loved* him until he *died.*

That book *changed* my life.

If you speak in a dialect that drops this *s, es, d,* or *ed,* you need to be especially careful to include the standard endings when you are writing. During your finishing stages, look for verbs that are in the present tense. Then look at the subject to determine whether the verb is third person. (*Third person* is the form that uses *he, she,* or *it* plus the verb.) If the verb is third person, and it is a regular verb, it needs to end in *s* or *es.* Be equally careful with the past tense of regular verbs; make sure your writing is not accidentally following your speaking.

Verb Errors

INAPPROPRIATE SHIFTS IN TENSE

Readers expect verb tenses to change only when there are changes in the time of the action being described. Most verb tense errors involve shifting verb tenses in ways that violate the action sequence being described. Sequence-of-tense errors were discussed at the beginning of the Quick View (page 215); a similar error in longer passages involves consistency of tense—shifts in tense that are unnecessary and inconsistent.

> **Inappropriate Shifts in Tense:** In 1895 Borglif *developed* the system of professional craft training that still *characterized* German factory development today. Under that system, young men *go* out to learn their trades under the leadership of a mentor, who *was* a senior craftsperson and basically *ran* the shop. The young men's schooling thus *is divided* into assisting a master craftsperson and getting hands-on experience.

If that passage were talking about something that occurred in 1895 but does not continue today, it should stay in past tense (for completed past action). But the words *still* and *today* in the first sentence indicate that the passage is describing something that occurred in 1895 and continues today. In this situation, you can leave the first verb in past tense (because it refers to 1895) but then switch immediately to present for the rest.

> **Revised:** In 1895 Borglif *developed* the system of professional craft training that still *characterizes* German factory development today. Under that system, young men *go* out to learn their trades under the leadership of a mentor, who *is* a senior craftsperson and basically *runs* the shop. The young men's schooling thus *is divided* into assisting a master craftsperson and getting hands-on experience.

Thus a past tense verb (*developed*) is followed by present tense verbs (*characterizes, go,* and so on), which reflect the continuing aspect of the action.

Exception: When you are writing about literature—unless you are writing about literary history—you should simply use the present tense, sometimes called the *literary present.*

> The central character of "The Love Song of J. Alfred Prufrock" *provides* an archetype of modern life. Prufrock *is* afraid to stand out from the crowd, afraid to speak up, afraid to be misunderstood. In his fear and timidity, he *leads* a more miserable life than he would if he once in a while let himself stand up and stand out. How to es-

cape this paralysis that *comes* from being too conscious of one's own consciousness *is* the postmodern dilemma.

(For more on verb tenses, see *Verbs,* pages 421–24.)

INAPPROPRIATE SHIFTS IN MOOD

299–302

The *mood* of a verb tells whether the verb expresses a fact or a factual condition (indicative mood); expresses doubt, a condition wished for, or a condition contrary to fact (subjunctive mood); or expresses a command (imperative mood). As with verb tense, readers expect verbs to shift in mood only for good reasons, not suddenly or arbitrarily. (For more examples of different moods of verbs, see *Verbs,* pages 425–27.)

Inconsistency in the mood of verbs is often caused by accidentally slipping into the imperative (a form in which the subject, *you,* is understood but not expressed):

First, a legal system—laws, police, courts, judges, and lawyers—needs

it needs to
to be established. Then begin to restore public services.
[The second sentence should be in the indicative, like the first sentence, rather than switching to the imperative.]

When you find you have accidentally shifted into imperative mood, revise each imperative sentence by inserting an appropriate subject and putting the verb into the indicative mood:

To bring the bow of the boat across the wind, the skipper begins by

hauling in the mainsail a little, quickly checking the water on what

will be the new course, and saying to the crew, "Ready about!" Next,

the skipper shouts,   *pushes*
shout, "Coming about!" and push the tiller all the way over.

PRACTICE

I. Revising Verb Errors

The following sentences are all from a sequence of paragraphs describing a series of events that have already occurred. Only the

Verb Errors

last sentence (number 9) refers to present circumstances. Revise each sentence to eliminate the verb problems. The first sentence has been done for you.

1. The note from the bank say only that the funds had been mislaid.

   Revised: The note from the bank <u>said</u> only that the funds had been mislaid.

2. Consequently, the customer request that her entire account be reviewed.

3. Mr. Thomas, the manager of the department where the problem apparently occurred, say no other information is available and the customer must have made a mistake.

4. Another person who works in the bank told me that Thomas regularly lay the blame for mistakes in his department on the bank's customers.

5. The lawyer for those clients are seeking other people who have grievances against the bank.

6. Checking account holders and one man who financed his house there has already come forward to join those filing formal complaints.

7. Either a detailed accounting or criminal charges is what the lawyer wants out of this episode.

8. The majority of the lawyer's clients is angry enough to take the matter to court.

9. The president of the bank and its many branches, a woman who until now had taken no particular interest in the case, want to talk to the claimants tomorrow.

II. Identifying and Revising Verb Errors

The following short passage contains a number of verb errors. Underline each verb error you find in the passage.

We live in an era when it was the duty of each citizen to ask what obligation citizenship carries with it. Today, that question can be extend two ways. First, we must ask what our obligation is to the planet we live on. Ask what our country's obligation is to the other countries we must live with. Today no one are able to tell where the obligations of citizenship end. Each person in each country probably have a different answer to these questions. But no matter who you are or where you lived, you can be sure those are the obligations you must carry. No matter how heavy they are, they cannot be lay down.

III. Identifying and Revising Inappropriate Shifts in Verb Tense

Rewrite the following passage to make the verb tenses consistent.

> As the deer entered the clearing, we remain crouched motionless behind the embankment. The slightest movement or sound—a caught breath or rustled leaves—would warn the quarry of our presence. From the instant the doe appeared, I knew I was no hunter and could not bring myself to do anything to harm it. It was therefore all the more shocking when I hear the explosion from my cousin's rifle. I dropped my own gun, clench my fists, and squeeze my eyes tightly shut. Waiting for an ominous silence, I was relieved to hear instead my cousin's curse and the sound of the deer crashing through the underbrush into the safety of the forest.

USING COMMAS

■ *QUICK VIEW*

Commas divide the words in a sentence into groups and thus clarify meaning. This Quick View shows where commas should be used and where they should not. The pages that follow explain these uses in more detail, grouping them into two categories: correct and incorrect uses.

Correct Uses of Commas

A comma is *necessary* in each of these ten situations:

1. To set off introductory elements

   With her long hair flowing free, Marina caught everyone's eye.

2. To set off nonessential (nonrestrictive) elements

   Antonio called one man, *his father,* to share the good news.

3. To separate the independent clauses of a compound sentence

   The newest mountain bikes are durable, *and* the best of them are also lightweight.

4. To separate coordinate adjectives

   Hamed's computer is a *newer, faster* one than mine.

5. To separate three or more items in a series

   Sam never dreamed that a subject like Latin American history could be so *complex, challenging, and interesting.*

6. To set off transitions, parenthetical elements, absolute phrases, and contrasts

   Then, *his hopes dashed,* he ran for the bus without looking back.

7. To set off nouns of direct address, tag questions, words such as *yes* and *no,* and interjections

   Yes, my friends, we have had a fantastic time, *haven't we?*

8. To set off phrases of attribution, such as "she said," that identify the source of a quotation

   "Let's head for the door," *Andre said* suddenly.

9. To separate the parts of dates, addresses, and numbers

   We will leave on *May 5, 1998,* to visit *Jackson Hole, Wyoming,*
   and several national parks nearby.

10. To prevent confusion

   The members of the winning team marched *in, in* no hurry
   to end their victory parade.

Incorrect Uses of Commas

A comma is *not necessary* in these ten situations:

1. Between a verb and its subject or object

   One effect of the Civil War/was a delay in western expansion.

2. After a coordinating conjunction (*and, but, or, nor, for, so, yet*)

   Texas separated from Mexico but/did not immediately join
   the Union.

3. Before and after essential (restrictive) elements

   Mark forgot the key/he needed/to open the padlock.

4. Before the first or after the last item in a series

   A happy dog will have/a shiny coat, bright eyes, and a healthy
   appetite/nearly all the time.

5. Between two compound elements

   Both the door/and its frame need repainting.

6. Between cumulative adjectives or adverbs

   Latonya still uses an old/manual typewriter.

7. Between an adjective and a noun or between an adverb and an
   adjective

   "Beanie babies" were one of those suddenly/popular toys.

8. After *such as* or *like* or before *than*

   His tests required more studying/than I was used to.

9. Before an indirect quotation

   Was it Milton's character Satan who said̷ he would rather rule in Hell than serve in Heaven?

10. With question marks, exclamation points, parentheses, and dashes

    Leon is like his father̷ (who played for the Dodgers).

CORRECT USES OF COMMAS

Many common errors in comma usage involve the failure to use commas where they should be used. The following pages discuss the ten most common uses of commas.

1. To Set Off Introductory Elements

A comma follows any introductory word, phrase, or clause unless there would be no chance of misreading. The comma separates the introductory information from the rest of the sentence. Here are examples showing different kinds of introductory elements that are followed by a comma:

> **Adverb:** *Suddenly,* steam erupted from the boiler in the basement.

> **Prepositional Phrase:** *On the other hand,* you may find it easier just to walk to the party.

> **Participial Phrase:** *Entering the bank,* she was astonished by the ten-foot Calder mobile hanging between the two rows of elevators.

> **Absolute Phrase:** *Her eyes blindfolded,* Stacy waited for the children to make the shout that would begin the game.

> **Infinitive Phrase:** *To do well in college,* he would have to find tutors who could meet with him regularly.

> **Dependent Clause:** *After she had worked at a day-care center for two years,* she decided against having children.

If the sentence has two (or more) such introductory elements, each one is normally followed by a comma:

> *At the beginning of the season, after the starting quarterback had been benched for disciplinary reasons,* the team fell apart.

Some writers omit the comma after a short introductory element when the omission would not cause even temporary uncertainty: "*Next week* they leave for England." However, using a comma with such introductory phrases is never incorrect.

Caution: Sometimes an opening phrase based on a participle or an infinitive may, in fact, be the subject of the sentence, so to follow it with a comma would create an error:

> Wearing infrared sunglasses/ can prevent damage to your eyes.

> To beat the school shot-put record/ was her only goal.

Using Commas

Similarly, if the introductory words begin a sentence that is in *inverted order* (the verb comes before the subject), no comma follows them:

> At the left of the stage / stood the security guards, waiting to escort the candidate back to her car.

2. To Set Off Nonessential (Nonrestrictive) Elements

When you insert additional information about someone or something into a sentence—information that is nonrestrictive, or not essential to the meaning—set it off with commas. Be sure in such cases to use a *pair* of commas, unless the nonrestrictive material is at the beginning or the end of the sentence.

You can check to see if an element is nonessential by deciding whether the sentence makes sense without it. In the first example below, the words "Robert Bly exaggerates the plight of modern man" convey the writer's meaning quite clearly; the clause set off by commas, "as his critics always point out," just adds detail.

> Robert Bly, *as his critics always point out,* exaggerates the plight of modern man.
>
> Lieutenant Worf, *growling and muttering under his breath,* escorted the visitor to the guest-of-honor seat.
>
> The sunset was framed with bright red clouds, *the most beautiful I've ever seen.*
>
> All the kids immediately got in line to ride on the Tilt-a-Whirl, *which is the most popular ride at the fair this year.*

Caution: As you revise your writing to set nonessential elements off with commas, be careful not to lose the distinction between nonessential elements and essential elements. If the added phrase or clause is essential for the reader's understanding of the sentence, then it is *restrictive* and should not be set off with commas:

> Behavioral modification programs are the best method / that adults can use to lose weight.
>
> We punish people / who commit crimes / by sending them to prison.

To review the distinction between essential and nonessential, consider the second example above: without the restrictive clause, the meaning seems to be that we punish all people by sending them to prison. But as the restrictive clause makes clear, the intended meaning is that only those who commit crimes are punished by being sent to prison. Because the clause provides an essential shaping of the sentence's meaning, it is not set off by commas. (For additional examples of the distinction between essential and nonessential elements, see *Restrictive/Nonrestrictive Clauses,* pages 336–37.)

3. To Separate the Independent Clauses of a Compound Sentence

Compound sentences have two or more independent clauses. When these clauses are joined by a coordinating conjunction (*and, but, or, nor, for, so,* and *yet*), a comma is needed before the conjunction to separate the clauses clearly. Without the comma, the intended division in the sentence might not be apparent:

> Pablo tried to phone Luis, and Julia ran across the street to see if the child was still at home. ^
>
> [If the beginning of the sentence is misread as "Pablo tried to phone Luis and Julia," the rest of the sentence—"ran across the street . . ."—makes no sense.]
>
> Mr. Combs didn't find his jade ring in the treehouse, for the children had hidden it in the bushes. ^

(For more on independent versus dependent clauses, see *Clauses,* pages 335–37.)

   Caution: Writers often have difficulty distinguishing between a compound sentence (two independent clauses) and a sentence with a *compound predicate* (two verbs but only one subject). Be careful that you do not erroneously insert a comma between the two parts of a compound predicate:

> Mary flew home/ and drove her car back later.
>
> The students in the residence hall must decide this issue for themselves/ or give up any hope of self-governance.

4. To Separate Coordinate Adjectives

When two or more adjectives relate equally to the noun they modify, they are called *coordinate adjectives,* and they are separated

Using Commas

by commas. If you can put *and* between the adjectives and not change the meaning, they are working individually and are thus coordinate:

> The *dark, gaping* hole quickly filled with water.

> His *bitter, dry, shriveled, chewy* fruitcake was not a family favorite.

If *and* does not make sense between the adjectives, you are using cumulative adjectives, which function as a unit, and no comma is needed:

> This printer has *three popular operating* features.

Note: Often, a noun or an adjective is placed before a noun to create a single concept from the two words: *table leg, rearview mirror, kitchen sink, light bulb, easy chair.* No comma should separate the essential modifier from the noun.

5. To Separate Three or More Items in a Series

You need to use commas to separate three or more items in a series—words, phrases, or clauses:

> Try to remember to *feed the dog, bring in the mail, and take out the trash.*

Be sure to insert a comma before the *and* to keep the units separate and to prevent any possibility of misreading:

> On the visit to our old summer camp, we enjoyed talks with old friends, nights under the stars, and sailboats on the lake.

> [Without the comma before *and,* this sentence could seem to mean that the nights were spent under sailboats.]

Exception: If there are commas within the items in a series, the punctuation mark that separates the series should be a *semicolon:*

> Marty set his table with plates that were red, white, and blue; napkins that were yellow, green, and brown; and a tablecloth that was gold, green, and black.

Caution: When only two items are combined with a conjunction, such as *and,* no comma is needed.

> His favorite food is a sandwich made with salmon/ and watercress.

6. To Set Off Transitions, Parenthetical Elements, Absolute Phrases, and Contrasts

You can add many types of explanatory phrases to your sentences to provide more information for your readers. These elements should be set off from the rest of the sentence with commas.

Transitions

Such transitions as *therefore, however, furthermore, indeed, then, in fact, to the contrary,* and *for instance* may be used to begin sentences or to connect parts of sentences. Use a comma to separate the transitional word or phrase from the rest of the sentence; if the transition occurs in the middle of the sentence, place a comma before and after it:

> *Therefore,* I am ready to leave now.
>
> John, *on the other hand,* walked away uninjured.
>
> The book I read, *for example,* was much longer.

When a conjunctive adverb, such as *however* or *nonetheless,* is used to begin the second of two independent clauses joined by a semicolon, the adverb is followed by a comma:

> The ball bounced right off the edge of the backboard; *therefore,* the referee stopped the play.
>
> Debbie took the subway across town; *in fact,* she rode it to the end of the line.

(See page 204 for a list of conjunctive adverbs and further discussion of their use.)

Parenthetical Elements or Interrupters

A parenthetical element is a word or a group of words that offers an aside—something that is clearly not necessary in the sentence, breaks up the flow of words, or seems like an afterthought. Such elements are usually set off with commas (although dashes or parentheses may be used instead):

> The biggest waves, *I think,* are yet to come.
>
> Your first chemistry course, *most people say,* is the hardest one.
>
> The contemporary novel, *according to my English teacher,* is not a very high form of art.

Absolute Phrases

An absolute phrase is a phrase that modifies the entire sentence; a comma separates such a phrase from the sentence it modifies. These phrases usually consist of a noun and a participle, as in the following examples:

> *The race having been postponed,* the boats were towed back in to San Diego harbor.

> *Their bus no longer functioning,* the team members decided to run the final mile to the game.

> *His pride shattered,* the lawyer had to admit that he hadn't planned his presentation very carefully.

(For more examples of absolute phrases, see *Phrases,* pages 373–77.)

Contrasting Elements

A word or a phrase that marks a sharp contrast with the rest of the sentence is usually set off with a comma or commas:

> The officers, *unlike the rest of the crew,* wanted the fleet kept together under one command.

> The casino, *not known for its high standards of entertainment anyway,* sank to a new low with this act.

7. To Set Off Nouns of Direct Address, Tag Questions, Words Such As *Yes* and *No,* and Interjections

Several kinds of short elements allow you to address readers directly but are not essential to the meaning of the sentence. These elements should be set off by commas.

Nouns of Direct Address

> The problem, *friends and acquaintances,* is one of character, not intelligence.

> Always remember, *future voters,* that your vote is worth nothing if you don't use it.

Tag Questions

> Luigi looks better after taking a vacation, *don't you think?*

> We're leaving right after the encore, *aren't we?*

Words Such As *Yes* and *No* and Interjections

Yes, I would agree with his point in general.

You ask if I agree with her; *no,* I don't.

Well, that's your opinion.

Oh, I suppose I'll go along with it this time.

[Mild interjections such as *oh* are usually followed by a comma (instead of an exclamation point).]

8. To Set Off Phrases Such As "She Said" That Identify the Source of a Quotation

Use commas to set off a quotation from the phrase that introduces it or identifies its source. Place a comma following a quotation *within* the closing quotation mark:

> *Mae West declared,* "When choosing between two evils, I always like to try the one I've never tried before."

> "Golf is a good walk spoiled," *said Mark Twain.*

9. To Separate the Parts of Dates, Addresses, and Numbers

The elements of dates or addresses are set off by commas when they appear as part of a sentence:

> Georgia O'Keeffe kept a house in *Abiquiu, New Mexico,* for her guests, but she often lived up the road, at Ghost Ranch.

> *December 7, 1941,* Pearl Harbor Day, is called "the day that will live in infamy."

Exception: No comma separates the zip code from the name of a state or the month from the year:

> Please send the package to 5522 Iroquois Drive, St. Paul, Minnesota⁄ 55106.

> He left town in April⁄ 1998.

Use the comma to separate the digits of long numbers into groups of three, counting from the right. The comma with numbers of four digits is optional (except in years, street numbers, and page numbers, where a comma is never used):

> On the new riverboat gambling ship, Carolyn made $*1,921* [*or* $1921] the first night, but she had been hoping for the $*1,234,999* grand prize.

Using Commas

10. To Prevent Confusion

Sometimes you need to insert a comma into a sentence just to prevent misreading:

> The police found the murderer, murdered.
>
> Those who can, do.

A comma can also clarify a sentence by replacing a word or words that have been omitted:

> My goal was to live more slowly; my method, to get lots of sleep.
>
> [The comma replaces the missing word, *was*.]

INCORRECT USES OF COMMAS

In the following ten situations, including a comma would be incorrect.

1. Between a Verb and Its Subject or Object

Especially when several words appear between a subject and its verb, a writer may insert an unnecessary comma between them:

> The gray brick building that looked like a fortress in the rain⁄ turned out to be a campus library.
>
> Droves of teenagers of every shape, size, and kind of dress⁄ swarmed into the streets.

Similarly, a writer may mistakenly insert a comma between the verb and its object when several words are between them:

> After leaving the small town where she was born, Delta found in the city⁄ a satisfaction that she had never known.

2. After a Coordinating Conjunction

Although compound sentences joined by coordinating conjunctions (*and, but, or, nor, for, so, yet*) require a comma before the coordinating conjunction, some writers regularly insert an unnecessary comma after the conjunction as well:

> The concept of codependency has entered many areas of human behavior today, and⁄ its definition is less clear with each new use.

Incorrect Uses of Commas

Terri took all her books home for the weekend, but/ she did not get any work done.

3. Before and After Essential (Restrictive) Elements

Words, phrases, and clauses that are necessary to the meaning of a sentence should not be set off by commas:

A majority of students/ whom we polled/ felt their classes were too big.

All the university administrators/ who returned our questionnaires/ thought the class size was just about right.

(For more examples, see *Restrictive/Nonrestrictive Clauses,* pages 336–37.)

4. Before the First or after the Last Item in a Series

Do not put a comma either before a series or after the last item:

Jen's strengths in/ running, jumping, and throwing/ made her a natural for the basketball team.

The biologists selected four trees for their studies of acid rain, soil erosion, and insect damage/ in the southern Rockies.

Bayfield, Superior, and Grand Portage/ make the points of a Lake Superior triangle that is rich in history for many different races and nationalities of people.

5. Between Two Compound Elements

Writers often mistake a compound predicate (a predicate containing two verbs and their modifiers) for a compound sentence (a sentence with two independent clauses). Having made this mistake, they then insert a comma between the two parts of the compound predicate:

Our directions told us that Thompson's advice was to be followed no matter what/ and warned us about the dangers of ignoring her.

These particles can become highly charged with negative ions under the right conditions/ and can create an increase in the whole field's electrical activity.

Check to see whether your sentence contains a compound verb (or a compound subject) or is a compound sentence; the only one that merits a comma by virtue of its being *compound* is the compound sentence.

Using
Commas

6. Between Cumulative Adjectives or Adverbs

If a group of adjectives or adverbs lean on each other and work together to modify the noun or the verb, they are *cumulative,* and they are not separated by commas:

> He wouldn't part with his faded/ Yankees/ baseball cap.

Note: If two or more adjectives modify a noun separately, or if two or more adverbs modify a verb separately, they are called *coordinate adjectives* or adverbs and should be separated by commas:

> The Nacra is a *fast, dependable* catamaran.

> The North Fork of the Little Pigeon River flows *clean, clear, and cold* through the Smokies.

7. Between an Adjective and a Noun or between an Adverb and an Adjective

If a series of adjectives modifies a noun, there should be commas between the adjectives but not between the last adjective and the noun:

> Jack chose to attend the school with the biggest, most current, and most accessible/ library collection.

Sometimes the adjective that modifies a noun will itself be modified by an adverb. Do not separate the adverb from the adjective with a comma:

> Our school has a barely/ adequate library.

8. After *Such As* or *Like* or before *Than*

The phrases *such as* and *like* should not be separated by a comma from the words following them:

> A real expert, such as/ Professor French, would disagree with you.

> The Colorado Rockies, like/ their northern counterparts, provide recreation for millions of skiers.

In a comparison, do not put a comma in front of *than:*

> The long way to the top is a more scenic path/ than this one.

> Marcelle plays drums better/ than Frank does.

9. Before an Indirect Quotation

Although direct quotations are usually set off by commas, indirect quotations (reported speech as opposed to quoted speech) are not:

> Bob Dylan once wrote/ that it takes a lot to laugh but a freight train to cry.

> Princess Diana maintained/ that one of the worst things in life was to feel unloved.

10. With Question Marks, Exclamation Points, Parentheses, and Dashes

If a direct quotation ends with a question mark or an exclamation point, do not also include a comma:

> "Prepare to jibe!"/ called the skipper.

> "Are you ready now?"/ asked the doctor.

When material is enclosed in parentheses or set off with dashes, there should be no commas:

> My mother's quilt/ (a family heirloom)/ has four generations of work in it.

> Several national parks/—including my favorite, Yosemite—/ are now requiring visitors to leave their cars at the entrance and ride tour buses in the park.

Using Commas

PRACTICE

I. Commas with Introductory Elements

In the following sentences, insert commas where they are needed after the introductory elements. The first one has been done for you.

1. When he came into the room he didn't notice the broken window.

   Revised: When he came into the room, he didn't notice the broken window.

2. Next you need to reserve a place for your pets at a kennel.

3. After the class started John came in the door looking surprised.

4. Hidden behind the staircase was the grandfather clock.

5. To complete a big project successfully you need lots of time.

6. Just standing on the high wire is incredibly difficult.

II. Commas with Restrictive and Nonrestrictive Clauses

Underline the restrictive or nonrestrictive clause in each of the following sentences and, where necessary, insert or delete commas. The first sentence has been revised for you.

1. Each player, who comes in after curfew, is fined one hundred dollars.

   Revised: Each player <u>who comes in after curfew</u> is fined one hundred dollars.

   [The clause is restrictive because it is essential to the meaning; thus it does not need commas.]

2. Beethoven's Ninth Symphony which is one of my favorites will be performed at the benefit concert next week.

3. Children who go to private schools often get a better introduction to computers than those who go to public schools.

4. Barbra Steinbren who is vacationing in Hawaii with her family will be the new vice president of marketing.

5. I went immediately to the only hospital in our town that offers multiple-resonance-imagery screening for back and spine problems.

III. Commas in Compound Sentences

Insert commas correctly into the following compound sentences. The first one has been done for you.

1. Victor began climbing down the ladder but he was stopped by a worker near the bottom.

   Revised: Victor began climbing down the ladder, but he was stopped by a worker near the bottom.

2. Television addicts often think about reading or gardening while they sit in front of the screen for many of them don't really enjoy the activity that takes up all their free time.

3. Freddie kept asking when we would get there and Jimmy kept complaining that his sister was pinching him.

4. Soap opera families all seem to live in huge houses and have beautiful clothes yet few of the adults seem to work for a living.

5. Cole could not find any wrapping paper so he decided to use the Sunday comics.

IV. Commas with Coordinate Adjectives

Insert commas if they are necessary to separate coordinate adjectives in the following sentences. The first one has been done for you.

1. After the grill overturned, the ground was covered with grimy burnt hot dogs.

   Revised: After the grill overturned, the ground was covered with grimy, burnt hot dogs.

2. Everyone knew about the sad red-haired orphan and her dog from either the popular cartoon strip or the Broadway play.

3. When Hilda came down the stairs, she was surprised to see a shiny new American sports car parked in the driveway.

4. Can you help us create a short lively talent show to benefit our charity?

5. The book was made into a sensationalized feature film.

V. Commas with Items in a Series

Insert commas into the following series where they are needed. The first sentence has been done for you.

1. My parents wanted me to go to college get a good job and then move back home.

   Revised: My parents wanted me to go to college, get a good job, and then move back home.

2. Jogging up and down the stadium steps doing push-ups and using free weights gave the athlete great strength.

3. For drug testing to be fair, it should be required for the employee and the employer.

4. He needs to either enter a graduate school and study counseling or get a job at a hospital.

5. She always catches a cold when her feet get wet when she doesn't dry her hair in the morning or when she forgets to wear a coat.

Using Commas

6. You can get an accounting job in this city if you have good college grades a recommendation from an accounting professor and some bookkeeping experience.

VI. Other Comma Uses

Insert commas correctly into the following sentences. The first one has been done for you.

1. We finished our project early; however the instructor didn't read it for a week.

    Revised: We finished our project early; however, the instructor didn't read it for a week.

2. Kaylesha for example always leaves early for class.

3. Yes Mrs. Foster it is time to leave for the reception.

4. At midnight on December 31 1999 everyone in Ann Arbor Michigan plans to head to the football stadium.

5. Her arms and legs aching Melissa kept struggling toward the finish line.

6. "Carla it seems has already decided against finishing this painting" said the art teacher.

VII. Unnecessary Commas

Delete any unnecessary commas in the following sentences. The first sentence has been done for you.

1. The film, that I had to watch, was long, dull, and filled with second-rate actors and actresses.

    Revised: The film that I had to watch was long, dull, and filled with second-rate actors and actresses.

    [The dependent clause, *that I had to watch,* is restrictive; thus it should not be set off with commas.]

2. The law specifies that women will receive equal treatment, and, that requirement applies to hiring practices.

3. Each patient brought a gift, of baked goods, produce, or handicrafts.

4. Stereotypes are common in American stage, screen, and performing arts, and do not always indicate poor writing by the dramatist.

5. Her ambition in life was to fly an F-16 jet, fighter, plane.

6. After he had solved a problem in math or physics, Feynman often lost, all interest in explaining the concepts to others.

7. The environment, the admiral grew up in, no longer exists.

8. What Lincoln actually had said was, that the war could not be allowed to go on past the election.

9. "Wouldn't it be nice to think so?", he responded.

10. Tom's crazy idea proved to be foolish, self-destructive, and, wrong.

VIII. Identifying and Revising Comma Errors

Rewrite the following paragraph, correcting the comma errors it contains.

With her mortarboard firmly on her head Tammy took her place in the graduation procession. She had always wanted to be the first in the family to get a college degree which would also help her get a good job. In her mind, either you could get a degree after high school or you could get a degree later but eventually everyone in the United States would need a college degree. When the chance came for her to go to college and pay for most of it herself she decided it was a chance she could not afford to pass up. Each course she took in her ambitious, undergraduate curriculum was another triumph for her. Another fifteen weeks of reading, staying up late at night, writing, studying, and sitting at uncomfortable desks, never scared Tammy. As she marched off the stage, Tammy clutched the diploma in one hand, and hurled her mortarboard into the crowd with the other.

Using
Commas

PRONOUN ERRORS

▪ QUICK VIEW

A *pronoun* is a word used in place of a noun or a noun phrase (called the pronoun's *antecedent*). This Quick View outlines the four most common types of problems with pronouns: vague or ambiguous reference, lack of agreement with the antecedent, inappropriate shifts in person, and biased uses of pronouns. The pages that follow explain the problems in more detail. (For a description of different types of pronouns, see *Pronouns*, pages 380–82.)

Vague or Ambiguous Pronoun Reference

The reference of each pronoun should be immediately clear. Unclear pronoun reference usually is caused either by lack of specificity or by too much distance between pronoun and antecedent.

the rainbow
Just as the plane was about to fly through the rainbow, it disappeared.

Lack of Agreement between Pronoun and Antecedent

Most pronoun mistakes involve disagreement in *number*—singular or plural—between pronouns and their antecedents (the nouns to which they refer). Disagreement occurs mainly in four situations.

1. Nouns joined with *and* usually take a plural pronoun:

After hunting all morning for my hammer and chisel, I decided I

them.
would never find it.

2. When two or more nouns are joined with *or* or *nor,* the pronoun that refers to them should agree with the closest noun:

Neither the challenging boats nor the defending champion returned

its
to their dock unharmed.

3. Most indefinite pronouns (words such as *each, one, anybody, somebody, no one,* and *everybody*) are treated as singular:

his
Each of the boys must accept their own share of responsibility.

(For a list of indefinite pronouns that are always singular, are always plural, or may be either, depending on the context, see *Pronouns*, pages 381–82.)

4. Pronouns that refer to collective nouns (words such as *team* and *group*) are singular or plural, depending on whether the noun emphasizes the group or the members individually:

their
The group realized the waiter had mixed up ~~its~~ orders.

Inappropriate Shifts in Person

Needless shifts between first (or third) person and second person can cause confusion. (*Person* is the point of view: first person, *I* or *we;* second person, *you;* or third person, *he, she, it,* or *they.*)

They
Good teachers listen closely to each question. ~~You~~ know that the answer may help many students.

Biased Uses of Pronouns

Pronoun choices need to be inclusive—to reflect the diversity of the human population. Use masculine pronouns only when you mean to indicate only males.

All students   *their*   *s*
~~Every student~~ will have ~~his~~ own e-mail account next year.

or

or her
Every student will have his own e-mail account next year.

VAGUE OR AMBIGUOUS PRONOUN REFERENCE

The reference of each pronoun should always be immediately clear to readers. Two kinds of problems are common here—problems with the *specificity* of the reference and problems with the *nearness* of the reference.

Problems with *Specific* Reference

To make sure each pronoun has a specific antecedent, you need to rewrite sentences that contain *ambiguous pronoun references*. In the sentence shown here, the problem is that the reader cannot be sure which person the pronoun refers to:

When Dr. Thomas made the first incision on Mr. Innis, ~~his~~ *Dr. Thomas's* heart began to beat faster.

[The sentence needs to make clear *whose* heart began to beat faster.]

Avoid using a pronoun to refer to an entire clause or sentence instead of to one specific noun:

When my mother got a job and wasn't home to cook on weeknights, I wasn't pleased ~~with it.~~ *that she stopped cooking.*

[Does "it" refer to mother getting a job or to mother not being home to cook?]

The ~~cook is new and doesn't know how~~ *new cook's inability* to operate this boiler~~, which~~/ could cause a problem.

[Is the problem the cook's newness, the cook's ignorance of the boiler, or the boiler itself?]

~~When~~ *If* you apply for a job, ~~you should~~ *you don't* learn about the company, ~~It~~ *when you apply for a job, you may not be hired.* ~~may not work out if you don't.~~

[*What* may not work out—your being hired or the job?]

Special Problems with *It*

You should avoid using the pronoun *it* to refer to a noun if the sentence also contains another type of *it* structure:

eating at the cafeteria
Although ~~it~~ usually doesn't make Charles happy, ~~to have to eat at~~
                                                  ^
~~the cafeteria,~~ he will do it every time rather than miss a meal.

Special Problems with This

Like other pronouns, *this* should not be used to refer to an entire
sentence or clause. At the beginning of a sentence, *this* is most
effectively used *with a noun* to indicate the exact meaning. (For
more examples of using *this* with a noun, see page 41.)

> My little brother refuses to get up and get dressed before the bus
>   *stubbornness*
> comes. This has made him late to school many times.
>   ^

Problems with Nearness of Reference

Sometimes, as shown in the preceding examples, a pronoun is
not clear because too many nouns are nearby that it might refer
to. In other cases, a pronoun's reference is not clear because the
noun it refers to is too far away. Unless you are sure that the reference is clear, a pronoun should not refer to a noun that appears
much earlier in a long sentence (or in a previous sentence). Because your reader may not remember that particular noun, your
meaning may be needlessly ambiguous.

> We realized the first-aid kit in one of our four vans was empty about
>
> five minutes after the health inspectors finished checking all our ve-
>   *that kit.*
> hicles. We were lucky that the inspectors overlooked ~~it.~~
>   ^
> [Will readers remember, so many words later, what *it* refers to?]

There are many ways to rewrite such sentences to make the pronoun reference clearer.

LACK OF AGREEMENT
BETWEEN PRONOUN AND ANTECEDENT

The pronoun you use to refer to a noun must be singular if the
noun is singular and plural if the noun is plural.

Mr. *James* decided that *he* wanted to go on to graduate school for further training in his chosen field.

If these *tables* were refinished, *they* would regain *their* original luster.

Agreement with Nouns Joined by *And*

When two or more nouns are joined by *and,* the pronoun that refers to them must be plural.

When *Bob and Jaime* left the dorm to take the test, *they* left Bob's calculator behind.

After a *dove and a canary* came out of the hat, *they* immediately flew out over the auditorium.

The only exception occurs when the two nouns describe the same person or form a single unit:

My best *friend and confidante* stood waiting by *her* car when I came out of the airport terminal.

In this new budget, *research and development* has lost *its* supremacy in our company.

Agreement with Nouns Joined by *Or, Nor, Either . . . Or,* or *Neither . . . Nor*

When two or more nouns are joined by *or, nor, either . . . or,* or *neither . . . nor,* the pronoun is singular if both nouns are singular, and plural if both nouns are plural.

Singular Nouns: If the state doesn't increase the education budget next year, *either the junior college or the technical school* will lose *its* accreditation.

Plural Nouns: *Neither the symphony members nor the owners* were willing to give up *their* plans for next year's schedule.

If one noun is singular and the other is plural, the pronoun agrees with the noun that is nearer to it.

Singular and Plural Nouns: *Either your floppy disks or your computer's hard drive* has a virus infecting *its* files.

Either your computer's hard drive or your floppy disks have a virus infecting *their* files.

Indefinite Pronouns

Many indefinite pronouns (*each, everyone, everybody, everything, anybody, anyone, either, neither, no one, someone,* and *something*) always take singular verbs, and singular personal pronouns are used to refer to them:

> As the ballerinas came back on stage, *each* bowed *her* head to the roaring crowd.

> The two young men were surprised to learn that *neither* was *his* father's sole heir.

A few indefinite pronouns (*both, few, many, others, ones,* and *several*) are always plural:

> Having slept through their alarms, *both were* late for *their* eight o'clock classes.

> *Others are* coming with us to see the play.

A few indefinite pronouns (*all, any, enough, more, most, none,* and *some*) may be either singular or plural, depending on their context. Compare:

> *Some* of the leaves *were* brown and wrinkled.

> *Some* of the leaf *was* brown and wrinkled.

Collective Nouns

When a collective noun (such as *team, group,* or *chorus*) applies to the group as a whole, use a singular pronoun to refer to that noun. When a collective noun refers to members acting individually, choose a plural pronoun.

Singular	Plural
Our *team* won *its* first conference championship this year.	The *team* ran out of the locker room to tell the coach that *their* uniforms had not arrived.

INAPPROPRIATE SHIFTS IN PERSON

Avoid shifts between first person (*I, we*), second person (*you*), and third person (*he, she, it, they*) while you are still referring to the same people or things.

The student *Students* should realize that in college you *they* are responsible for setting your *their* own schedule *s*.

or

You
~~The student~~ should realize that in college you are responsible for setting your own schedule.

you
When ~~one~~ first enters the Lincoln Memorial, you are struck by a feeling that Lincoln is really there.

or

visitors   *they*
When ~~one~~ first enters the Lincoln Memorial, ~~you~~ are struck by a feeling that Lincoln is really there.

(See also *Parallelism,* pages 273–77.)

BIASED USES OF PRONOUNS

When you use a singular pronoun or noun, such as *everyone* or
each student, choose a singular pronoun to refer to it. If you are
talking about a male student, *he* is appropriate, as is *she* for a female student. But if you mean to include both males and females,
do not use *he,* because it excludes women. To be inclusive, you
have three options:

- Use *he or she* (*him or her, his or hers*).
- Change the antecedent to the plural so that you can use *they* (or
  them or *theirs*).
- Rewrite the sentence without the pronoun.

or her
Every contestant should bring three copies of his winning essay to
the grand prize luncheon.

or

All   *s*   *their*   *s*
~~Every~~ contestant should bring three copies of ~~his~~ winning essay to
the grand prize luncheon.

or

Each   *whose essay won a prize*
~~Every~~ contestant should bring three copies ~~of his winning essay~~ to
the grand prize luncheon.

Overusing *he or she* can make your writing awkward ("He or she should bring his or her books to his or her classes"). To incorporate unbiased language without interrupting the flow of your writing, choose carefully among the three options for pronouns. Remember also not to stereotype certain roles for certain genders: for instance, if you are writing about a secretary or a pilot, you should carefully consider the three options instead of assuming that a secretary would be female or a pilot male. (For a more detailed discussion about avoiding bias in your writing, see *Biased Uses of Language,* pages 324–28.)

PRACTICE

I. Making Sure Each Pronoun Clearly Refers to a Specific Noun

Revise the following sentences to clarify pronoun reference. The first sentence has been done for you.

1. I did not go up to the front desk to sign in again after the first part of my physical, <u>which</u> caused a problem for the receptionist.

    Revised: I did not go up to the front desk to sign in again after the first part of my physical, <u>and my failure to sign in</u> caused a problem for the receptionist.

2. Carmen told Clara that she couldn't go to her party.

3. When Linda came out of the restaurant and saw her father standing in the middle of the street hailing a cab, she was not pleased about it.

4. Although Brian likes working with desktop publishing on his Macintosh computer, he does not plan on getting a job that involves it.

5. In the hall closet, the children tried to search for their escaped turtle without overturning any of the boxes and umbrellas or making any noise. They did not want their mother to catch them doing that.

6. The teachers looked out the window and saw all the preschoolers running around the yard acting like pirates on a raid. This drove them crazy.

II. Making Sure You Use the Right Pronoun

Decide whether the pronouns in the following sentences are used correctly. Rewrite the sentences, changing the pronouns and the verbs to singular or plural where necessary. The first sentence has been done for you.

1. Either James or Andre needs to bring <u>their</u> glove to the ballpark.

    Revised: Either James or Andre needs to bring <u>a</u> glove to the ballpark.

    or

    Either James or Andre needs to bring <u>his</u> glove to the ballpark.

2. At the beginning of the play, the director signals the cast to take its position on the stage.

3. Regina, Sergei, and Victor, Russian friends of my mother, like to tell the class about his native culture.

4. Either the father or the sons will have to work harder if he wants to finish the entertainment center by the first of the month.

5. The service club donates its time to renovating homes for the needy.

6. Every woman in the club wanted their names to appear at the top of the grand prize board.

III. Avoiding Inappropriate Shifts

Correct the inappropriate shifts in the following paragraphs to make the point of view consistent. The first problem in paragraph A (sentence 2) has been revised for you.

Paragraph A

(1) Before the first day of class, you should make sure that you know where each building is. (2) Then <u>the student</u> can find out if <u>she</u> will have time to get to <u>her</u> classes.

Revised: (2) Then <u>you</u> can find out if <u>you</u> will have time to get to <u>your</u> classes.

(3) If you won't have time to walk, you might consider buying a bicycle from a local store. (4) They may have used bicycles as well as new ones. (5) Students should also buy good bicycle locks. (6) Otherwise, he or she may have a bike stolen.

Paragraph B

(1) When one gets to the new workout center, one is immediately greeted by a counselor. (2) They will help you decide on the right combination of free-weight and Nautilus repetitions for you. (3) If you like one of the staff members, you can choose them to help you with your workout each time you come in. (4) These guided visits help the client follow a workout program that will be safe and effective for her.

IV. Avoiding Biased Uses of Pronouns

Rewrite the following sentences, trying all three options for eliminating biased pronoun use. (Some of these sentences will not work all three ways.) The first sentence has been done for you.

1. Every bicyclist should bring his own water to the road race.

   Revised: Every bicyclist should bring his or her own water to the road race.

   All bicyclists should bring their own water to the road race.

   All bicyclists should bring water to the road race.

2. Do you know anyone who bakes her own bread?
3. If the interviewer does not seem to be listening to you, you should look him straight in the eye.
4. When an executive finally moves into the large corner office, he may forget about all the people who helped him get there.
5. Every winner of the Iditarod trans-Alaska sled-dog race for the past ten years will be at the ceremony to receive his new plaque.
6. Each student should choose an internship that will help him get his first job.

V. Identifying and Revising Pronoun Errors

Rewrite the following paragraph, correcting any pronoun errors.

To do photocopying in our library, each student takes his money to a machine, puts enough in it to cover as many copies as he wants at five cents a page, and receives a card that will let him do exactly that much copying at any copy machine in the building. Each of these machines take only cards, not cash. Because of this, you will not find dollar-bill-changing machines in our library or students walking around with hands full of nickels. They have been replaced by card-activated copiers. The advantage of this is that those dollar-bill-changing machines hardly ever worked. The disadvantage is that anyone who wants to make copies are going to have to go first to the machine that makes copy cards. If it is not working, he won't be able to use the copier at all.

USING APOSTROPHES

This Quick View shows the four most common kinds of errors with apostrophes: in possessive case, in contractions, in some plurals, and in pronoun homonyms. The pages that follow explain the problems in more detail.

Apostrophes in the Possessive Case

Nouns

Nouns show possession with an apostrophe and an *s;* if the plural form already ends in an *s,* the apostrophe is placed after this *s:*

the *book's* conclusion	his *boss's* car
all the *girls'* keys	the *linemen's* shoes

Whether both parts of a pair of nouns show possession depends on whether both share possession:

Jon and Annie's tapes [They jointly own the tapes.]

Jon's and Annie's tapes [They each own some of the tapes.]

Pronouns

Two types of pronouns—*personal* pronouns and *indefinite* pronouns—form their possessives in very different ways:

- **Personal pronouns,** such as *I, you,* and *they,* form their possessives by switching to a different form (*I* becomes *my* or *mine*) or by adding an *s* (*it* becomes *its,* and *their* becomes *theirs*).

   Everything I have is *yours.*

   This tarp is *hers;* that one is *ours.*

- **Indefinite pronouns,** such as *one* or *anyone,* form their possessives by adding an apostrophe and an *s* (*one's* or *anyone's*):

   Are you *anybody's* lab partner?

   Denise is *everyone's* friend.

Apostrophes in Contractions

Contractions are shortened forms of two words combined into one, such as *don't* for *do not, weren't* for *were not,* or *can't* for *can not*. The apostrophe in a contraction replaces the missing letters:

> I *can't* understand why you *didn't* like it.

> Samantha *wouldn't* have entered the race if her roommates *hadn't* dared her.

Apostrophes to Form Plurals

Apostrophes also appear in the plurals of letters, numerals, and words referred to as words:

> Remember to remove some of those *and*'s from your sentences and cross your *t*'s.

> Europeans draw a line through their *7*'s so that they won't look like *1*'s.

Its versus *It's* and Other Pronoun Homonyms

The word *it* is a personal pronoun and, like other personal pronouns, forms its possessive simply by adding an *s*, with no apostrophe:

> The lion shook *its* head and roared.

When you add an apostrophe and an *s* to *it*, you create the contraction for *it is:*

> Tell me when *it's* safe to come out.

APOSTROPHES IN THE POSSESSIVE CASE

Nouns

Use the apostrophe to indicate the possessive case of nouns. The apostrophe is equivalent to the preposition *of,* another marker of possession:

the friend of my brother →	my brother's friend
the problem of the children →	the children's problem
the end of the day →	the day's end
the dog of the boys →	the boys' dog

In these cases of possession, the placement of the apostrophe also shows whether the noun (the owner) is singular or plural.

With Singular Nouns

For singular nouns, add the apostrophe and then *s:*

the author's creativity [one author]

a week's pay [one week]

the valley's residents [one valley]

Note: When a singular proper noun ends in *s,* the possessive form may be written with just an apostrophe or with an apostrophe and *s.* Most authorities prefer adding the apostrophe and *s:*

James's calendar [*or* James' calendar]

With Plural Nouns

For nouns with *regular plurals,* add the apostrophe after the *s:*

the teachers' decision [more than one teacher]

the carpenters' tools [more than one carpenter]

the heroes' parade [more than one hero]

the colonies' concerns [more than one colony]

the Kennedys' ambitions [more than one Kennedy]

the buses' fumes [more than one bus]

Using Apostrophes

For nouns with *irregular plurals,* use that plural form and then add an apostrophe and *s:*

women's rights

children's toys

alumni's phone-a-thon

two deer's hides

For Compounds and Word Groups

For compounds and word groups, add the apostrophe and *s* only to the final word:

her sister-in-law's party

the attorney general's office

Ken Griffey, Jr.'s batting average

For Pairs of Nouns

To indicate *individual ownership* for pairs of nouns, add the apostrophe and *s* to each noun:

Carmela's and Juana's coats [two separate coats]

the judge's and the defense attorney's opinions [two separate opinions]

To indicate *joint ownership* for pairs of nouns, add the apostrophe and *s* to the final noun:

Jaime and Sarah's house [a house owned jointly]

the father and mother's preferences [shared preferences]

Pronouns

Not all pronouns are made possessive by adding an apostrophe and an *s*. How a pronoun indicates possession depends on the type of pronoun.

Personal pronouns do not use apostrophes to show possession. Personal pronouns show possession by either switching to a different form (*him* or *he* becomes *his*) or simply adding an *s* (*their* becomes *theirs; your* becomes *yours*).

Personal Pronoun	Possessive Form
I	my, mine
you	your, yours
he, she, it	his, her, hers, its
we	our, ours
you	your, yours
they	their, theirs

Indefinite pronouns show possession by adding an apostrophe and an *s:*

one's friends	anyone's remarks
somebody's mother	another's livelihood
everybody's happiness	

(For more on the types of pronouns, see *Pronouns,* pages 380–82.)

APOSTROPHES IN CONTRACTIONS

A contraction is a shortened form of two words combined into one. When you form a contraction, you must show that some letters are missing. Signal the missing letter or letters with an apostrophe:

can + not → can't	I + am → I'm
will + not → won't	I + will → I'll
does + not → doesn't	we + are → we're
did + not → didn't	you + are → you're
would + not → wouldn't	they + are → they're
should + not → shouldn't	

Caution: When you use contractions, the tone of your writing becomes informal—almost conversational. Contractions are not recommended in academic and professional writing. If you are in doubt about how your reader will respond to a contraction, do not use it!

Using
Apostrophes

APOSTROPHES TO FORM
PLURALS OF LETTERS AND NUMERALS

To form the plural of a letter or a numeral or of a word considered as a word, add an apostrophe and *s*. These words and numbers—but not the apostrophe and *s*—are generally placed in italics:

Watch your *p*'s and *q*'s.

We cannot distinguish his *3*'s from his *8*'s.

We said our *thank you*'s and left quickly.

To form the plural of an abbreviation followed by a period, use the apostrophe and *s:*

two Ph.D.'s   two V.P.'s

When an abbreviation or acronym is written without periods, its plural does not contain an apostrophe:

MIAs   IOUs   UFOs   VCRs

With decades, do not include an apostrophe:

the 1960s

ITS VERSUS *IT'S* AND
OTHER PRONOUN HOMONYMS

Remember that *it,* like other personal pronouns, forms its possessive without an apostrophe. But you need to use an apostrophe when you are forming the contraction of *it is: it's*. Three other pairs of *pronoun homonyms* can also cause confusion for writers.

Pronoun Homonyms

Contraction	Possessive
It's hot today.	*Its* heat slows me down.
Who's driving today?	*Whose* keys are these?
You're my one chance.	*Your* chance will come.
They're coming soon.	*Their* turn will come soon.

Because *its, whose, your,* and *their* are the possessive forms of personal pronouns (also called *possessive adjectives*), they do not use apostrophes to form possessives. The only pronouns that form possessives with apostrophes are *indefinite pronouns* (such as *one* or *someone*).

PRACTICE

I. Use of Apostrophes in Possessive Case

Correct the apostrophe errors in the following sentences. The first sentence has been done for you.

1. The author borrows one of <u>Shakespeares</u> plots.

   Revised: The author borrows one of <u>Shakespeare's</u> plots.

2. At first, Dick was surprised by the discuses weight.
3. The teachers raises made them all happy.
4. Emersons and Hawthornes homes were not far apart.
5. Is this ballpoint yours or mine?
6. The coach wants everybodys cooperation on this trip.

II. Use of Apostrophes in Contractions and Plurals

Correct the apostrophe errors in the following sentences. The first sentence has been done for you.

1. This package <u>cant</u> go through the mail this way.

   Revised: This package <u>can't</u> go through the mail this way.

2. Your computer wont read my disks.
3. No one knows how many cs and rs are in *occurrence*.
4. This isnt the last home game of the year.
5. We arent coming back until next month.
6. Were helping each other proofread for *however*s that should be preceded by semicolons.

III. *Its* versus *It's*

In each blank in the following sentences, insert either *its* or *it's*, as appropriate. The first sentence has been done for you.

1. _____ a shame that Keats died so young.

   Revised: <u>It's</u> a shame that Keats died so young.

Using Apostrophes

2. My cat likes to have _____ belly scratched.
3. Our small plane lost _____ takeoff clearance before we even left the gate.
4. _____ time to give this new play _____ premier performance.
5. When did our basketball team lose _____ desire to win?
6. Gina believes that _____ never too late to begin again.

IV. Identifying and Revising Apostrophe Errors

Rewrite the following passage, adding missing apostrophes and deleting unnecessary ones.

Everyone thought that this would be our teams year to win the championship. Its center was a senior, and the only ambition of her's that anyone had ever hear'd was to win a national championship ring just like her sisters ring. The teams only problem was that when a shot needed to be taken and the point guard and the center looked at each others eyes, they couldnt tell whether the shot should be taken by this one or that one. The point guard always thought the shot was the centers, and the center always thought the shot was the point guards. Each of the other player's thought the shot was someone elses, too. By last week, the teams unselfishness had meant that theyd only won one close game all year, and the coachs hair was turning grayer than her cars paint because she could'nt get anybody to take a shot when things got close. It wasnt that her player's were afraid to shoot; in fact, theyre all quite confident shooters. Its that their all so unselfish. Last Friday the coach had to make a rule: "When theres only one minute or less left in the game, dont pass the ball more than three time's. Whoevers hands are on the ball after the third pass, the shots her's!" Now maybe well win some close game's and the centers hand will get a championship ring to match her sisters.

PROBLEMS WITH MODIFIERS

QUICK VIEW

This Quick View presents five common problems with modifiers; these are explained in detail in the pages that follow. Correct use of modifiers helps make written English more precise.

Misplaced Modifiers

Misplaced modifiers are words, phrases, or clauses placed too far away from the words they modify:

With a temperature of 5000 degrees, Darren could see that the engine was running much too hot.

[The original makes it sound as if Darren were running quite a temperature!]

Dangling Modifiers

Dangling phrases or clauses have no word to modify:

Pouring the brown, soapy water through a filter, ^*we could see* the first real indications of the pollution ~~could be seen.~~

[There is no word in the sentence for the introductory phrase to modify; the person doing the pouring is not mentioned.]

Squinting Modifiers

Squinting modifiers are words, phrases, or clauses that could modify either what comes before or what comes after:

Chayyal said *definitely* she would be here.

[Did she definitely make the statement or will she definitely be somewhere?]

or

Chayyal said *definitely* she would be here.

Overstacked Modifiers

Overstacked modifiers are so numerous that they obscure the meaning:

> **Overstacked:** This *much-debated, incredibly expensive, multinationally constructed, limited use, too small, excessively fragile, dangerously unsafe* space station should not be built.

> **Revised:** This *much-debated* and *incredibly expensive* space station should not be built. Even though it is *multinationally constructed,* it will be of *limited use* because it is *too small, excessively fragile,* and *dangerously unsafe.*

Improper Adverb or Adjective Forms

To add *ly* or not to add *ly*? What is the *comparative* form of *round*? This final section discusses modifiers' suffixes:

Although he did not agree with the ruling, the defendant did his community service as ~~cheerful~~ *cheerfully* as possible.

Captain Janeway found the universe to be ~~more infinite~~ *bigger* than she had thought.

MISPLACED MODIFIERS

Modifiers must be placed as close as possible to the word(s) they modify. *Misplaced modifiers* are words, phrases, or clauses that are located closer to words they don't modify than to the words they do modify:

> Pat showed the new pool to her guests *that had just been filled with* water.
>
> [The sentence needs to be revised to make it clear that the pool, not the guests, had just been filled.]

If you find a modifier that has drifted away from its object, change the sentence to get them back together.

> Thirty-two trout were caught by fishermen *that had been banded.*
>
> *Hanging over the fireplace,* Jack was showing off his new painting.
>
> As we were flying
> ~~Flying~~ over Chicago, the Sears tower looked even more impressive ~~to us.~~
>
> One exception to the rule is the interest earned on bonds issued by a state or local government or a municipality, *which is tax exempt.*

DANGLING MODIFIERS

Whatever modifiers refer to must be named in the sentence. *Dangling modifiers* are usually phrases that begin with the *-ed, -ing,* or *to + verb* form of a verb (*verbal phrases*) and do not clearly refer to any other word or phrase in the sentence. These modifiers can confuse readers:

> you can easily see
> *Driving through downtown,* the effects of the fire ~~are easy to see.~~
>
> [The sentence needs to be revised so that *driving* has something to modify.]

If the object that a modifying clause or phrase is intended to describe is not named in the sentence, rewrite the sentence to include the object explicitly.

the plane was bound to have
With ice one-inch thick on its wings, an accident ~~was inevitable~~.

the students on the team had to cut corners
To take the tournament championship, ~~corners had to be cut~~ when it

came to schoolwork.

Because I was
~~Being~~ a high school senior, my parents didn't want to move until the

school year ended.

Exception: One construction looks like a dangling modifier, but it is in fact acceptable. An *absolute modifier* is a word or a phrase that modifies a whole sentence:

Jack being an honest person, there was nothing else for him to say.

[The opening phrase places a condition on the rest of the sentence; it follows an earlier discussion of his honesty.]

The judge having considered the circumstances, she ruled that the forensic pathologist's testimony should be allowed.

[An earlier discussion describes the circumstances; the opening phrase modifies the whole sentence.]

That being said, the trial moved on.

[Presumably, the words that were said are cited in the preceding sentence.]

(For more on absolute phrases, see *Phrases,* page 377.)

SQUINTING MODIFIERS

A *squinting modifier* is unclear because it could modify more than one thing in the sentence—usually the word or phrase before it as well as the word or phrase after it:

Tom told the bank *with great difficulty* he could get the money.

[Was it hard for Tom to tell them, or hard to get the money?]

or

Tom told the bank *with great difficulty* he could get the money.

If you find you have written a sentence with a squinting modifier in it, rewrite the sentence to make clear exactly what the modifier refers to.

t ~~~~~~~~~~~~~~~~~~ *0*
The otters in Abrams Creek [only] are affected by the presence of humans in the campgrounds.

[Are the Abrams Creek otters the only animals affected, or is the presence of humans the only thing that affects the Abrams Creek otters?]

or

The otters in Abrams Creek (only) are affected by the presence of humans in the campgrounds.

OVERSTACKED MODIFIERS

291–92

In government, military, scientific, and technical writing, modifiers are often stacked one on top of the other until no one knows what goes with what. The modifiers in such stacks could be nouns, adjectives, or prepositional phrases. These *overstacked modifiers* are one of the main reasons that the jargon of the Pentagon and other bureaucracies is so difficult to understand:

> **Overstacked:** The *insufficiently correlated atmospherically disturbed nitrogen-binding negative-charge ionized* molecules glow.

> **Revised:** A few of the molecules glow. Although the data about these glowing molecules are *insufficiently correlated* right now, they seem to be *nitrogen-binding* molecules that are *negatively charged* and *ionized*. Apparently, they glow when they are *atmospherically disturbed*.

Unstack overstacked modifiers to make the sentence clear, even if you have to use a few more words (or sentences) to do so.

Overstacked	Revised
The purpose of this research is to determine the feasibility of the finite-element method as a predictor for actual laboratory testing using a *three-dimensional, nonlinear, transient, dynamic, stress-and-strain finite-element* code developed at Livermore National Laboratory for analyzing average tibias and	The purpose of this research is to determine the feasibility of the finite-element method as a predictor for actual laboratory testing. The research will analyze average tibias and fibias under varying conditions of impact loading, using a *finite-element* code developed at Livermore National Laboratory.

Problems with Modifiers

fibias under varying conditions of impact loading.

The code is *three-dimensional* and *nonlinear,* allowing representation of *transient* and *dynamic stresses* and *strains.*

IMPROPER ADVERB OR ADJECTIVE FORMS

The two most common problems with adverbs and adjectives are confusion about whether to add an *ly* and confusion about the correct *comparative* and *superlative* forms.

To Add *ly* or Not?

Most adverbs are formed by adding *ly* to an adjective. Although conversational English often ignores this distinction, written English always observes it.

Spoken	Written
The coach told us to play the next five minutes as *slow* as possible.	The coach told us to play the next five minutes as *slowly* as possible.

The absence of an *-ly* ending generally means that the modifier is an *adjective*—but the words that modify verbs, adjectives, or adverbs need to be *adverbs:*

Adjective	Adverb
Paul walked with a *heavy* step out the door.	Paul walked *heavily* out the door.

Comparatives and Superlatives

Many adjectives and adverbs change form as they move from the *positive* form (*big*), to the *comparative* (*bigger*), and to the *superlative* (*biggest*). *Big,* like most one-syllable adjectives and like two-syllable adjectives that are accented on the first syllable, forms its comparative or superlative by adding *er* or *est.* (For a word that ends in *y,* the *y* changes to *i* when *er* or *est* is added.)

For adjectives that are longer than two syllables and for most adverbs, *more* and *less* are used to form comparatives and *most* and *least* are used to form superlatives. A few common modifiers have irregular forms, such as *good-better-best, bad-worse-worst,* and *some-more-most.*

There are no degrees of comparison for words that describe absolute concepts. It is illogical to speak of something being "more infinite," "less round," or "most (or very) unique."

The new Pearl Jam CD is their ~~most excellent~~ *best* one.

It is ungrammatical to use double comparative or superlative forms such as "more prettier" or "most prettiest."

Shanelle was ~~more~~ happier than I had ever seen her before.

(For sample lists of positive, comparative, and superlative forms of common adjectives and adverbs, see *Adjectives* and *Adverbs,* pages 320–22. For words not covered in that list, consult a good dictionary.)

PRACTICE

I. Correcting Modifier Problems

Correct the modifier problems in the following sentences. The first one has been done for you.

1. With one last look at the sun setting beyond Golden Gate Bridge, the plane headed for New York City.

   > **Revised:** <u>After giving the passengers</u> one last look at the sun setting beyond Golden Gate Bridge, <u>the pilot headed</u> the plane for New York City.

2. Daneeka thought that Professor Longhair's music was more unique than Doctor John's.

3. I like to dance even more when the music plays real slow.

4. To drive that kind of car the way it should be driven, long stretches of straight roads would be needed.

5. Running the FUZBOL program, the data can be compared in separate sets.

6. Shaquille told the referee only that he had been fouled before by Carlus.

7. Once a stable platform indicator disengagement stage connector light has been illuminated, the primary verification procedure for primary apogee burn initiation checklist can be reviewed.

8. Driving for the first time in a big city, Amir's car overheated and stalled.

9. Having grown up in California, the cost of property in the mountains of Tennessee was a pleasant surprise to Russell.

10. In the final analysis, no residents apparently had their health harmed by eating geese shot by hunters that had hatched and been raised on polluted reservoirs.

II. Identifying and Revising Modifier Problems

Rewrite the following short paragraph, correcting the modifier problems in it.

The freeway will come through by the spring of next year in the neighborhood where we lived before we moved to the suburbs of the city across the bay. Riding on the school bus there, most days trucks full of potatoes could be seen lined up waiting for processing. One day my friend Pat told me with great disgust his mother had packed a mashed potato sandwich in his lunchbox on the bus. He thought that was the most disgustingest thing she had ever put in his lunchbox. That is the last and most clearest memory I have of Pat. Now the potato plants have been torn down to build a massive freeway interchange, the last symbol of my old neighborhood's agricultural heritage.

FAULTY PARALLELISM

This Quick View describes the most common errors involving parallelism; the pages that follow explain those errors in more detail. *Parallelism* is a similarity of form in words, phrases, or clauses that have similar functions in a sentence or a paragraph. *Faulty parallelism* is the lack of parallel structure:

> Lucinda likes *swimming, skating,* and *~~to ski~~*. [*skiing*]

> In that dormitory, all the students have to tell the counselors *where they are going* and *~~their study schedule~~*. [*when they will be studying.*]

Readers expect parallel word structures especially when there is some underlying parallelism of meaning. In particular, the following four situations generally signal a need for parallelism.

Items in Lists

Words, phrases, or clauses in a list or series should all have the same grammatical structure:

> You can find information on authors in three ways: *ask* a librarian, *type* the author's name into the on-line catalogue, or *~~by looking~~* in [*look*] *Contemporary Authors.*

Items Joined by Coordinating Conjunctions

Words or phrases joined by coordinating conjunctions should have the same structure:

> They went *to a party* and *movies.* [*to the*]

Parts of a Sentence Joined by Correlative Conjunctions

Elements joined by correlative conjunctions, such as *either . . . or* and *not only . . . but also,* should be parallel:

> Domingo is not only *a great striker* but also *plays great at goalie.*
>   ^a

Comparisons or Contrasts

Two elements that are compared or contrasted should be expressed in parallel structures:

> Some politicians would rather *be talking* about government waste
>   ^talk
> and mismanagement than *try* to do anything about them.

ITEMS IN LISTS

Items in a list, such as "swimming, skating, and skiing," need to have the same grammatical structure. For example, the first sentence below has been corrected so that each item appears in the *-ing* form, and the second one has been corrected so that each item appears in the same order:

> From the park, we could hear *the banging of drums, the wailing of gui-* tars, and ~~cymbals crashing.~~ *the crashing of cymbals.*

> We read and discussed *Love Medicine* by Louise Erdrich, *Beloved* by Toni Morrison, *Woman Warrior* by Maxine Hong Kingston, and ~~Gretel Ehrlich's~~ *Heart Mountain* *by Gretel Ehrlich.*

ITEMS JOINED BY COORDINATING CONJUNCTIONS

Words or phrases linked by a *coordinating conjunction* (*and, but, or, nor, for, so,* and *yet*) must have parallel structure. For example, repeat any preposition (such as *in, on,* or *for*) used in the first phrase; repeat the *to* if the first phrase is an infinitive:

> Her concern was not *for a high-paying job* but *for a learning experience.*

> She decided *to cut* the old permanent out of her hair and ~~try changing~~ *to change* her hair color.

PARTS OF A SENTENCE JOINED BY CORRELATIVE CONJUNCTIONS

You also need to use parallel structures for parts of a sentence connected by *correlative conjunctions* (*both . . . and, either . . . or, neither . . . nor, not only . . . but also, whether . . . or*). To make the meaning clear, use the same structure after each of the two parts of the conjunction.

Faulty Parallelism

I had to drop
I knew that either I had to study more or ~~the~~ course. ~~should be dropped.~~

lose,
Whether we win or ~~a loss results,~~ we will know that we did our best.

COMPARISONS OR CONTRASTS

Parallel structures are also needed to clarify the meaning of comparisons or contrasts, which are usually signaled by the word *than:*

getting
Stephen thought finding a girlfriend was more important than good grades.

Saving all the bibliographic information in a computer file is easier

writing
than ~~to write~~ it all down on paper.

PRACTICE

I. Correcting Problems with Parallelism

Rewrite the following sentences, correcting any errors in parallelism. The first one has been done for you as an example.

1. Sam couldn't wait to get to camp, where he could ride horses, go on a hike, and swimming.

   Revised: Sam couldn't wait to get to camp, where he could ride horses, hike, and swim.

2. Carlos cannot decide whether he wants to return to Puerto Rico after college or if staying in Atlanta would be a better plan.

3. Since the new baby has arrived, they eat at home more than trips to a restaurant.

4. She seems to like the new hair dryer better than she liked the old one.

5. She should be hired because of her desire to improve our computer networking, the fact that she has four years of technical training and a college degree, and she has a good work record.

6. The professor cited three reasons for Hitler's rise to power: the bad economy, the citizens believed that their country had been persecuted after World War I, and everyone needed a national German identity.
7. Three reasons were given for the concert's cancellation: the lead singer had a bad cold; the ticket sales were low; and because the drummer had left the band.

II. Identifying and Revising Problems with Parallelism

. Rewrite the following short paragraph so that it uses parallel structures correctly and effectively.

My favorite hobbies have always been fishing, hiking, and to waterski. Throughout junior high and high school, I found that spending a little time outdoors doing one of these activities not only made the rest of my week go better, and actually helped me make better grades. This September, when I entered State Tech, I immediately began to miss my outdoor time and worried about only being indoors all the time. My worries disappeared, however, when I discovered how easy it was to go for a swim in the Aquatic Center's huge outdoor pool and joining the State Tech Hiking Club. Now I know that spending outdoor time as a freshman at State Tech is even easier than it was when I was in Lawton High School.

MIXED CONSTRUCTIONS

This Quick View describes the most common kinds of mixed constructions; the pages that follow explain them in more detail. A *mixed construction* is a sentence whose parts do not fit together well. This problem has two principal causes: the subject and the predicate do not belong together, or two clauses do not work together logically.

Mismatched Subject and Predicate

One book we read in high school was *Walden,* by Thoreau.
[Thoreau is the name of the author, not of the book.]

Mismatched Clauses

When planes take off late, *the delay* causes airlines to lose passengers.
["When planes take off late" is a dependent clause, not a subject.]

or

When planes take off late causes airlines to lose passengers.

Mismatches with *Is When, Is Where,* or *The Reason . . . Is Because*

Being really alone is *finding* when you find nothing in your mailbox, not even junk mail.
[Words or phrases linked by *is* should be parallel in structure.]

or

You know you are Being really alone is when you find nothing in your mailbox, not even junk mail.

MISMATCHED SUBJECT AND PREDICATE

The subject and the predicate (the verb plus its object or other complements) of a sentence should make sense together. If they do not, the result is one type of *mixed construction*. (A more specific name for this version of the error is *faulty predication*.) Writers most frequently make this error when several words interrupt the flow between the subject and the verb:

Building a new little league park would ~~be~~ *create* a great *place* for the boys

and girls to have fun.

[It is the *park* that would be a great place, not *building* it.]

or

~~Building~~ *A* new little league park would *be* a great *place* for the boys

and girls to have fun.

Because she
~~Tina, who~~ did not have flood insurance, ~~caused her to feel~~ *Tina felt* anxious

during the hurricane.

or

Her lack of
~~Tina, who did not have~~ flood insurance, *Tina* caused ~~her~~ to *feel* anxious

during the hurricane.

If you find you have written a sentence that seems jumbled or mixed, as these examples are, you will probably need to rework the sentence from scratch. To get a fresh start, try saying what you mean out loud, and then write down the words that way.

MISMATCHED CLAUSES

Sometimes a writer will begin a sentence with one type of structure and end it with another, thus creating a confusing combination:

after   , but she is also experiencing
Not only does her head ache, the accident ~~caused~~ neck pain.

[Pairing *not only* with *but also* helps to logically relate the clauses.]

Mixed
Constructions

After running ten miles, ~~was the reason~~ Sandra became dehydrated.
["Running" can be a reason for becoming dehydrated; "after running" cannot be.]

In this kind of mixed construction, a sentence starts in one direction but then—without warning—goes off in another. The solution is to decide which of the two directions you want and then to make the other part of the sentence fit smoothly into that path.

MISMATCHES WITH *IS WHEN, IS WHERE,* OR *THE REASON . . . IS BECAUSE*

In sentences stating definitions, constructions such as *is when, is where, is why,* and *the reason . . . is because* can cause confusion and awkwardness. Using *reason* with *because* is repetitive; *where* should be used only for locations; and *when* should be used only for time. Although these wordings are fairly common in spoken language, they produce illogical statements and should be avoided in formal writing:

A sanction *is* ~~when one nation imposes~~ *the imposition of* a penalty *by one nation* on another for misconduct.

A breach of contract *is* ~~where one party fails~~ *one party's failure* to live up to the terms of the contract.

~~The reason~~ *He* didn't go to the party ~~is because~~ he doesn't have a tuxedo.

PRACTICE

I. Correcting Mixed Constructions

Rewrite the following sentences, eliminating any mixed constructions you find in them. The first one has been done for you.

1. Although she found that child care was hard to pay for, not only that but she needed to work.

Revised: Although she did not have enough money for child care, she needed to work.

2. The reason Congress should reduce foreign aid is because we have too many needy people here at home.

3. If teenagers want to fit in with their peers is the main reason they start smoking.

4. Walking every day for about five miles can be a good distance for effective weight loss.

5. More than seventy samples to analyze was the reason the work took so long.

6. A blocking foul is when the defender's feet are not set before the player with the ball gets there.

II. Identifying and Revising Mixed Constructions

Rewrite the following paragraph, eliminating the mixed constructions it contains.

One way to identify being a member of Generation X is when your favorite movies all are based on cartoon heroes or other imaginary characters. The reason for our fascination with raised-from-the-dead rock stars, lycanthropes, poltergeists, and other morphs is because we have found real people never live up to our expectations. Not only do the few would-be heroes in real life always seem to turn out to have dark sides, politics, sports, and religion have a shortage of people willing even to try to live up to high ideals of behavior. Every night, more than a network newscast full of politicians on the take, sports stars gambling or on drugs, or various religious leaders preaching hatred and violence is why we turn to characters made up of fantasies. Away from real life is where we find our role models. When we watch a steady diet of nothing but fantasy films is one reason we are called Generation X.

FOR ESL WRITERS

⊕ ▶ FOR ESL WRITERS

▪ *QUICK VIEW*

This Quick View provides a list, with short examples, of the most common writing problems encountered by students whose native language is not English. The pages that follow explain these problems in more detail. Many of the discussions are also touched on in other places in this book, where they have been marked with a globe icon.

Articles and Nouns (pages 285–91)

- **Four rules for using the articles *a, an,* and *the:*** *The friends* who study *chemistry* work together on *a supercomputer.*
- **Articles with names of places:** Asia, South America, *the* Atlantic Ocean, *the* West
- **Nouns made from adjectives:** *The elderly* can take advantage of many discount travel offers.

Adjectives (pages 291–93)

- **Order of cumulative adjectives:** *the small, square, wooden card* table
- ***-Ing* and *-ed* verbs used as adjectives:** The *bored* tourist thought it was the most *boring* museum of the trip.
- ***No* and *not:*** *No* audience members left early. They did *not* want to miss the encore.

Prepositions (pages 293–94)

- **Phrasal prepositions:** according to, across from, out of
- **Phrasal constructions:** preferable to, thankful for

Verbs (pages 294–304)

- **Two-word verbs:** admit to, agree on, agree with
- **Missing verbs:** Luis *is* at home.
- **Helping verbs:** He *can* win. He *has* eaten. He *could be* playing.

- **Verbs in conditional sentences:** If the store *closes* early, she *will come* by our house.
- **Verbs followed by gerunds and infinitives:** They *finished dancing*. They *offered to help* her. They *expect* him *to stay*.

Sentence Structure (pages 304–07)

- **Understood subjects:** *Finish* your lunch.
- ***It* and *there* structures:** *There were* clouds earlier. Now *it is* raining.
- **Direct and indirect questions and quotations:** The clerk asked, "Would you like to charge your purchase?" I said I would pay in cash.
- **Relative clauses:** He liked the movie *that he had rented*.

The chapter concludes with a list of on-line references for ESL writers.

ARTICLES AND NOUNS

Four Rules for Using the Articles *A, An,* and *The*

The words *a, an,* and *the* are called *articles. A* and *an* are *indefinite articles,* and *the* is the *definite article.* They are used to modify nouns.

As the flowchart (Figure 20) shows, the two keys to understanding when to use *a, an,* and *the* are the distinction between *general* and *specific* nouns and the distinction between *countable* and *uncountable* nouns. To use the four rules, you must first understand those two key distinctions.

General Nouns and Specific Nouns

First you need to decide whether you are looking at a *general* noun or a *specific* noun. Although some nouns are usually used in a general sense and others usually in a specific sense, the context is

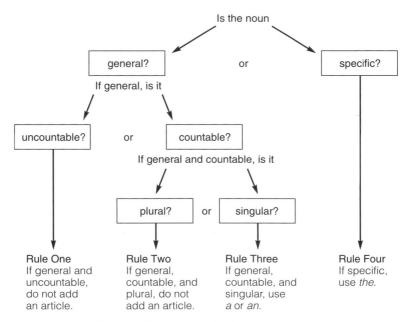

Figure 20. Flowchart and Summary of Rules for Using Articles

the only sure way to judge whether a noun is general or specific. Consider the following three uses of the noun *door:*

General Nouns

Doors are available in many different materials and styles.

Every room in my parents' house had a *door.*

Specific Noun

Kim shut the *door* and locked it.

General nouns name an entire category or a representative member of a category:

Air is necessary for *life.*

These plants need *water.*

Mexico City is surrounded by *mountains.*

A *city* offers more *services* than a *town.*

My sister has an unnatural fear of *spiders.*

Specific nouns refer not to a general category but to one particular thing (or group of things), which is known to the reader:

The *air* in here is stale.

Please hand me the ice *water.*

Let's go to the *mountains* this weekend.

Ottavo's dream was to go to the big *city.*

The *spiders* we found were not poisonous.

Several situations can make a noun specific: (1) a superlative (such as *biggest*) or an ordinal (such as *first*) adjective precedes the noun; (2) an identifying phrase or clause follows the noun; (3) the noun names something unique; and (4) the noun has been previously mentioned. The following paragraphs give examples of these situations.

1. Some adjectives can change a noun from general to specific. **Superlative adjectives** (*most, biggest, bluest*) make the nouns they modify specific:

General	Specific
A *famous tree* in Austin was poisoned.	The *oldest tree* in Austin was poisoned.

A *runner* was disqualified for drug use.	*The fastest runner* was disqualified for drug use.

Ordinal adjectives (*first, second, third*), which specify a noun's place in some order, can also change a noun from general to specific:

General	Specific
A *violin concerto* would be a good addition to the program.	*The first violin concerto* ever performed in public was by Mendelssohn.

A few other adjectives, such as *top* and *current,* can also make a general noun specific.

2. Sometimes a **phrase or clause following a noun identifies it** in such a way that the meaning of the noun becomes specific:

General	Specific
Trust is an important factor in medicine.	*The trust of a patient in a doctor* is an important factor in medicine.
Time will be a factor on this test.	*The time that you take answering each question* will be a factor on this test.

3. Some nouns are specific because they refer to **things that are unique:** the *sun,* the *moon,* the *ground,* the *sky,* the *past,* the *present,* the *future.*

DeWan looked at *the sky* for signs of rain.

Amelia will win *the championship.*

4. Sometimes an otherwise general noun is treated as specific because that **noun has been mentioned earlier.** Typically, the definite article (*the*) is used for each mention after the first:

Esteban approached the choice of *a major* by rating each subject from 1 to 5 on the following questions: How much do I enjoy the work in *the major*? What job opportunities exist for new graduates in *the major*?

Uncountable and Countable Nouns

General nouns can be countable or uncountable. **Uncountable nouns** refer to things that are not broken into units; they have no plural form and they cannot be used with words that indicate quantity, such as *many* or *few*.

> *Love* is a powerful emotion.
>
> *Chemistry* is the hardest class I have.
>
> The doctor said I should eat less *salt*.
>
> *Honesty* is the best policy.

See the box "Types of Uncountable Nouns" for the kinds of words that are usually uncountable nouns.

Types of Uncountable Nouns

Words in the following categories are usually uncountable nouns:
- Substances without definite shapes: *air, cement, dirt, flour, gasoline, paper, rain, snow, steel, water*
- Kinds of food and drink: *beer, bread, candy, fish, lettuce, milk, nuts, rice, soup, tea, water, yogurt*

- Abstractions: *anger, bravery, determination, gravity, happiness, justice, liberty, respect, truth*

- Continuous processes: *digestion, education, living, photosynthesis, turbulence*

- Fields of study: *biology, chemistry, economics, mathematics, music, physics, zoology*

Other common uncountable nouns include *advice, equipment, furniture, garbage, information, jewelry, luggage, machinery, money, traffic,* and *vocabulary.*

Countable nouns refer to things that can be counted; they can be used with quantity words, such as *many* and *few*, and they have singular and plural forms.

> Next term they hope to find *an apartment* off campus.
>
> Are there *many apartments* available near campus?

Examples of singular countable nouns are *apartment, bicycle, car, cloud, computer, couch,* and *friend*.

Some nouns can be uncountable in one context and countable in another:

He does good *work*. [uncountable]

He created two art *works*. [separate, countable pieces]

I love *chocolate*. [uncountable]

Let me have two *chocolates* from that box. [separate, countable pieces]

Rule One: No Article before General, Uncountable Nouns

If you decide that a noun is both *general* and *uncountable,* do not add an article:

Alfredo has decided to study ~~the~~ economics.

Jianyi went to buy ~~the~~ sugar.

E
~~The~~ ~~e~~ducation has always been stressed in Maria's family.

Again, the noun's use in context determines its type. If the first example were "Alfredo has decided to study *the economics* of the automotive industry," the noun would be specific, and *the* would be correct. The way the noun is used, not the noun itself, determines the need for the article.

Note—Quantity Terms and Uncountable Nouns: Uncountable nouns can be modified by certain quantity terms, such as *cup of, gallon of,* and *pound of:* "a cup of water," "a gallon of milk," or "7.5 pounds of sand." When uncountable nouns are preceded by quantity terms, the nouns themselves still do not take a plural form (that is, "7.5 pounds of *sand*," not "7.5 pounds of *sands*"). The words *some, more,* and *any* can be used to indicate nonspecific quantities: "some sand," "more sugar," "any milk."

Rule Two: No Article before General, Countable, Plural Nouns

If you decide that a noun in a sentence is both *general* and *countable,* then you must decide whether it is *singular* or *plural.* If the noun is plural, it is not preceded by an article:

When Anna talks about ~~the~~ computers, she is very easy to understand.

A
~~The~~ ~~a~~pples are one of nature's healthiest foods.

Felicia takes ~~the~~ grades more seriously than I do.

Rule Three: Use A or An before General, Countable, Singular Nouns

If you decide that a noun is *general, countable,* and *singular,* add *a* or *an.* If such a noun begins with a *consonant* sound, use *a.* If it begins with a *vowel* sound, use *an:*

> James saw *a truck* in front of the dorm.

> Last week we read *an article* by Carl Sagan.

Rule Four: Use The before Specific Nouns

Specific nouns—words that clearly refer to one or more specific things—take *the* for an article. We return to the example used at the beginning of this discussion of articles:

> Kim shut *the door* and locked it.

Here *door* clearly refers to one specific door; thus *door* is preceded by *the,* as is the plural, *doors:*

> Kim shut *the doors* and locked them.

Articles with Names of Places

Most place names in English are not written with articles—*America, Europe, Indochina, South America.*

> I hope to go to *Canada* or *Mexico* next summer.

One exception is collective names and plurals; they are preceded by *the.* Examples include *the United States, the sub-Saharan states, the United Kingdom.*

> *The European Community* faces an uncertain future.

Other exceptions are land masses, bodies of water, and geographical regions; they are generally preceded by *the.* Examples include *the Asian subcontinent, the Southern Hemisphere, the Atlantic Ocean, the Mediterranean, the Baja Peninsula, the Appalachian highlands.*

> Few people know *the prairie* as well as Aldo Leopold did.

> *The West* was the last frontier.

Nouns Made from Adjectives

An adjective usually modifies a noun, but an adjective is also occasionally used as a noun. When it is, the adjective is always in singular form, even if it names something plural. For example, instead of writing a sentence in which *young* is used as an adjective,

> *Young* people especially are invited to this concert.

we might write a sentence in which *young* is used as a noun:

> *The young* especially are invited to this concert.

Even though *young* in the second sentence refers to a number of people (and the verb, *are*, is plural), it is not put in plural form. Here are some more examples of singular nouns made from adjectives:

The *lucky winners* are going home to celebrate.

The ~~luckies~~ *lucky* are going home to celebrate.

The *tall people* are chosen first when we play basketball.

The talls are chosen first when we play basketball.

Some citizens do not vote, but the *responsible ones* do.

Some citizens do not vote, but the responsibles do.

ADJECTIVES

Order of Cumulative Adjectives

In English, adjectives usually *precede* the nouns they modify, and certain types of cumulative adjectives in a series precede other types in a series. Instead of modifying the noun individually, as coordinate adjectives do, cumulative adjectives build on each other, with each adjective to the left of the noun modifying the entire unit that follows it. In the sentence "Several bright floral prints hang in the living room," *bright* modifies *floral prints,* and *several* modifies the entire phrase.

Eduardo bought ~~an~~ *a* old blue beautiful house for his family.

Cumulative adjectives have a customary ordering in English. Although there are exceptions, here is how the order works generally:

- Articles and pronouns go first: *a, an, the, his, her, our, several, few, every,* and so on.
- Evaluative words go next: *beautiful, ugly, handsome, pretty, committed, tasty, appealing,* and so on.
- Words about size go next: *big, small, huge, tiny,* and so on.

- Words about length and shape go next: *short, long, square, round, oblong, triangular, wide, narrow,* and so on.
- Words about age go next: *old, young, fresh, stale,* and so on.
- Words about color go next: *red, green, blue,* and so on.
- Words about nationality go next: *Canadian, Irish, Mexican, Puerto Rican, Vietnamese,* and so on.
- Words about religion go next: *Catholic, Protestant, Muslim, Buddhist,* and so on.
- Words about material makeup go next: *concrete, wooden, brick, stone, steel-and-glass,* and so on.
- Nouns used as adjectives go next: *swim* (as in *swim team*), *rope* (as in *rope ladder*), *fish* (as in *fish market*), and so on.
- The noun being modified goes last: *teacher, student, house, books, ideas,* and so on.

Note—Cumulative versus Coordinate Adjectives: *Cumulative* adjectives, such as those listed above, build on each other and are not separated by commas. *Coordinate* adjectives, in contrast, modify the noun separately and are separated by commas, as in "Eric turned out to be a loud, messy, annoying roommate." You can identify adjectives as cumulative if you cannot insert *and* between them or change their order, as you can with coordinate adjectives:

Example: My small red toy boat moved over the surface of the lake.

Test for Cumulative: My *and* small *and* red *and* toy boat moved over the surface of the lake.

[Since inserting *and* between the adjectives doesn't work, the adjectives are cumulative.]

Another Test for Cumulative: Small red toy my boat moved over the surface of the lake.

[The awkwardness of the changed order of the adjectives suggests that, in their original ordering, they were working together, not separately. Thus they are cumulative, not coordinate.]

-Ing and *-Ed* Verbs Used as Adjectives

Adjectives can be formed from both the present participle (*-ing* form) and the past participle (*-ed* form) of verbs. The *-ing* form indicates that the word modified produces an effect; the *-ed* form indicates that something has affected the word modified:

The *exciting* movie is still playing.

[The movie produces excitement.]

The *excited* girl waited in the lobby.

[The girl has been excited: that effect has been produced in her.]

Produces an Effect	Has an Effect Produced on It
amazing	amazed
boring	bored
depressing	depressed
disappointing	disappointed
interesting	interested
satisfying	satisfied
surprising	surprised
worrying	worried

Even though you may not always hear the *-ed* ending in speech, remember not to omit it in your writing:

The *worried* girl waited for her mother.

No and Not

Not is an adverb that modifies an adjective or a verb: When *not* is used with an adjective, it precedes the adjective:

That salesclerk is *not* helpful.

When *not* negates a verb, it is placed between a helping verb and a main verb or between a *be* verb and a participle:

Clarissa does *not* plan ahead.

She is *not* coming to the party.

No is an adjective, and therefore it modifies a noun:

Clarissa makes *no* plans in advance.

PREPOSITIONS

Phrasal Prepositions

English has a number of phrasal prepositions, including the following:

according to	down from	out of
across from	in addition to	prior to
because of	in between	with the exception of

To write fluent, idiomatic English, you need to be careful not to use the wrong combination.

The student center is across ~~to~~ the law school.

(*from* marked above, ^ below)

Phrasal Constructions

Several other *phrasal constructions* in English can be difficult if English is not your native language. These constructions usually follow a verb and take the form of an adjective (or a noun) plus a preposition:

ability at, with	identical to, with	preferable to
angry at, with	impatient for, with	receptive to
capable of	independent of	superior to
deserving of	inferior to	thankful for, to
free of, from, to	necessity for, of, to	worthy of, to

Because the meaning of the phrase depends partly on the preposition, you need to be careful to use the correct preposition in these constructions. If you're unsure of the correct combination, check an unabridged dictionary during the finishing stage of your writing.

VERBS

Two-Word Verbs

Many combinations of a verb and a preposition have a special (idiomatic) meaning in English. The following sentences illustrate these accepted combinations, including the ones in which the preposition can follow the object of the verb:

They were *accompanied by* their parents.

He was *accused of* a crime.

She can *adapt to* new situations.

The manager will never *admit to* his errors.

We never *agree on* the best vacation spot.

Do you *agree with* me?

Jana *called off* the wedding.

Or Jana *called* the wedding *off*.

How much will he *charge for* admission?

How does this album *compare with* his last one? [The two albums are in the same category.]

He *compared* the crowd *to* an army of ants. [A figurative comparison is being made.]

The two buildings are *connected by* an underground tunnel.

I am *connected with* that group.

We *differ on* that question.

She *differs from* her suitemates.

Carlos *dropped in* on his old roommate.

He always *gets up* early.

Come *join in* the party.

Join with us in supporting Belinda for class president.

I will *look into* this problem.

Mother asked me to *look up* her old friend from Seattle.

Or I will *look* her *up*.

Sarah *objects to* your decision.

These seats are *occupied by* the dancers' families.

I have been *occupied with* raising children for ten years.

She didn't want to *part from* her grandmother.

She didn't want to *part with* her inheritance.

She *ran across* an old friend.

Are you *worried about* the meeting?

The clerk *waits on* the customer.

I will *wait for* a taxi.

Consult a dictionary for the correct combinations when you are not sure about which preposition to use with a verb. Most dictionaries, especially unabridged dictionaries, give examples of sentences in which such combinations are used properly.

Missing Verbs

In some languages, you can omit the verb if the meaning is clear without it. In English, this omission (usually of a form of *be*) is not allowed:

is
Cara⌄very pretty.

is
Rosa⌄in the park near the corner.

In English, neither the present participle (the -*ing* form) nor the infinitive (the *to* + *verb* form) may be used as the main verb of the sentence:

is
Prim⌄playing golf.

is
Samuel ~~to be~~⌄my friend.

or

wants
Samuel⌄to be my friend.

Helping Verbs

Some verbs, called *helping* or *auxiliary verbs,* do not appear alone in sentences but instead are always combined with another verb, the main verb. The helping verb completes the meaning of the main verb:

h.v. m.v.
Lisa can go to the party.

h.v.   m.v.
You should eat your vegetables.

The helping verbs called *modals* normally function *only* as helping verbs:

Modal Helping Verbs

can	might	should
could	must	will
may	shall	would

The other helping verbs are forms of *do, have,* and *be,* shown in the following list:

Helping Forms of *Do*

do	does	did

Helping Forms of *Have*

have	has	had

Helping Forms of *Be*

| be | am | is | are |
| was | were | been | being |

These helping verbs appear with only certain forms of the main verb, as explained in the following sections.

Modal Helping Verbs

The modal helping verbs listed on the preceding page are always used with the base form of the verb, which is the form used with *to* in an infinitive (*to* + *verb*):

Examples of Base Forms

become	dive	grow	sing
begin	drink	keep	speak
build	drive	know	stand
buy	eat	make	swim
choose	get	read	take
come	give	run	teach
dig	go	say	

Modal helping verbs do not change form to agree in number with the subject:

He cans̸ go.

Modal helping verbs are never followed by any verb except the base form:

He will ~~goes.~~ *go.*

She should writes̸ every day.

Paulina will ~~bringing~~ *bring* the tablecloth.

His collie could ~~catched~~ *catch* a flying disc.

Do, Does, *and* Did

Like the modal helping verbs, the forms of the helping verb *do* occur only with the base forms of verbs. However, unlike the modals, *do* changes to agree in number with the subject. A form of *do* can be combined with base forms of main verbs in the following ways:

- To express a negative meaning along with *not:*

  You *do* not need that green registration form.

  He *did* not want to stay with his parents.

- To ask a question:

  Do you want your dessert?

  Does it ever rain in the winter here?

- To emphasize a main verb:

  You *do* look delightful today.

  This makeup *does* make your face look more round.

Have, Has, and Had

The helping verbs *have, has,* and *had* are used with the past participle form of the verb (usually ending with *ed*):

Regular Past Participles—Formed with *ed*

Base Verb	Past Participle
like	liked
receive	received
talk	talked
touch	touched

Irregular Past Participles

Base Verb	Past Participle
break	broken
bring	brought
build	built
buy	bought
catch	caught
choose	chosen
do	done
drink	drunk
eat	eaten
forget	forgotten

get	gotten
grow	grown
keep	kept
lead	led
read	read
say	said
sing	sung
speak	spoken
swim	swum
take	taken
teach	taught
throw	thrown

The combination of a form of *have* plus the past participle creates the *perfect tenses,* which indicate action that has occurred over time and continues into the present (with *have* or *has*) or that had occurred over time and ended in the past (with *had*):

I *have sung* with this choir many times.

He *has eaten* my pound cake each week.

Sarah *had liked* math until she got to algebra.

Helping Verbs in Progressive Tenses

Forms of *be* (*be, am, is, are, was, were,* and *been*) are used as helping verbs with the present participle (the *-ing* form) of the verb to form the progressive tenses, those that indicate continuing action in the past, present, or future:

- **To discuss a continuous action that was completed in the past,** use *was* or *were* with the present participle:

  Fredericka *was planning* a trip to Mexico.

  Her brothers *were working* for the railroad company.

- **To discuss an ongoing action in the present,** use *am, is,* or *are* with the present participle:

  I *am standing* on the street outside his house.

  Carlos *is refinishing* his father's desk.

  They *are driving* home from Alaska.

- **To discuss possible actions or future actions,** use a modal (*can, could, may, might, must, shall, should, will,* or *would*) plus the helping verb *be* plus a present participle:

  I *could be playing* golf right now.

  They *should be leaving* soon.

  I *will be starting* school next week.

- **To discuss actions that began in the past and have continued to the present,** use *has* or *have* plus the helping verb *been* plus the present participle:

  That cord *has been hanging* there for weeks.

  Your friends *have been telling* me all about you.

- **To discuss actions in progress in the past that were completed before another past occurrence,** use *had* plus the helping verb *been* plus the present participle:

  We *had been working* there on the day before it rained.

  I *had been skating* there twice before the rink closed.

Exceptions: Some English verbs (called *state-of-being verbs*) may *seem* to imply a continued action, but they do not take the progressive form:

State-of-Being Verbs

appear	desire	like	prefer
appreciate	dislike	love	recognize
believe	doubt	mean	seem
belong	hate	need	suppose
cost	know	own	want

love
I ~~am loving~~ him.

weighs
He ~~is weighing~~ 195 pounds.

Helping Verbs in Passive Sentences

Passive voice makes the subject of the sentence the *receiver* of the verb's action, rather than the *agent* or *actor* for the verb. To create a passive sentence, use a form of *be* (*am, is, are, was,* or *were*) with a past participle (the *-ed* form of the verb):

> The scholarship *is awarded* to the student with the highest SAT score.
>
> The letter *was received* last Tuesday.

Some forms of the verb *be* (*be, being, been*) need an additional helping verb as well as the past participle to create a passive form:

- *Be* must be preceded by a modal (*can, could, may, might, must, shall, should, will, would*):

  > The money *will be spent* this week.
  >
  > This crime wave *must be stopped.*

- *Being* must be preceded by *am, is, are, was,* or *were:*

  > I *am being criticized* daily by the new boss.
  >
  > The small group of single mothers *was being helped* by the new program.

- *Been* must be preceded by *has, have,* or *had:*

  > He *has been ignored* by his father-in-law.
  >
  > The desks *had been moved* last week.

Verbs in Conditional Sentences

Conditional sentences use two clauses to express the dependence of one action or situation on another action or situation. The clause containing the condition begins with *if, unless,* or *when.* Conditional sentences can be identified as one of four kinds: statements of fact, predictions and advice, unlikely possibilities, and nonfactual conditions and wishes.

- **In factual conditional sentences** (such as those that state scientific truths or describe habitual behaviors), the present tense is used in both clauses:

  > If the temperature *drops* below 30 degrees, ice *forms* on this bridge.
  >
  > When Mary *enters* her father's study, he always *puts* his books away.

- **In conditional statements that predict the future or offer advice or opinions,** the *if* or *unless* clause contains a present tense verb, and the main clause contains the modal *will, can, may, might,* or *should* followed by the base form of the verb:

If you *marry* him, you *will please* your parents.

Children *will* not *rest* unless you *remind* them to do so.

- **In statements speculating about an unlikely condition in the present or the future,** use a past tense verb in the *if* clause. The main clause contains the modal *would, could,* or *might* followed by the base form of the verb:

    If I *won* the lottery, I *would retire* immediately.

    Tandra *could make* the team if she *ran* the mile 20 seconds faster.

- Conditional sentences are also used to discuss **events that are not factual,** such as wishes that cannot be granted. These sentences, even though they do not concern the past, have *were* (not *was*) in the *if* clause; then the main clause contains *would, could,* or *might* followed by the base form of the verb:

    If I *were* king for a day, I *would provide* health care for everyone.

    If my father *were* still alive, he *would walk* me down the aisle.

Verbs Followed by Gerunds and Infinitives

The *gerund* is the *-ing* form of the verb used as a noun, as in the sentence "I like *swimming*." The infinitive is the base form of the verb preceded by *to,* as in "I like *to swim*." Either form can serve as the subject or the object of a sentence:

Walking can be great exercise.

To walk again was the accident victim's dream.

He likes *eating*.

He likes *to eat*.

As the following sections show, several different rules apply when verbs are followed by gerunds or infinitives, depending on the nature of the verb in question.

Verb + Gerund or Infinitive

Some verbs can be followed by a gerund or an infinitive without any change in meaning:

begin	like
can't stand	love
continue	start
hate	

"I hate *driving*," for example, means the same as "I hate *to drive*."
With other verbs, such as *stop* and *remember,* the meaning
changes depending on whether it is followed by the gerund or
the infinitive form. That is, "I *stopped calling* my mother" means
"I no longer called her," but "I *stopped to call* my mother" means
"I interrupted what I was doing to call her."

Verb + Gerund

Some verbs may be followed by a gerund but not by an infinitive:

appreciate	enjoy	practice
avoid	finish	recall
deny	miss	resist
discuss	postpone	suggest

He finished ~~to play~~ *playing* golf by noon.

She enjoys ~~to study~~ *studying* for her finals.

Verb + Infinitive

Verbs that describe something anticipated or planned may be followed by an infinitive but not by a gerund:

agree	decide	mean	promise
ask	expect	offer	wait
beg	have	plan	want
claim	hope	pretend	wish

He offered ~~helping~~ *to help* me.

We planned ~~leaving~~ *to leave* after the ceremony.

Verb + Noun or Pronoun + Infinitive

With some verbs that take an infinitive, a noun or a pronoun
must come between the verb and the infinitive in order to name
the person who is affected by the action:

advise	cause	encourage
allow	command	instruct

order	require	urge
persuade	tell	

me
He caused to quit my job.

Lucinda
Treena encouraged to return to college.

A few verbs may be followed either by an infinitive or by a noun or pronoun plus an infinitive:

ask	need	would like
expect	want	

He *wants Frederico to keep* his class ring.

He *wants to keep* his class ring.

SENTENCE STRUCTURE

The regular order for an English sentence is *subject/verb/object,* as in *She/sent/a letter.* Indirect objects can follow the verb or be replaced with a prepositional phrase that follows the direct object: "She sent *her new roommate* a letter" or "She sent a letter *to her new roommate.*" You will find a thorough discussion of this order and of each type of English sentence on pages 394–99. What follows here are explanations of several trouble spots in sentence structure.

Understood Subjects

In some languages, the subject of a sentence may be omitted if the writer judges that readers will know it. In written English, the subject may be omitted only in second-person constructions, in which the second-person pronoun *you* may be omitted as an *understood subject:*

Second-Person Construction	Understood Subject
You go get the car.	Go get the car.

In any other situation, you need to be sure that the subject of the sentence—however familiar you think it may be to the reader—is stated:

the catalyst
Next, we will add a catalyst to the mixture; will speed up the reaction.

It and *There* Structures

Sentences can begin with *it* or *there* and a *be* verb if the subject has been moved to another position in the sentence. In these sentences, the *it* or the *there* performs an important function and cannot be omitted:

There are
~~Are~~ many ways to speed up this chemical reaction.

It is
~~Is~~ Luis's turn to write up the procedure.

Direct and Indirect Quotations and Questions

When you want to include a direct quotation (either a few words, a sentence, or a question), you must place the exact words in quotation marks. When you use an indirect quotation or question, which summarizes or paraphrases the speaker's words, however, you report the speaker's words without quotation marks:

Direct Quotation: She said, "I finally found the tickets."

Indirect Quotation: She said that she finally found the tickets.

Direct Question: Laura asked, "Has he folded the laundry?"

Indirect Question: Laura asked if he had folded the laundry.

Direct and Indirect Quotations

The following examples illustrate some of the changes you must make to turn a direct quotation into an indirect quotation:

1. The indirect quotation has no quotation marks and requires an inserted *that.*

   Direct Quotation: Our teacher said, "The guest enjoyed our class."

   Indirect Quotation: Our teacher said *that* the guest enjoyed our class.

2. When direct quotations use the first person (*I*), this pronoun changes to the third person (*her* or *she*) in the indirect quotation.

   Direct Quotation: "*I*'m ready to leave," she announced.

   Indirect Quotation: She announced that *she* was ready to leave.

3. Direct quotations of commands become indirect quotations with the addition of to before the verb.

Direct Quotation: The camp counselor said, "Shut that window."

Indirect Quotation: The camp counselor said *to* shut that window.

4. Creating indirect quotations may require some rewriting of time expressions or rephrasing of conversation.

Direct Quotation: His grandmother said, "You know, Bob, I think I should begin buying your school clothes tomorrow."

Indirect Quotation: *Bob's* grandmother said that she *would* begin buying *his* school clothes *the next day.*

Direct and Indirect Questions

When you change a direct question to an indirect question, the word order is no longer that of the direct question, and the verb tense and the person may change (from *I* to *he* or *she*). Add *if, whether,* and question words such as *why* and *when* to introduce indirect questions:

Direction Question: Nguyen asked, "Are the cookies done?"

Indirect Question: Nguyen asked if the cookies were done.

Direct Question: "Should I go home during the Thanksgiving break?" wondered Rachel.

Indirect Question: Rachel wondered whether she should go home during the Thanksgiving break.

Direct Question: The child asked, "Why can't I go to the circus?"

Indirect Question: The child asked why she couldn't go to the circus.

(For additional help with incorporating quoted material into your writing, see pages 81–86.)

Relative Clauses

An adjective clause that modifies a noun or a pronoun and begins with *who, that,* or *which* is called a relative clause. An adjective clause should be placed right after the noun it modifies:

Luisa entered the plane, which was a new 747 jet, with her son.

Tzusheng returned the book that he had borrowed to the library.

Omission of That

Although the general rule is that relative clauses begin with a relative pronoun (*who, that,* or *which*), the pronoun *that* may be omitted when there is no possibility of misreading:

> At the Comedy Club last night, Marta showed her audience [that] she knows how to make people laugh.

However, when *that* is the subject of the relative clause, it must be included:

> The grocery store *that* was closest to our house went out of business last month.

Repeated Objects

When you use a relative clause to describe the object of sentence, the relative pronoun refers to that object; you do not need another pronoun at the end of the clause:

> Pedro saw the tennis racket that he wanted it.

www.

On-Line Resources for ESL Writers

If you simply type "ESL" into the text box of your favorite Web browser, you should find plenty of ESL resources on the Web. We tried a simple Yahoo! search and discovered 3 categories of ESL listings (each containing multiple sites) and 280 individual sites. Here are some sites that we found using a more sophisticated search technique and that we explored in more detail:

- To review the TOEFL test for free, try <http://testwise.com/ review.html>, a service of Teletext USA, a TOEFL preparation company.

- For general ESL resources, take a look at ESL Net, at <http://esl.net/>, or try the excellent index of ESL resources on the Web at the University of Illinois at Urbana-Champaign <http://www.lang.uiuc.edu/r-li5/esl/>. In fact, you might want to look at the entire Lingua Center at <http://deil.lang.uiuc. edu/lchomepage.html>.

- The grammar and writing page of Capital Community-Technical College has a number of useful features for ESL learning, including on-line quizzes, at <http://webster.commnet.edu/HP/pages/ darling/grammar.htm>.

(continued)

(continued)
- Dave Sperling's ESL Help Center <http://www.eslcafe.com/help/> allows students to send in ESL questions via e-mail and receive answers on-line.

- For a great list of ESL links, try the page maintained by Professor Christine Meloni at The George Washington University in Washington, DC <http://gwis2.circ.gwu.edu/~gwvcusas/>. An even more comprehensive set of links, presented in an interesting format, can be found on the "Frizzy University Network" (that's "FUN" for short) at <http://thecity.sfsu.edu/~funweb/Welcome.html>.

- Finally, you can dive into a whole "ring" of ESL pages that have been joined together into "The ESLoop" (that's a clever way of spelling "the ESL loop"). Once you get to any page in the loop (in Web terminology, it's actually a "ring"), such as the loop's home page <http://www.linguistic-funland.com/esloop/>, you automatically have access to all the other pages. In January of 1998 the loop included 64 sites.

PRACTICE

I. Articles and Nouns

Revise the following sentences to eliminate errors involving articles. The first one has been done for you.

1. Four trees had fallen, and they blocked street.

   Revised: Four trees had fallen, and they blocked <u>the</u> street.

2. We decided to make an honesty an important quality in the person we hired.

3. Six of the hours you take as part of your undergraduate work must be in the physics.

4. When the Lake Erie became polluted, the New Yorkers quit vacationing there.

5. Captain Picard says his goal is to explore the space, final frontier.

6. Her home was only seven blocks away from library.

7. Of the two movies, comedy was better than musical.

8. Sasha was first one to go through the line.

9. Northwestern United States is home to many Indian tribes.

10. The careless will fail this test, but the carefuls will pass it easily.

II. Adjectives

Rewrite the following sentences, correcting any problems you see with adjective order, -*ing* and -*ed* forms, or the use of *no* or *not*. The first one has been done for you.

1. His <u>square</u> <u>coffee</u> <u>small</u> table has lost a leg.

   Revised: His <u>small</u> <u>square</u> <u>coffee</u> table has lost a leg.

2. She felt annoying when her son left his clothes on the floor.
3. Jaime no wanted to leave.
4. Will you bring your blue new African beautiful jacket?
5. That was the most bored movie I have ever seen.
6. All of you will no fit in the car.
7. The particle theory of physics supports the idea of very large one explosion at the start of the universe.

III. Prepositions

Rewrite the following sentences, correcting any problems you see with the prepositions or two-word verbs. The first one has been done for you.

1. According <u>with</u> the forecast, it will rain all day today.

   Revised: According <u>to</u> the forecast, it will rain all day today.

2. My teacher and I differ by what my grade should be.
3. Last year three more countries declared themselves independent to their former colonial rulers.
4. Our basketball team just did not seem to be able to get for the game up.
5. In this essay, the writer objects with the idea of private gun ownership.
6. The seismograph is not capable for detecting tremors that small.
7. Teri moved out of the apartment because her roommate's loud music.
8. After the storm, we were just thankful for to be someplace warm and dry.
9. Are you concerned to your grades?
10. I am thankful you for your help.

IV. Verbs

Rewrite the following sentences, correcting any problems you see with the verbs. The first one has been done for you.

1. Tomas studying Latin this semester.

    Revised: Tomas is studying Latin this semester.

2. A firm declare a loss if three conditions are met.
3. Digging the foundations through solid rock maked the project cost more.
4. Cattle cans go through the gate that is open.
5. For registration, you not need your advisor's signature.
6. The hotel's management can approved the new union agreement.
7. Too many times the government breaked its promise to the Cherokee.
8. Uzma's book had laid out in the rain all night.
9. The Mayans had being dominant in their region for more than 500 years.
10. I might being on the honor roll this December.
11. Each additional gigabyte of memory has been costing only an additional hundred dollars.
12. Donita will have being picked by three sororities by tonight.
13. If money market investment continue to rise, inflation will surely rise with it.
14. When the space station is completed, many countries benefits from the use of it.
15. If the new atom-smasher built in Mexico, it would creates thousands of new jobs.
16. The otters traveling nearly twenty miles from where we left them.
17. Simple honesty means one does not to lie.
18. A new graduate cannot avoid to worry about the job market.
19. Anna promised meeting me after class.
20. The new editor required to submit three copies of each article.

V. Sentence Structure

Rewrite the following sentences, correcting any problems you see with the sentence structure. The first one has been done for you.

1. You don't have to stay long, but is important that you come to see her.

   Revised: You don't have to stay long, but <u>it</u> is important that you come to see her.

2. Tamara took the car back to the airport that she had rented.

3. Myra finally found a bathing suit that she wanted to buy it.

4. My friend told me study more.

5. Lisa asked if I can go?

6. Is true that Eddie passed the test.

7. Larissa said, I can't understand that teacher.

VI. Identifying and Revising ESL Errors

The following short paragraph contains a number of typical ESL errors. Rewrite it, correcting those errors.

Abdullah nearly have all the researches for thesis completed, and he says his other coursework will be finish next week. The work has gone slow because his gray, old car is his only way to get to a campus. He could not worked last week because his car had been broken down. He can begin writing his report when he finishes the work in the chemistry lab which he has not complete that. Earliest day Abdullah will finish is Wednesday, so earliest he can turn in report is Friday. Other than buying Abdullah a new car is no way to speed up the progress on his report. The better his car cans go, the faster his work it can get done.

THE BASICS FROM A TO Z

PART THREE

The Basics
from A to Z

A

ABBREVIATIONS

Abbreviations, shortened versions of words or phrases, enable writers to save space, but they should not be overused. A dictionary will list the proper forms of abbreviations not shown here.

Personal and Professional Titles

Common personal and professional titles can be abbreviated when they precede a proper name. These abbreviations are followed by periods:

Dr. Cameron Jameson	St. Francis
Mrs. Lazarra	Mr. Morgenstern
Gen. Abrams	Ms. Martinez

Ms. designates either a married or an unmarried woman, and it is followed by a period even though it is not an abbreviation. *Miss* is not followed by a period.

Religious, military, academic, and **governmental titles** should be abbreviated only if they are followed by a complete name (both a first and a last name):

Rev. Jesse Jackson	the Reverend Jackson
Gen. Douglas MacArthur	General MacArthur
Sen. Edward Kennedy	Senator Kennedy
Gov. Christine Whitman	Governor Whitman
Prof. Rami Adeleki	Professor Adeleki

When abbreviations for family designations, titles, or academic degrees follow a name, they are preceded by a comma:

Fredson Franks, Jr.

You may place an appropriate label before or after a name but not in both places:

Dr. Charles Boudreaux *or* Charles Boudreaux, M.D.
[*not* Dr. Charles Boudreaux, M.D.]

Religious and professional titles should never be abbreviated when they are used as nouns (that is, when they are used without a proper name):

St. Paul	He is a saint.
Dr. Maria Conchada	She is my mother's doctor.
Prof. Barbara Adams	She is a famous professor of Greek.

Abbreviations for academic degrees—such as B.A., M.A., Ph.D. (or BA, MA, PhD in the style preferred by the Modern Language Association)—can be used without proper names:

> After a high school teacher encouraged him to get a B.A., Mr. Parker started college at age 72.

Familiar Abbreviations and Acronyms

An acronym is an abbreviation that can be pronounced as a word, such as *UNICEF, NATO, NOW,* and *AIDS*. These familiar terms are commonly written without periods. Familiar abbreviations, such as *NFL, SAT,* and *CBS,* also appear in writing without being spelled out or explained. When these abbreviations stand for three words or more, they are commonly written without periods: FBI, CD-ROM. However, documentation styles vary in their use of periods in some common abbreviations, such as B.A./BA and A.D./AD.

Unfamiliar Abbreviations and Acronyms

If a new term (with an unfamiliar abbreviation or acronym) appears only once or twice in your paper, you may choose to write it out each time. If you use it frequently, however, cite the abbreviation or acronym in parentheses right after you introduce the term, omitting the periods if the abbreviation is of three or more words. Thereafter use the abbreviation or acronym by itself:

> The new program, called *Writing Across the Curriculum (WAC),* has funding from a local foundation. *WAC* provides computer labs and tutorial services for students, staff, and faculty.

Abbreviations with Numerals

The following abbreviations are acceptable when they are used with numerals:

450 B.C. [BC]	"before Christ"
A.D. [AD] 70	*anno Domini;* Latin for "in the year of the Lord"; it precedes the date
11:15 A.M. [a.m.]	*ante meridiem;* Latin for "before noon"
12:15 P.M. [p.m.]	*post meridiem;* Latin for "after noon"
2500 rpm	revolutions per minute
32 mpg	miles per gallon
225° F	Fahrenheit scale
24° C	centigrade or Celsius scale

Do not abbreviate these terms when you use them without numerals:

before the birth of Christ.
The Roman Empire began to falter ~~B.C.~~
　　　　　　　　　　　　　　　　　　　　^

　　　　　　　　　　　　　　　　　　　　　　　　miles　*kilometers.*
Americans are more accustomed to distances shown in ~~mi.~~ than in ~~km.~~
　　　　　　　　　　　　　　　　　　　　　　　　　　　^　　　　　　^

　　　　　　　　　　　　　　　morning.
He has trouble getting up in the ~~a.m.~~
　　　　　　　　　　　　　　　　　　　　^

Geographic Locations

290

In formal writing, spell out names of cities, states, countries, and continents. Also spell out words such as *street, avenue, road, park, mount,* and *river* when they are used in proper names:

> In *New York City* this summer, ice skaters from *New Hampshire* will study with experts from *Russia.*

> The house on *Marmsley Road* is famous for its high walls, which protect it from the frequent overflowing of the *Ressem River* near *Mount Frederick.*

The abbreviation *U.S.* (or *US*) can be used for *United States*—but only as an adjective:

As a Noun	**As an Adjective**
I was glad when my uncle finally came to *the United States.* [not U.S.]	The *U.S. team* slowly entered the hockey rink.

The abbreviation *D.C.* (or *DC*) is accepted for *District of Columbia* in the phrase *Washington, D.C.*

Days and Months

Spell out days of the week and the names of months:

> On *December* 15, Corinne finally finished the quilt she had begun on the first *Monday* in *January.*

Units of Measurement

Except in tables and graphs, spell out all units of measurement:

> John, who is six *feet* tall, lost forty *pounds* after he began eating fewer *ounces* of meat and reducing the *grams* of fat in his diet.

Publication References

Except in bibliographies, spell out terms concerning books and journals, such as *chapter* and *page:*

> In the second *edition* of the first *volume,* Jorge changed the *preface* to acknowledge his wife's contributions.

> On the last *page* of the last *chapter,* Sherlock Holmes finally identified the murderer.

Latin Abbreviations

Reserve the common Latin abbreviations for use in bibliographies and for informal comments placed in parentheses. These abbreviations generally do not appear in formal writing:

cf.	*confer*	compare
e.g.	*exempli gratia*	for example
et al.	*et alii*	and others
etc.	*et cetera*	and so forth
i.e.	*id est*	that is
N.B. or NB	*nota bene*	note well
vs. or v.	*versus*	versus

Wanda needed a tutor to help her with several basic math skills—

such as

~~e.g.,~~ using fractions and figuring percentages.

and other activities.

At camp, I enjoyed horseback riding, swimming, boating, ~~etc.~~

or

many activities, such as   *and*
At camp, I enjoyed horseback riding, swimming, boating, ~~etc.~~

Company Names

Company names can generally be written without the final *Inc., Ltd., Co., Bros.,* or *Corp.* (*Sears* or *Sears Roebuck* instead of *Sears Roebuck & Co.*). If you want to cite the full name, you may use the abbreviations. (No comma is needed between the company name and the abbreviation.) If these terms occur elsewhere in a name, spell them out and capitalize them (*Aluminum Company of America*). If a word such as *company* or *incorporated* appears by itself, it should be spelled out and written in lowercase. Use the ampersand (&) only if it is part of an official title or company name, such as *Barnes & Noble Booksellers:*

> The new advertisements portray Ford Motor Co. [*or* Ford] as an all-American business.
>
> The Corporation for Public Broadcasting sponsors environmental programs.
>
> Standard & Poor's *Register of Corporations* lists the correct name for most companies.

No abbreviation should be used with a theatrical or dance company (*Martha Graham Dance Company*) or a military unit (*Company B*).

Symbols

Symbols such as @, +, =, #, ¶, and ¢ are not used in formal writing, although they may appear in graphs and tables. Use of the dollar sign ($), however, is acceptable with numbers (*$125, $350 billion, $11.98*), although you should spell out the word *dollars* with numbers that can be expressed in one or two words. Similar use of the percent sign (%) with a figure is usually acceptable:

> So far, we have spent less than *three percent* (3%) of the $240,000 that was budgeted for this project.
>
> I bet you *five dollars* that Carlos will not bring back even ten cents from his vacation.

ABSOLUTE PHRASES

An absolute phrase, consisting of a noun or pronoun and a participle, modifies a whole sentence instead of a single word. It is separated from the rest of the sentence by a comma:

Her bags packed, she was ready to leave for the airport.

Other things being equal, he would prefer to hire someone with database experience.

(See *Phrases,* page 377, for more examples of absolute phrases.)

ACTIVE VOICE

A sentence is in active voice if the subject of the sentence is the do-er of the sentence, as in "Kathryn hit the free throw." In passive voice, the subject receives the action of the do-er, as in "The free throw was hit by Kathryn." (For discussions of active and passive voice, see pages 39–44, and *Verbs,* pages 424–25.)

ADJECTIVES

Adjectives modify nouns or pronouns, adding specific descriptive information about them:

The pale child stood by his mother.

That dented Toyota has 100,000 miles on it.

When *several small* bubbles floated to the surface, we knew the diver was still alive.

Most adjectives have comparison forms (called **positive, comparative,** and **superlative**). The comparative of short adjectives is usually formed by the addition of *er,* and the superlative is usually formed by the addition of *est.* Adjectives of two or more syllables are usually made comparative with the addition of the word *more* (or *less*) and are made superlative with the addition of *most* (or *least*). Here is a list of these forms for some commonly used adjectives; for others, consult a dictionary:

Comparison Forms of Adjectives

Positive	Comparative	Superlative
bad	worse	worst
big	bigger	biggest
careful	more careful	most careful
good	better	best
hot	hotter	hottest
lucky	luckier	luckiest
quick	quicker	quickest
silly	sillier	silliest
tough	tougher	toughest
weak	weaker	weakest

Some adjectives also have ordinal forms, which allow you to place things in an ordered sequence (*first, last,* and so on).

Several types of pronouns can also be used as adjectives: personal (*his* jalopy), demonstrative (*this* cable), indefinite (*few friends*), and interrogative (*Which* show should I watch?). Other types of adjectives include articles (*a, an,* and *the*) and numbers (*two, twenty-ninth, seven million*).

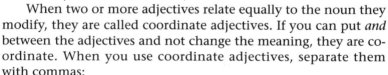

When two or more adjectives relate equally to the noun they modify, they are called coordinate adjectives. If you can put *and* between the adjectives and not change the meaning, they are coordinate. When you use coordinate adjectives, separate them with commas:

The Fordson was a *small, inexpensive, reliable* tractor.

When two or more adjectives work together to modify a noun (and could not logically be combined with *and*), they are called cumulative adjectives (or unit modifiers), and they are not separated by commas:

The Russian tractor offers *few optional* features.

(For more examples of coordinate and cumulative adjectives, see pages 233–34 and 292.)

ADVERBS

Adverbs modify verbs, adjectives, other adverbs, or an entire clause. Many adverbs are formed by adding *ly* to an adjective: *pretty, prettily;*

quick, quickly; terrible, terribly; bad, badly. (Note that a *y* at the end of an adverb becomes an *i* when *ly* is added.) Other commonly used adverbs include *very, well, almost, soon, never,* and *not:*

> He strolled *confidently* through the shopping mall.
> [The adverb *confidently* modifies the verb *strolled.*]
> The *very* big dog did not respond to his owner's commands.
> [The adverb *very* modifies the adjective *big.*]
> They *almost never* leave before the bingo game ends.
> [The adverb *almost* modifies the adverb *never,* and *never* modifies the verb *leave.*]
> *Unfortunately,* we have no way to balance this budget.
> [The adverb *unfortunately* modifies the rest of the sentence.]

Like adjectives, some adverbs have **positive, comparative,** and **superlative forms.** One-syllable adverbs are typically made comparative with the addition of *er* and made superlative with the addition of *est.* For longer adverbs, *more* (or *less*) is used to form the comparative, and *most* (or *least*) to form the superlative. Here is a list of these forms for some commonly used adverbs; for others, consult a dictionary:

Comparison Forms of Adverbs

Positive	Comparative	Superlative
carefully	more carefully	most carefully
far	farther, further	farthest, furthest
happily	more happily	most happily
well	better	best

AGREEMENT

The verb in a predicate should agree in number with its subject: *"Carolina and Margaret are* friends." Pronouns should agree in number, person, and gender with their antecedents: "The *women* are demanding to see *their* lawyers." (For thorough discussions of agreement, see pages 218–21 for subject-verb agreement, and 249–50 for pronoun-antecedent agreement.)

ANTECEDENTS

An antecedent is the noun to which a pronoun refers. In "When Bill saw his coat, he wondered what the cleaners had done to it," *Bill* is the antecedent of *he*, and *coat* is the antecedent of *it*. (See pages 249–50 for a full discussion of pronoun-antecedent agreement.)

APOSTROPHES

The apostrophe is a small but important mark of punctuation: it is used to indicate possession (*Lula's kitchen*); to mark omissions in contractions (*can't, I'll*); and to form plurals of letters, numerals, and abbreviations ending in periods (*B.A.'s*). (For a complete discussion of apostrophes and help with common errors, see pages 257–64.)

APPOSITIVES

An appositive is a noun or a noun phrase that is placed near another noun and renames it in some way:

> Dr. Tran's yacht, *Windward II*, won the race.

Appositives, like other modifiers, can be one word or a group of words; they can also be classified as **restrictive** (essential to the meaning of the sentence) or **nonrestrictive** (nonessential). Restrictive appositives are not set off by commas; nonrestrictive appositives are. Writers sometimes forget that distinction and set restrictive appositives off with unnecessary commas:

> **Restrictive Appositive:** Robert Altman's movie *Nashville* has become an American classic.

Without the name of the movie, the sentence would be "Robert Altman's movie has become an American classic," and it would be nearly meaningless—Altman has made too many movies. Because the sentence needs to identify a particular movie (that is, to restrict the meaning of *movie*), *Nashville* is necessary to the meaning of the sentence—it is a restrictive appositive—and does not need commas around it.

> **Nonrestrictive Appositive:** Ralph's truck, *a new Ford Ranger,* has a Texas Longhorns sticker on the back.

Here, the kind of truck Ralph drives is not essential to the meaning of the sentence; its being a Ford Ranger is just extra information. Thus "a new Ford Ranger" is a nonrestrictive appositive and is set off by commas.

ARTICLES

The articles *a, an,* and *the* precede nouns. *A* is used before nouns beginning with consonant sounds; *an* is used before nouns beginning with vowel sounds (*a dog, an antelope, an hour*). The article *the* implies a specific reference:
285–91

> *The* thimble fell under the rug. [one particular thimble]
>
> *A* thimble fell under the rug. [a single, but unspecified, thimble]

B

BASE FORMS

The base form of the verb is the form listed in a dictionary, the infinitive without the marker *to,* such as *shout, dance, be,* and *sing.* (For more examples of the base form of verbs, see pages 297–98.)

BIASED USES OF LANGUAGE

The way language is used can suggest or reveal bias—discrimination against people on the basis of their gender, age, race, religion, ethnic group, or physical abilities. When you write, you should look for instances of bias in your language and eliminate them.

Gender-Biased Uses of Language

Avoid using gender-biased language, which can stereotype or demean both women and men.

Degrading and Patronizing Language

Martha Blair, ~~a pert little blonde,~~ is running for city council.

office staff is
The ~~girls in the office, including that new one with really great legs,~~ ~~are~~ taking up a collection to pay for the party.

Occupational and Social Stereotypes

shirts come out of the dryer smelling fresh.
With the new fabric softener, ~~women can get their husbands' shirts to smell fresh.~~

their work schedules are *doctors need patient spouses.*
Because ~~his~~ work schedule ~~is~~ ever changing, ~~a doctor needs a patient wife.~~

working.
A dental assistant should always wear ~~her~~ gloves while ~~she works.~~

Use of *He* to Designate Both Genders

A singular pronoun must be used with a singular construction like *everyone* or *each student*. *He* is appropriate if you are clearly talking about a male student, as is *she* for a female student. But if you mean to include both women and men, then you should not use *he*. To be inclusive, you have three options:

1. Use *he or she* (*him or her* or *his or her*)

   Each child should write about *his or her* personal experience.

2. Change the construction to a plural and use *they* (*them, their*)

   The *children* should write about *their* personal experiences.

3. Rewrite the sentence so that it does not need a pronoun

   Each child should write about *a* personal experience.

Overusing the phrase *he or she* can make writing awkward ("He or she should bring his or her books to his or her classes"). Carefully plan your use of all three options to incorporate non-biased language without interrupting the flow of your writing.

Gender-Biased Word Choices

The following list of gender-neutral terms can help you eliminate gender-biased word choices:

Gender-Biased	Gender-Neutral
chairman	chair, presiding officer, moderator
congressman	member of Congress, representative, senator
fireman	firefighter
lady lawyer	lawyer
mailman	letter carrier
mankind	people, humanity
man-made	synthetic, manufactured, hand-made
manpower	personnel, staff
policeman	police officer
seamstress	tailor
stewardess	flight attendant
to man	to staff, to operate
workman	laborer, worker

Other Biased Uses of Language

Just as language may suggest bias based on gender, it may also suggest bias based on age, race, religion, ethnic group, or physical abilities. The guidelines to follow here are designed to help you avoid degrading language and stereotyping in your writing. Here are a few examples of each bias type:

Age

Be careful to avoid negative stereotypes and sentimentalized depictions of any age group—babies are not always angelic and older people are not always forgetful. Do not make unnecessary references to age:

> We are seeking a number of new, ~~young~~ employees who will bring fresh ideas and enthusiasm to this year's sales effort.

[Bringing fresh ideas and enthusiasm to a job is not the sole province of youth; anyone, regardless of age, can do that. Besides, discrimination in hiring based on age is illegal.]

Race

If identifying people by race or ethnic group is relevant to your topic, use the most specific term you can. For example, if a person is Mexican American, use that term rather than the more general *Hispanic* or *Latino.* Do not mention race or ethnic identity, however, unless it is to the point:

Our new history teacher, ~~a bright young black man~~ *Clifford Reilly* from the University of Chicago, will assist Sarah Perkins in the Guidance Office this year.

[*Bright, young, black,* and *man* are needless here; notice that Sarah Perkins is not similarly characterized. These characteristics are no more relevant to the announcement than identifying Sarah Perkins as fairly intelligent, middle-aged, and white would be.]

Religion

Avoid generalizations about belief systems and organized religions. If you are writing about a particular religion or an individual's religious practices, use the terminology preferred by that group or person and try to maintain a neutral tone:

The coach lectured us at halftime about our poor play on defense with ~~all the~~ *so much* fervor ~~of a Bible-thumping preacher who had discovered the seven deadly sins.~~ *that the veins stood out on his forehead, sweat rolled off his arms, and he finally lost his voice.*

[The references to the Bible and the seven deadly sins are needless and may be taken as showing disrespect to matters some people take very seriously—one person's colorful metaphor is another person's holy book. Avoid such needless references.]

Ethnic Group

Avoid ethnic stereotypes—such as the Jewish mother or the inscrutable Asian—as well as expressions that originated with a negative characterization of a particular group.

it would be unacceptable for her to take back the video game she

I told LaShondra ~~if she took back the video game she had given me,~~

had given me as a gift.

~~she would be no better than an Indian giver.~~

[Phrases such as *Indian giver*, *Dutch treat*, or *Scotch courage* are needless and insulting to the groups named—who usually are not otherwise mentioned in the context of the phrase anyway.]

Physical Abilities

Do not define people by their disabilities or impairments. Instead of *an arthritic*, write *a person with arthritis*. Avoid language that characterizes a person with a disability as a victim. Instead of *a person confined to a wheelchair*, write *a wheelchair user* or *a person who uses a wheelchair*.

people with disabilities.

We will make special provision at our restaurant for ~~the disabled and~~

~~the handicapped.~~

[The expressions *disabled* and *handicapped* define people on the basis of physical limitations. The guideline here is to put the individual first, as shown in the revised sentence.]

BRACKETS

Brackets are used to enclose an explanatory comment within a quotation or within parentheses.

Within a Quotation

Use brackets to add your own words to a quotation to make it grammatically complete, especially in cases where an ellipsis mark indicates that part of the quotation has been omitted. The added words should not alter the original meaning of the complete quotation:

> Murray Ross thinks that fans idealize football players: "they tend to . . . [become] embodiments of heroic qualities such as 'strength,' 'confidence,' 'perfection.'"

Additional information that explains the quotation can also appear in brackets:

The first reporter gave the basic facts: "He [Deniston] has been found in a room at his club [the YMCA on Second Avenue]."

With *Sic*

When you must use a quotation that contains a spelling error, you need to let your readers know the error is the original author's, and not yours. Place the word *sic* (Latin for "just so") in brackets after the misspelled word. (Because *sic* is Latin, many writers put it in italics.)

> According to Louis Strauss, Fred Newton Scott of the University of Michigan "had at command, beside his spendid [*sic*] background in English literature and his thorough mastery of the history of rhetoric, a wide knowledge of the arts of painting and music and of many literatures."

Within Parentheses

Use brackets to supply additional information to statements made within parentheses:

> Aubrey's will excluded all his family members (including his only son, Paul Frontmain [from his first marriage]).

> The new governor's pet projects (like the Lake Fund and the Office of Environmental Quality [OEQ]) have been opposed by legislators from his own party.

C

CAPITALIZATION

The First Word in a Sentence

Capitalize the first word of a sentence, either your own or one being quoted:

> Can you meet me tomorrow?

> Erica's cleaning will be ready in an hour.

> Lucia finally blurted out, "Aren't you ready to go?"

Two Clauses Joined by a Colon

When you join two sentences with a colon, you do not have to capitalize the second sentence. This capitalization is optional, but you should use one style consistently throughout a paper:

> Ruth-Ann is an irresponsible student: she generally comes in late and without her homework.
>
> *or*
>
> Ruth-Ann is an irresponsible student: She generally comes in late and without her homework.

Sentence within Parentheses

A full sentence within parentheses should begin with a capital letter and be punctuated as a separate sentence within the parentheses:

> The plant growth was generally slow in the first year. (See Table 1.)
>
> Place the darts of the armhole and sleeve together. (The sleeve's darts will be one inch longer.)

Poetry

When you are quoting poetry, use a capital letter to begin each line only if the author uses one. In the following poem, for example, Cathy Song begins some lines with capital letters and some with lowercase letters. In your paper, you would quote her lines exactly:

> I call to the children.
> We can see the mountains
> shimmering blue above the air.
> If you look really hard,
> says my son the dreamer,
> leaning out from the laundry's rigging,
> the work shirts fluttering like sails,
> you can see all the way to heaven.
>
> —"Heaven," 11. 56–63

Proper Nouns and Adjectives

Capitalize proper nouns (names of specific persons, places, or things) and proper adjectives (those created from proper nouns). Do not capitalize common nouns (names of general classes or types of persons, places, or things) unless they begin a sentence or appear as part of a title or proper noun:

Proper	Common
Darwin, Darwinian	scientist, scientific
America, American	nation, national
Lake Pontchartrain	lake

Capitalize the following types of proper nouns:

Names of Individuals and Adjectives Derived from Them

Toni Morrison	Harry Connick, Jr.
Elizabethan poetry	Freudian slip

Geographic Names, Nationalities, Ethnic Groups, and Languages

San Diego	Fort Sill
Australia	Park Avenue
Adriatic Sea	Ethiopian famine
Rocky Mountains	Canadian coins
Saudi Arabian	Serbo-Croatian
Pakistani	English

Buildings and Other Structures

Danforth Hall	Golden Gate Bridge
Washington Monument	Eiffel Tower

Associations and Teams

American Medical Association
National Organization for Women
Key Club
Atlanta Braves

Ships, Trains, Airplanes, and Spacecraft

U.S.S. *Kidd*	*Enola Gay*
Orient Express	*Challenger*

Note: The names of ships, trains, planes, and spacecraft are italicized.

Historical Documents, Events, Eras, and Calendar Terms

Magna Carta	August
Battle of Vicksburg	Tuesday
Middle Ages	Fourth of July
Great Depression	New Year's Eve

Religions and Religious Terms
Judaism, Jews, Jewish
the Church of Jesus Christ of Latter-Day Saints
Protestant
Jesus Christ
Buddha
the Bible
Kaddish (*or* kaddish)

Businesses and Trade Names
First National Bank
Steven-Darniere Motors
General Foods
Honda Prelude
Rice Krispies

Note: The article *the* is usually not capitalized if it appears with a proper noun:

the Renaissance
the Ford Escort
the Bill of Rights
the Boston Celtics

Exceptions: The Netherlands, The Hague.

Titles of Books, Movies, and Other Works

Capitalize the titles of books, magazines, articles, essays, movies, plays, television shows, songs, and paintings. Within such titles, articles (*a, an,* and *the*), prepositions, conjunctions, and the *to* of infinitives are not capitalized unless they begin the title:

Gone with the Wind
"Driving to Town Late to Mail a Letter"
"Anecdote of the Jar"
Handel's *Messiah*
Van Gogh's *Sunflowers*

Note: Titles of long works—such as books, magazines, movies, plays, and symphonies—are italicized. Titles of shorter works—

such as short stories, articles, and songs—are enclosed in quotation marks. Titles of paintings and sculptures are italicized.

Personal Titles

Capitalize titles when they appear before a proper name. When they are used alone or after a proper name, they should not be capitalized:

Governor Lawton Chiles—*but* Lawton Chiles, governor of Florida

Professor Mikiso Hideki—*but* Mikiso Hideki, a history professor

Senator Mary Landrieu—*but* Mary Landrieu, senator

Exception: Many writers capitalize the word *president* when it appears alone if it refers to the president of a national government.

Academic Institutions and Courses

Capitalize names of academic institutions and courses. Capitalize the names of specific universities, departments, and courses, but not the common nouns for schools or departments. *English, French,* and names of other languages are always capitalized, but names of other subject fields are capitalized only in official course titles:

University of Washington—*but* a good university

Department of English—*but* the department office

Physics 122—*but* an introductory physics course

Fundamentals of Calculus—*but* a freshman calculus course

Do not capitalize words used to designate school terms:

fall term	spring semester
winter quarter	summer school

Names of Relatives

Common nouns such as *mother, father,* or *brother-in-law* are not capitalized. When they are used as proper nouns—either as substitutes for a name or as part of a name—they are capitalized:

My father and his sister grew up in Africa.

When they were first married, Father and Mother often went to local square dances.

> After the party, Aunt Laura, Uncle Stephen, and Dad rode down to the coast with my cousin.

Geographic Regions

Capitalize terms for specific regions of the United States and for people from those regions. Do not capitalize compass directions, such as *north* and *south:*

> People from the South think that Midwesterners sound like radio announcers.
>
> Johnson and his family live west of town, on the southern fork of Highway 68.

Seasons

Do not capitalize seasons. Although months and days of the week are capitalized, seasons of the year are not:

fall	spring
winter	summer

CASE

Nouns and pronouns in English can be used as subjects, as objects, or as modifiers in possessive forms. These uses correspond to three cases: **subjective** (the subject form), **objective** (the object form), and **possessive** (the possessive modifier form). Whereas nouns in English (unlike many other languages) change form only for possessive case (*girl, girl's*), pronouns have different forms for each case:

Pronoun Cases

	Subjective	Objective	Possessive
Singular	I	me	my, mine
	you	you	your, yours
	he	him	his
	she	her	her, hers
	it	it	its
Plural	we	us	our, ours
	you	you	you, yours
	they	them	their, theirs

CLAUSES

A clause is a unit of words with a subject and a verb. There are two kinds of clauses, *independent* and *dependent* (sometimes called main and subordinate). An **independent clause**—with a subject and a predicate—can stand alone as a sentence:

> She left home.
>
> The young mother had taken her son to the park.

306–07

A **dependent clause** also has a subject and a predicate, but it is introduced by a word such as *that, while,* or *when* that makes it need an independent clause to complete its meaning. Notice the difference in these two examples:

Independent Clause	Dependent Clause
The rain fell in big, heavy drops.	While the tourists ran to escape the downpour.

The dependent clause, if left by itself, would be a sentence fragment. It needs to be combined with an independent clause to make a grammatically complete statement:

> **Combined:** The rain fell in big, heavy drops while the tourists ran to escape the downpour.

(For a complete discussion of revising sentence fragments, see pages 193–200.)

Sentences that combine a dependent and an independent clause are called *complex sentences* and are perhaps the most common ones in English.

The words that introduce dependent clauses are relative pronouns or subordinating conjunctions:

Relative Pronouns

that	whichever	whomever
what	who	whose
whatever	whoever	
which	whom	

Subordinating Conjunctions

after	as if	because
although	as soon as	before
as	as though	even if

even though	since	until
how	so that	when
if	than	whenever
in order that	that	where
in that	though	wherever
once	unless	while

Types of Dependent Clauses

Dependent clauses can be used as nouns or as modifiers. As modifiers, they can be either adjectives or adverbs:

Dependent Clauses as Nouns

The adults had forgotten *that rain can be fun.*

What the children knew was a special thing.

Dependent Clauses as Adjectives

The weather radars had screens *that were lit up green, gold, and red.*

The city, *which had been dozing through another hot summer afternoon,* shook itself into new life.

Dependent Clauses as Adverbs

When the rain stopped, things slowly went back to normal.

No big changes had occurred *where I live.*

The city streets, however, were brighter *than they had been before.*

Restrictive versus Nonrestrictive Relative Clauses

Many writers fail to distinguish between modifying clauses that are essential to the meaning of the sentence (restrictive clauses) and those that are not essential (nonrestrictive clauses). Restrictive clauses usually narrow or specify the meaning of the sentence in an essential way. They are almost always introduced with *that.* Nonrestrictive clauses, usually introduced with *which,* merely add additional information. Nonrestrictive clauses are set off by commas; restrictive clauses are not:

Restrictive	Nonrestrictive
The room *that was painted red* held her grandfather's chest.	The room, *which was painted red,* held her grandfather's chest.

The difference in the meaning of the two sentences is signaled to readers by the presence or absence of commas around the clause. In the first sentence, the writer is distinguishing one room from others—the information is thus essential. The dependent clause restricts the meaning of "room" to this particular room—the red one. In the second sentence, the words "which was painted red" simply add detail. (See *Restrictive and Nonrestrictive Clauses,* page 389.)

Clauses and Sentence Fragments

Another common writing error involves giving a dependent clause an initial capital letter and a mark of terminal punctuation, thus creating a sentence fragment:

Dependent Clause Fragments

When the bus comes.

Once I get my next check.

Whenever you think it's a good idea to go.

(For a full discussion about revising sentence fragments, see pages 193–200.)

CLICHÉS

Clichés are phrases that have been used so much that their meaning is no longer clear and forceful: *crazy as a loon, nose to the grindstone, with his heart in his hands.* You should avoid them because they blunt your meaning rather than sharpen it. (For a list of clichés and more on how to eliminate them from your writing, see page 43.)

COLONS

A colon can be placed after a complete sentence to indicate that it will be further explained by an example, a list, or a quotation. Colons also have other uses, such as separating numbers in time designations, as in *8:30.* The following pages discuss all these uses as well as unnecessary colons and spacing and capitalization with colons.

Between Two Independent Clauses

A colon can be used between two independent clauses as a substitute for a semicolon if the second clause further explains the first one or provides an example:

> Today a new policy has gone into effect: if you don't have a reserved parking place in the parking garage, you may not drive into it at all.

> Luisa is so disorganized: yesterday she lost her briefcase and the file cabinet key.

To Introduce Lists

A colon is used to introduce a list placed at the end of a sentence that contains a subject, a verb, and an object or complement:

> For our camping trip, we need to rent the big items: backpacks, tents, sleeping bags, and a stove.

Note: The words in front of the colon must be a complete sentence. Thus, beginning the example above with "The things we need are: . . ." would be an incorrect use of the colon.

With an Appositive (or One-Word List)

A colon can also be used to introduce an appositive at the end of a sentence:

> Keith had forgotten only one thing: his plane tickets.

With Direct Quotations

A colon should be used to introduce either a short quotation or a longer, indented quotation if it follows a complete sentence:

> This is what the consultant actually said: "People in other parts of the world will not like this ad series."

> Here are the consultant's exact words:

>> If your ad assumes people "read" pictures from left to right, you're going to be in trouble in cultures that "read" graphics from right to left.

Special Uses

Although the four preceding uses of colons can be seen as instances in which the colon replaces the words *that is,* there are other special uses of colons.

- **After the Salutation of a Letter:** In a formal letter, such as a business letter, use a colon after the salutation:

    Dear Professor Rickards:

- **Between a Title and a Subtitle:** The colon separates a main title (of a book, for example) from its subtitle:

    She didn't want to read *The Right Moves: Succeeding in a Man's World without a Harvard MBA.*

- **In Citations:** Many systems of documenting research sources require the use of a colon between the place of publication and the name of the publisher:

    MLA Style: Boston: Houghton, 1990.

    APA Style: Washington, DC: U.S. Government Printing Office.

- **In Time References:** The colon is used to separate the hour and the minutes in time references:

    I'll meet you at 7:45 tonight.

- **In Scriptural References:** The chapter and verse in scriptural references can be separated with a colon or with a period:

    We'll be studying John 2:7.

    We'll be studying John 2.7.

- **For Proportions:** Colons are often used to indicate ratios and proportions:

    Mix the gasoline and oil at a 3:1 ratio.

Unnecessary Colons

Two common mistakes involve unnecessary colons. In each case, the colon should be removed.

Between a Complete Verb and Its Object or Complement

The ingredients you'll need are:/kidney beans, tomato sauce, red pepper, chili powder, oregano, and cayenne.

After For Example, Such As, or Including

You will need to report on one of Sherry Turkle's books, such as:/*The Second Self.*

There were several causes for the structural failure, including;/corro-

sion, poor welds, and impurities in the steel itself.

For example;/the child's roving eyes and blank stares may be symp-

toms of Attention Deficit Disorder.

Spacing after a Colon

Skip one space after a colon when it is used to introduce a clause, an example, part of a bibliographic citation, or a subtitle. Do not skip a space in constructions like *8:30* and *4:1*.

Capitalization after a Colon

If the material following a colon does not constitute a complete grammatical sentence, do not capitalize the first letter:

The Boeing 767 has these advantages over older passenger jets: $\mathcal{S}$ize,

economy of operation, and reliability.

If the material following a colon is an independent clause, you may either capitalize or lowercase the first letter: capitalization is optional. Whichever style you choose, be consistent in the use of capital or lowercase letters in all similar instances in a paper.

Our library has a big advantage despite the small size of its collection: the [*or* The] planners worked very hard to make materials as
accessible as possible.

COMMAS

The comma is a mark of punctuation that separates elements within a sentence. As illustrated in the following examples, these elements can be words, phrases, or clauses:

When Luther left for college, he took his stereo, computer, and microwave oven.

After hearing the weather report, Carmelita went to find her raincoat, galoshes, and umbrella.

New mothers and fathers quickly learn how to make funny faces,
how to keep walking on aching feet, and how to operate a wind-up
swing.

(For a complete discussion of commas and help with common errors, see pages 228–45.)

COMMA SPLICES

A comma splice is a sentence error that occurs when two independent clauses are separated only by a comma:

The flood waters were rising more each hour, *but* many families refused to evacuate.

(For a full discussion about identifying and correcting comma splices, see pages 201–08.)

COMPARISONS

Make Comparisons between the Same Types of Items

Two things being compared must be logically comparable:

He drove his His *race car* came around the track quicker than any *other driver* I have ever seen.

[The comparison should be between two drivers or two race cars, not between a car and a driver.]

or

His *race car* came around the track quicker than any *other race car* ~~driver~~ I have ever seen.

Compared with *Marsha,* *Sheri has terrible* Sheri's *study habits* ~~are terrible.~~

[The comparison should be between the two women or between their study habits, not between *Marsha* and *study habits.*]

or

~~Compared with Marsha,~~ Sheri's *study habits* are *much worse than Marsha's study habits.* ~~terrible.~~

The *courses* here are more advanced than *the courses at* the previous *school* I attended.

[The comparison should be between courses, not between courses and a school.]

Make Comparisons Complete

A complete comparison clearly indicates the two items being considered:

Jana is happier/ *than she was last week.*

This margarine is better tasting/ *than butter.*

Don't Make Ambiguous Comparisons

Make sure the reader can easily tell what items are being compared:

Carmen looks more like Thania than Juana/ *does.*

or

Carmen looks more like Thania than Juana. *she looks like*

I have more confidence in the store manager than the district

manager/ *does.*

or

I have more confidence in the store manager than the district *I have in*

manager.

Indicate Degrees of Comparison Properly

Remember that comparative words ending in *er* and comparative phrases using *more* (*lovelier, more cooperative*) are used for comparing two items. Comparison words formed with *est* and comparative phrases using *most* (*loveliest, most cooperative*) are for more than two:

She is *stronger* than her cousin.

She is the *strongest* athlete in her class.

She is *more helpful* than her brother.

She was the *most helpful* worker at the convention.

If you are unsure about the correct comparative form of any word, you can look it up in the dictionary. (These forms are discussed in *Adjectives,* pages 320–21, and *Adverbs,* pages 321–22.)

Use *Other* with *Any* in Comparisons

Remember that the word *other* (or another modifier) needs to be used with the word *any* to indicate that you are comparing a member of a group with other members of that same group:

This book is better than *any* ~~other~~ book I have read.

or

This book is better than *any* book I have read~~previously.~~

Daytona Beach is more crowded than *any* ~~other~~ beach.

or

Daytona Beach is more crowded than *any* ~~California~~ beach.

Use *As . . . As* and *If Not . . . Than* Correctly

Remember that the comparison *as . . . as* (*as hot as, as relaxed as*) must always have the second *as*, even when this phrase is combined with *if not . . . than* (*if not hotter than, if not more relaxed than*).

In Louisiana, September is *as* hot *as, if not* hotter *than,* August.

COMPLETE VERBS

The complete verb is the main verb of a clause. In "Because she was running quickly, she was able to reach her bus," the complete verb of the dependent clause is *was running;* the complete verb of the independent clause is *was able to reach.* (For a full discussion of verbs, see pages 417–27.)

COMPLEX SENTENCES

A complex sentence is one with both an independent clause and a dependent clause: in "Thoreau did much of his writing while he was at Walden Pond," "Thoreau did much of his writing" is the independent clause, and "while he was at Walden Pond" is the dependent clause. (For more on the construction of complex sentences, see page 394. For a full discussion of sentence structure, see *Sentences,* pages 392–99.)

COMPOUND-COMPLEX SENTENCES

A compound-complex sentence has two or more independent clauses and at least one dependent clause: in "Even though we were exhausted, Carla had to study, and I had to drive back to Des Moines," the dependent clause is "Even though we were exhausted," and the independent clauses are "Carla had to study" and "I had to drive back to Des Moines." (For a full discussion of sentence structure, see *Sentences*, pages 329–99.)

COMPOUND SENTENCES

A compound sentence has two or more independent clauses: in "Wind erosion is destructive, but tropical deforestation is deadly," the two independent clauses are "Wind erosion is destructive" and "tropical deforestation is deadly." (For more on the construction of compound sentences, see pages 203–05. For a full discussion of sentence structure, see *Sentences*, pages 392–99.)

CONJUNCTIONS

Conjunctions connect words or groups of words to one another. There are three kinds of conjunctions: *coordinating, correlative,* and *subordinating.* One kind of adverb, the *conjunctive adverb* (see pages 346–47), is also used as a conjunction, but it has to be preceded by a semicolon to join two independent clauses.

Coordinating Conjunctions

Coordinating conjunctions (*and, but, or, nor, for, so,* and *yet*) can connect words, phrases, or clauses:

> Playing Opie Taylor *and* Richie Cunningham on television taught Ron Howard about techniques of acting, lighting, *and* set design.
>
> She will have to clean up her room soon *or* evacuate it.
>
> Carmella felt nervous about moving away, *so* she decided to go to a junior college in her hometown.

When a conjunction joins two words or phrases, no comma appears between them ("Opie Taylor and Richie Cunningham";

"clean up her room soon or evacuate it"). In a series of three or more words or phrases, a comma separates each item ("techniques of acting, lighting, and set design"). When a coordinating conjunction joins two independent clauses, as in the last example above, a comma precedes it.

Note: Coordinating conjunctions can also be used to begin sentences when you want to indicate the connection between the ideas in two sentences. This technique is informal and should be used sparingly:

> The judge thought the trial would be over by Friday. *But* he had not foreseen the defense's long witness list.

Correlative Conjunctions

Correlative conjunctions (*either . . . or, neither . . . nor, not only . . . but also, both . . . and*) can join words, phrases, or clauses:

> *Not only* the boys *but also* their parents are expected to participate in each Tiger Cub activity.

> All applicants for the directorship should have *either* studied geriatrics in college *or* worked in a senior citizens center.

> *Either* you should begin doing the work, *or* you should drop the class.

When you use either coordinating or correlative conjunctions, make sure that the units being joined have the same grammatical form:

> Raymonda *likes to eat* a big breakfast but ~~eating~~ *she eats* almost nothing for
>
> lunch.

> Francine is not only *a talented actress,* but also ~~she is~~ *an excellent student.*

> Rafael knows both *how to play* clarinet and ~~playing~~ piano.

Joining units with different grammatical forms is called *faulty parallelism*. (Faulty parallelism is discussed in detail on pages 273–77.)

Subordinating Conjunctions

Subordinating conjunctions can be used to introduce a dependent (or subordinate) clause, which consists of the subordinating conjunction, a subject, a complete verb, and its object or complement ("when I left home last week"). The subordinating conjunction generally explains the connection between the main clause and the additional information given in the dependent clause. These conjunctions specify time, location, causation, and other logical connections.

Subordinating Conjunctions

after	even though	that
although	if	though
as	in order that	unless
as if	in that	until
as soon as	no matter how	when
as though	once	whenever
because	since	where
before	so that	wherever
even if	than	while

Subordinate clauses can be placed before or after the main clause of the sentence. They cannot appear by themselves because they are not independent clauses or complete sentences. As in these examples, a comma follows the dependent clause when it begins the sentence; generally, no comma is needed when the dependent clause ends the sentence:

Although she cannot come to the party on Tuesday, she is making two appetizers to be served there.

Until I was eight, I thought that French kissing created babies.

The train came down the track *before Lawanda was ready to leave her parents.*

Don't come out of your room *until you are ready to apologize.*

CONJUNCTIVE ADVERBS

Conjunctive adverbs are transition words such as *however, therefore,* and *thus.*

Conjunctive Adverbs

accordingly	besides	conversely
also	certainly	finally
anyway	consequently	furthermore

hence	moreover	specifically
however	nevertheless	still
incidentally	next	subsequently
indeed	nonetheless	then
instead	otherwise	therefore
likewise	similarly	thus
meanwhile		

When two independent clauses are joined by a semicolon, a conjunctive adverb is often used at the beginning of the second clause to provide a transition. The adverb is preceded by a semicolon and followed by a comma.

> She studied carefully for the test; *however,* no amount of review could have prepared her for question five.

CONNOTATIONS AND DENOTATIONS OF WORDS

Words that have similar dictionary definitions (denotations) may have different connotations: a different emotional impact and set of associations. For example, *sports car* is defined as "an automobile equipped for racing," but it may connote rich, young people on exciting adventures. Such connotations cause people to buy these cars. What connotations do the following words have for you?

surgeon	college	politician	red
cigarette	home	graveyard	pumpkin pie

By carefully gauging the connotations of your word choices, you can convey the meaning and associations that you intend:

> The tourists *looked* at the movie star.

> [Notice how the sentence would change if you substituted *gawked* or *stared* for *looked.* Although the three words have similar meanings, the connotations are very different.]

> He was attracted by the *odor* surrounding her.

> [For many people, *odor* has an unpleasant connotation, so it is not quite the right word to use here. *Smell* would have the same problem. The word with the right connotation is *fragrance* or *aroma.*]

(For more discussion of how word choice affects writing, see *Word Choice,* pages 427–28.)

CONTRACTIONS

A contraction is two words condensed into one, accomplished by omitting one or more letters and adding an apostrophe in their place: *isn't* for *is not, aren't* for *are not, couldn't* for *could not.* (For a fuller discussion of contractions, see page 261.)

D

DASHES

The dash is dramatic; it draws the reader's attention to a word or a phrase. It can signal a sudden change, or it can emphasize an introductory list or parenthetical material. It should be used sparingly—just in the situations mentioned here and not as a substitute for the semicolon or the colon—so that it does not lose its particular power.

On a word processor or a typewriter, use two hyphens without a space between them to create a dash. In some software programs, a dash can be created by pressing a specific combination of keys or selecting the long dash from the symbols menu. No space is needed between the dash and the words on either side of it.

To Signal a Sudden Change

Use the dash as the strong signal of a sudden change in thought or tone, a new direction in the sentence:

> I'm sure we will get our raises soon—or never.

> Kevin proved his courage and manliness in the Marines—by scrubbing the barracks every afternoon.

After an Introductory List

Use the dash between an introductory list and the main part of the sentence. This construction leads the reader to consider an emphasized list of traits and then apply it to the subject:

Cold, calculating, ruthless, conniving—our boss is commonly described with these terms.

Shy, cautious, clean, nurturing—these traits of snakes receive little attention because most people think of snakes as dangerous and evil.

Chauffeur, coach, medic, cook, housekeeper, laundry specialist, counselor, homework helper—a parent's jobs are unending.

To Emphasize Parenthetical Material

Use the dash (or two dashes if the addition occurs within the sentence) to emphasize an added explanation, illustration, or comment. If the added material contains commas, the dashes help mark its separation from the rest of the sentence:

Liechtenstein—not quite as large as Washington, D.C.—is a constitutional monarchy located in the Alps between Austria and Switzerland.

Barrier islands—sandy areas that protect the mainland from storms—change location every ten to fifteen years.

Salisbury offered the best of traditional England—a breathtaking cathedral, cobblestone streets, old pubs with flower baskets hanging outside.

DEPENDENT CLAUSES

Although it may contain a subject and a predicate, a dependent clause cannot stand on its own as a sentence because it begins with a word such as *when* or *if* that makes it dependent on some other clause to complete the meaning. In the sentence "When the snow melts, there may be floods," the words "When the snow melts" are a dependent clause. (For a full discussion of dependent and independent clauses, see *Clauses*, pages 335–37.)

DICTION

Diction means the choice of words. The criteria for such decisions include appropriateness, specificity, and conciseness. (For help with diction, see *Word Choice*, pages 427–28, and *Revising Sentences*, pages 39–44.)

DICTIONARY USE

To succeed as a writer, you will need a desk dictionary, such as *The Random House College Dictionary, The American Heritage College Dictionary,* or *Merriam-Webster's Collegiate Dictionary.* Their entries provide a great deal of information, such as that in the following entry from *The American Heritage College Dictionary* (3rd ed.). From it you can learn a number of things about the word being defined: spelling, word division, and pronunciation; part of speech; and meanings, usage labels, word origins. Depending on the dictionary you choose, you can also look up synonyms and antonyms, biographical and geographical names, or the history and evolution of a word. (For information on using dictionaries and other reference books for research papers, see pages 59–73.)

> **scream** (skrēm) *v.* **screamed, scream·ing, screams.** — *intr.* **1.** To utter a long, loud, piercing cry, as from pain or fear. **2.** To make a loud, piercing sound. **3.** To speak or write in a heated, hysterical manner. **4.** To have or produce a startling effect. — *tr.* To utter or say in or as if in a screaming voice. — **scream** *n.* **1.** A long, loud, piercing cry or sound. **2.** *Informal.* One that is hilariously or ridiculously funny. [ME *screamen,* poss. of Scand. orig.; akin to ON *scræma.*] — **scream′ing·ly** *adv.*

Spelling, Word Division, and Pronunciation

In each dictionary entry, you first see the correct spelling of the word. If there is more than one acceptable form, both will be listed with the preferred spelling given first (for example, "*judg·ment* also *judge·ment*").

The main entry also shows how the word is divided into syllables. *Scream,* which has no dot markers, is a one-syllable word. *Judg·ment* has two syllables. If you need to split a word at the end of a line, make that division only at a syllable break: thus *scream* cannot be divided.

The main entry also indicates how to write compound words. If only syllable markers appear in the word, it is written as one word (*touchdown*). If a hyphen appears in the entry, write the word with a hyphen (*touch-type*). If two words appear with a space between them, write them as two separate words (*touch football*). If a two-word combination does not appear in the dictionary, then it is two words: *easy touch* does not appear in the dictionary because these are simply two separate words that create a common phrase but not a compound.

The correct pronounciation of the word appears in parentheses. The symbols used there are explained through examples in a pronunciation key generally located at the bottom of each page. The long *e* shown in *scream,* for example, is like the *e* sound in *be.* If two pronunciations are given in the dictionary entry, both are acceptable, but the first one is the more common one: *economics,* for example, can be pronounced with a short *e* or a long *e,* but the pronunciation with the short *e* is listed first.

Part of Speech

The dictionary entry next gives the part of speech, using the following abbreviations:

n.	noun
s.	singular noun
p.	plural noun
v.	verb
tr.	transitive verb
intr.	intransitive verb
adj.	adjective
adv.	adverb
pron.	pronoun
prep.	preposition
conj.	conjunction
interj.	interjection

In the sample entry for *scream,* the first four definitions are for the word as an intransitive verb, the next one is for a transitive verb, and the next two are for a noun.

Along with the part of speech, the dictionary provides the **principal parts** of the word. For verbs, it lists the past tense and past participle (listed once if they are the same), present participle, and third-person singular (*screamed, screaming, screams*). For nouns, no plural is listed if the plural is formed by adding *s* or *es.* Because no plural is given for *scream,* the plural is *screams.* But the entry for *child* has "*n. pl. children*" (meaning "noun, whose plural form is 'children'"). For adjectives and adverbs, dictionaries usually provide the comparative and superlative forms: *high* is followed by *higher* and *highest.*

Meanings, Usage Labels, Word Origins, Synonyms, and Antonyms

The meanings are given next, sometimes with illustrations of their usage. Usage labels indicate that the word has a usage that may not be acceptable in all contexts. These labels include *archaic, British, dialect, informal, nonstandard, obscene, obsolete, offensive, poetic, regional, slang,* and *vulgar.* A guide to the dictionary, usually located at the beginning, will provide the precise meaning of each usage label. The definition of *scream* as "one that is hilariously or ridiculously funny" is listed as informal. The origins of the word appear in brackets after the list of meanings. Some entries conclude with a list of synonyms or antonyms that help define the exact meaning of the word.

Biographical and Geographical Entries

Besides offering definitions of words, dictionaries provide brief discussions of notable people and locations. In some dictionaries, such as *Webster's Collegiate Dictionary,* this information is placed in separate sections at the end. Other dictionaries, such as the *Random House College Dictionary,* have these entries along with the definitions.

Other Types of Dictionaries

For more information about definitions and usage, and for the most complete listing of American vocabulary, consult an unabridged dictionary, such as *Webster's Third New International Dictionary of the English Language.*

For information concerning the meaning of a word in earlier centuries as well as illustrations of these usages by well-known writers, consult the twenty volumes of the *Oxford English Dictionary.* The word *scream,* for example, was once commonly used to mean the "characteristic shrill cry" of a bird, as in "The eagles answer'd with their scream," from Sir Walter Scott's *The Lady of the Lake* (1810). This usage has been less common in the twentieth century.

Other dictionaries cover specialized terms of specific disciplines, often in lengthy entries explaining their origins and current importance. Page 62 lists some examples of specialized dictionaries.

DIRECT OBJECTS

The direct object is the word that receives the action of a verb in a sentence in which the subject is the actor or agent. In such a sentence, the subject names the do-er, the verb names what is done, and the direct object names who or what the verb acts upon. In "Susan bought new boots," *boots* is the direct object.

DOUBLE NEGATIVES

A double negative is the nonstandard use of two negatives in a sentence that is intended to have a negative meaning: "Shakespeare *can't* have *nothing* like that in mind." One of the negatives must be eliminated: "Shakespeare can't have *anything* like that in mind."

E

ELLIPSIS MARKS

Three spaced periods (the ellipsis mark) are used to indicate omissions from quotations or to mark a hesitation.

For Omissions in Quotations

The ellipsis mark indicates that a word, phrase, sentence, full paragraph, or more has been left out of a quotation. An ellipsis mark is not necessary to indicate that material preceded or followed your excerpt.Your reader will understand that the quotation, whether a few words or a few paragraphs, is part of a larger work.

The three dots of the ellipsis mark within a quotation indicate that material has been omitted. If the omission follows a sentence, its period precedes the ellipsis mark (making, in effect, four dots). These omissions should enable you to emphasize the key lines and ideas from a source; they should not be used to modify the author's arguments:

> **Original:** There has always been a poignancy in watching human activity and settlement crowd out existing animals and plants so that their numbers gradually dwindle and disappear. The dodo, the passenger pigeon, and the golden parakeet are examples of animals that were once abundant and have now vanished. The buffalo, the whooping crane, the rhinoceros, the tiger, the African elephant, the sperm whale, and many other large animals may soon follow them. No one wants to see such rare and exotic creatures driven to extinction.
>
> —William Tucker, *Progress and Privilege*

> **Shortened Quotation with Ellipsis Mark:** After naming animals that are now extinct, William Tucker mentions another sad possibility for Americans: "the buffalo . . . may soon follow them."

> **Shortened Quotation with a Period and Ellipsis Mark:** William Tucker maintains that recent extinctions have frustrated human observers: "There has always been a poignancy in watching human activity and settlement crowd out existing animals and plants so that their numbers gradually dwindle and disappear. . . . No one wants to see such rare and exotic creatures driven to extinction."

> **Misleading Use of the Ellipsis Mark:** William Tucker, that animal nut, dreams of a world without people, a time when "human activity and settlement . . . dwindle and disappear."

For a Pause or Hesitation

The ellipsis mark can indicate a pause, a reluctance to speak further, or an intentionally unfinished statement. If the omission follows a complete sentence, the ellipsis mark should be preceded by a period:

> He remembers many joyous moments from his marriage . . . and too many fights over nothing.

> "I'm not sure how I feel . . . ," said Mother. "Don't press me to decide."

> It's a bird. . . . It's a plane. . . . No, it's Superman!

END PUNCTUATION

Three punctuation marks can signify the end of a sentence: the period, the exclamation point, and the question mark.

Period

The period is normally used at the end of a declarative sentence:

> Sandy approved the revised schedule gladly.

With Indirect Questions and Exclamations

A sentence that reports a question but does not ask it is an indirect question, which ends with a period:

> Kerry asked if Tanesha's signature was legible.

> The physicist wondered if the new discovery could be explained by any existing theory.

> Mustapha wondered where all the people had gone.

Similarly, if a sentence reports an exclamation, it should end with a period. In the following examples, the first is an exclamation and appropriately ends with an exclamation point. The second reports an exclamation, and it appropriately ends with a period:

> Stop that noise!

> The teacher said to stop that noise.

Question Mark

Question marks are used after direct questions:

> Where are Ben and Amy today?

> How much did you pay for your accounting book?

> Why have you waited so late to register?

Indirect questions (such as "Linda asked if I was finished with her book") do not end with question marks but with periods.

With Quotations

A question mark may appear either inside or outside the quotation marks that set off a direct quotation, depending on whether the material within the quotation marks is a question or the question is about the material within the quotation marks:

"Where are you going?" Juanita asked.

Was it Richard Nixon who said, "I am not a crook"?

When did you memorize "How Do I Love Thee?"

In the first example, the material within the quotation marks asks the question; thus the question mark is inside the quotation marks. In the second example, the material outside the quotation marks asks the question (the quotation itself is not a question); thus the question mark is outside the quotation marks. In the third example, both the sentence itself and the quotation are questions; however, only one question mark should be used, the one within the quotation marks.

Exclamation Point

Exclamation points are used after sentences or other groups of words that express strong feelings:

Slide!

Drop that gun!

Home at last!

Some writers tend to overuse exclamation points; they should be used sparingly.

Indirect exclamations (such as "Paul shouted at Rosemary to bring in the lawn furniture before the rain started") do not end with exclamation points but with periods.

F

FAULTY PREDICATION

Faulty predication is the use of a predicate (the complete verb plus any object, predicate adjective, or predicate noun and all their modifiers) that does not fit with the subject of the sentence. "One test *is* an infrared spectrometer" is an example of faulty predication. The sentence should be revised to read "One test *involves the use of* an infrared spectrometer." (For more on mismatched subjects and predicates, see pages 278–79.)

FIGURATIVE LANGUAGE

A *figure of speech,* or figurative language, is an expression in which words are used in an imaginative rather than a literal sense. The two chief figures of speech are the simile and the metaphor. A *simile* is an explicit comparison between two things that are essentially unlike, usually introduced by the word *like* or *as.* Humorist Dave Barry chooses the simile, for example, to complete a description of his son's new haircut:

> The hair on the top was smeared with what appeared to be transmission fluid and sticking up in spikes, which made it look like a marine creature striking a defensive posture.

A *metaphor* is an implied comparison of unlike things, made without *like* or *as,* as in this Dave Barry comment on his sons' messiness:

> Little boys are Pod People from the Planet Destructo.

Both similes and metaphors can enhance your writing by bypassing strict logical connections and providing instead a more forceful and imaginative expression of meaning.

Simile

> San Francisco sits like a thimble on the little thumb of its peninsula.
>
> —Bob Thompson
>
> Before the girls got to the porch I heard their laughter crackling and popping like pine logs in a cooking stove.
>
> —Maya Angelou

Metaphor

> Our tension itself was fire, we ourselves were forever burning—to live, to get down the foreboding in our souls, to make good.
>
> —Alfred Kazin
>
> Necessity is the mother of invention.
>
> —Proverb

Do not overuse such figurative language, and avoid mixed metaphors that leave readers with a jumbled or confusing picture:

> We tried to turn back the tide, but the genie was out of the bottle.
> [Are they controlling the waves or dealing with spirits?]
> He acted like a lazy dog with his head in the clouds.
> [This one certainly creates an odd picture.]

FORMAL WRITING

Formal writing is the kind required for the papers you will prepare for college classes, the articles you will write for publication, and the letters and reports that will be a regular part of your career work. The grammatical and stylistic usage discussed in this book is an essential component of formal writing. For your personal letters or daily journals, a more informal, colloquial style may be appropriate.

FRAGMENTS

A fragment is a part of a sentence punctuated as though it were a complete sentence with a capital letter for the first word and with end punctuation:

> The neighborhood renewal project still faced considerable opposi-
>
> tion. Even after the city council discussed it for three years and
>
> signed several contracts.

In general, fragments are not appropriate in formal writing. (For a complete discussion of fragment types and methods of correcting them, see pages 193–200.)

FUSED SENTENCES

A fused sentence is one that combines two independent clauses into one sentence with no punctuation between them.

Congress
The economy was slipping.~~they~~ decided to lower taxes.
                      ^

(This error, also called a *run-on sentence,* is discussed fully on pages 209–14.)

G

GERUNDS

302–04

A gerund, one kind of verbal, is the *-ing* form of the verb used as a noun. In "Writing is more difficult than math," *Writing* is a gerund. (For more on gerunds and other verbals, see *Verbals,* pages 416–17.)

H

HELPING VERBS

296–302

Helping verbs, such as *can, would, have,* and *do,* combine with the principal forms of verbs to create the different tenses in English. (For a complete discussion, see *Verbs,* pages 421–24.)

HYPHENS

A hyphen is used to divide a word at the end of a line and to link compound words or word parts.

At the End of a Line

To divide a word at the end of a line, make the break between syllables (*break-fast, mor-ning*) and put a hyphen at the end of the first unit to indicate that the rest of the word will appear on the next line. Dictionaries show where the syllable breaks occur. If the word already has a hyphen, like *brother-in-law* or *ex-husband,* make the break after the hyphen: do not add extra hyphens to these words. Also, make sure that each part of the divided word has at least two letters: thus *i-con* should not be separated; *a-non-y-mous* should not be divided after the *a*. Do not divide one-syllable words (even long ones like *friend* or *spring*), abbreviations (*USA, UNICEF*), contractions (*don't, wouldn't*), or numerals (*250; 1,000,000*).

Occasionally, you may be asked not to divide words at the ends of lines. If you use a word processor, you should be able to turn off the hyphenation command.

With Compound Words

A hyphen is often used to join two or more words that function as a single word:

> double-jointed, long-range, off-key [adjectives]
>
> double-decker, Johnny-come-lately, mother-of-pearl [nouns]
>
> double-park, hand-feed, pinch-hit [verbs]

If you are not sure whether a compound has a hyphen, check a dictionary. Many compounds are written as one word without a hyphen or as two words. The nouns *double-crosser* and *double-talk* have hyphens, for example, but *double dribble, double feature,* and *double date* are written as two words. The adjectives *low-down* and *low-key* are hyphenated; the adjectives *lowbred* and *lowborn* are written as one word with no hyphen.

If you decide to make your own combination to create a memorable effect, hyphenate your original coined compound. Do not overuse this dramatic technique, however.

> He said that his sister was one of those *nobody-loves-me* pouters.
>
> Students view the university's new *no-drop* policy as a *drop-dead-if-you-have-problems* rule.

With Compound Adjectives

When you use a compound adjective not listed in a dictionary, insert a hyphen if the compound adjective precedes a noun; do not hyphenate the compound if it follows the noun:

Hyphen before Noun	No Hyphen after Noun
The exterminator entered the *rat-infested* warehouse.	The exterminator entered the warehouse, which was *rat infested*.

She no longer buys those *ill-fitting* discount dresses.	She no longer buys those discount dresses, which are *ill fitting.*
The *well-respected* attorney refused to take the case.	The attorney who refused to take the case is *well respected.*

You should also use hyphens to clarify combinations of modifiers that would be ambiguous without them. Hyphenation can make clear whether the phrase *three quarter inch nails* means "three-quarter-inch nails" (nails that are three-fourths of an inch long) or "three quarter-inch nails" (three nails that are each one-fourth of an inch long).

With Very and with Adverbs Ending in ly

Do not hyphenate compounds that contain *-ly* adverbs or *very* plus an adjective:

> The *plainly visible* lighthouse led us to the shore.

> The *very large* orchestra could not fit onto the school's stage.

With Numbers and Fractions

Use hyphens if you spell out numbers from *twenty-one* to *ninety-nine,* both when the numbers stand alone and when they are part of a larger number:

twenty-seven	thirty-two thousand
forty-eight	ninety-five billion

To spell out a fraction as an adjective, place a hyphen between the fraction's two parts. Hyphenation is not required when the fraction is used as a noun:

As Adjective	As Noun
one-eighth full	containing one eighth of the liquid
a two-thirds majority	a majority of two thirds

To refer to inclusive numbers of pages, you can use a hyphen or you can use the words *to* and *from,* but not a combination of the two:

> We need to read *pages 89–174* for class tomorrow.

> [or *from page 89 to page 174,* but not *from page 89–174*]

With Prefixes and Suffixes

Most words with prefixes and suffixes do not contain hyphens:

deactivate	irregular	precautionary
advancement	continuance	

Only in the following cases will you need a hyphen in a word with a prefix or a suffix:

- Hyphenate a prefix with a capitalized base word:

  pre-Columbian architecture   anti-American activities

  mid-October

- Hyphenate a prefix with dates:

  pre-1954   post-1865

- Use a hyphen with single-letter prefixes:

  T-shirt   A-frame   x-ray

- Use a hyphen with *all-, ex-, self-,* and *-elect:*

  all-conference   ex-wife

  self-righteous   president-elect

- Use a hyphen to differentiate homonyms. For example, since *recount* means "to narrate," *re-count* needs a hyphen to mean "count again." Compare *recollect* and *re-collect, recover* and *re-cover.*

- Use a hyphen to separate an awkward combination of vowels or consonants:

  re-arm   de-escalate   anti-inflammatory   fall-like

Compare these with *reload, debrief, antiballistic, childlike.*

I

INDEPENDENT CLAUSES

An independent clause is a group of words that contains a subject and a predicate and can stand alone as a sentence. In the sentence "When the Warblers did an encore, many people started to dance," the words "many people started to dance" form an independent clause. (For a full discussion of independent and dependent clauses, see *Clauses,* pages 335–37.)

INDIRECT OBJECTS

Some verbs, such as *buy, bring, lend,* and *sell,* may have a direct object and an indirect object. The indirect object is who or what receives the direct object and the action of the verb. The indirect object usually precedes the direct object in the sentence. In "Mai sold Dave her used history book," *Dave* is the indirect object, and *book* is the direct object. An indirect object can also be replaced by a prepositional phrase following the direct object: "Mai sold her used history book *to Dave.*"

INFINITIVES

The infinitive is the base form of the verb preceded by the infinitive marker *to,* as in *to shout, to dance,* and *to sing.* (For information about infinitive phrases, see *Phrases,* pages 375–76.)

INTERJECTIONS

Interjections—such as *oh, wow, ouch, ah,* and *all right*—are exclamations used to express surprise or emotion. They are generally followed by a comma or an exclamation point:

> Wow!
>
> Oh, how beautiful that new ZX is!

INTERNET ADDRESSES

Uniform Resource Locators (URLs) should be placed within angle brackets (< >) wherever they appear as part of a paragraph. If angle brackets are used, breaking the address across two lines is acceptable, but the break should be made in a logical location, such as before or after a slash or after a period:

> <http://www.mayfieldpub.com>

(For more information on searching the Internet and document-ing sources found there, see pages 67–74 and 87–130.)

INTERROGATIVES

Interrogative pronouns, adjectives, and adverbs—such as *what, where, why, whose,* and *which*—are used to ask questions: "Whose car are we taking?"

INTRANSITIVE VERBS

Intransitive verbs are verbs that do not take objects (for example, "The fish *died.*") *Go, laugh, persevere, sit,* and *tremble* are other ex-amples of intransitive verbs. (Transitive verbs, page 415, are those that can take objects.)

ITALICS (OR UNDERLINING)

When you write longhand or use a typewriter, use underlining as the equivalent of the italics found in word-processed documents and printed materials. The following sections discuss the appro-priate uses of underlining or italics.

With Titles

Use italic type (or underlining) for titles of complete works: books, magazines, newspapers, plays, long poems, movies, television shows, record albums or compact discs, ballets, operas, musical compositions, and works of art:

> To advertise the debut of *Gone with the Wind,* MGM studios created a separate feature section for the *Atlanta Constitution.*

> Within a year Whoopi Goldberg appeared in the movie *The Associ-ate,* the television show *In the Gloaming,* and the Broadway play *A Funny Thing Happened on the Way to the Forum.*

> The *Mona Lisa* is so small that the crowds generally obscure it from view.

Use quotation marks for the title of a short work or for a part of something larger—a short story; an essay or article from a book, magazine, or newspaper; a short poem; a song; and episode of a television show or radio show; or a chapter or subdivision of a book:

The Blues Traveler song "Run-Around" from the album *Four* features John Popper on harmonica.

When *Newsweek* published "Why Johnny Can't Write," many schools began to reexamine their curricula in English.

In his poem "To An Athlete Dying Young," A. E. Housman described the difficulties of the aging sports hero.

Exception: Do not use either italics or quotation marks to refer to the Bible, books of the Bible, or legal documents:

The Book of Matthew, in the New Testament, contains some of the Bible's best-known parables of Jesus.

The states would not accept the Constitution without the Bill of Rights.

For Foreign Words and Phrases

Foreign words or phrases—those that are not also English words—should be italicized (underlined):

When he hears *"Sicilia est insula"* coming from the class next door, Mr. Mauldin knows that the first-year Latin students have begun their oral drills.

The mountain laurel, an evergreen shrub whose scientific name is *Kalmia latifolia,* has clusters of pink or white flowers that hide its poisonous leaves.

If a foreign word has been accepted into English—if it appears in an English dictionary—it should not be italicized (or underlined). Many common English words have been borrowed from other languages:

alumnus (Latin)

habeas corpus (Latin)

judo (Japanese)

pasta (Italian)

For Names of Ships, Aircraft, Spacecraft, and Trains

The U.S.S. *Nautilus,* an atomic submarine, made the first voyage under the polar ice cap in 1958.

After the successful *Pathfinder* mission to Mars in 1997, NASA began making plans for a base there.

Lindbergh's *Spirit of St. Louis* hangs in the Smithsonian Museum; the *Enola Gay,* which dropped the bomb on Hiroshima, was removed from a World War II exhibit and placed in a warehouse.

For Special Uses of Words, Letters, Numbers, or Phrases

Italicize (underline) words, letters, numbers, and phrases used as such:

The letter combination *ough,* which is pronounced differently in *dough* and *cough,* confuses many young readers.

The sign often seen in restaurants, *Wait for the Hostess to Be Seated,* doesn't really mean that this employee should sit down first.

Is that last number a *3* or an *8*?

You can also use italics (underlining) occasionally to emphasize a word or a phrase. If you employ this technique too frequently, though, it will lose its effect.

Why don't *you* see who's at the door?

If Roger had been on time to his appointment, *he* would have been a witness to the robbery.

J

JARGON

Within scientific and technical circles, the controlled and careful use of a specialized vocabulary can serve an important purpose: to convey information quickly and exactly. But for other audiences, such words may obscure meaning. Jargon, the special vocabulary of a trade or a profession, should be used only within the group for which it is appropriate (and then only in moderation). Music historians, for instance, might discuss the polyphony or dodecaphony of a certain symphony or the guitaristic techniques of Segovia, but they need to either avoid or define that vocabulary when they address other audiences.

An extension of jargon is the inflated terminology sometimes used to impress—or confuse—readers. Compare these two versions of the same statement:

Needlessly Inflated	Clearer
Dr. Frederiks finalized her interface with the staff by requesting office input.	Dr. Frederiks ended the staff meeting by asking for advice.

The following are examples of typically overinflated words from government, business, and military circles. Simpler, clearer alternatives are shown in parentheses.

Overinflated Words (and Simple Synonyms)

ameliorate (improve)   interface (talk)

facilitate (help)   optimal (best, most favorable)

finalize (finish)   prioritize (set priorities)

impact (affect)   systematize (make rules for)

indicator (sign)   utilize (use)

input (advice)

(For additional discussions of word choice in writing, see *Word Choice*, pages 427–28, and *Revising Sentences,* pages 39–44.)

L

LINKING VERBS

Linking verbs link, or join, a subject with a predicate noun or a predicate adjective: "Josepha *is* a teacher." "She *appears* friendly." Common linking verbs include *appear, be, become, feel, look, seem, smell, sound,* and *taste.* (For more on predicate adjectives and predicate nouns, see *Sentences,* page 394.)

M

MODAL AUXILIARIES

  Modal auxiliaries—such as *will, would, shall, should, may, might, must, can,* and *could*—are a subset of the helping verbs. These

296–301

verbs do not change form as they change number. They are used with the principal parts of verbs to show ability (*can*), possibility (*may*), intent (*shall*), obligation (*should*), or necessity (*must*).

MODIFIERS

A modifier is any word or word group that describes, limits, or qualifies another word or word group. Modifiers include adjectives and adverbs as well as phrases and clauses that function as adjectives or adverbs:

> The *hungry* customers harassed the waiter.
>
> The grass grew *quickly*.
>
> Theo mocked his *golfing* partner.
>
> I own the car *that has a dented fender*.

(For information about errors with modifiers, see pages 265–72.)

N

NOUNS

Nouns are words that name persons and animals (*teacher, daughter, brontosaurus*), places (*town, ocean*), things (*table, incubator*), and concepts (*freedom, creativity*). (For help with the proper articles to use with nouns, see pages 285–93.)

285–93

Common nouns name people, animals, objects, places, things, or concepts in a general (nonspecific) way (*girl, dog, city, university, religion*). **Proper nouns** name specific people, animals, places, things, or concepts (*Louisa, Fido, Tulsa, University of Florida, Christianity*). Proper nouns begin with capital letters. **Collective nouns** name groups: *team, crew, chorus*. When a collective noun refers to the group as a whole, it is treated as singular. When it refers to members of the group who are acting individually, it is treated as plural. (For examples, see pages 219–20.) **Mass nouns** name something that is not usually countable (*sugar,* *sand, gravel*) or qualities (*peace, tranquility, fortitude*). They usually remain singular.

Plural forms of most nouns are made by adding an *s* or *es* (*pictures, heroes*). A few nouns use irregular endings for their plurals (*child—children; man—men; mouse—mice*).

Nouns can also be written in **possessive forms** to indicate ownership. You form the possessive by adding an apostrophe plus *s* to a singular noun, an apostrophe to a plural noun, or an apostrophe plus *s* to a plural noun that doesn't end in *s* (*John's friend, the boys' dog, the children's classroom*).

NUMBERS

Write as words any numbers that can be expressed as one or two words; use numerals for numbers expressed in more than two words:

one friend	2,800 years ago
seven times	$197.50
twenty-two boxes	2,970,000 pebbles

Large round numbers can be written with words or numerals. To emphasize the size of the amount, use numerals:

ten million dollars *or* $10 million *or* $10,000,000

In most scientific and technical disciplines, the practice is to write out numbers from one to nine and to use numerals for ten and above and with units of measurement. Be sure to be consistent.

Special Uses

- At the **beginnings of sentences,** always write numbers as words:

  Ninety-two
  9̶2̶ contestants chose the first answer.

- For **time of day,** use numerals with A.M. and P.M. (or a.m. and p.m.) designations. Use words with *o'clock:*

  11 A.M. (a.m.) *or* 11:00 A.M. (a.m.)

  or eleven o'clock in the morning

- For **dates,** usage varies, as you see in the examples:

  With a Year Included

  April 8, 1992 *or* 8 April 1992 [*not* April 8th, 1992]

  Without a Year Mentioned

  April 8 *or* April 8th *or* the eighth of April

  For Decades

  the 1990s *or* the nineties

  For Centuries

  the twentieth century

  nineteenth-century literature

  For Inclusive Years

  from 1971 to 1991 *or* 1971–1991 [*not* from 1971–1991]

- In **addresses,** use numerals for house, apartment, and suite numbers and for zip codes:

  Apartment 23C, 1412 Caldwell Street, Tallahassee, Florida 32304

  With Abbreviations

  Apt. 23C, 1412 Caldwell St., Tallahassee, FL 32304

  For Numbered Streets

  12 West Ninth Street *or* 12 W. 9th St.

  1779 North 110 Street *or* 1779 North 110th Street

  or 1779 N. 110th St.

- Use numerals for **decimal numbers** and for **numbers with symbols:**

4.78 percent	.0769 cubic feet	twenty dollars
five percent	eighteen degrees	$21.75
7%	74°F	

  In text, however, you can write out a number if it can be expressed in one or two words. In such cases, also write out *percent, degrees,* and *dollars* (other symbols are not used in text, only in graphs and charts).

- Write **identification numbers** as numerals:

Highway 61   Physics 122

Channel 13   Richard III

- Write **pages** and **divisions of books and plays** as numerals:

    part 3

    page 97

    chapter 7

    act 1, scene 6 *or* Act I, Scene vi

- With **measurements,** especially in scientific and technical writing, use numerals, whether they are smaller or greater than nine:

    When iodine entered the beaker, it eroded 39 cells and left 2 unchanged.

    The blocks for this fireplace mount need to be 12 feet long, 3 feet wide, and 2 feet deep.

O

OBJECT COMPLEMENTS

An object complement follows and modifies a direct object. The complement may be a noun, an adjective, or a word group functioning as noun or an adjective. *Disaster* is the object complement in the sentence "Meleta declared the party a disaster."

P

PARALLELISM

Parallelism refers to similarity of form of pairs or series of words, phrases, or clauses. In the sentence "We tried *hiking the trails, rafting the rivers,* and *exploring the back-country* on our vacation," the italicized phrases are grammatically parallel. (For help with correcting faulty parallelism, see pages 273–77.)

PARENTHESES

To Set Off Supplementary Material

Parentheses separate information from the main part of the sentence and minimize its importance. If the information is significant to the meaning of the sentence, place it within dashes (which provide emphasis) or commas:

> There are 110,000 species of moths and butterflies (one thousand butterfly species in the United States alone).

> The Public Affairs Information Service (PAIS) provides important statistics on the expanded role of women in Third World agriculture.

To Enclose Letters or Numerals in a List within a Sentence

> We need to take three immediate actions to solve our budget problems: (1) disconnect the office WATS lines, (2) discontinue spending for entertainment, and (3) suspend all travel allocations.

Punctuation with Parentheses

When parentheses enclose an element within a sentence, commas and periods are placed after the closing parenthesis:

> When we entered the main entrance (called the Thompson Lobby), we saw the large signs for the City Consortium of Actors (CCA).

When parentheses enclose an entire sentence, the sentence should begin with a capital letter and end with a period or other end punctuation placed before the closing parenthesis:

> Columbus made four voyages to the New World, visiting what are now the Bahamas, Jamaica, Cuba, Puerto Rico, Trinidad, and Venezuela. (He first came in search of a westward route to India.)

PARTICIPLES

A participle is a verb form that functions as part of a verb phrase (*Paulette is leaving; the guests have eaten*) or as an adjective (*the required course; the students waiting in line*). When functioning as an adjective, the participle is a verbal and can combine with other

292–30

words to make a participial phrase. In "The cars sitting in the showroom were too expensive," the participial phrase is *sitting in the showroom*. (For more examples of participles, see *Verbals,* pages 416–17, and *Verbs,* pages 417–21. For information on misplaced participial phrases or modifiers, see pages 265–70.)

PARTS OF SPEECH

There are eight parts of speech:

- **Nouns**—words that name a person, animal, place, or thing
- **Pronouns**—words that substitute for nouns
- **Verbs**—words that express action or state of being
- **Adjectives**—words that modify nouns or pronouns
- **Adverbs**—words that modify verbs, adjectives, or other adverbs
- **Prepositions**—words that show a relationship between their object and the rest of the sentence
- **Conjunctions**—words that connect words, phrases, or clauses
- **Interjections**—exclamation words

(Each part of speech is discussed more fully in its own entry here in part 3.)

PASSIVE VOICE

A sentence is in the passive voice if the subject of the sentence receives the action of the do-er, as in "The mayor was surrounded by shouting reporters." In the active voice, the subject of the sentence is the do-er, as in "Shouting reporters surrounded the mayor." (For discussions of active and passive voice, see pages 39–44, and *Verbs,* pages 424–25.)

PHRASES

A phrase is a group of grammatically related words that lacks either a subject or a complete verb. There are eight kinds of phrases.

Noun Phrases

A noun phrase includes a noun and its modifiers:

> Judy took off *her dripping raincoat.*

Notice that *her dripping raincoat* cannot stand alone as a sentence; it does not have a complete verb. (The word *dripping* is a participle here—a verbal rather than a complete verb.)

Verb Phrases

A verb phrase includes a main verb and helping verbs:

> Judy's raincoat *is dripping* on the floor.

The phrase *is dripping* contains no subject; the verb phrase in combination with the noun phrase *Judy's raincoat* does make a complete sentence, however. The combination of the auxiliary, or helping, verb *is* with the participial form *dripping* creates a complete form of the verb *drip.*

Prepositional Phrases

A prepositional phrase consists of a preposition (such as *to, at,* or *of*) and its object (a noun or pronoun and any modifiers):

> I took my shoe *to the repair shop.*
>
> *At the shop,* a new heel costs ten dollars.
>
> I paid with the last *of my money.*

Gerund Phrases

The gerund is a verb form that ends in *ing* and functions as a noun. Here are some examples of gerund phrases:

> *Replacing heels* is a lucrative business.
>
> I specialize in *wrecking shoes.*

In the first sentence, *replacing* is a gerund and the noun *heels* is its object; together they make up a gerund phrase that functions as the subject of the sentence. In the second sentence, *wrecking* is the gerund, and *shoes* is its noun object; together they make up a gerund phrase that functions as the object of the preposition *in.*

Sometimes the gerund in a gerund phrase has a subject. Suppose we want to say that when Carmen wrecked her shoe, Bob thought it was funny—wrecking her shoe made Bob laugh:

Carmen's wrecking her shoe made Bob laugh.

Carmen is the subject of the gerund phrase; the subject of the gerund is put into possessive form—*Carmen's.*

Infinitive Phrases

302–04

The infinitive is the base form of a verb preceded by *to*—*to run, to fly, to dream.* Infinitives can be combined with subjects, objects, and complements to form infinitive phrases, as the following examples show:

Infinitive Phrase with Subject

I wanted *Casey to open the door.*

Asking *her to give me a hand,* I got into the game free.

In the first sentence, *Casey* is the subject of the infinitive *to open,* and *the door* is its object. Together they make up an infinitive phrase that functions as the direct object of the sentence. In the second sentence, *her* is the subject of the infinitive *to give, me* is its indirect object, and *a hand* is the direct object of the infinitive. Together they make up an infinitive phrase that functions as the object of the participle *Asking.*

Infinitive Phrase with Object

To pitch a perfect game was Wanda's big dream.

What I wanted was *to throw a pitch to Wanda.*

In the first sentence, *to pitch* is the infinitive, and *a perfect game* is a noun phrase that is its object. The infinitive phrase functions as the subject of the sentence. In the second sentence, *to throw* is the infinitive, and *a pitch to Wanda* is a noun phrase functioning as its object. (*What I wanted* is a dependent clause functioning as a noun—the subject of the sentence.)

Infinitive Phrase with Complement

Asking *Wanda to be the team captain* made her happy.

Here *Wanda* is the subject of the infinitive *to be,* and *captain* is the complement (here a predicate noun renaming Wanda). The infinitive phrase is the object of the gerund *Asking,* and the gerund phrase is the subject of the sentence.

Participial Phrases

The participle is the *-ing* or *-ed* form of the verb used as a modifier. Present participles are the *-ing* forms of verbs; past participles are the *-ed* forms of regular verbs. (See *Verbs,* pages 418–21, for the past participle forms of irregular verbs.) In participial phrases, participles can have objects, complements, and modifiers:

Participial Phrase with Object

Lupe turned down my invitation to dinner, *cracking a smile* and *breaking my heart.*

[The words *smile* and *heart* are objects of the participles *cracking* and *breaking.*]

Participial Phrase with Complement

Turning red with embarrassment, I started to walk away.

[*Turning* is the participle, *red* is an adjective functioning as its complement, and *with embarrassment* is a prepositional phrase modifying *red.* The participial phrase modifies *I,* the subject of the sentence.]

Participial Phrase with Modifier

Slowly increasing her smile, she suggested dinner at her apartment instead.

[*Slowly* is an adverb modifying the participle *increasing.*]

Appositive Phrases

An appositive is a noun or a noun phrase that renames another noun or noun phrase in some way. Thus an appositive phrase is a group of words functioning as an appositive:

Faculty objected when the trees in the parking lot, *Chinese elms,* were removed to create a walkway.

The big box of 64 crayons introduced several generations of children to the colors *burnt umber and sienna.*

Appositive phrases can be restrictive or nonrestrictive (essential or nonessential), and the distinction is signaled by the absence or presence of commas. In the first sentence above, the appositive phrase is nonessential to the meaning. In the second sentence, the appositive phrase is essential. (For examples of restrictive and nonrestrictive appositives, see *Appositives,* pages 323–24.)

Absolute Phrases

An absolute phrase, consisting of a noun or pronoun and a participle, modifies a whole sentence instead of a single word. It should be set off from the rest of the sentence by commas or dashes:

> Then we left the stadium—*Celeste catching the subway for home and me walking on air.*
>
> *The rain having freshened the air,* we decided to go for a walk.

Note: There is an important distinction between an absolute phrase, which modifies an entire sentence, and a dangling modifier, which is an error because it does not modify anything in the sentence. (For more on recognizing dangling modifiers, see pages 267–68.)

> **Absolute Phrase:** *Her dinner finished,* she left the cafeteria and headed to the library.
>
> [Here the absolute phrase—having a subject and a past participle—describes the situation and the reason for her action: it modifies the entire main clause.]
>
> **Dangling Modifier:** *Running quickly,* the train was reached.
>
> [Here the participle is dangling, an error, because it does not modify any word in the sentence. The sentence should be rewritten as *Running quickly, I reached the train.*]

Phrases and Sentence Fragments

A common writing error is to treat a phrase as if it were a complete sentence—to start it with a capital letter and end it with a mark of end punctuation (a period, a question mark, or an exclamation point). Here's what this kind of sentence fragment looks like:

> Dripping on the floor.   Opening the door.
>
> To the game.   Having cracked a smile.
>
> That she could be interested in me.

In each case, the phrase needs to be joined to a complete (independent) clause to eliminate the sentence fragment. (For more on recognizing and correcting these fragments, see pages 193–200.)

PLAGIARISM

To plagiarize means to claim authorship falsely. Giving the impression that another person's words, ideas, images, or data are your own constitutes plagiarism. (For guidelines for acceptable uses of other people's words and ideas, see pages 81–86.)

POSSESSIVES

The possessive case shows ownership or a comparable relationship: *Lucia's car, a day's pay.* It replaces a phrase beginning with *of: the car of Lucia, a day of pay.* The possessive case of singular nouns and indefinite pronouns is indicated by an apostrophe plus *s* (*the child's braces, somebody's galoshes*). Plural nouns ending in *s* are followed by an apostrophe to indicate possession (*the singers' recital*), and plurals not ending in *s* are followed by an apostrophe and *s* (*men's attitudes*). Personal pronouns (such as *he, she,* or *it*) have their own possessive case forms (*his, hers,* or *its*). They never use apostrophes to show possession. (For more on possession and the apostrophe, see pages 259–61. For more on forms of pronouns, see *Pronouns*, pages 380–82.)

PREDICATE ADJECTIVES

A predicate adjective follows a linking verb (such as *is, looks, smells, becomes, appears, seems*) and modifies the subject. In "Monty Python films are always funny," the word *funny* is a predicate adjective.

PREDICATE NOUNS

A predicate noun, also known as a predicate nominative, follows a linking verb (such as *is, looks, smells, becomes, appears, seems*) and renames the subject. In "The Beatles were George, Paul, John, and Ringo," the series *George, Paul, John, and Ringo* is the predicate noun.

PREDICATES

The predicate of a sentence is the complete verb plus any object, predicate noun, or predicate adjective and all their modifiers. Thus it is everything in the sentence except the subject and its modifiers. In "My best friend Vick likes to spend Sunday afternoons watching football and playing the piano," the predicate is *likes to spend Sunday afternoons watching football and playing the piano.* (For a full discussion of sentence elements, see *Sentences,* pages 393–94. For information on faulty predication, see pages 278–81.)

PREPOSITIONS

A preposition expresses the relationship that its object (a noun, pronoun, or noun clause) has to the rest of the sentence:

> The Cheshire cat perched *in* the tree.

> Jamie reached the finish line *before* her friend.

In the first example, the preposition *in* describes a spatial relationship: it tells where the cat perches. In the second, *before* shows a time relationship. The object of *in* is *tree;* the object of *before* is *friend.* The entire unit—the preposition, its object, and the object's modifiers—is called a prepositional phrase.

Listed here are some common prepositions:

about	below	for
above	beneath	from
across	beside	in
after	between	inside
against	beyond	into
along	by	like
among	concerning	near
around	despite	of
as	down	off
at	during	on
before	except	onto
behind	excepting	out

outside	throughout	until
over	to	up
past	toward	upon
regarding	under	with
since	underneath	within
through	unlike	without

Phrasal prepositions consist of more than one word. Here are some examples:

293–94

according to	due to	in spite of
along with	except for	instead of
aside from	in addition to	next to
because of	in front of	out of
by way of	in place of	with regard to

PRINCIPAL PARTS OF VERBS

The principal parts of verbs are their basic forms. Except for *be*, all verbs in English have these five forms:

- **The base form**—the one that combines with *to* to form the infinitive: *walk, ring*
- **The -s form**—the third-person-singular form: *walks, rings*
- **The past tense**—as in "Last week they *walked* out" or "Last week we *rang* the bell twice."
- **The past participle**—as in "We have *walked* together many times" or "We have *rung* the bell before."
- **The present participle**—as in "They are *walking* here now" or "They are *ringing* the bell now."

The irregular verb *be* has eight different forms: *be, is, am, are, was, were, been, being*. (A full discussion of verbs appears on pages 417–21.)

PRONOUNS

Most pronouns substitute for nouns or noun phrases and function in sentences as nouns do. They allow writers to continue discussing a person or a thing without repeating the noun:

Dauphine looked for *her* biology textbook, but *she* could not find it.

In this example, *her* stands for *Dauphine's*, and *she* stands for *Dauphine;* the writer uses *it* to avoid repeating *biology textbook*. In other words, *Dauphine* is the antecedent of *her* and of *she; textbook* is the antecedent of *it*. (Errors in using pronouns are discussed on pages 246–56.)

Types of Pronouns

- **Personal pronouns** (*I, you, he, she, it, we, they* in the subjective case; *my, mine, your, yours, his, her, hers, its, our, ours, their, theirs* in the possessive case; and *me, you, him, her, it, us, them* in the objective case) refer to specific people or things:

    I am sorry that *you* don't like *his* friends and that *you* refuse to play music with *them*.

- **Reflexive pronouns** (*myself, yourself, himself, herself, itself, oneself, ourselves, yourselves, themselves*) refer to the subject of the sentence or clause, indicating that it receives the action of the complete verb:

    If that rope breaks, you will hurt *yourself*.

- **Intensive pronouns** have the same forms as reflexive pronouns. They are used to emphasize a noun or a pronoun:

    The manager *himself* could not open the safe.

- **Indefinite pronouns** (including *all, anybody, anyone, both, each, either, enough, everybody, everyone, everything, few, many, most, neither, none, no one, one, ones, other, others, some, somebody, someone*) do not substitute for specific nouns, but they function as nouns:

    Somebody took *everything* from the office.

Most indefinite pronouns (*anybody, anyone, each, either, everybody, everyone, everything, neither, no one, one, somebody, someone*) are singular and thus take singular verbs:

    Each of the carts *is* here.

    Anybody is eligible to win.

    Everything here *is* on sale.

A few of them *(all, any, enough, none, more, most, some)* can be either singular or plural, depending on the noun or pronoun they refer to—which is usually the object of a prepositional phrase that follows the pronoun:

Plural	Singular
Some of the *books were* second editions.	*Some* of the *book is* inspiring.
More of *them are* paperback than hardback.	*More* of this *author is* what I want.
Most of *them are* dog-eared and well read.	*Most* of her *work is* similar.
Any of *them are* excellent choices.	*Any* of *it is* worth the price you pay.

A few indefinite pronouns *(both, few, many, ones, others)* are always plural:

Both of the *basketballs are* in the garage.

Many of the *stragglers are* still looking for seats.

(More examples and a list of indefinite pronouns can be found on pages 250–51.)

• **Demonstrative pronouns** *(this, that, these, those)* point to nouns, clarifying the group under discussion:

Those are the presents that should be taken to the homeless shelter.

• **Interrogative pronouns** *(who, whom, whose, which, what)* are used to ask questions:

Who took my jacket?

• **Relative pronouns** *(who, whom, whose, which, that, what, whoever, whomever, whichever, whatever)* introduce dependent clauses by relating the additional information to the rest of the sentence. Each relative pronoun should refer to a specific noun:

You look like the boy *who* came to the party last week.

(The role of relative pronouns in introducing dependent clauses is discussed in *Clauses,* pages 335–37. The use of relative pronouns as subjects is discussed on page 221.)

PUNCTUATION

To find out how to use a particular punctuation mark, go to its entry on the pages shown here.

QUOTATION MARKS

Quotation marks set off source materials, some types of titles, and words intended in a special sense. You will need to understand not only the correct use of quotation marks but also the correct punctuation to go along with them. (Additional examples of the use of quotation marks for quoting source materials may be found on pages 81–86. The specific requirements of MLA and APA documentation are found on pages 91–128.)

When to Use Quotation Marks

With Short Quotations from Source Materials

Use double quotation marks (") to enclose brief direct quotations from written or oral source material—four lines or less of prose or three lines or less of poetry for Modern Language Association

(MLA) documentation style or less than forty words for American Psychological Association (APA) documentation style:

> "The first mistake," writes Isaac Asimov, "is to think of mankind as a thing in itself."

> According to Alexander H. Leighton, residents described the bomb that hit Hiroshima as "a black smoky mass, lit up with color."

The division between lines of poetry is indicated by a slash (/) with a space on each side:

> In the opening lines of "The Tyger" by William Blake—"Tyger! Tyger! burning bright / In the forests of the night"—the speaker calls out to the animal.

> When Hamlet declares, "To be or not to be: / that is the question," he is considering whether suicide is the best answer to his plight.

With Longer Quotations from Prose and Poetry

Unlike short quotations, longer quotations are not enclosed in quotation marks. Instead, they are set separately from the main text and indented. If the author of the quoted passage includes quotations, copy the quotation marks as they appear in the original:

> In the chapters about America in *Martin Chuzzlewit,* critic G. K. Chesterton sees wit rather than Charles Dickens's more typical humor. As an example of this wit, Chesterton offers the following interchange from the novel:
>
>> The republican gentleman who receives Martin on landing is horrified on hearing an English servant speak of the employer as "the master." "There are no masters in America," says the gentleman. "All owners are they?" says Martin. (viii)

For the MLA style of documentation, a quotation that is longer than four lines of prose or three lines of poetry is indented one inch (or ten spaces) from the left margin. For APA style, a quotation that is more than forty words is indented half an inch (or five spaces) from the left margin.

With Short Excerpts of Dialogue

Like quotations from source materials, dialogue is put in quotation marks. Generally each person's lines are written as a separate paragraph:

"Should we walk into the park here?" Cara asked her mother, indicating a small gap in the hedge.

"No," her mother replied, "I would rather wait until we come to the main entrance where the lighting is better."

If you quote only a few words from two or more speakers, you do not have to begin a new paragraph for each one:

Samuel yelled, "Stop, Stop," as the girl put her hands on the keyboard, but she ignored him. Then he heard her cry out, "Help me," as all the text on the screen disappeared.

You do not need quotation marks around the single word *yes* or *no:*

I won't take ⁄no⁄ for an answer.

Juan said ⁄no⁄ when his son asked for another ice-cream cone.

With Paragraphs of Dialogue

If a speaker's words continue for more than one paragraph, use quotation marks at the beginning of each paragraph but at the end of only the last one.

With Thoughts

To state a thought, as though you or another speaker were saying it internally, use quotation marks, as with a direct quotation:

I finally said to myself, "I am so tired of this vacation."

"How can I stop this log from rolling down the hill?" Bradley wondered.

With Titles

Use quotation marks to cite the title of a short work or a part of something larger—a short story; an essay or article from a book, magazine, or newspaper; a short poem; a song; an episode of a television or radio show; or a chapter or subdivision of a book. Italicize or underline the title of a long work—a book, an epic poem, a magazine, a newspaper, a record album, a television show, or a movie:

In an article for *Writer's Digest* entitled "Digging Up Stories with Stephen King," W. C. Stroby says that King writes for at least four hours every morning.

"Sixth Avenue Heartache," from the album *Bringing Down the Horse,* propelled The Wallflowers to instant fame.

Milton's poem "Lycidas" reflects his reading of Dante's epic, *The Divine Comedy.*

A Note on Your Own Titles: Quotation marks are for *quoting* a title. When you write an essay, do not put your own title in quotation marks.

With Words Intended in a Special or Ironic Sense

You may—infrequently—place a word or a phrase in quotation marks to indicate that you are modifying its usual meaning:

Her "perfect man" turned out to have two children and a wife in New Jersey.

His mother finally found out the truth about his "big promotion."

Do not use quotation marks to enclose a cliché or slang:

Faulty: That "dude" was "sitting on the fence."

Improved: That dude was sitting on the fence.

Better: That man remained neutral.

With Word Usage and Definitions

Use quotation marks (or italics) when you discuss a particular word or its definition:

The word "friendship" was not in his vocabulary.

"Slink" means "to move in a quiet, furtive manner."

With Quoted Material That Contains Quotation Marks

If the quotation contains material within quotation marks (such as a quotation, a title, an ironic phrase, or a definition), you will need both double and single quotation marks. (On a computer, the single marks are made with the apostrophe key.) The single quotation marks enclose the material that the author placed in quotation marks. The double marks enclose the entire passage being quoted:

Original	Quoted
America has given the Negro people a bad check, a check which has come back marked "insufficient funds." —Martin Luther King, Jr.	When Martin Luther King called justice "a check which has come back marked 'insufficient funds,'" he was describing America's lack of commitment to equality under the law.
"You Better Leave Segregation Alone" came out of the Nashville Freedom Rides and was based on a hit by Little Willie John, "You Better Leave My Kitten Alone." —Bernice Reagon	In the 1960s, according to Bernice Reagon, civil rights advocates wrote protest lyrics that could be sung to old blues tunes: "'You Better Leave Segregation Alone' came out of the Nashville Freedom Rides and was based on a hit by Little Willie John, 'You Better Leave My Kitten Alone.'"

Punctuation with Quotation Marks

- Place **periods** and **commas** within quotation marks:

  "Come on," he said. "You don't fool me."

  "When I go to baseball games," she told me, "I start getting nervous right after 'The Star-Spangled Banner.'"

- Place **colons** and **semicolons** outside quotation marks:

  In the nineteenth century, quiltmaking was popularly known as "patchwork"; this practical use of fabric scraps provided one of the few creative outlets for women.

  Emily Dickinson wrote about the fine sewing required for "esthetic patchwork": "I'll do seams—a Queen's endeavor / Would not blush to own."

- **Question marks** and **exclamation points** should be placed *inside* quotation marks when they are part of the quotation:

  The short-order cook leaned over the counter and asked me, "Do you take your eggs over easy?"

  Is any line of poetry more famous than "How do I love thee?"

  [With a question within a question, only one question mark is used, and it is placed within the quotation marks: *Why was Laura yelling, "Can I eat now?"*]

When she asked if she could join the boys' hockey team, the coach first said, "Absolutely not!"

When a question mark, an exclamation point, or a dash is not part of the quotation, it belongs *outside* the quotation marks:

Why did you yell "Fire"?

Don't expect me to listen to "Dance Fever"!

"And Richard Cory, one calm summer night, / Went home and put a bullet through his head"—those final lines of Edwin Arlington Robinson's poem have always shocked me.

• When **parenthetical documentation** (MLA style) is used for a short quotation, the page numbers (or line numbers of poetry) that are placed in parentheses come after the quotation marks and before the period:

"Tread softly," wrote William Butler Yeats, "because you tread on my dreams" (8).

QUOTATIONS

To quote a person or another source is to repeat the words of that person or source. Quotations can be presented word for word (*direct quotation*) or rewritten in your own words (*paraphrase*). (For more on using quotations, see pages 81–86.)

R

RELATIVE CLAUSES

A relative clause is a dependent clause that begins with a relative pronoun (*which, that, what, who, whoever, whomever, whom, whose, whatever, whichever*). In "The President defended the estimates that he had made before," the words *that he had made before* are a relative clause. (For more on dependent clauses, see *Clauses*, pages 335–37.)

RESTRICTIVE AND NONRESTRICTIVE CLAUSES

The presence or absence of commas helps readers distinguish between modifying clauses or phrases that are essential to the meaning of a sentence (restrictive) and those that are not essential (nonrestrictive). Nonrestrictive elements are set off by commas; restrictive elements are not. Writers sometimes fail to distinguish between essential and nonessential elements, usually incorrectly setting off with commas an element that is essential to the sentence's meaning (restrictive).

Commas with Nonrestrictive Clauses

The car, a 1965 yellow Mustang convertible, caught my eye immediately.

The test of adulthood, as my neighbor likes to say, is the ability to say no.

No Commas with Restrictive Clauses

The bank robber/ whose picture was shown on television last night/ was recognized today by his neighbors.

The book/ that I haven't been able to find all year/ has been recalled by the library.

Compare these two sentences:

Essential Clause: The clip-art files *that can be customized* are in the main directory.

Nonessential Clause: The clip-art files, *which can be customized,* are in the main directory.

What is the difference between the two sentences? The first one tells us the location of the clip-art files that can be customized and implies that there are other clip-art files that cannot be customized. The clause "that can be customized" restricts the meaning of the sentence in an essential manner: the sentence is not about the location of all the clip-art files, only the ones that can be customized. The second sentence is about the location of all the clip-art files. The fact that they can be customized is just extra information and not essential to the sentence's meaning; hence, the nonrestrictive clause is set off by commas.

Appositives (nouns or noun phrases renaming a noun) may also be classified as essential or nonessential; for more on restrictive and nonrestrictive appositives, see *Appositives,* pages 323–324.

RUN-ON SENTENCES

A run-on, or fused, sentence is the combination of two independent clauses into one sentence with no punctuation between the two clauses: "The battle over salary increases seemed to be deadlocked neither side wanted to compromise." (This error and ways to correct it are discussed on pages 209–14.)

S

SEMICOLONS

The semicolon can join two or more independent or main clauses that are not linked by a coordinating conjunction (*and, but, for, nor, or, so,* or *yet*). It is used when the two clauses are closely related in meaning:

> He can't stop worrying; he can't seem to control any part of his life.
>
> Stella peered out the window; she was surprised by what she saw in the street below.

Note: When the first clause ends with a quotation, the semicolon goes after the quotation marks:

> The young man says, "Nothing can stop me"; the older man says, "I wish I'd spent more time with my family."

With Conjunctive Adverbs

If the second of two independent clauses begins with a conjunctive adverb—such as *however, therefore, furthermore, moreover, thus, instead,* or *indeed*—you still need the semicolon. These adverbs are generally followed by a comma:

> People use words like *Kleenex, Dramamine, Band-Aid,* and *Coke* to refer to product types; *however,* these terms are actually trademarks of specific manufacturers.

The conjunctive adverb does not have to be placed right after the semicolon. Set off by commas, it can appear later in the sentence:

People use words like *Kleenex, Dramamine, Band-Aid,* and *Coke* to refer to product types; these terms, *however,* are actually trademarks of specific manufacturers.

(For a full list of conjunctive adverbs, see *Conjunctive Adverbs,* pages 346–47.)

With Complex Sentences

The semicolon can combine not only two independent clauses but also two or more complex sentences (sentences that contain both an independent and a dependent clause):

> When the mechanic crawled under the car, he saw a corroded muffler and shaft; when he crawled out, the car owner saw a large bill to be paid.

With Coordinating Conjunctions

If the independent clauses you are joining are long and complicated, perhaps having several commas or conjunctions, you can use a semicolon along with a coordinating conjunction to create a clear division between the two main parts:

> The warm-water ocean and endless sunny weather, heralded in the state's tourist advertisements, make southern California's beaches popular for swimmers; *and* the high, straight waves, which rival Australia's, make these beaches a mecca for surfers.

With Series

For clarity, use semicolons to separate items in a series when the items are long and contain commas:

> Leading the meeting were Frederica Nipp, president; Raul Garcia, vice president; Louisa Lane, secretary and treasurer; and Laura Holmes, student representative.

Errors to Avoid

• Do not use a semicolon to join a dependent and an independent clause. Use a comma:

> When he came into the room, he heard water dripping from the faucet.

Some people put tag questions like "don't you think?" at the end of their statements, a habit that makes them seem uncertain and unconfident.

- Do not use a semicolon to introduce a list. Instead, use a colon if the list follows a sentence having a subject, a verb, and an object or complement:

Three college teams have names that refer to army units: the Volunteers of the University of Tennessee, the Tar Heels of the University of North Carolina, and the Colonials of George Washington University.

- Do not overuse the semicolon. Reserve it for two independent clauses of related meaning:

The urban development committee has finally come up with a workable plan. They have decided to use the old post office as the site for the only licensed gambling hall *because* other privately owned locations seemed to invite criminal influence. The site will house no restaurants or motel rooms; these new businesses might detract from the current facilities for tourists.

SENTENCES

A sentence is a group of words that (1) makes sense on its own, (2) includes a subject and a predicate, and (3) begins with a capital letter and ends with a period, a question mark, or an exclamation point. Omission of the subject or the verb creates a sentence fragment. (For help recognizing and correcting sentence fragments, see pages 193–200.)

Parts of Sentences

- The main parts of sentences in English are the *subject* (usually built around a noun or a pronoun) and the *predicate* (built around a complete verb):

> Rain fell.

- The **subject** of a sentence is a noun or a pronoun about which the predicate asserts or asks something. It may also include modifiers (usually adjectives) of the noun or pronoun:

> *The dusty, summer-smelling rain* fell.

Some sentences, such as instructions or commands, begin with an understood subject—*you:*

> [*You*] Insert the address into your file with the "merge files" command.

- The **predicate** of a sentence is the part that says something about the subject. The predicate includes the complete verb and its modifiers. The predicate may also include a direct object, an indirect object, a predicate adjective, or a predicate noun.

> The rain *was falling lightly.*

- The **direct object** receives the action of the complete verb:

> The rain hit *Bob's just-washed car.*

Here *car* is the direct object, receiving the action of the predicate verb, *hit; Bob's* and *just-washed* are adjectives that modify the direct object.

- The **indirect object** tells to or for whom or what something is done:

> Lucia gave *Simon* her book.
> Lucia gave her book *to Simon.*

Here *book* is the direct object, receiving the action of the complete verb: it is what Lucia gave. *Simon* and the prepositional phrase *to Simon* are both indirect objects, telling for whom the action was performed.

- The **object complement** follows and modifies a direct object:

> Officials considered the town *a disaster area.*

Here *area,* the object complement, modified by *a disaster,* renames and further describes the direct object, *town.*

- The **predicate adjective** follows a linking verb (such as *is, looks, smells, becomes, appears, seems*) and modifies the subject:

> The rain was *gray against the sky.*

Here *gray* is a predicate adjective, modifying the subject *rain,* and *against the sky* is a prepositional phrase modifying *gray.*

- The **predicate noun** follows a linking verb (such as *is, looks, smells, becomes, appears, seems*) and renames the subject:

> The rain was *a deluge.*

Here *deluge* is a noun, renaming *rain*—it is not some aspect or attribute of the rain (as *gray* was in the previous example) but rather another name for the same thing.

Structures of Sentences

Sentences may be classified as simple, compound, complex, or compound-complex, depending on how many independent and dependent clauses they contain. An independent clause is a subject-verb unit that makes a complete statement and can stand on its own. A dependent clause begins with a subordinating word (such as *when, if,* or *since*) and thus needs to be linked to an independent clause to complete its meaning. (For more about independent and dependent clauses, see *Clauses,* pages 335–37.)

- A **simple sentence** contains only one independent clause:

> Drug abuse clearly is destroying our cities.

- A **compound sentence** has two (or more) independent clauses:

> Elementary-school teaching provided some employment opportunities for nineteenth-century women, but high-school teaching was reserved for men.

- A **complex sentence** contains an independent clause and a dependent clause:

> When drug-related crime makes whole neighborhoods unsafe after dark, drug abuse clearly is destroying our cities.

• A **compound-complex sentence** has two or more independent clauses and one or more dependent clauses:

> When you first enter the master's degree program in public administration, you may find America's foreign policy difficult to understand, but the professor's lectures will clarify it for you.

• A sentence is in **inverted order** when the verb appears before the subject for effect:

Inverted Order	Usual Order
Then came the day of reckoning.	Then the day of reckoning came.

Sentence Variety

Using different types of sentence structures can add variety to your writing, provide more detail, and express subtle relationships among ideas. In some situations, a steady diet of simple sentences may be exactly right; in others, a variety of structures is preferable. You can add a word, a clause, or a phrase to the front of a sentence as an **opener,** to the middle of a sentence as an **interrupter,** or to the end of a sentence as a **closer.**

ADD AN OPENER

Openers can stipulate the *time of an action:*

> *Today,* Joey begins his soccer lessons.

> *When you are finished washing the dishes,* let's go for a walk.

Openers can also state *necessary conditions* for an occurrence:

> *If the weather clears,* we will have a picnic.

> *Whenever his sister yells at him,* Ramon pretends to be deaf.

As modifiers, openers can also *emphasize a trait* or a descriptive detail that defines the subject:

> *With purple garters hanging from his knees,* Jonathan stood out from the crowd.

As in the preceding examples, openers are usually connected to the main clause with a comma.

(continued)

(continued)
ADD AN INTERRUPTER

A well-placed interrupter can *add information* about the subject or the predicate, enhancing the reader's understanding and perhaps also creating emphasis:

> She went, *along with her sister,* to every school dance that spring.

> Sarah Spivey—*the kindergarten troublemaker*—held the knife in her hand.

As in the examples above, interrupters are usually enclosed in paired commas or dashes.

ADD A CLOSER

A closer can *add descriptive details* to the general picture created in the independent clause, building a cumulative effect:

> He stood alone in the hall, *his socks bunched around his ankles, his shoes untied, and his sweater dragging the ground.*

A closer can also *offer an explanation* for an action or a situation discussed in the independent clause or in other ways add detail about a topic:

> He refuses to clean up his room, *probably to irritate his mother.*

> The table has been leaning on three legs *ever since the big fight.*

> He likes to take a walk every day *after he finishes the supper dishes.*

A short closer can also *highlight a word or two,* giving them extra emphasis:

> Rayonda hated one thing about camp—*her bunkmate.*

When the closer is a dependent clause, no punctuation is needed to separate it from the main clause. Other closers can be preceded by a comma or a dash.

MAKE YOUR OWN PATTERN

These additions (openers, interrupters, and closers) can be used in combination to convey various kinds of information accurately and vividly:

> *When the movie started,* the projection booth began burning *because no one had covered the chemical solutions.*

> *By four o'clock,* Fred and Emile, *longtime enemies,* could no longer stand being in the same room.

Types of Sentences

One way to designate sentence types is to classify them as simple, compound, complex, or compound-complex. Another way is to describe them as *cumulative* (or *loose*), *periodic,* or *balanced.* This rhetorical classification scheme is based more on style than on grammar.

• **Cumulative sentences:** Writers use cumulative (or loose) sentences most of the time, at least in first drafts. Such sentences state the main point and then provide additional information:

> Mr. Nguyen will pick us up in front of the theater after the movie ends.

In earlier centuries, the cumulative sentence was frowned upon. Although such sentences are the norm today, memorable effects can be achieved by writers who deliberately vary their sentence types with an occasional periodic or balanced sentence.

• **Periodic sentences:** In periodic sentences, modifiers come before the main clause, which appears at the end. These sentences come to a definite and powerful stop. Perhaps the simplest (but not the only) way to achieve this effect is to add several openers and place the verb at the end, as in the following:

> After the show ended, after the crowds had left, once the costumes had all been put away, and the lights had all gone dark, the man who for the previous three hours had hypnotized thousands in the role of king and conqueror finally allowed himself to weep.

However, periodic sentences do not have to be long or end with a verb:

> When I saw two ways of life before me, one easy and one hard, I chose the latter.

Periodic sentences often profit from repetition:

> As long as the white man sent you to Korea, you bled. He sent you to Germany, you bled. He sent you to the South Pacific to fight the Japanese, you bled.

> —Malcolm X

- **Balanced sentences:** Balanced sentences usually have two (or more) similar structures in them:

> Run that through your calculator! It may come out Hard, it may come out Easy. But it will come out whole, and it will last forever.
>
> —E. B. White, in an article against calculating the readability, or appropriate grade level, of literature

Balanced sentences often use antithesis. They make a statement one way and then make a different statement in a very similar way—thus creating in the second clause a mirror-image of the first:

> The press is so powerful in its image-making role; it can make a criminal look like he's the victim and make the victim look like he's the criminal.
>
> —Malcolm X

> Ask not what your country can do for you—ask what you can do for your country.
>
> —John F. Kennedy

Combining Sentence Types

Here is a short passage from one of the best writers of this century. Notice how the sentence type changes and how the resulting variation in style gives life to the author's writing. See how many of the kinds of sentences described above you can find in it:

> Style cannot go beyond the ideas which lie at the heart of it. If they are clear, it too will be clear. If they are held passionately, it will be eloquent. Trying to teach it to persons who cannot think, especially when the business is attempted by persons who also cannot think, is a great waste of time, and an immoral imposition upon the taxpayers of the nation. It would be far more logical to devote all the energy to teaching, not writing, but logic—and probably just as useless. For I doubt that the art of thinking can be taught at all—at any rate, by school-teachers. It is not acquired, but congenital. Some persons are born with it. Their ideas flow in straight channels; they are capable of lucid reasoning; when they say anything it is instantly understandable; when they write anything it is clear and persuasive. They constitute, I should say, about one-eighth of one percent of the human race. The rest of God's children are just as incapable of logical thought as they are incapable of jumping over the moon. Trying to teach them is as vain an enterprise as trying to teach a streptococcus the principle of Americanism. The only thing to do

with them is to make Ph.D.'s of them, and set them to writing hand-books on style.

—H. L. Mencken, cited in *Speaking of Rhetoric*

SIMPLE SENTENCES

A simple sentence contains only an independent clause: "Cole is playing a video game." (For a discussion of all types of sentence structures, see *Sentences,* pages 392–99.)

SLANG, REGIONALISMS, AND NONSTANDARD FORMS

In your college writing, avoid using slang terms, regional terms, or other words that would not be understood or accepted by your readers. These are usually terms that either do not appear in the dictionary or are marked as *slang* or *regional:*

Regional	Standard
He won't stay by the neutral ground for Rex. [*regionalisms from New Orleans*]	He won't stand in the median during the Rex parade at Mardi Gras.
Big hat, no cattle. [*regionalism from Texas*]	A person who puts on that big a display may be overcompensating for not having anything.

Slang	Standard
That teacher's threads are gross to the max.	That teacher's clothes are wrinkled and dirty.

You may, however, want to use regional or nonstandard words in dialogue if they represent the person's real speech patterns or, very rarely, if you want to get the reader's attention.

Standard English is generally required for writing in academic, business, and professional fields. Nonstandard English may be acceptable when spoken within a group sharing the same regional or social heritage, but it should be avoided in writing:

Dialect	Standard
He don't know what she mean by that.	He doesn't know what she means by that.

(If you speak a nonstandard dialect, you should examine the ways it differs from standard English. You may find explanations of some of those variations as they relate to verb endings on page 223. For more on standard versus nonstandard English, see pages 414–15.)

SLASHES

Use the slash to separate two or three lines of poetry quoted within your text. Add a space before and after the slash:

> W. H. Auden's poem "The Unknown Citizen" concludes with these ironic lines: "Was he free? Was he happy? The question is absurd: / Had anything been wrong, we should certainly have heard."

You can also use the slash to indicate a pair of options, with no space before or after the slash:

> Internships are generally offered as pass/fail courses.

SPELLING

Some words are frequently misspelled, like those listed on the following pages. Knowing basic spelling rules (pages 405–12) can help you avoid some mistakes, as can knowing the difference between commonly confused words (pages 413–14). However, you should always keep a dictionary handy when you are writing and check it whenever you are not sure about the spelling of a word.

Keep a list of the words that you frequently misspell and then review it as you proofread. For particularly troublesome words, you might also jot down the reason for the spelling to help you understand the correct choice. Of course, if you are using a word processor, you can also run its spell checker. But do not rely on it totally. For example, your computer's spell checker will not help you with the confusing pairs of words listed on pages 413–14.

Words Frequently Misspelled

The following words are often misspelled. You might study them in groups of ten or twenty. If you are unsure of their meanings, consult a dictionary.

A

absence
abundance
acceptable
accessible
accidentally
accommodate
accumulate
accuracy
achievement
acquaintance
acquire
acquitted
address
adolescent
advice
advising
aggravate
aggressive
alcohol
allotted
all right
a lot of
always
amateur
analysis
analyze
annihilate
announcement
annual
anywhere
apiece
apology
apparent
appearance

appropriate
approximately
arguing
argument
article
aspirin
assassination
athlete
athletics
attacked
attendance
authentic
awkward

B

bachelor
bargain
basically
belief
believed
beneficial
benefited
biscuit
border
boundaries
breath
breathe
brilliant
bulletin
bureaucracy
burglar
business

C

calendar
category
ceiling

cemetery
changeable
chief
chocolate
choice
choose
chosen
coarsely
column
commission
commitment
committed
committee
compelled
competence
conceited
conceivable
condemn
confidence
conscience
conscientious
conscious
consistency
consistent
control
controlled
controlling
controversial
convenience
convenient
coolly
correlate
counterfeit
courteous
criticism

criticize
cruelty
curiosity
curious

D

dealt
deceive
defense
definitely
definition
descend
desirable
desperate
develop
development
dictionary
difference
dilemma
dining
disappearance
disappoint
disapprove
disastrous
discipline
disease
dispensable
disturbance
divine
dormitory

E

ecstatic
effect
efficiently
eighth
eligible
embarrass

environment
equipped
especially
everything
exaggerate
exceed
excel
except
exercise
exhaust
existence
expense
experience
extraordinary

F

familiar
fascinate
February
financially
forehead
foreign
forfeit
forty
forward
friend

G

gauge
generally
government
governor
grammar
grammatically
grief
guaranteed
guard
guidance

H

happened
harass
height
heroes
heroin
heroine
hindrance
humor
hypocrisy

I

ignorance
illogical
imitate
immediately
immense
incidentally
incredible
independent
indispensable
inevitable
infinite
influential
initiative
innocence
intellectual
intelligence
interest
irrelevant
irresistible
irritated

K

knowledge

L

laboratory
legitimate

leisure
liable
library
license
lightning
literature
lively
loneliness
lonely
lose
loose
lying
M
maintenance
maneuver
manual
manufacture
marriage
material
mathematics
meant
medicine
mere
messenger
millennium
miniature
mischievous
missile
mortgage
muscle
mysteriousness
N
naturally
necessary
nickel
niece

ninety
ninth
noticeable
nuclear
nuisance
O
occasionally
occur
occurred
occurrence
occurring
omission
omitted
opinion
opponent
opportunity
opposite
optimism
origin
P
paid
pamphlet
parallel
particular
pastime
peculiar
performance
permanent
permissible
physical
physician
pleasant
poison
possess
possession
possibly

practically
prairie
precede
preferred
prejudice
presence
prevalent
privilege
procedure
proceed
professor
prominent
pronunciation
propaganda
prophecy
prophesy
psychiatry
psychology
publicly
pumpkin
pursue
Q
quiet
quit
quite
quizzes
R
realize
really
realty
receipt
receive
recognize
recommend
reference
referred

referring

regular

relieve

remembrance

repetition

restaurant

rhythm

ridiculous

roommate

S

sacrifice

safety

salary

satellite

schedule

secretary

seize

separate

sergeant

severely

sheriff

similar

since

sincerely

skiing

sophomore

speech

sponsor

strength

strict

stubbornness

studying

subtlety

succeed

successful

succession

sufficient

suicide

summary

superintendent

supersede

suppose

suppress

surely

surprise

surround

susceptible

suspicious

swimming

symbol

sympathize

T

technique

temperament

tendency

than

their

themselves

then

therefore

thorough

though

thought

through

till

tomorrow

tournament

traffic

trafficked

tragedy

transferred

tremendous

tried

tries

truly

twelfth

tyranny

U

unanimous

unconscious

undoubtedly

unmistakably

unnecessary

until

usage

useful

using

usually

V

vacuum

valuable

varies

various

vegetable

vengeance

venomous

vice

view

vigilance

villain

violence

visible

vitamins

W

waive

warring	whichever	wreck
weather	wholly	write
Wednesday	wield	writing
weird	wintry	written
where	withdrawal	**Y**
wherever	woman	yield
whether	women	

Spelling Rules

Many of the difficulties involved in commonly misspelled words can be solved through an understanding of spelling rules.

Words With ie and ei

The full rule can help you determine which spelling to choose:

I before e

believe, friend, field, piece, relieve, niece, brief, grief, chief, hygiene, yield, siege, cashier, frontier

Except after c

receive, deceive, perceive, conceive, deceit, ceiling, conceit

Or When Pronounced ay

neighbor, weigh, eight, freight, beige, vein, sleigh

Or in Weird Exceptions Like Either and Species

neither, leisure, seize, foreign, height, caffeine, forfeit, ancient, conscience

Prefixes

Prefixes, such as the ones in the box "Common Prefixes," are placed at the beginning of words to qualify their meaning. Prefixes do not change the spelling of the word they are added to, even when the last letter of the prefix and the first letter of the word are the same:

co + founder = cofounder

de + merit = demerit

dis + appear = disappear

il + literate = illiterate

im + mature = immature

ir + relevant = irrelevant

mis + apply = misapply

mis + step = misstep

un + able = unable

un + necessary = unnecessary

A note on hyphens: A hyphen after a prefix is sometimes necessary to differentiate between two meanings, between *recreate* and *re-create* or *reform* and *re-form*, for instance. Hyphens are also sometimes used to make words more easily pronounceable, especially when two vowels are joined: *co-author, de-escalate,* or

Common Prefixes

Prefix	Meaning	Example
a-	without; on or in	amoral, aboard
co-, com-, con-	jointly, with	copilot, compose, contact
de-	take away from	deactivate, defang
dis-	negation, rejection	discredit, discharge
ex-	out of	exclude, exclaim
il-, im-, in-, ir-	not	illegal, immobile, inaction, irrational
inter-	between	interact, interbreed
mal-	bad	maladjusted, malformed
mis-	wrong	misspell, mistake
non-	not	nonfiction, nonsense
pre-	before	prefix, prepay
pro-	support, onward	prorevolutionary, project
re-	again, back	reread, return
un-	not	unable, unfeeling

pro-abortion. Consult a dictionary if you are not sure whether a word with a prefix should have a hyphen.

Suffixes

Suffixes are placed at the ends of words to form new, related words. For example, you can build on the word *love* by adding suffixes:

lov*able*	love*liest*
lov*er*	love*less*
love*ly*	lov*ing*

Some of the most common suffixes and their meanings are shown in the box "Common Suffixes" on page 408.

Spelling Rules for Suffixes

• **Drop an unpronounced *e*** at the end of a word if the suffix starts with a vowel:

grade → gradation

create → creator

love → lovable

sane → sanity

space → spacious

favorite → favoritism

Exceptions: The final unpronounced *e* may be maintained (1) to distinguish homonyms:

dye + ing = dyeing [*not* dying]

singe + ing = singeing [*not* singing]

(2) to clarify pronunciation:

shoe + ing = shoeing [*not* shoing]

be + ing = being [*not* bing]

(3) to keep the sound of *c* or *g* soft:

notice + able = noticeable

embrace + able = embraceable

courage + ous = courageous

manage + able = manageable

Common Suffixes

COMMON SUFFIXES ADDED TO CREATE NOUNS

Suffix	Meaning	Example
-ance, -ence	quality or condition	riddance, independence
-cy	state or quality	bankruptcy, privacy
-dom	state of being	boredom, freedom
-er, -or	one who	adviser, actor
-ism	a practice, doctrine, or behavior	terrorism, capitalism, heroism
-ity	state or quality	authenticity, equality
-ment	condition or means	environment, measurement
-ness	state of being	nervousness, kindness
-sion, -ation, -tion	action or process	immersion, imagination, ambition

COMMON SUFFIXES ADDED TO CREATE VERBS

Suffix	Meaning	Example
-ate	operate upon	regulate, concentrate
-en	cause to be or become	shorten, cheapen
-fy	make or cause to be	terrify, unify
-ing	doing an action	forming, running
-ize	cause to be or become	dramatize, sterilize

COMMON SUFFIXES ADDED TO CREATE ADJECTIVES

Suffix	Meaning	Example
-able, -ible	capable of being	debatable, edible
-ful	characterized by	masterful, playful
-ious, -ous	of or characterized by	conscientious, joyous
-ive	having a tendency toward	disruptive, restive
-less	without	endless, penniless

COMMON SUFFIXES ADDED TO CREATE ADVERBS

Suffix	Meaning	Example
-ly, -ally	having a characteristic	forcefully, slowly

- **Keep an unpronounced** *e* if the suffix starts with a consonant:

  arrange → arrangement

  fate → fateful

  bore → boredom

Exceptions: judgment, argument, ninth, likable, truly, wholly

- **Change** a *y* to *i* before all suffixes except *ing:*

  try → tries, tried (trying)

  carry → carries, carried, carrier (carrying)

  vary → varies, varied, variable, variance, variation (varying)

  pretty → prettily, prettiness, prettier

Exceptions: Verbs ending in *y* preceded by a vowel do not change the *y* before *s* or *ed:* play, plays, played; destroy, destroys, destroyed.

- **Double the final consonant** if the word ends in a vowel and a consonant and has one syllable or an accented last syllable and if the suffix begins with a vowel:

  hop → hopping

  hit → hitter

  stop → stoppable

  begin → beginning

  occur → occurrence

  refer → referring

- **Do *not* double the final consonant** in the following cases:

  When the final consonant is preceded by more than one vowel or another consonant:

  wait → waiting

  walk → walked

  crawl → crawling

  report → reporter

When the suffix begins with a consonant:

red → redness

master → masterful

assign → assignment

When the word is not accented on the last syllable:

benefit → benefited

panel → paneled

focus → focusing

fatal → fatality

combat → combatant

When the accent shifts from the last syllable to the first after the suffix is added:

confer → conference

refer → referee

- **Use _ly_ to form the adverb** if the base word does not end in _ic_. If the word ends in _l_, keep it when you add _ly:_

slow → slowly

ridiculous → ridiculously

forceful → forcefully

real → really

formal → formally

cruel → cruelly

- **Use _ally_ to form the adverb** if the base word ends in _ic:_

basic → basically

characteristic → characteristically

realistic → realistically

rhythmic → rhythmically

Exception: public + ly = publicly

Plurals

Most nouns are made plural by adding an *s* to the singular:

dogs, lamps, schools, problems

the Smiths and the Morgans

brothers-in-law [in such compounds, the chief word is made plural]

• **For nouns ending in *f* or *fe*,** change the ending to *ve* before adding *s:*

thief → thieves

life → lives

knife → knives

leaf → leaves

Exceptions: chief → chiefs; belief → beliefs. Note that *beliefs* is the plural of the noun *belief,* and *believes* is the third-person singular of the verb *believe* (*I believe, he believes*). Similarly, *relief* and *grief* are nouns, but they generally appear just in the singular; *relieve* and *relieves* and *grieve* and *grieves* are verbs.

• **For nouns ending in *y* preceded by a vowel,** add an *s* to form the plural:

joy, joys

holiday, holidays

valley, valleys

buy, buys

• **For nouns ending in *y* preceded by a consonant,** change the *y* to *i* and add *es:*

company, companies

specialty, specialties

anxiety, anxieties

• **For nouns ending in *o* preceded by a vowel,** add an *s:*

rodeo, rodeos

zoo, zoos

patio, patios

• **For nouns ending in *o* preceded by a consonant,** you will need to memorize the spelling or consult a dictionary for the plural because some add *es* and some add *s*. Here are the plurals of some of the most common of these words:

hero, heroes

potato, potatoes

tomato, tomatoes

veto, vetoes

memo, memos

pro, pros

piano, pianos

solo, solos

• **For nouns ending in *s, ch, sh,* or *x,*** add *es* to form the plural:

Jones, the Joneses

class, classes

church, churches

clash, clashes

box, boxes

• Some nouns, many of which were derived from other languages, have **irregular plurals:**

woman, women

man, men

child, children

foot, feet

tooth, teeth

alumna, alumnae (female)

alumnus, alumni (male or both male and female)

medium, media

phenomenon, phenomena

deer, deer

sheep, sheep

series, series

species, species

Words Commonly Confused

Many people make spelling errors because they confuse words that sound and look similar. Some of these words are *homonyms*—words that are spelled differently but pronounced the same—and some are pronounced nearly the same. Here is a list of such words. Other commonly confused words are listed in the Glossary of Usage, pages 429–443.

board	to get on a plane or a ship; flat piece of wood
bored	uninterested
boarder	one who pays a homeowner for food and lodging
border	a boundary
brake	a device for slowing or stopping motion
break	to crack or destroy
desert	dry land; to abandon
dessert	a sweet served after a meal
device	something made for a purpose, a useful machine
devise	to plan or invent
diary	a private journal
dairy	a farm for producing milk
die, dying	to become dead, becoming dead
dye, dyeing	to color, coloring
forth	forward, onward
fourth	between third and fifth
gorilla	an ape
guerrilla	a revolutionary soldier
hear	to listen to
here	in this place
heard	past tense of *hear*
herd	a group of animals
heroin	a drug
heroine	a courageous woman
human	characteristic of people
humane	kind, compassionate

personal	private, individual
personnel	employees
plain	simple; flat land
plane	airplane; tool
quiet	silent
quit	to discontinue or give up
quite	entirely, really
right	correct; opposite of left
rite	ceremony
write	to form letters
scene	setting; public display
seen	past participle of *see*
thorough	complete, accurate
through	by way of
wear	to be clothed in
were	past tense of *be*
where	in what place
weather	climatic conditions
whether	if

STANDARD ENGLISH

English is written (and spoken) in many different ways. People who learned English outside the United States often have learned British English (or even Indian English). People from the eastern mountains of the United States may learn another dialect, Appalachian English. There are, in fact, many forms and dialects of English. Some are geographically based; others are racial or ethnic in origin (such as Black English, sometimes called Black English Vernacular, or Spanish Influenced English). The form of English used for communication in education, business, industry, government, and the professions in the United States is called **Standard American English** (SAE). The standards established by colleges and universities for student writing are often those of SAE. When prospective employers look at your writing, chances are they are looking for SAE.

Writing in Standard American English (or revising your writing to conform to it) involves selecting particular options in vocabulary, grammatical forms, spelling, capitalization, and punctuation. How to select those options is explained in parts 2 and 3 of this handbook. SAE avoids slang, vernacular (spoken) forms, and regional or ethnic dialects. (For a discussion of nonstandard forms, see page 223.) Each of these forms of English (often called "nonstandard") has its own time and place to be used, and over time various pieces of these forms do become acceptable as SAE. But when you are writing (or speaking formally) in an academic setting, or in business, government, and the like, Standard American English needs to guide the choices you make. (See also *Formal Writing,* page 358.)

SUBJECTS

304

The subject of a sentence is a noun (or a substitute for a noun) that performs the action expressed in the predicate of the sentence. In "The contractor offered the mayor a bribe," the subject is *contractor.* (For more on parts of sentences, see *Sentences,* pages 393–94.)

SUBORDINATE CLAUSES

The term *subordinate clause* is another name for a dependent clause. In "When Avia entered the lab, all the tutors were eating at the counter," the subordinate or dependent clause is *When Avia entered the lab.* (For more on dependent clauses, see *Clauses,* pages 335–37.)

T

TRANSITIVE VERBS

A transitive verb is a verb that can take an object; verbs such as *bring, give, hit, insert,* and *take* are transitive verbs. (*Intransitive verbs,* page 364, do not take objects.)

V

VERBALS

Verbals are forms of verbs that function as nouns, adjectives, or adverbs. There are three types of verbals: *gerunds, infinitives,* and *participles.* They can take subjects, objects, and complements and can be modified by adverbs, but they cannot be used as complete verbs.

- **Gerunds** end in *ing.* Thus they have the same form as present participles. Gerunds and gerund phrases always function as nouns:

> Camilla loved *skating.*

> *Eating at authentic Mexican restaurants near the hotel* consumed all his time at the Santa Fe conference.

- **Infinitives** are the base form of the verb plus *to.* Infinitives and infinitive phrases can function as nouns, adjectives, and adverbs:

> *To graduate* was his only goal. [noun]

> Taking a quick straw vote would be a good way *to assess the group's general preferences.* [adjective]

> *To improve your golf game,* watch the instructional series available at your video store. [adverb]

- **Present** and **past participles** are the *-ing* and *-ed* verb forms. The past participle of some irregular verbs ends in *en, n,* or *t.* Participles and participial phrases function as adjectives:

292–30.

> The *freezing* children finally saw a rescue truck.

> *Running quickly,* they got away from the fumes.

> *Exhausted from the two-hour session,* the young debaters waited to hear their scores.

Participles and Infinitives in Verb Phrases

When functioning as part of a complete verb, a participle must be preceded by some form of the verb *be* or *have;* the form of that verb indicates the tense:

The car *is driven* daily.

The car *has been driven* daily.

The man *has driven* daily.

Unlike other verb forms, participles and infinitives, when they are part of a verb phrase, do not change to indicate tense:

	Verbals	Complete Verbs
Present	The trucker likes *to drive.*	The trucker *drives.*
Past	The trucker liked *to drive.*	The trucker *drove.*
Future	The trucker will start *to drive.*	The trucker *will drive.*

Participles and infinitives, unlike complete verbs, also have the same form in singular and plural in the present tense:

	Verbals	Complete Verbs
Singular	The trucker starts *driving.*	The trucker *drives.*
Plural	The truckers start *driving.*	The truckers *drive.*

(For more on gerunds, infinitives, and participles and how they are used, see *Phrases,* pages 374–76.)

VERBS

94–304

The verb is the part of a sentence that connects the subject with everything else. The verb may tell what the subject does, name an action done to the subject, or describe the subject's state of being. Verbs provide much of the force and precision of written English.

Subjects and verbs always need to agree in *number*—singular or plural. They also need to agree in *person*—first, second, or third. No matter where the subject appears in the sentence, the number of the subject determines whether the verb will be in the singular or plural form. (For a full discussion of subject-verb agreement, see pages 218–21.)

Forms of Verbs

The forms of most verbs change to indicate the verb's tense—the time of a verb's action. Verb tenses have three forms; they may be *simple* (present, past, or future), *perfect* (present perfect, past perfect, or future perfect), or *progressive* (indicating continuous action). Most dictionaries list the principal parts of all verbs in this order: base form (the infinitive form without the marker *to*), past tense, past participle, present participle, and present tense in the third-person-singular form. (When the past tense and the past participle are the same, the form will be printed only once.) Verb tenses are explained in more detail later in this entry.

Except for the verb *be,* all verbs in English have five forms:

Base Form: I (*talk, swim*). [The base form is usually the present tense of the first person singular.]

-s Form: He/she/it (*talks, swims*).

Past Tense: Last week they (*talked, swam*).

Past Participle: We have (*talked, swum*) many times before.

Present Participle: They are (*talking, swimming*) now.

The verb *be* has eight forms:

be, am, are, is, was, were, been, being

Irregular Verbs

All regular verbs have past tense and past participle forms that are the same: they end in *ed* or *d*. Irregular verbs, however, have irregular past tense and past participle forms. As you can see from this list, many of these verbs are used frequently:

Principal Parts of Irregular Verbs

Base	Past Tense	Past Participle
arise	arose	arisen
awake	awoke, awaked	awoken, awaked
be	was, were	been
beat	beat	beat, beaten
become	became	become
begin	began	begun
bid	bid [or bade]	bid [or bidden]

Base	Past Tense	Past Participle
bite	bit	bitten, bit
blow	blew	blown
break	broke	broken
bring	brought	brought
build	built	built
burst	burst	burst
buy	bought	bought
catch	caught	caught
choose	chose	chosen
come	came	come
cost	cost	cost
cut	cut	cut
deal	dealt	dealt
dig	dug	dug
dive	dived, dove	dived
do	did	done
draw	drew	drawn
dream	dreamed, dreamt	dreamed, dreamt
drink	drank	drunk
drive	drove	driven
eat	ate	eaten
fall	fell	fallen
fight	fought	fought
find	found	found
flee	fled	fled
fly	flew	flown
forget	forgot	forgotten, forgot
freeze	froze	frozen
get	got	got, gotten
give	gave	given
go	went	gone
grow	grew	grown
hang (suspend)	hung	hung
hang (execute)	hanged	hanged
have	had	had

Base	Past Tense	Past Participle
hear	heard	heard
hide	hid	hidden
hold	held	held
hurt	hurt	hurt
keep	kept	kept
know	knew	known
lay (put)	laid	laid
lead	led	led
leave	left	left
lend	lent	lent
let (allow)	let	let
lie (recline)	lay	lain
lose	lost	lost
make	made	made
pay	paid	paid
prove	proved	proved, proven
read	read	read
ride	rode	ridden
ring	rang	rung
rise (get up)	rose	risen
run	ran	run
say	said	said
see	saw	seen
send	sent	sent
set (place)	set	set
shake	shook	shaken
shoot	shot	shot
shrink	shrank	shrunk, shrunken
sing	sang	sung
sink	sank	sunk
sit (be seated)	sat	sat
sleep	slept	slept
slide	slid	slid
speak	spoke	spoken
spin	spun	spun

Base	Past Tense	Past Participle
spring	sprang, sprung	sprung
stand	stood	stood
steal	stole	stolen
sting	stung	stung
strike	struck	struck, stricken
swim	swam	swum
swing	swung	swung
take	took	taken
teach	taught	taught
tear	tore	torn
throw	threw	thrown
wear	wore	worn
write	wrote	written

If you are not sure whether a verb is irregular, consult a dictionary. When you look up the base form of an irregular verb, it will be followed by its principal parts. (For more information on errors with irregular verbs, see pages 222–23.)

Lie *and* Lay

Writers often confuse *lie* and *lay* because their principal parts are similar. *Lay,* a transitive verb, means "to put or place something"; *lie,* an intransitive verb, means "to recline or rest in a flat position." After choosing the right verb, you must use the correct principal part:

Base	Past Tense	Past Participle	Present Participle
lay (put)	laid	laid	laying
lie (recline)	lay	lain	lying

She was *lying* on the floor.

Have you seen where I *laid* the silverware?

He has *lain* in that bed for a week.

Tense

The three *simple tenses* are *present, past,* and *future.* The three perfect tenses are *present perfect, past perfect,* and *future perfect.* Each of these tenses has a *progressive* form. They are constructed with the principal parts of the verb, as shown on the following pages.

Simple Tenses

The simple tenses indicate fairly simple time relationships:

• The **simple present** indicates action occurring as it is being mentioned or occurring regularly. This tense uses the base form or, for third-person singular, the -*s* form:

	Singular	Plural
1st person	I talk/swim	we talk/swim
2nd person	you talk/swim	you talk/swim
3rd person	he/she/it talks/swims	they talk/swim

• The **simple past** (the -*ed* form for regular verbs) indicates action completed in the past:

	Singular	Plural
1st person	I talked/swam	we talked/swam
2nd person	you talked/swam	you talked/swam
3rd person	he/she/it talked/swam	they talked/swam

• The **simple future** (*will* or *shall* plus the base form) indicates action that will occur in the future:

	Singular	Plural
1st person	I will talk/swim	we will talk/swim
2nd person	you will talk/swim	you will talk/swim
3rd person	he/she/it will talk/swim	they will talk/swim

Perfect Tenses

The perfect forms indicate action that was or will be completed before another action or time. They consist of a form of *have* plus the past participle:

Present Perfect

	Singular	Plural
1st person	I have talked/swum	we have talked/swum
2nd person	you have talked/swum	you have talked/swum
3rd person	he/she/it has talked/swum	they have talked/swum

Past Perfect

	Singular	Plural
1st person	I had talked/swum	we had talked/swum
2nd person	you had talked/swum	you had talked/swum
3rd person	he/she/it had talked/swum	they had talked/swum

Future Perfect

	Singular	Plural
1st person	I will have talked/swum	we will have talked/swum
2nd person	you will have talked/swum	you will have talked/swum
3rd person	he/she/it will have talked/swum	they will have talked/swum

Progressive Forms

299–301

Each of the six tenses above has a progressive form to indicate a continuing action. These verbs consist of a form of *be* plus the present participle:

Present Progressive

	Singular	Plural
1st person	I am talking/swimming	we are talking/swimming
2nd person	you are talking/swimming	you are talking/swimming
3rd person	he/she/it is talking/swimming	they are talking/swimming

Past Progressive

	Singular	Plural
1st person	I was talking/swimming	we were talking/swimming
2nd person	you were talking/swimming	you were talking/swimming
3rd person	he/she/it was talking/swimming	they were talking/swimming

Future Progressive

	Singular	Plural
1st person	I will be talking/swimming	we will be talking/swimming
2nd person	you will be talking/swimming	you will be talking/swimming
3rd person	he/she/it will be talking/swimming	they will be talking/swimming

Present Perfect Progressive

	Singular	Plural
1st person	I have been talking/swimming	we have been talking/ swimming
2nd person	you have been talking/ swimming	you have been talking/ swimming
3rd person	he/she/it has been talking/ swimming	they have been talking/ swimming

Past Perfect Progressive

	Singular	Plural
1st person	I had been talking/swimming	we had been talking/ swimming
2nd person	you had been talking/ swimming	you had been talking/ swimming
3rd person	he/she/it had been talking/ swimming	they had been talking/ swimming

Future Perfect Progressive

	Singular	Plural
1st person	I will have been talking/ swimming	we will have been talking/ swimming
2nd person	you will have been talking/ swimming	you will have been talking/ swimming
3rd person	he/she/it will have been talking/swimming	they will have been talking/ swimming

Helping or Auxiliary Verbs

The base form of the verb can also combine with helping or auxiliary verbs such as *do, can, could, may, might, will, would, shall, should,* and *must:*

296–30?

> The boys do run.
>
> She can go.
>
> He should clean his room.

Active and Passive Voice

The voice of a verb indicates how the subject relates to the action expressed by the verb. When the subject is the actor (the do-er), the sentence is *active.* When the subject receives the action expressed by the verb, the sentence is *passive:*

Active	Passive
Marcos kicked the ball.	The ball was kicked by Marcos.

The passive may be appropriate to emphasize the recipient of an action rather than the performer:

Princess Diana was killed in a Paris tunnel.

In other cases, however, the active voice will express meaning more emphatically and vigorously:

Princess Diana touched the lives of sufferers worldwide.

To revise a passive sentence, first identify the agent—the do-er of the action—and put the agent into the subject slot. Then make other changes as needed:

An aide leaked word to the press
~~The existence~~ of five complaints of sexual harassment against the

senator ~~was leaked to the press.~~

chief clerk made the
The error ~~was made~~ during fund transfer.

(For more examples of revising passive sentences, see pages 39–40.)

Only transitive verbs, verbs that take direct objects, can be made passive. Two intransitive verbs, *occur* and *happen,* seem to have passive meanings, but they cannot be used in the passive voice:

A revolution ~~was being~~ occurred in the small village.

A problem ~~was~~ happened in my office today.

One special class of verbs, called *psychologically reversed verbs,* take active subjects in the passive voice. You might want to remember this list of past participles and their special usage to indicate a state of mind: *interested, tired, bored.*

I *was interested* in the ballgame when it began, but I *was bored and tired* by the fifth inning.

Mood

The mood of a verb tells whether the verb expresses a fact or a factual condition (*indicative mood*); expresses doubt, a condition wished for, or a condition contrary to fact (*subjunctive mood*); or expresses a command (*imperative mood*):

Indicative

His bike *had been stolen* for the third time.

Her essay *won* the prize for this year.

Shakespeare's works *will live* forever.

Subjunctive

If it *were* mine to give, it would be yours.

I wish Cheryl *were* here to see this.

Dr. Smith requests that you *make* another appointment.

Imperative

Look over here!

Take the dog home!

Read that book!

Verbs change form to show their different moods. Most native speakers of English have no trouble with indicative and impera- tive moods. Their problems come with the subjunctive. The form of the subjunctive is easy: it is the base form of the verb (the one the dictionary gives first—the infinitive form without the marker *to*). The only exception involves the verb *be*, which has a present subjunctive form (*be*) and a past subjunctive form (*were*). The past subjunctive is used only for conditions of doubt, conditions wished for, and conditions contrary to fact.
301–02

The subjunctive is used in four instances:

1. To express conditions of doubt, conditions wished for, or condi- tions contrary to fact:

   I wish I *were* a rich person.

   Would that they *weren't coming* this weekend.

2. In *if* clauses that describe conditions that are contrary to fact, hypothetical, or improbable:

   If I *were* in charge, things would be different.

   If that *were* my boat, I'd take good care of it.

3. In *that* clauses following verbs of asking, insisting, requesting, making a motion, or wishing:

I move that Dorothy *be* elected.

She requested that I *bring* my brother.

4. In a few common expressions:

As it *were*...   that we might *be* free of...

Be that as it may   *Come* what may

(For a discussion of mood errors, see page 225.)

VOICE

Voice refers to the relationship between the subject and the action expressed by the verb. If the subject acts, the sentence is in **active voice.** If the subject receives the action of the verb, the sentence is in **passive voice:**

Active	Passive
The staff must wear uniforms.	Uniforms must be worn.

(For additional examples of active and passive voice, see *Verbs,* pages 424–25. For help with revising sentences in the passive voice, see pages 39–40.)

W

WORD CHOICE (DICTION)

Choosing Specific Language

Word choices range along a continuum from the most general to the most specific:

General ←——————→ Specific

mammal	dog	German Shepherd
food	appetizer	steak tartare
people	children	Darlene and Tommy standing in the mud and rain with dirt caked all over them

You generally want to use the most specific and appropriate words possible and avoid needless abstraction and wordiness. For example, describe the 450-pound sumo wrestler in specific terms rather than just calling him "big." Describe in detail the giant, three-scoop ice-cream cone dripping with caramel swirls and nuts rather than just calling it "good." Help your readers feel as if they are at the midnight beach party under a sky full of northern lights, eating Four-Alarm Chili, and listening to the sound of the harbor's fog horn with a jazz guitar in the background—rather than just saying the beach party was "nice." Making specific word choices does not require a large vocabulary, just careful use of the words you already know. Try to do without words such as *good, interesting, important, nice, thing, real, area,* and *aspect:* they don't say much.

Avoiding Pretentious Word Choices

Try to avoid flowery or stilted phrases, overwriting that calls attention to the words instead of the ideas. Especially in prose, this type of phrasing sounds affected:

Overwritten	Improved
When the last glimmer of the sun fell behind the horizon, in the long ago days of my youth, I felt the shiver of fear as I climbed the stairs to my room.	When I was a child, I was afraid to go upstairs to bed at night.
The heroine of our little drama let the moments trickle past in a recurvated chaise.	She waited in her rocking chair.

Considering Your Reader

In choosing the right words for any piece of writing, you also should consider the nature of the audience. Different levels of formality and different kinds of word choice are appropriate for different readers. (See pages 7–8 for more on adjusting your writing to the reader. Further discussion of problems with word choice can be found on pages 39–44 and in *Jargon,* pages 366–67.)

GLOSSARY OF USAGE

This glossary of usage offers help with many common errors: words that are commonly confused (such as *affect* and *effect*), homonyms (words that sound alike, such as *principle* and *principal*), words that are often misspelled (such as *all right* and *a lot*), and nonstandard or slang words (such as *ain't* and *OK*) that should be avoided in formal writing. (For additional words that are commonly confused, see *Spelling*, pages 413–14.)

a, an   Use *a* before a consonant sound; use *an* before a vowel sound: *a dog, an animal.* When a word begins with a silent *h*, it begins with a vowel sound, so use *an: an hour, an herb,* but *a house, a horse.*

accept, except   *Accept* is a verb meaning "to receive willingly." *Except* is a preposition meaning "excluding":

> I will accept all the nominations except the last one.

adapt, adopt   *Adapt* means "to adjust to a situation":

> She will adapt to college life easily.

Adopt means "to take into the family" or "to accept a course of action or belief":

> We adopted a child.

> She adopted a new code of ethics for all employees.

advice, advise   *Advice* is a noun meaning "guidance"; *advise* is a verb meaning "to counsel":

> We advised him to seek advice from a college counselor.

affect, effect   *Affect* is a verb meaning "to influence":

> Her performance affected me.

Effect is generally used as a noun meaning "the result":

> She had heard about the dangerous effects of that prescription drug.

Effect can also be a verb meaning "to bring about":

> The new diplomat immediately effected important changes.

ain't   *Ain't* is nonstandard. Use *am not, isn't,* or *aren't.*

all right *All right* should always be written as two words, never as *alright.*

allude, elude *Allude* means "to refer to indirectly":

> At the end of his speech, he briefly alluded to his son's drinking problem.

Elude means "to evade or escape from":

> How did he elude the police?

allusion, illusion An *allusion* is an "indirect mention." An *illusion* is a "false belief or appearance":

> The doctor made an allusion to the patient's illusions of greatness.

a lot *A lot* is always two words:

> She has a lot of friends.

already, all ready *Already,* an adverb, means "before" or "previously." *All ready,* an adjective, means "completely prepared":

> I already told you that I am all ready to leave for the camping trip.

altar, alter *Altar* is a noun meaning "the elevated front part of a church." *Alter* is a verb meaning "to change":

> The new priest wants to alter the arrangement of flowers on the altar.

altogether, all together *Altogether* means "entirely, completely." *All together* means "in a group":

> I altogether agree with you that we cannot go all together to the wedding.

among, between Use *among* for three or more items; use *between* with two:

> The tasks were divided among the ten volunteers.

> Park your car between these two posts.

amoral, immoral *Amoral* means "neither moral nor immoral." It also means "not concerned with right and wrong." *Immoral* means "morally wrong":

> Her sex education lectures have an amoral perspective.

> Taking those books was an immoral act.

amount, number *Amount* refers to items in bulk or mass; *number* is for countable items:

> You will need a larger amount of flour, baking soda, and sugar to make a large number of cakes.

an See *a, an*.

and etc. A redundant phrase: use *etc.* by itself. See also the entry for *etc.*

and/or Avoid this construction, since it can be awkward and confusing:

> The decision will be made by the teacher and/or adviser.

> [If you mean *both*, use *and*. If you mean *either one*, use *or*. If you mean *either one or both*, write "by the teacher, by the adviser, or by both."]

anybody *Anybody* is singular.

anyone *Anyone* is singular.

anyone, any one *Anyone* means "any person at all." *Any one* refers to a member of a group:

> Anyone can purchase any one of the paintings in the show.

anyplace Nonstandard for *any place* or *anywhere*.

as Do not use *as* to mean "because" or "since": the resulting sentence may be confusing, since *as* can also mean *when*.

> We left the pool because [not *as*] it was raining.

See also *like, as*.

bad, badly *Bad* is the adjective form; *badly* is the adverb:

> The bad wound healed badly.

being as, being that Nonstandard for *because*.

beside, besides When they mean *except,* these two are interchangeable. In addition, *beside* means "by the side of" and *besides* means "in addition to":

> She sat beside the bed.

> He is getting a monthly living allowance besides his regular salary.

be sure and   Use *be sure to* in formal writing:

> Be sure to [not *and*] bring in the dog tonight.

between   See *among, between.*

biannual, biennial   *Biannual* means "twice a year"; *biennial* means "once every two years."

breath, breathe   *Breath* is a noun meaning "the air inhaled and exhaled." *Breathe* is a verb meaning "to inhale and exhale":

> When her breath became regular, I began to breathe more easily.

burst, bursted, bust, busted   *Burst* is the standard verb form:

> The balloon burst.

Bursted, bust, and *busted* are nonstandard forms.

capital, capitol   *Capital* means "a city that is a government seat." *Capitol* means "a building where a legislature meets":

> As soon as our train arrived in the capital, we looked up to see the dome of the capitol.

choose, chose   *Choose* is the present tense verb; *chose* is the past tense.

cite, sight, site   *Cite* is a verb meaning "to refer to." The noun *sight* means "the ability to see" or "something that is seen." The noun *site* means "a location":

> Remember to cite your sources in your research paper.

> He lost his sight when he was five.

> The vacant lot was the site of the new parking lot.

cloth, clothes   *Cloth* means "fabric." *Clothes* means "garments like shirts and pants":

> The tailor used only fine silk cloth to make the clothes for her trip.

complement, compliment   *Complement* means "to make whole or bring to perfection." *Compliment* means "praise":

> That color complements your eyes.

> Her new haircut received many compliments.

conscience, conscious   *Conscience* is a noun that means "a sense of right and wrong." *Conscious* is an adjective that means "being aware of your existence and feelings":

Shoplifting the candy bothered her conscience.

He was conscious of his own prejudices.

continual, continuous   *Continual* means "of frequent recurrence." *Continuous* means "without stop."

The continual ringing of bells at nearby churches bothered the office staff, but they never noticed the continuous hum of the Xerox machine.

could of   Nonstandard for *could have:*

She could have [not *could of*] been a wonderful president.

council, counsel   *Council* is a noun that means "an assembly of leaders." *Counsel* means "advice" (noun) or "to give advice" (verb):

The student council offered to counsel the new freshman class.

criteria   The plural of *criterion.*

data, datum   *Data* is, technically, the plural form of *datum.* In many fields, *data* is now treated as the only form, as singular or plural, depending upon the context.

differ from, differ with   *Differ from* means "to be unlike." *Differ with* means "to disagree with":

My suggestions differ from the manager's.

I differ with his decisions.

disinterested, uninterested   *Disinterested* means "impartial, objective." *Uninterested* means "not interested":

Umpires should be disinterested.

Fans often become uninterested when their team falls behind.

due to   *Due to* should be used to mean "because of" only after a form of the verb *be:*

Darla left the house because of [not *due to*] her husband's violence.

Freida's success was due to hard work.

each   *Each* is singular.

effect   See *affect, effect.*

e.g.   In formal writing, replace the Latin abbreviation *e.g.* (for *exempli gratia*) with *for example* or *for instance.*

either   *Either* is singular.

elicit, illicit   *Elicit* is a verb meaning "to bring out" or "to evoke." *Illicit* is an adjective meaning "unlawful":

> The police officer shoved the suspect into a chair and began to elicit information in an illicit manner.

elude   See *allude, elude.*

emigrate from, immigrate to   *Emigrate from* means "to leave one country or region":

> Many people emigrated from England in search of religious freedom.

Immigrate to means "to enter another country and live there":

> He left Sarajevo and immigrated to Italy.

eminent, imminent   *Eminent* means "exceptional" or "distinguished." *Imminent* means "about to happen":

> The eminent historian announced that war was imminent.

etc.   In formal writing, avoid the Latin abbreviation *etc.* (for *et cetera,* meaning "and so forth"). Instead of ending a list with *etc.,* begin it with *such as, for example,* or *for instance.*

everybody, everyone   *Everybody* and *everyone* are singular.

everyday, every day   *Everyday* is an adjective meaning "ordinary." Do not confuse it with the phrase *every day* meaning "each day":

> On every day except Sunday, I use my everyday plates and silverware.

everyone, every one   *Everyone* is an indefinite pronoun. *Every one,* the pronoun *one* modified by the adjective *every,* means "each individual or thing in a particular group":

> Everyone waited until every one of the jewels was found.

except   See *accept, except.*

explicit, implicit   *Explicit* means "expressed directly"; *implicit* means "implied, unstated":

> The pilot gave explicit instructions to the ground crew.

> Their immediate smiles and nods indicated their implicit agreement.

farther, further   *Farther* refers to additional distance. *Further* refers to additional time, quantity, or extent:

As we drove farther from home, I told Dennis that I didn't want to discuss the matter any further.

fewer, less   *Fewer* refers to items that can be counted; *less* refers to bulk or mass amounts:

fewer days, less time; fewer cups, less sugar

firstly   *Firstly* sounds stilted, and it leads to the awkward series *firstly, secondly, thirdly, fourthly,* and so on. Use *first, second, third* instead.

get   *Get* has many slang and colloquial uses. In formal writing, avoid using *get* to mean the following: "to evoke an emotional response" (*That song gets to me*); "to annoy" (*Her pouting gets to me*); "to take revenge on" (*I plan to get her back*); "to finish" (*We got done*); "must" (*I've got to study*); and "have" (*I've got three tests this Friday*).

good, well   *Good* is an adjective, and *well* is nearly always an adverb:

The good friends dance well together.

Well may be used as an adjective to refer to health:

She is well.

good and   Nonstandard for *very:*

I am very [not *good and*] angry with you.

had ought   The *had* is unnecessary:

She ought [not *had ought*] to finish college.

hanged, hung   *Hanged* is the past tense and the past participle of the verb *hang* meaning "to execute":

In the nineteenth century, many petty criminals were hanged.

Hung is the past tense and past participle of the verb *hang* meaning "to fasten or suspend":

The large decorations were hung on piano wire.

hardly   Avoid expressions such as *can't hardly* and *not hardly,* which are considered double negatives:

I can [not *can't*] hardly wait for the party to begin.

he   At one time *he* was used to mean "he or she." Today such usage is not considered appropriate. (For alternatives, see pages 325–26.)

he/she, his/her   In formal writing, use *he or she* or *his or her.*

hisself   Nonstandard for *himself.*

hopefully   *Hopefully* means "in a hopeful manner":

> We waited hopefully while Tran was in surgery.

Do not use *hopefully* to mean "it is to be hoped":

> I hope that [not *Hopefully*] you will get the lead part in the play.

i.e.   In formal writing, replace the Latin abbreviation *i.e.* (for *id est*) with its English meaning, *that is.*

if, whether   Use *if* in a statement of condition and *whether* to express alternatives:

> If you go to college, whether to a private or state school, you will need to fill out financial aid forms.

illicit   See *elicit, illicit.*

illusion   See *allusion, illusion.*

immigrate to   See *emigrate from, immigrate to.*

imminent   See *eminent, imminent.*

immoral   See *amoral, immoral.*

implicit   See *explicit, implicit.*

imply, infer   *Imply* means "to suggest without stating directly"; *infer* means "to draw a conclusion":

> The lawyer implied that her client had been treated unfairly at three universities, but the judge inferred that the defendant had been a bad teacher.

in, into   *In* generally indicates "location or condition within"; *into* indicates movement or a change in condition:

> He ran into another car while he was driving in the rain.

in regards to   Nonstandard for *in regard to* or *regarding.*

irregardless   Nonstandard for *regardless.*

is when, is where   These constructions are often incorrectly used in definitions:

> A beefalo is a hybrid between an American buffalo and a domestic cow.
> [Not "A beefalo *is when* an American buffalo is bred with a domestic cow."]
> Washington, D.C., is the capital of the United States.
> [Not "Washington, D.C. *is where* the capital of the United States is."]

its, it's   *Its* is a possessive pronoun; *it's* is a contraction of *it is:*

> It's pleasing to see that dog leave the pound with its new owner.

later, latter   *Later,* referring to time, is the comparative form of *late. Latter* refers to the second named of two; the first is called the *former:*

> I had hoped to see Naomi and Chris, but only the latter was home. Naomi wasn't expected until much later.

lay   See *lie, lay.*

lead, led   *Lead* is a noun referring to a metal and a verb meaning "to go before." *Led* is the past tense of the verb *to lead:*

> The tests led to the conclusion that the child had lead poisoning.

learn, teach   *Learn* means "to gain knowledge"; *teach* means "to impart knowledge":

> Her parents must teach [not *learn*] her to eat with a spoon.

less   See *fewer, less.*

liable   *Liable* means "obligated" or "responsible." Do not use it to mean "likely":

> You're likely [not *liable*] to fall if you walk on that high wall.

lie, lay   *Lie* is an intransitive verb meaning "to recline or rest in a flat position." Its principal parts are *lie, lay, lain. Lay* is a transitive verb meaning "to put or place." Its principal parts are *lay, laid, laid:*

> Do you need to lie down?
> Where did I lay those leather gloves?

like, as   *Like* is a preposition. It should be followed by a noun or a noun phrase. *As* is a subordinating conjunction that introduces a dependent clause:

> You look like a friendly person.

> You don't know her as I do.

loose, lose   *Loose* is an adjective meaning "not fastened." *Lose* is a verb meaning "to misplace" or "to fail to win":

> Rosa began to lose the race when her rear wheel became loose.

lots, lots of   *Lots* and *lots of* are slang substitutes for *many, much,* or *a lot.* Avoid using them in formal writing.

maybe, may be   *Maybe* is an adverb meaning "possibly." *May be* is a verb phrase:

> Maybe we will win the relay race.

> The results may be a surprise to the fans.

may of, might of   *May of* and *might of* are nonstandard for *may have* and *might have:*

> They may have [not *may of*] already left.

media, medium   *Media* is, technically, the plural form of *medium.* *Media* is often treated now as the only form, as singular or plural, depending upon the context.

moral, morale   *Moral* is an adjective meaning "conforming to standards of goodness." *Morale* is a noun meaning "the spirit of an individual or group":

> His moral decision to stand up for his staff increased the morale of the whole group.

most   *Most* should not be used to mean *almost:*

> Almost [not *Most*] everyone enjoyed the concert.

myself, yourself, himself, herself, ourselves, themselves   The *-self* pronouns are reflexive or intensive pronouns and thus must have an antecedent.

> Reflexive: I hurt myself.

> Intensive: I will teach you myself.

Do not use *myself* in place of *I* or *me:*

The police next questioned Trudy and me [not *myself*].

neither *Neither* is singular.

none *None* is singular.

nowheres Nonstandard for *nowhere*.

number See *amount, number*.

of Use the verb *have,* not the preposition *of,* after the verbs *could, should, would, may, might,* and *must:*

You should have [not *of*] seen her new interview suit.

off of The *of* is unnecessary. Use *off:*

She fell off [not *off of*] the balcony.

OK, O.K., okay All three spellings are acceptable, but you should avoid these slang expressions in formal writing.

passed, past *Passed* is the past tense of the verb *to pass;* thus it means "went by" or "received a passing grade." *Past* means "of a former time" or "beyond in time or position":

She passed her test.

He passed the car driven by our past president.

The accident occurred just past the new entrance ramp.

phenomena The plural of *phenomenon*.

plus Do not use *plus* to join two independent clauses:

The oleander bushes need clipping, and [not *plus*] the roses need fertilizer.

precede, proceed *Precede* means "to come before." *Proceed* means "to go onward" or "to move in an orderly fashion":

As Juana proceeded to the final turn of the walk race, she realized that three contestants had preceded her.

principal, principle *Principal* is a noun meaning "the head of a school" or "a sum of money." It is also an adjective meaning "first in importance." *Principle* is a noun meaning "a basic truth or standard":

The principal asked the school board, "Do we have the principal to rebuild the science building?"

My principal reason for leaving home was that I disagreed with my stepfather's principles of discipline.

proceed   See *precede, proceed.*

provided, providing   *Provided* can serve as a subordinating conjunction meaning *if. Providing* cannot be used this way:

> We will begin providing a larger budget for urban housing provided we receive a new federal grant.

quote, quotation   *Quote* is a verb; *quotation* is a noun. Do not use *quote* as a shortened form of the noun:

> She supported her arguments with quotations [not *quotes*] from current journals.

raise, rise   *Raise* is a transitive verb meaning "to move upward." It takes a direct object:

> She raised the banner above her head.

Rise is an intransitive verb meaning "to go up." It does not take a direct object:

> When the sun comes up, the temperature rises.

real, really   *Real* is an adjective; *really* is an adverb. *Real* is sometimes used informally as an adverb, but you should avoid this use in formal writing:

> They were really [not *real*] tired.

reason is because, reason why   Both of these phrases are redundant. Use *reason is* or *reason is that* instead.

> The reason [not *The reason why*] he chose a technical college is unclear.

respectfully, respectively   *Respectfully* means "in a manner that shows respect." *Respectively* means "each in the order given":

> She acted respectfully toward her older cousins.

> The three childhood friends, Margaret, Paula, and Suelinda, became a college teacher, a lawyer, and a counselor, respectively.

rise   See *raise, rise.*

set, sit   *Set* is a transitive verb meaning "to put" or "to place." Its principal parts are *set, set, set. Sit* is an intransitive verb meaning "to be seated." Its principal parts are *sit, sat, sat:*

> She set the tray of cucumber sandwiches near the bench where her mother-in-law sat.

should of   Nonstandard for *should have:*

He should have [not *should of*] filled the tank with gas before he left town.

sight, site   See *cite, sight, site.*

sit   See *set, sit.*

somebody, someone   *Somebody* and *someone* are singular.

something   *Something* is singular.

sometime, some time, sometimes   *Sometime* is an adverb meaning "at an indefinite or unstated time":

The plane will leave sometime soon.

Some time is two words (a noun and its modifier) that mean "a period of time":

I had not seen my sister for some time.

Sometimes is an adverb meaning "now and then":

Sometimes I go jogging at the track.

stationary, stationery   *Stationary* means "not moving." *Stationery* is a type of writing paper:

I stood stationary while the dean pulled out her stationery to write my parents.

suppose to   Nonstandard for *supposed to.*

teach   See *learn, teach.*

than, then   *Than* is a conjunction used in comparisons; *then* is an adverb meaning "at that time in the past" or "next":

Then he decided that he liked contact lenses more than glasses.

that, which   *That* introduces essential (or restrictive) clauses. In "The next set will begin with the song that Harvey wrote," the restrictive relative clause *that Harvey wrote* identifies the specific song being referred to. *Which* can introduce either essential or nonessential (nonrestrictive) clauses, but many writers reserve *which* for nonrestrictive clauses. In "The song, which Harvey wrote, has three different choruses," the nonrestrictive relative clause *which Harvey wrote* simply provides additional information. (For further discussion of restrictive and nonrestrictive clauses, see page 389.)

theirselves   Nonstandard for *themselves.*

them   Do not use *them* in place of *those:*

Martha bought those [not *them*] blouses for her sister.

there, their, they're   *There* is an adverb meaning "in that place" and an expletive in the phrase *there is:*

There is a homeless man lying over there.

Their is a possessive pronoun. *They're* is a contraction of *they are:*

They're sure that they left their skates near the door.

thru   In formal writing, avoid this colloquial spelling of *through.*

to, too, two   *To* is a preposition usually meaning "in a direction toward"; *too* is an adverb meaning "also"; *two* is a number:

Gerald went to the soccer game.

Two famous Argentinians were playing, and pro scouts were there too.

try and   Nonstandard for *try to:*

We agreed to try to [not *try and*] stop arguing about our in-laws.

uninterested   See *disinterested, uninterested.*

use to   Nonstandard for *used to.*

wait for, wait on   *Wait for* means "to be in readiness for" or "to await." *Wait on* means "to serve":

We are waiting for [not *on*] the rain to slacken.

ways   Use *way* when referring to distance:

Her house is a long way [not *ways*] from her garden.

well   See *good, well.*

where   Do not use *where* in place of *that. Where* should be used only for locations:

I heard that [not *where*] the new American cars are just as well made as Japanese cars.

whether   See *if, whether.*

who, which, that   Use *who* or *that,* but not *which,* to refer to persons. See also *that, which.*

who, whom   *Who* is used for subjects; *whom* is used for objects.

> Who wrote the sentence?

> She is the woman whom I love.

who's, whose   *Who's* is a contraction of "who is"; *whose* is a possessive pronoun:

> Who's going to your graduation?

> Whose bedspread is this?

your, you're   *Your* is a possessive pronoun; *you're* is a contraction of "you are":

> Your dog has won the first prize.

> You're the best trainer at the meet.

WEB GLOSSARY

Boolean logic   A system for searching a database that uses the operators AND, OR, and NOT to look for two variables.

Bookmark   A tool provided by most Web browsers that enables you to save Web page URLs so that you can return to them at any time.

browser   An interface for reading information on the World Wide Web, either graphical (such as Netscape or Explorer) or textual (such as Lynx).

byte   A unit of information in a computer, equal to 8 bits.

DNS (domain name system)   The convention for translating the names of hosts into Internet addresses; see also *URL*.

domain name   The part of the Internet address (URL) that specifies the area on a computer reserved for a particular organization, such as mayfieldpub.com. In this example, .com stands for "commercial"; other types of organization designations include .edu for "educational" and .gov for "governmental."

download   To transfer information from one computer to another, or to transfer information from a network to your computer.

e-mail   Electronic mail; one of the most popular uses of the Internet; it can be sent to an individual or a list.

FAQ (frequently asked questions)   List of common questions about a particular product, service, or topic.

FTP (file transfer protocol)   The standard protocol for transferring files across the Internet. Most browsers have one-way FTP; for two-way (the ability to send as well as receive), you can acquire FTP software for both Macintoshes (Fetch) and PCs (WS_FTP).

GIF (graphics interchange format)   File format for images that are viewable on the Web; see also *JPEG*.

Gopher   A menu-driven information system created at the University of Minnesota.

hits   The number of times a particular page is accessed, or the number of successful matches you receive during a keyword search.

home page   The main, or starting, page for a series of Web pages.

HTML (hypertext markup language)   The formatting language of the World Wide Web.

HTTP (hypertext transfer protocol)   The protocol for reading HTML programs from the Web.

hypertext   A text link that takes you to another file on the Internet. A hypertext document contains hypertext or hyperlinks or both.

Internet   A global network of linked computers; home to the World Wide Web, newsgroups, bulletin boards, Gopher, and on-line forums.

ISP (Internet service provider)   A company that provides subscribers access to the Internet.

JPEG or JPG (joint photographic expert group)   File format for images that are viewable on the Web; see also *GIF.*

link   Short for *hyperlink.* A link, textual or graphic, that takes you to another file on the Internet or another location in a document.

modem   A device that allows a remote computer to communicate via phone lines to networks and other computers.

netiquette   Etiquette on the Internet. The guidelines for preferred behavior when communicating with others on the Internet.

page   Any Web document viewable with a browser.

platform   The operating system that your computer runs, for example DOS (disk operating system), Windows, or Macintosh.

protocol   Information format. The protocol lets two computers know what type of information is being transferred. The protocol for transferring information across the Internet is given in the first part of the URL (e.g., http, ftp, gopher, telnet).

RAM (random access memory)   The amount of available short-term memory in a computer directly correlating to the speed of your processor—the more RAM you have, the faster your computer is.

ROM (read-only memory)   The unchangeable portion of the computer's memory containing the start-up instructions for your system.

search engine   A program that allows you to perform keyword searches to locate Web documents.

server   A computer accessible to other networked computers.

shareware   Copyrighted software that is distributed on a trial basis; you eventually have to pay for it if you want to continue to use it beyond the trial period. The cost is generally minimal.

SMTP (simple mail transfer protocol)   The standard protocol for transferring e-mail from one computer to another across the Internet.

subject tree   A hierarchical directory of information.

surfing   Exploring the Internet by clicking links from one page to another.

URL (uniform resource locator)   An address for an Internet location.

virus   A self-replicating destructive program that can be downloaded from the Internet or obtained via an infected file on a diskette. A few viruses are harmless and even amusing, but most can destroy the data on your hard disk.

Web page   A document accessible on the Web.

World Wide Web   The segment of the Internet that uses primarily HTTP.

CREDITS

INDEX

A

a, an, 285–91, 323–24, 429
  summary of rules, 285
abbreviations, 315–19
  of academic degrees, 315
  acronyms, 316
  of company names, 319
  of days, 318
  faulty, 317
  of geographic locations, 317
  Latin, 318–19
  of months, 318
  numerals with, 316–17
  plurals of, 262
  of publication references, 318
  symbols, 319
  of titles, 315–16
  unfamiliar, 316
  with units of measure, 318
absolute concepts, and comparatives, 271
absolute modifiers, 268, 377
absolute phrases, 320, 377
  commas with, 236
abstractions
  needless, 427–28
  worn-out, 43
accept, except, 429
acronyms, 316
  plurals of, 262
active sentences, 39–40
active voice, 39–40, 320, 424–27
  revising for, 39–40
  See also passive voice; voice
adapt, adopt, 429
A.D., B.C., 316
addresses, commas in, 237
ad hominem fallacy, 151–52
adjective clauses, 306–07, 336
adjectives, 320–21
  capitalization of, 330–32
  comparative, 270–71, 320–21
  compound, hyphens in, 360–61
  coordinate, 233–34, 292, 321

  cumulative, 233–34, 292, 321
  ESL problems with, 291–93
  improper forms of, 270–71
  as nouns, 290–91
  ordinal, 287, 321
  past participles as, 292–93
  positive, 320–21
  possessive, 262–63
  present participles as, 292–93
  pronouns as, 321
  superlative, 270–71, 286–87, 320–21
adopt, adapt, 429
adverbs, 321–22
  comparative, 270–71, 322
  conjunctive, 204–05, 346–47, 390–91
  improper forms of, 270–71
  -ly endings, 270–71
  positive, 322
  superlative, 270–71, 286–87, 322
advice, use of conditional sentences for, 301–02
advice, advise, 429
advise, advice, 429
affect, effect, 429
age-biased language, 326–27
agreement, 322
agreement errors, 218–21, 246–51
  pronoun-antecedent, 249–51
    Quick View, 246–47
  subject-verb, 218–21
    Quick View, 215–17
aims for writing, 6
ain't, 429
aircraft, names of, 331
all ready, already, 430
all right, 430
all together, altogether, 430
allude, elude, 430
allusion, illusion, 430
almanacs, 61–62
a lot, 430
already, all ready, 430

periodicals
  citation of articles
    APA style, 125–27
    MLA style, 103–05
  titles
    capitalization of, 332–33
    italics for, 364–65
    quotation marks for, 364–65,
      385
periodic sentences, 397
person
  of pronouns, inappropriate shifts
    in, 251–52
  of verbs, 417, 422–24
personal, personnel, 414
personal pronouns, 381
  possessive, 260–61
personal response notes, 76–77
persuasive letters, 186–89
phenomena, 439
phrasal constructions, 293–94
phrasal prepositions, 293–94, 380
phrases, 373–77
  absolute, 320, 377
  appositive, 377
  dangling modifiers, 267–68
  empty and wordy, 42–43
  gerund, 374–375
  infinitive, 231, 375–376
  introductory, commas after,
    231–32
  misplaced modifiers, 267
  noun, 374
  participial, 231, 376
  prepositional, 231, 374
  as sentence fragments, 377
  signal, 85
  squinting modifiers, 268–69
  verb, 374
physical ability, biased language
  about, 328
pie charts, 137–38
placement of adjective clauses,
  306–07
place names, articles for, 290
plagiaphrasing, 84–85. *See also*
  paraphrasing sources
plagiarism, 77–78, 378
plain, plane, 414

planning, 13–17
  devices, 15–17
  for essay exams, 161–65
  main idea, 13
  for oral presentations, 167–68
  organizational pattern, 14
  papers, 14–17
  thesis, 13
  time for essay exams, 162
plays
  divisions, 371
  titles
    capitalization of, 332–33
    italics for, 364–65
plurals
  of abbreviations, 262
  irregular, 412
  of letters and words, 323
  of numbers, 323
  spelling of, 410–12
plus, 439
P.M., A.M., p.m., a.m., 317
poems
  quotations from, 98, 330
  titles
    capitalization of, 330
    quotation marks for, 384–85
possessive adjectives, 262–63
possessive case, 259–61, 334, 378
  apostrophes with, 259–61
  of indefinite pronouns, 261
  individual possession, 260
  joint possession, 260
  of nouns, 259–60
  of pairs of nouns, 260
  of personal pronouns, 260–61
  of pronouns, 260–61
possibilities, unlikely, conditional
  sentences for, 301–02
PowerPoint presentations, 172–73
practice, for oral presentations, 173
precede, proceed, 439
predicate adjectives, 378, 394
predicate nominatives. *See* predicate
  nouns
predicate nouns, 378
predicates, 379
  compound, 233
predication, faulty, 279, 356–57

Boxes and Illustrations

NOTES

NOTES

NOTES

NOTES